Habitants and Merchants in
Seventeenth-Century Montreal

Studies on the History of Quebec /
Études d'histoire du Québec

John Dickinson and Brian Young
Series Editors / Directeurs de la collection

Habitants and Merchants in Seventeenth-
Century Montreal
Louise Dechêne

Habitants and Merchants in Seventeenth-Century Montreal

LOUISE DECHÊNE

Translated by Liana Vardi

McGill-Queen's University Press

Montreal & Kingston • London • Buffalo

60106514

© McGill-Queen's University Press 1992
ISBN 0-7735-0658-6 (cloth)
ISBN 0-7735-0951-8 (paper)

Legal deposit fourth quarter 1992
Bibliothèque nationale du Québec

Printed in Canada on acid-free paper

This book has been published with the help of a
grant from the Social Science Federation of
Canada, using funds provided by the Social
Sciences and Humanities Research Council of
Canada.

This book is a translation of *Habitants et Marchands
de Montréal au xviie siècle*, published by les Editions
Plons, Paris, in 1974 and reprinted by Les Éditions
du Boréal, Montreal, in 1988. Translation of the
original work was supported by a grant from the
Canada Council.

Canadian Cataloguing in Publication Data

Dechêne, Louise, 1932–
    Habitants and merchants in seventeenth-
    century Montreal
    (Studies on the history of Quebec)
    Includes bibliographical references.
    Translation of: Habitants et marchands de
    Montréal au XVIIe siècle.
    ISBN 0-7735-0658-6 (bound)
    ISBN 0-7735-0951-8 (pbk)
    1. Montréal (Quebec) – Social conditions.
    2. Montréal (Quebec) – Economic conditions.
    3. Canada – History – To 1763 (New France).
    4. Montréal (Quebec) – Population – History.
    I. Title. II. Series.
    HN110.M63D4213 1992   971.4'28014   C92-090231-6

Contents

Tables

Preface

The English translation of *Habitants et marchands de Montréal au XVIIe siècle* has been many years in the making; almost twenty years separate this publication from the original edition. During this interval, research on early Canada has advanced rapidly on two fronts: the study of French settlements and the history of Indians and Indian-European relations. In the first area, colonial trade, agriculture, demographic and social reproduction, family, religion, and various cultural manifestations are some of the themes which have been investigated by a new generation of scholars. Many seventeenth- and eighteenth-century parishes have been the subject of doctoral dissertations and these findings have begun to appear in print. New issues have been raised and old ones are being reformulated. In short, the history of New France is very much alive and in the mainstream of social history.

But these are relatively recent developments. When I undertook this community study of early Montreal, the political narrative dominated the field and it paid scant attention to the colonists as such. Canadians were lumped together under the ill-defined labels of *habitants* or *coureurs de bois*, the terms being more or less interchangeable. They were presented as brave, vain, footloose, and improvident, happy to let the government and the Church take care of their needs. Plots could vary but colonial society remained an abstraction. It was not an object of research. Cole Harris's 1966 book, *The Seigneurial System in Early Canada*, stood as an exception. Based on official and legalistic aggregate data, it did not come closer to the settlers' experience, but its analytical approach, focus on the rural landscape, and discussion of the important issues marked a turning point. For me it acted as an incentive to probe in these directions.

My training had been largely in the history of Ancien-Régime France and, initially, strictly practical considerations (the impossibility of travelling abroad) made me choose a Canadian setting for my research. The French historians of the 1960s, as often noted, placed a heavy emphasis on structures and continuities and a great faith in numbers, but the lessons from the Continent went beyond these methodological aspects. In these carefully crafted books, replete with minute observations, one gained a sense of time and context, one learned a way of dealing with people of the past with sensitivity and respect. Could such methods, designed for stable, socially differentiated human groups, be used to study early Montrealers? If the settlers really had followed erratic ways of life outside the normal pattern of European and colonial history elsewhere, the answer would have been no. But the minute I began to investigate the many traces left by the immigrants and their children, this assumption proved false. Local evidence showed the seriousness of purpose of these peasants, concerned with the security of their families, and of merchants and traders seeking respectability and profits. Beneath the apparent chaos of the new settlement, lasting patterns very soon emerged in economic activity as well as in cultural attitudes. The issue of change *versus* continuity is the underlying theme of each chapter and, if one sums up the partial findings, the emphasis clearly falls on the side of continuity. Old institutions took root, hierarchy prevailed as the base of public order, and, in spite of the advantages of the New World environment, the old material, social, and cultural constraints still commanded the rhythm of development. In this small fur trade outpost and the surrounding countryside, another traditional society was spontaneously recreated, albeit with its own distinctive features.

More recent research on rural Canada in the early modern period generally supports this view and in some cases reinforces it. Allan Greer's *Peasant, Lord, and Merchant* (1985), a major study of power relations and the peasant economy in three parishes settled in the mid-eighteenth century, is one example. However, some of the arguments I put forth twenty years ago, especially those in the conclusion, need to be modified in view of the theoretical and empirical advances in the field. Influenced by models that were popular in the 1970s, I exaggerated the separation between agriculture and the mercantile sector. This led me to assume that uniformity of farm production and egalitarian inheritance arrangements, so visible among these seventeenth-century Montreal peasants, would be enduring features. New evidence has shown that, on the contrary, inequality increased over time and was linked to an important system of local exchange in goods and services that fed into larger markets. Fortunately, these rash projections into the future were few and, in general, the analysis did not stray too far from the evidence. And when I had doubts about the solidity of certain hypotheses, I shared them with the readers.

There are many facets of the life of early Montrealers that the book ignored or treated too superficially. In some instances, this was due to a lack of documentation. It was very frustrating, for example, to find next to nothing about the Indian village located on the island or about the summer fur fair, a high point in the annual calendar for Montrealers and their native visitors. Other omissions were a matter of choice. There was no time to deal adequately with the nascent artisanal community, to investigate the impact of wars and the military presence, or to pay more attention to religious attitudes, to mention only a few of the neglected topics. As important as they were, these came lower in the order of priorities. Because so little was known about this population it was essential to start at the beginning and, for me, this meant the nature of immigration and the socioeconomic foundations of the urban and rural settlements, trade, and agriculture. In spite of everything that has been written of late criticizing this conventional materialist approach, I still think it is the most appropriate. This does not imply any rejection of the new analytical tools today's historians are using, but why should these exciting innovations make the former approach to community studies obsolete? How can we find our way around this peoples', or any peoples', culture, make sense of their rituals, read their emotions, interpret their submission and their resistance, if we remain ignorant of the basic facts about their material and social environment?

Because it brings these facts to light, and because it raises problems which are still relevant to present debates, this book may deserve a second life. But that is for the reader to judge. Thanks are due to McGill-Queen's University Press, who never ceased to believe in this project, particularly to Joan McGilvray, who tried to make me share her optimism, and also to Liana Vardi who made the original translation, and Allan Greer and Thomas Wien, who took time to revise part of it.

Introduction

The problem underlying and inspiring this study is how a colonial society was formed and shaped by European settlers under the twin influences of tradition and North American experiences. Its subject is therefore transition and adaptation, a subject that Canadian historians have tended to neglect by concentrating on imperial policies, metropolitan rivalries, and administrative decisions. Those who have delved into the social aspects of the French regime have turned to the brief lull between two wars in the eighteenth century, when the colony's particular features were already more or less in place. Works on the earlier period of gestation usually focus on political and military events, or on important personages; the colonists appear only as coureurs de bois whom the authorities try to settle. To link this picture to that of the habitants of a later century who, from their barn doors, fought off the invaders who threatened their homeland, one must examine the evolution of this society step by step, for it has left more records than the reactions of a handful of administrators or memorialists unmoved by daily life, or of travellers in search of the picturesque, all of whose impressions, endlessly reprinted, have served only to bolster the preoccupations of various authors and interpreters.

The study requires an analysis of immigration, of the origins of the settlers, followed by study of the socio-professional categories that arose in this specific context and income levels and lifestyles. Yet once this is done, will we have reached a fuller understanding of the new realities, still couched in traditional terms, of the forces governing this particular social structure? Description is simply not enough, for should a deeper analysis corroborate that Canadian society did indeed move away from its origins in the Ancien Régime, this shift would demand an explanation. Our investigation must begin by focusing on the system of production and exchange, and on the interplay between these two sectors, so that we may gauge the exact role of the participants. Our survey will also deal with social linkages rooted in other times and other places, which were first imposed upon and then gradually incorporated into the local organization.

The interplay of various influences upon the colonists – the environment, the economy, the cultural baggage of the immigrants, the institutions of the Ancien Régime, and the new society emerging rapidly from this network – is very complex. Capturing this changing, multifaceted reality is an ambitious project, and it could not have been realized for the whole of New France. The colony was small, but the settlers were as scattered as the sources a researcher would need to consult. That is why this work became a monograph on the Island of Montreal. A local study can be significant if it covers the essential characteristics that shaped a larger destiny. Montreal, a nexus of activity, answers those requirements. The fur trade led to the creation of this inland trading post, but the agriculture that developed alongside was similar to that of other parts of the colony. It provides an excellent standpoint from which to examine the links between a commercial centre and its hinterland. The focus may indeed be confined to a small group, but in 1720 its five thousand inhabitants were one-fifth of the Canadian population of European origin. The sample is therefore relatively important and, given the well-circumscribed locale, it becomes possible to gather documentation substantial enough to yield a basic analysis of conditions that were widespread.

The only statistical information available for the whole of the colony survives in the odd census, so chary of details during the seventeenth century. There is nothing on the migratory movements, nothing on the volume of trade prior to 1729, nothing on the actual occupation of the land or on agricultural yields. There are no cadastral surveys or market price lists or major tax rolls. The administrative correspondence between Quebec and Versailles is incomplete for the first decades and especially poor in descriptions of material life. By contrast, for the Island of Montreal, a well-run seigneury, quantitative and qualitative evidence is fairly abundant, and includes lists of immigrants and of censitaines, tax rolls, court records, and seigneurial correspondence. I undertook a simple compilation of parish-register data with the sole aim of establishing the link between demographic patterns and the way of life. These records are difficult to use because of the relative importance of migration movements in the seventeenth century. Besides, demographers at the University of Montreal have undertaken a massive project on family reconstitution for the entire colonial population, and it would have been pointless to anticipate their research.

I obtained most of my information from notarial records. I took down every partnership, obligation, hiring contract, and merchant inventory, and this enabled me to trace the nature and evolution of trading activities. A variety of deeds relating to agriculture, land grants, land sales and leases, and rural estate inventories, once organized, threw new light on life in the countryside. Notaries also provided information on social and family relations. I had to work with thousands of deeds, and sometimes the results fell short of my expectations, but always, with supplementary evidence, they yielded elements of information.

There are other limitations to this research, the first a chronological one. I meant to show how the economic system and the society came to be, how, by the first quarter of the eighteenth century, the process had been completed, and how the initial phase of adaptation and quick transformation came to an end. What began in tentative and chaotic fashion evolved into a coherent and lasting organization. From then on the colony did not cease to develop – far from it – but it adopted a more normal pace.

This study does not pretend to cover every issue affecting Canada over the seven decades from 1642 to around 1713. Montreal's political history was strongly linked to French imperial destinies, but I purposely left this aspect aside, since others have dealt with it before me and done it well. I am obliged to them for providing me with the key to those events. Nor do I propose to discuss the factors that hindered the colony from developing along the lines of the English colonies. The problems lay elsewhere: in the unfavourable location and in the France of Louis XIV, which did not encourage emigration. I was interested in what actually happened and not in what might have been in other places and circumstances. Yet I cannot pretend that focusing on Montreal can provide a complete picture, since many of the links between France and Canada stopped in Quebec. Nevertheless, I believe that one gains useful insights by illuminating the hinterland. For what mattered in the long run was the local organization and the society it nurtured rather than the metropolitan companies. I did not see any point in expounding on the general aspects of civil, military, or religious institutions, and so concentrated on those that had a direct bearing on the life of Montrealers, lightly touching on familiar matters while stressing lesser-known features, such as the seigneury, the family, and the parish.

This book, therefore, integrates a number of separate investigations that aim to address the same problem. Each was carried out with as much rigour as possible, but only some of the queries could be answered fully. I suggest some hypotheses for the remainder, and I sometimes put forth an interpretation, without attempting to hide the weaknesses in the argument. Is this not the way in which our knowledge of the past advances? If my inadequacies stimulate other research in these areas, my work will have been useful.

I would like to thank all those who helped me to bring this study to fruition, especially Professor Robert Mandrou of the Hautes Etudes and the University of Paris X, Nanterre, who agreed to supervise the work and who provided unstinting support. The list of colleagues and friends to whom I turned for advice and who were always so encouraging is too long to reproduce. May each one read individual thanks in these lines. I also wish to record my gratitude to the Canada Council, to McGill University, and to the University of Ottawa, whose financial help allowed me to carry out this research, and to Suzanne Mineau and Rita Wallot for their invaluable assistance, as well as to the numerous archivists and librarians who made access to the many documents I needed easier for me. François, Geneviève, and Julie all accepted that I would be spending most of these last years in the seventeenth century. I thank them for their patience.

The Island of Montreal in 1702, after a plan drawn by the seigneurs

Source: L. Beauregard, "Géographie historique des côtes de l'île de Montréal." *Cahiers de géographie du Québec* 28, nos 73–74 (1984): 53

PART ONE

The Population

This study begins with the people, natives and Frenchmen, who gradually congregated around a concept, a fort, a store. Of the former we know too little. Historians traditionally have consigned them to the background, and for lack of evidence we are unable to take this petty and static vision much further, to describe the roles they played in this particular establishment. The French left their mark in census material and parish registers, and these permit a detailed reconstruction of immigration that is completed by a broad sketch of demographic trends.

CHAPTER ONE

Native People

1 LOCAL TRIBES

Between the sixteenth and seventeenth centuries the population of the Great Lake and Laurentian regions experienced major shifts. The Iroquoians, semi-sedentary horticulturists who had occupied lowland villages such as Hochelaga on Montreal Island during Cartier's voyages, had left by the time the French came to settle in 1642. The length of their stay along the river, the reason for their retreat, as well as their prior links to the Algonkians, have received various interpretations. The quasi-nomadic habits of a large number of some Iroquois groups and the horticultural concerns of a large number of Algonkian tribes argue against any strict identification between language and lifestyle. A capacity for quick adaptation to the environment and for borrowing from neighbouring groups must have reduced the cleavages existing between these cultures.[1]

The French established themselves on what was practically unoccupied ground, but their presence, like that of the Dutch along the Hudson, stimulated trade and, as a consequence, exacerbated ancient rivalries among Iroquoian tribes located on either side of Lake Ontario.[2] The Five Nation Confederacy's destruction of Huronia in the decade that followed the founding of Montreal proved a short-lived triumph. Huron control of northern markets fell to the Ottawa and other Algonkians who became the French's major suppliers. Worried that their furs might be diverted towards New Amsterdam, the French strove to consolidate their alliances and to subjugate the Iroquois. This policy proved a tortuous one, expansionist and aggressive on the commercial front but militarily faint-hearted and defensive.[3] The War of the League of Augsburg fused such rivalries within the larger Anglo-French conflict, and native peoples appeared mostly as mercenaries in the pay of the Europeans.[4]

About 80,000 Indians lived within an 800-kilometer radius of Montreal in present-day Quebec and Ontario.[5] Within a 250-kilometer radius the Iroquois territory contained a total of some 50,000 people and some villages with over 1,000 inhabitants; this was the only area of relatively high population density. About 4,000 Algonkians still dwelt along the North Shore, while a few scattered bands of Mohicans crossed the hazy boundaries of New England to the French settlements. These were Montreal's closest neighbours. The Ojibwa, reckoned at 20,000, formed a more compact group to the west, between the Ottawa River and other concentrations along Lake Michigan, but they only visited the colony occasionally. As for the Northern Cree, they rarely ventured downstream. The Montagnais did not travel west, and the Micmacs and Abenaki seldom penetrated the Montreal plain before the eighteenth century. Despite this geographic dispersal, links were soon forged between the Indians distributed along the huge Saint Lawrence basin and the French who occupied the valley. Proselytism, trade, and warfare stimulated readier contacts than the layout of settlement would suggest.

The studies undertaken by anthropologists and ethno-historians provide a clearer understanding of the nature of pre-Columbian civilization and the sort of tensions that arose from contact with the Europeans.[6] If contemporary eyewitness accounts can help to shed light on the cultural make-up of these societies and on their subsequent transformations, the very same documents can in turn be read to assess changes in the perceptions of the onlookers.[7] This last approach has, however, proved both less fruitful and less satisfactory because we still know too little about the outlook of the community experiencing this contact. For surely neither the Jesuits, who, according to circumstances, denounced the original sin they had come to extirpate or exalted the innate virtues of their catechumens and even displayed some cultural relativism, nor La Hontan, who voiced the bitterness and hopes of the early eighteenth century, nor any of the administrators or chroniclers, could be said to represent the mass of settlers.[8]

Only rarely does a chapter devoted to the impact made by native civilization soar beyond material and technical borrowings – foodstuffs or medicinal plants, means of transport, and hunting, fishing, or fighting methods.[9] A description of the mores of the coureurs be bois follows such enumerations, with the inevitable characterization of the Canadian as sturdy, carefree, insubordinate, even corrupt, as some would have it – features hastily imputed to Indian influence.[10] Except for a few works, such as Marcel Giraud's, the physical setting and the process of acclimatization get short shrift. Giraud concludes in his excellent study of the Canadian Métis that the Laurentian colony never felt the pull of native society to the point of surrendering its own identity. But harsh living conditions, coupled with unavoidable links with native peoples, bred a familiarity that heralded the closer ties forged in the interior and paved the way for the eventual integration of a sizable portion of Canadians into the other culture.[11] Whether they simply facilitated later associations or were strong enough to alter the character of the peasantry within half a century, such contacts are still poorly understood. Yet before we take this analysis further, it is imperative to clarify the mentality of the immigrants and the influences under which they laboured.

The structure of colonial society played as significant a role in determining the perceptions of native civilization as did the nature, frequency, and intensity of contacts. To define these relations, to find out which traits of Indian behaviour were really perceived by the average colonist, would be a challenging and exciting study, but it can only be done for the entire colony. It is impossible, given our limited focus and the scarcity of local sources, to impart more than a few observations that might eventually help to reveal the impact of each culture on the other and traces of this conflict in values that supposedly engendered regressive acculturation.[12]

We are emphasizing the perceptions of the settlers and not those of a minority like the coureurs be bois. For every Etienne Brûlé one could probably find twenty inhabitants who never ventured beyond the Lachine rapids and another score whose experience of the wilds was a brief and painful campaign endured rather than welcomed.[13] The vision of native peoples elaborated during the tentative contacts that preceded actual settlement undoubtedly reflect Indian harmony and pride, which the traveller, venturing alone in the wilds, would discover and retain the more easily if he were predisposed to accept the values he encountered.[14] But we believe that the ordinary contacts within the French settlement were of a different kind.

2 RESIDENTS AND VISITORS

At first the natives came spontaneously to meet the French. They brought them furs and lingered willingly around their settlements. Montreal soon had its contingent of Indians, and even if conversion was perfunctory, the seventy-six baptisms performed by the resident Jesuit in 1643 alone prove that native families remained in the vicinity. Baptisms continued to figure in parish registers until 1653 (although less frequently) and attest to the regular flow of visitors and to tentative settlement.[15] In the wake of the upheavals that accompanied the invasion of Huronia, various Algonkian and Iroquoian bands, cut off from their tribes by war, famine, and epidemics, moved to the valley. Merchants and missionaries, all pursuing their own interests, persuaded a number to settle in the colony. In a period of increasing peril, when settlers stuck close to their fields and few regular shipments of pelts came in from the west, the small Indian nucleus nestled by the storehouses could ensure a steady if not plentiful supply of furs. Merchants readily extended credit to these Indians, while the priests kept an eye on their families during the long hunting season. The authorities encouraged these settlements and showed great liberality towards such valuable military auxiliaries. One would be hard put to say whether the Indians viewed the material benefits as a mere by-product of conversion or as a major incentive.

In the first two decades of colonization the Indians were free to settle where they liked.[16] The Sulpicians placed several families on their Gentilly property and, in 1671, opened La Montagne mission, half a league from the town. Almost simultaneously, the Jesuits founded the mission known as Sault-Saint-Louis, or Kahnawake on their South-Shore seigneury of Laprairie-de-la-Madeleine. In both cases they were dealing with partly sedentary Indian hunters and farmers, mainly Iroquois in the case of the Jesuits, or Iroquois by adoption or enslavement in the case of the Sulpicians.[17] These missions relocated periodically, both to distance themselves from the taverns and to replace exhausted corn soils. In 1696 La Montagne was transferred north to Sault-au-Récollet, and in 1721 to the seigneury of Lac-des-deux-Montagnes. The Jesuits moved their Sault settlement on three separate occasions progressively further west.[18] The Sulpicians ministered separately to a small group of Algonkians located at the end of the island, in Baie d'Urfé (and later on the Ile aux Tourtes).[19]

Table 1 shows that resident Indians outnumbered the French up to 1666–68, after which their relative population size dropped rapidly. Epidemics, notably smallpox, which hit in 1687, took a heavy toll on the missions' populations, after which numbers stagnated. The sample is too small, however, to permit a thorough analysis. The table indicates quite clearly, however, that the ratio between women and children under fifteen rarely exceeded 1 and that in 1688 and 1695 it lay between 0.7 and 0.4. Similar rough calculations show that in the same period this ratio for the European population varied between 2 and 2.7. The imbalance between the sexes, always noticeable among the Indians, was certainly increased by the regular participation of men in military campaigns.

Table 1
Indian population settled in the vicinity of Montreal, 1666–1716

Year	1666	1685	1688	1692	1695	1716
Houses	–	104	106	117	–	–
Men	–	197	202	140	206	270
Boys fifteen and over	–	44	43	73	46	92
Women	–	255	195	233	288	362
Girls fifteen and over	–	36	40	22	32	55
Children of both sexes, younger than fifteen	–	372	136	253	129	398
Total Indian population	1,000(*)	904	616	721	701	1,177
French population enumerated on the Island of Montreal	659	1,720	1,413	1,341	2,161	4,409

Source: Colonial census, AC, G1, 460 and 461. Missions were no longer included after 1716.
*As there is no mission census prior to 1685, an approximation of 1,000 inhabitants was retained, although it may be too low since everyone agrees that their population dwindled between 1650 and 1685. The Montreal region was less affected, however, than those of Trois-Rivières and Quebec.

The extra Indian women found husbands among their own people beyond the mission walls, and the consequent resurgence of paganism created moral dilemmas for the Sulpicians.[20] Contemporaries all remarked on the natives' low birthrate. Talon, the intendant, ascribed it to the heavy tasks allotted the women as well as to prolonged breast-feeding, both of which practices he imagined changing through police regulations.[21] Yet aside from such factors, could this not be another example of the cataclysm that shrank the number of native peoples from Baffin Island to Tierra del Fuego? Infants succumbed to European viruses and to new foodstuffs that replaced a traditional diet.[22] Women, still responsible for the heavy labour and often mistreated by husbands they could no longer divorce, began to despair. The need to love and procreate languished, along with the will to live, in these first generations torn between two worlds. "We rarely see the natives age," one governor remarked.[23]

New arrivals were not sufficient to arrest the demographic slump. Whatever allure the colony had once held for the Indians evaporated. The Jesuits concentrated their efforts on far-off Algonkian missions and lost faith in mass conversions among the Iroquois, whose wavering allegiance had now fallen to the English. The extension of the fur-trading network meant that merchants were no longer keen to attract hunters and western middlemen to nonproductive areas. From time to time an Iroquois family having difficulties in its homeland or slaves escaping their condition might seek asylum in the missions, but this trickle was too weak to reverse the trend. The trend reversed itself in the eighteenth century with the establishment of a new mission on the West Island and the integration of prisoners captured in French raids on New York and New England during the War of the Spanish Succession.[24] Some of the captives were Indian, but most were women and children of European extraction. They were adopted, and the missionaries lost no time in converting them. This procedure raised such outcries in the neighbouring colonies that the authorities of New France were careful to publish no statistics. The Indians' legitimate booty could not be forcibly removed. Vigorous English protests and a bishop's pastoral spurred wealthy Canadians to buy back some of the prisoners. Others managed to escape; some of the women found husbands in the colony, and New England envoys secured the return of a group of prisoners. Several children who had been taken very young were left with their adoptive families and figure in the 1716 mission census.[25] The mission population continued to rise in the eighteenth century through the slow but regular absorption of newcomers or Métis and presumably through natural increase, which suggests that the Indians were slowly adapting. Between 1735 and 1752 the Sault-Saint-Louis mission still contained about a thousand people, as did the one at Lac-des-deux-Montagnes, located further from Montreal.[26]

There were also a few Indians settled outside the missions, in the town and in the *côtes*. A number had stayed behind when the missions moved on; others had rejected clerical tutelage while still desiring to trade with the colonists, and others yet had been turned out of the missions for improper behaviour.[27] The authorities encouraged Canadian families to hire Indian children – a covert form of adoption. These youngsters were free when they came of age.[28]

Slavery, made official in 1709, gradually replaced adoption, which had always been negligible. Since the 1685 Code Noir did not at first apply to New France, the colonists were loath to invest in goods they could not legally secure. The slave trade only took off with the settlement of Louisiana, where Indians were sold to plantations or were transported to the West Indies, two Indians being worth one black. Western tribes – the Cree, Assiniboine, and especially the Pawnees from Missouri – were the objects of this traffic. Both fur traders and trading-post officials regularly brought slaves back to the colony, and according to Marcel Trudel, by the middle of the eighteenth century, merchants, civil officials, and military officers owned on the average two slaves apiece.[29] Slaves were quite rare in our period, however, as is confirmed by estate inventories, and there were certainly not more than fifty or so on the Island of Montreal in 1716. Their presence raised the number of Indians unaccounted for and dispersed among the island's French population to about two hundred.

Mission Indians enumerated with the French were Christian and therefore royal subjects.[30] France long cherished the hope that the colony might absorb the entire native population. What better way indeed of nurturing the King's loyal subjects?[31] "The native population should be encouraged to live with the French by giving them land and common farms, by educating their children and having them marry."[32] Although this policy remained in effect, after 1675 the metropolitan authority ceased to concern itself with this matter or indeed with peopling Canada.

The Jesuits, who did not equate conversion with assimilation, frustrated the French policy by attempting to isolate new converts, even inside the colony. Their detractors, headed by Governor Frontenac and the Sulpicians, claimed that they made no attempt to alter native lifestyles and did not teach the Indians how to read or speak French for fear of the corrupting influence of the settlers, who might weaken their hold over them.[33] The Sulpicians prided themselves on following royal directives. "We believe," one of them declared, "that they profit by living among us, and not in their own land; that they must be taught our language, that their women must wear skirts and their men hats and pants; that they must adopt French housing; learn animal husbandry, and how to sow wheat and root vegetables; and that they must be able to read and hear mass and be taught the holy rites."[34] Less generous as proselytizers and more fussy about matters of dogma and morals, the Sulpicians did not glorify the primitive state and encouraged racial integration, which they felt would elevate rather than corrupt the Indians. For "congress with the French was only dangerous in unruly Michili-mackinac, where no French woman dared venture. Inside the colony, with its married women and rather strict laws, the natives fared better than in their sin-infested, magic-ridden homeland."[35] Such principles would bend in the face of widespread drunkenness, yet the Sulpicians held fast to their methods. At Kahnawake, however, which had no school, and where they were never completely cut off from their New York tribesmen, the Iroquois did not learn French. Since the Indians seem to have refused to gibber in French, the colonists had to acquire a smattering of various native languages. Yet surprisingly few Indian words entered the French tongue until the middle of the eighteenth century.[36]

The missions cannot be regarded as "true reservations cut off from civilization" along the lines of Latin American *reduciones*.[37] Whether they advocated or opposed segregation proved immaterial to the Sault-Saint-Louis Indians, who had as many dealings with the settlers as their Montreal counterparts. The Jesuits' aims could not be achieved without a complete overhaul of the economic foundations of the missions, which remained anchored in the fur trade and thus in the life of the colony.[38]

Besides, there was no point fencing in sedentary Indians while the town gates were thrown wide open to visitors from the west. Every August Montreal welcomed hundreds of members of various nations to its annual fur fair.[39] Although numbers dwindled after 1680, once the furs were gathered at source, the fair itself survived until the turn of the century.[40] It continued to be attended by as many as five hundred to one thousand Indians hoping for better terms than those afforded by the voyageurs, and by envoys on official visits, whom the governor greeted with great ceremony.[41] The fair was held on the communal plot stretching between the town and the river, in principle the only authorized trading ground. The visitors camped in and around this area, located beyond the urban enclosure. Anyone could buy furs, but those who rented a stall had the ascendency, while soldiers and archers did a brisk trade on their own behalf or that of their officers under the guise of protecting the Indians from local cupidity.[42] In this ebullient atmosphere, where deals were struck on the spot without witnesses or interpreters, disorder proved unavoidable. At best, the worst violence was averted.[43]

One intendant actually suggested lodging the visitors on a small island, under guard, "to avoid their being insulted and so that the French do them no harm," but the run of conflicts did not justify such extreme measures.[44] Having sold their furs, the Indians lingered on the island, and for a few weeks the publicans and peasants who retailed illegal brandy made excellent money. Having thus jettisoned part of the European goods they had come to fetch, the visitors mended their canoes and returned home. They enlivened the town with their presence until late September.

3 CONTACTS

In addition to these disheartening summer encounters, the settlers came into regular daily contact with Indian residents. Some suburban residents attended Mass at La Montagne, which was closer than the parish church. For a long time settlers in Rivière-des-Prairies depended on the offices of the Sault-au-Récollet missionary, while the Jesuit mission provided a similar service for the Laprairie-de-la-Madeleine colonists, who were without a church.[45] These weekly meetings provided opportunities for Indian and French to become better acquainted.

At La Montagne their children attended the same school. The nuns imparted various skills deemed appropriate for the girls, such as knitting, while the schoolmaster taught the boys French, reading, writing, woodwork, and Latin canticles for the church.[46] Royal subsidies for native education allowed the neighbouring colonists' sons to learn more than the weekly catechism, all that was taught to youngsters in other côtes.

The Indians erected their bark-and-branch housing near the fort surrounding the mission buildings and sowed corn and beans on land to which they held no legal title. The Crown had placed the land under trusteeship and "for excellent reasons established the Reverend Fathers of the Company of Jesus as trustees and guardians of the Indians of New France, for the said Indians have been deemed incapable of managing the Property they are given." The monarch conferred seigneuries on the Natives "with the proviso that the said Indians will be and always remain under the guidance, direction, and protection of the Fathers."[47] Their trustees allocated them part of these seigneuries and gradually granted the remaining parcels to French colonists. This meant that the Indians could no longer clear the land gradually and break in new ground to replace exhausted soils in their customary manner.[48] Once French farms surrounded the mission, the Indians were forced to relocate further afield and start from scratch. The natives never regained the ownership of the seigneuries, which simply devolved to the Company of Jesus.

Conditions were different on the Island of Montreal, which belonged outright to the Sulpicians. No one can accuse them of usurpation, since they never granted any land to the Indians. "We have been told," wrote their procurator "that no land is transferred to the Indians in return for seigneurial dues, that such is not the custom in New France, but that they get only the usufruct of the lots placed at their disposal."[49] The issue came up repeatedly. "The decision not to grant land owing Cens and Rentes to the Indians should be strictly obeyed, for as they are unreliable, these parcels would soon escheat to the Crown. One can, however, set aside and verbally allot them an amount they can properly clear and cultivate. Yet if these Indians subsequently depart either to transfer their dwellings elsewhere or for some other reason, the Seminary will have to repossess and would be well advised to rent these parcels rather than to treat them as uncleared lots."[50]

Yet we know that the Indians were reluctant to leave La Montagne.[51] Either their petitions or those of the peasants who coveted their admirably situated lots spurred the procurator to confirm his stance. He declared that Indian lands were to merge with the demesne, that their harvest should certainly not be appraised, and that the Indians should be prevented from renting out land they did not own. For should this happen, the foreseeable result would be that the takers would not pay dues and thus fail to recognize seigneurial rights. It was best that the rent "be collected by the seigneurs who might then assist the Indians."[52] The subsequent move from Sault-au-Récollet to Lac-des-Deux-Montagnes incited a similar response: "the plots cleared by the Indians will provide the Seminary with a whole new parish."[53]

The Indians, as Jesuit wards or Sulpician usufructuaries, were being dispossessed, but it took six or seven generations before this realization dawned and they grasped the meaning of private property.[54]

The missionaries convinced some families to build European-style housing at La Montagne, not far from the seigneurial domains, the farmer's quarters, the orchard, fishpond, and dovecote.[55] The settlers' fields lay scattered below. Since corn matured later than wheat, the French would damage Indian crops when they let their animals loose on harvested fields; common grazing in these parts was therefore put off until the middle of September. Indians soon added animal husbandry to horticulture and kept some chickens, pigs, or sometimes a cow.[56] In traditional fashion, these activities were relegated to the womenfolk, but they could neither plough the land nor grow European crops that required more time and other tools without male assistance. This agricultural produce hardly answered basic subsistence requirements or filled new needs. Whatever added income they could muster by peddling small objects in the town, or dressing hides for the voyageurs, still failed to cover the cost of blankets, tools, and now necessary utensils.[57] Missionary hand-outs of clothing, seeds, or food such as eels, remained mere expedients.[58]

The mission was still highly dependent on the fur trade, but military service interfered with such activity. Indians at Sault-Saint-Louis and Montreal furnished two to three hundred warriors, who fought in every campaign side by side with the colonial militias.[59] They received no other remuneration than their upkeep during the campaign and whatever they could loot.

When their services were not required, the men went off trapping in the fall and were absent most of the winter.[60] Merchants advanced them muskets, powder, shot, knives, and other implements used for the journey or by their families, which they eventually repaid with pelts.[61] The Indians honoured their debts. The authorities were quick to denounce the occasional default, for the entire system rested on a pyramid of credit erected on countless small loans to the Indians. In estate inventories such claims are included among short-term sound debts.[62] The rest of the Indians' income would too often be frittered away in drink and bring little to the community.[63] Although a few young Indians served apprenticeships, most of the second and third generations were engaged in fur trading and wars, just as their forebears had been.

Although no evidence is available, the men may well have participated in the building of roads, ditches, palisades, and the like. Yet there was no economic pressure to retrain them for such tasks. They were expert at fashioning the bark canoes used by both the voyageurs and the troops, and the absence of notarized contracts for this activity implies that it rested mainly in Indian hands. Under what conditions, and for what profit? We cannot say.

But contemporary accounts suggest men wandering through the côtes and the streets of the town looking for fun and friendship. "We drank some cider at Laverdure, then beer at Crespeau's and afterwards went door-to-door to say our farewells before the wintering," three Sault-au-Récollet Indians recalled.[64] That two alehouses were wanted in a village of a hundred men only confirms this impression of idleness. While such authorized establishments fulfilled a necessary social function, the Indian who really wished to get drunk had to get his brandy elsewhere. An endless barrage of edicts, decrees, ordinances, and pastorals prohibited the sale of alcohol to the Indians – a measure of the ineffectuality of such edicts.[66] Loud and quarrelsome, these drunken figures sent packing from the town by the archers would regain the mission of an evening, terrifying the peasants on their way, for there were enough cases of rape, injury, or murder to unnerve the population and to raise an outcry against these unfortunate drunkards.[67] The protests became even more shrill against the Indians' intoxicators and the sluggish authorities who neither protected nor punished. Torn between the Indians, who denied responsibility for crimes committed under the influence and who rejected French criminal statutes (to which they were deemed answerable), and settlers who clamoured for justice, the authorities bided their time.[68] They buried themselves in useless trials, undertaken to silence the one group, then dropped to pacify the other.[69]

4 INTERMARRIAGE

Despite initial official encouragement, intermarriage remained far from common. The three thousand livres set aside annually as a dowry to settle sixty Indian brides with French husbands were soon allocated elsewhere.[70] There are only seven mixed marriages registered on the Island of Montreal between 1642 and 1712, but this is hardly the whole picture, for it should not be forgotten that unions were usually blessed in the bride's parish, in many cases a mission for which no registers are extant. And it could be that the ethnic origins of Indians with French last names would not be recorded. Yet even with such omissions the proportion of interracial unions remained quite low, even for the early period, with its excess of males. Only later, in the west, would the temporary relationships between voyageurs and Indian girls who rendered invaluable assistance become long-lasting and often be legitimized by missionaries.[71] But such unions were usually confined to the hinterland.

The colonist who settled on the land or practised some craft had no incentive to take an Indian wife. We know of one case where the Sulpicians urged one of their servants to marry a girl from La Montagne and settle down in the mission.[72] But the reverse – Indian women integrated within the French community – was more common, though the evidence is elusive. If they survived their first confinement, how many of these brides, uprooted too suddenly, went back to their people? If mixed marriages are difficult to find, it is probably because such alliances were usually contracted by obscure individuals – a fact overshadowed by a few striking exceptions.[73]

Miscegenation was therefore usually a matter of illegitimacy, although a priori neither Iroquois mores nor the life of the missions encouraged promiscuity. These Indians were monogamous; the easy dissolution of marriages encouraged fidelity, and while girls were given much freedom, they took care if they wanted a husband.[74] Christianity imposed a stricter code, but if ancient restrictions no longer applied, it proved difficult to impose new ones. The governor reported that young noblemen took advantage of Indian women whom they kept in the côtes, and it was said that some mission women led scandalous lives. Such behaviour, often associated with alcohol, incurred the Indian community's disapproval and repudiation. Women with shorn heads were not unknown in the missions.[75]

The integration of illegitimate and adopted children soon altered the ethnic character of these sparsely populated Indian villages. But the handful of Indians slowly absorbed by white society and the half-breeds scattered around the missions were hardly sufficient to effect a racial transformation of the larger group.[76]

Even on this reduced scale, the difference between the behaviour of voyageurs and settlers recalls the contrast between Spanish and Anglo-Saxon patterns of colonization, the one with heavy and the second with limited interbreeding. This divergence can be traced, according to Chaunu, to specific circumstances rather than to psychological attitudes: namely, the relative size of the two groups in question and the type of economic activity.[77]

5   COLLECTIVE PERCEPTIONS

Except for references to the missionaries' trials and to policies formulated to deal with the natives, seventeenth-century sources yield only these few vague and negative traces to describe the Indian communities established around Montreal. After their initial enthusiasm, officials did no more than ensure that the Indian settlements quietly filled their expected functions: to provide furs and to be warriors.

After all, since the colonists' perceptions were shaped at the very time when Indian civilization was rocked by violent culture shock, could they view the Indians as anything other than pitiful savages? However trying their own circumstances, the first settlers had come face to face with a more beleaguered group. No matter what they had endured before emigrating, the Europeans encountered native people who suffered even greater alienation. After two decades of hard work the settler had a house, a cleared stretch of land, and status within rural society. Two decades after its establishment conditions at La Montagne remained as uncertain as ever. The life the Indians led in the colony was as precarious as it had always been, growing more disjoined and more dependent every day.[78] If we are correct in assuming that most settlers crossed the seas to escape endemic poverty and to find an alternative to vagrancy, could their perception of the Indians they dominated – a perception spawned by regular contacts – act as a model to decipher the character of this peasantry in the making?

CHAPTER TWO

The French Population

.

1 PATTERN OF IMMIGRATION

In the spring of 1642 a party of fifty Frenchmen, representing the Société de Notre Dame de Montréal pour la conversion des Sauvages de la Nouvelle France,[1] set foot on the island that the Compagnie des Cent Associés donated for the furtherance of such pious plans. In the first ten years some one hundred and fifty individuals arrived in the settlement. The age pyramid from the 1666 census illustrates the initial difficulties: few remained in the upper cohorts, where these first immigrants should logically figure, for just a handful had persevered in this isolated spot, so vulnerable to Iroquois attacks.[2]

The arrival of about another two hundred persons in 1653 and 1659 revitalized a settlement few had expected to survive. As defence against ambush improved, the colonists ventured beyond the palisades to clear the land and build new houses. They married. The same bimodal pyramid clearly pinpoints this recovery, and census data indicate that from then on Montreal kept pace with the rest of the colony.[3] Immigration continued to be slow and irregular, with a short period of relative intensity between 1653 and 1672 that left a favourable annual balance in migration – about three hundred settlers – in the colony.

Three factors account for the rise in the population of Montreal: immigration from France, local migrations, and natural increase. One would need to estimate the latter in order to isolate gains through immigration, but this proved impossible: the under-registration of deaths, the uneven reliability of census data, and the added complication of regional instability all combine to blur the results.

About twelve hundred to fifteen hundred immigrants settled on the Island of Montreal between 1642 and 1714; 75 per cent remained.

Half came before 1670, after which arrivals sharply declined; but between 1695 and 1705 a sudden upsurge rectified this lag. If a sizable
proportion came off the boats, newcomers also included four hundred discharged soldiers and people from other parts of the colony.

For 1681 – that is, immediately following the first wave of
arrivals – immigration can be categorized as in Table 2. Indentured
servants constituted the largest group, half of the males, excluding
those still in service who potentially could go home. A smaller
contingent of soldiers accounted for less than one-fifth of immigrants, while another fifth from miscellaneous backgrounds paid for
their own passage. Nearly three-quarters of the women who embarked set off alone in search of husbands.

These categories could be reshuffled so that temporary immigrants might be distinguished from permanent settlers. The first
group would comprise soldiers and indentured servants with short-
term contracts and return tickets. Yet can one really ascertain the
long-term intentions of unmarried workers who left for a three-year
stint in Canada rather than trek across France and neighbouring
countries?[5] Did distance imply more in that period? What about the
soldier who enlisted for six years and had no say in his destination?
Similarly, few merchants and officers perceived their transfer as
definitive. In fact, only whole families or single women left France
with no intention of returning.

Can one distinguish between forced and voluntary departures?
Strictly speaking, forced migration could apply to women or to the
odd prisoner forcibly enrolled into the colonial troops.[6] Actual
deportation to New France was insignificant in the seventeenth
century, but a broader definition of the term might well include
almost everybody. Obviously people emigrated because of economic
duress. But as long as they decided when to leave and where to go,
or at least decided when to stay, can one not speak of voluntary
relocation for economic reasons? There is little doubt that repulsion
played as great a part as attraction. Yet economic difficulties,
distress, and uncertainty characterized the entire century, and those
who crossed the ocean to escape this fate were few. This thin trickle
cannot be linked to the period's major crises.[7] Rather, it was the
result of individual and serendipitous encounters, which prompted
men to move beyond the usual migratory circuits. A country and a
century so conspicuously concerned with increasing population gave
little encouragement to such departures, and the response was on a
similar scale.[8]

Eschewing, therefore, any elaborate model, I now describe the
various groups of immigrants.

Table 2
Distribution of Montreal's population in 1681 according to the type of immigration[4]

Total enumerated		1,389
Born in the colony		888
Male immigrants		340
Ecclesiastics	10	
Officers and volunteer noblemen	12	
Merchants	15	
Volunteers with families	16	
Single volunteers (uncertain)	7	
Discharged soldiers	59	
Settled former indentured servants	150	
Indentured servants in 1681	71	
Female immigrants		161
Nuns	17	
Servants in 1681	4	
Women and girls accompanying husband or parents	26	
Women and girls on their own	114	

Source: Census AC, G1, 460

2   FAMILIES

Twenty-four of the 111 families living in Montreal in 1666 had already been formed in France.[9] Kin groupings comprised only 15 per cent of arrivals prior to the first census,[10] and later on this proportion fell even lower. We know of only four instances where a family head arrived separately and then brought out his dependents.[11] Usually the whole family emigrated as a unit, albeit a modest one, with just one or two children. Half consisted of old couples or widowers with grown-up children. Thirteen families embarked together in 1659, from their native Aunis, La Rochelle, and, especially, the village of Marans. Such groups were likely to be related or to have forged strong bonds before the crossing, and they shared such kinship ties with several unmarried engagés, or indentured labourers, who arrived at the same time. These families were poor, and the religious communities that recruited them advanced their fares in return for labour and other forms of payment. Although they were not bound by work contracts, their material and social position differed little from that of the engagés. The Sovereign Council, however, looked askance at immigrants with a one-way passage, who might come to depend on colonial largesse.[12]

Some of the Société de Notre-Dame's early recruits fared quite well, reflecting personal qualities that the tiny settlement and harsh living conditions brought to the fore. Natives of Igé en Perche, a carpenter, his wife, and five children, had accompanied the founders in 1642 and were followed a year later by his sister, her husband (a *laboureur*, it would seem), and their four children. In 1646 the carpenter returned home to sell his property and still had 800 livres due to him from the proceeds when he left for Montreal, again taking two young fellow-villagers into his service: they were followed by at least three more in the next few years.[13] The rather sizable emigration from this village containing but fifty households seems to have been inspired by local example rather than by poverty. Such immigrant families generally solidified the already enviable positions they had achieved in their places of origins. The first syndics and churchwardens issued from their ranks, and chance alliances worked in their favour. Single merchants and the choicest of early recruits married their daughters, disdaining the shipload of females sent over by the Crown to steady the *engagés*. This group of families along with a few single settlers ensured the survival of the trading post in the earliest decade, and such antecedence granted them the special status they would enjoy for two generations.

3 GENTLEMEN-SOLDIERS

Between 1642 and 1662 a score of men arrived in Montreal for whom soldiering was emblematic of their station rather than an occupation. The pronounced martial character of French society had been recently refuelled by the wars of religion and the Fronde. But while some of the gentilshommes who came to Canada belonged to the lower nobility, others were members of a provincial bourgeoisie with similar tastes for combat and a hankering after easy promotion.[14] These men formed the core of Ville-Marie's first notables. Not a one, including the local governor, had ever held a commission in the army (for, had they been discharged, their rank would certainly have appeared in the records). In short, they were the well-born who had failed to become officers and who had either served in the ranks or as members of some local company raised by provincial aristocrats. This was still common practice and did not, in and of itself, signify a loss of status.

Among the early arrivals, "fort soldiers" of good birth received fiefs and arrière-fiefs. Those serving as staff officers were remunerated by the Compagnie des Habitants, and they supplemented these payments with profits from the fur trade, which rapidly consumed their energies. A modicum of education allowed some to occupy the civil offices available in the seigneury. They were also used to lead the militia. After 1685, when Canada received a definite military organization, officers' commissions would be awarded in these families in recognition of past services and as a nod to their genteel birth. The second generation kept alive the military ideals that had brought their fathers to the colony.[15] These first Montrealers and other gentilshommes who had settled in Quebec or Acadia in Louis XIII's reign shared a chivalric tradition that encompassed both individual bravery and banditry.[16] These values corresponded so closely to those of Indian society that, instead of influence, we might well speak of encounter.[17]

While volunteers with similar social backgrounds still arrived in the second half of the seventeenth century, they were less soldiers than adventurers. They included Norman gentilshommes such as Dominique La Motte, who, in the wake of de la Salle, arrived too late and had problems meshing into a society where military promotion played such an important role and even adventure was prey to centralizing pressures.

The colonial authorities encouraged this sort of immigration in the decade that followed the establishment of royal government. The Sovereign Council supported for a year, at the King's expense, "six young men of good extraction who had paid for their crossing."[18] The intendant welcomed with open arms a young gentleman who had come to Canada "to get a feel for the lay of the land." "If persons of such quality follow suit," he exulted, "Canada will soon be filled with people who might adequately ensure its survival."[19] Several unhappy incidents combined with the proliferation of the local petty nobility soon dampened such enthusiasm.

4 INDENTURED LABOUR

The system

The system of indentured labour in the colonies represented no more than a variant of short-term service contracts. It was not unusual to part with one's freedom for specific periods, usually fairly lengthy or even perpetual – that is to say, indeterminate – if one became an apprentice, a servant, a soldier, or a sailor. Although Debien feels that indentureships in Canada derived from fishing contracts, it seems more likely that their origins lie in the widespread patterns of servitude familiar to people in the interior and on the Atlantic coasts of France.[20] In the early seventeenth century the

Virginia Company quite naturally had recourse to indentureship in order to people its plantations. This was considered preferable to forced conscription, and the system was favoured for similar reasons by French planters in the West Indies.[21]

Trading companies and a few colonists began by enlisting their labourers personally. They subsidized their crossing, provided for their keep, and paid their wages. For the system to be worthwhile, it had to generate sufficient profits to offset unavoidable losses by death, illness, or desertion, above and beyond the expected cost of enrolment and transport. The higher the number and the lengthier the contract, the better the chances of absorbing expected and unexpected expenditures. This implied that whatever these men produced had to find quick and profitable outlets. Yet, given the wretched development of Canada in the first half of the seventeenth century, the question is not why settlement lagged but rather how the colonists managed in these unfavourable conditions to bring over several hundred labourers. The only remunerative activity, the fur trade, did not require as many, so non-lucrative motives had to be invoked to promote this slight but steady inflow. Once the warehouses had a large enough contingent, the Church and its followers took over this unprofitable recruitment.

Almost all of the two hundred and fifty people who came to the Island of Montreal between 1642 and 1653 were hired by the Société de Notre-Dame, at a resounding loss. Having thus immobilized 300,000 livres, the society had to sit tight until the workforce generated returns, by land clearance and other labour, that, could recover some of that huge capital investment. The society hovered on the brink of bankruptcy.[22] Defraying the expense of recruitment, travel, and a few personal effects had exhausted its reserves. The society could simply not afford to support for five years the one hundred or so hands drafted in 1653 and pay the wages they were promised. Non-economic motivations (survival of the establishment for evangelical purposes) prompted further recruitment to replace the dead or missing. For a while yet furs would provide the only source of profit. The society did not disdain them, but its representative, de Maisonneuve, had to share the returns with his servants through fear of losing both returns and servants.

Granting these penniless men their freedom was no solution, for they required seeds, tools, and trade goods to make it on their own. This explains those curious transactions that freed the *engagés* upon landing, although they had to acknowledge a debt of 300 to 500 livres towards the governor to cover their fare and past and future advances.[23] These private agreements specified that those who settled permanently in Montreal would not be held accountable. Two-thirds of the 1653 contingent refused their freedom under such conditions, which underlines the temporary nature of their immigration as well as their doubts concerning the company's liquidity.[24] Ten years later, three of the assenters sued the governor to obtain their so-called bonus, or, alternatively, to void the debt acknowledgement they had signed, which restricted their freedom of movement and mortgaged their lot.[25] They lost the suit, and those who left the seigneury had to refund the amount.[26]

In fact, prior to 1655 indentured servants who came to Montreal found no masters. Around Quebec, by contrast, the system operated quite normally. The leaders of the Compagnie des Habitants did quite well for themselves: ships arrived that needed refitting; the price of wheat was high; and the first colonists needed workers to clear the land. These had to be fed, and a chain reaction set in that made it profitable for a time to import labour. Between 1655 and the creation of the Compagnie des Indes occidentales in 1664, the merchants of La Rochelle, Rouen, and the colony enlisted more men than the requisite *engagé* per ton of freight demanded by the Quebec Council.[27] This suggests that those who traded in this workforce got something out of it, as did those who had been shipping them to the Caribbean islands since 1645 or to the English colonies since 1625.[28] The buyer refunded the passage and various advances to these traders, who could make a profit if the buyer's estimates were high. As will be argued below, well-placed and enterprising colonists benefited from the system in other ways.

Montreal did not remain long on the sidelines. Merchants arrived along with the priests of the Compagnie de Saint-Sulpice, the Société de Notre-Dame's successors.[29] It was the latter who brought over a sizable group of families, servants, and single women in 1659, while merchants' recruits came up from Quebec. From then on, indenture contracts ran their usual course.

When Canada came under the administrative control of the French Ministry of Marine in 1663, settlement became a priority. Colbert wanted to send colonists, but the Sovereign Council argued that the two hundred men shipped annually by the Compagnie des Indes occidentales, between 1664 and 1667, would be put to better use as contract labour.[30] The Council's insistence is further proof that the system set up by the merchants was quite profitable. Metropolitan shippers did well by recruiting for the state, while colonial merchants profited from a cheap labour pool that cleared their land at the very time when government expenditures and the arrival of troops stimulated an unprecedented boom. Labour needs were soon met, however, and following this expansionary phase the number of *engagés* sent to New France dropped dramatically. As in earlier days, most were recruited directly, either by private individuals or by religious communities.[31] French outfitters had trouble meeting the official quota, based on their freight tonnage.[32]

Once it had been established, the local agricultural system based on family farms required little outside labour. Even New England, which was more developed, did not depend much on indentureships.[33] Montreal homesteaders relied on their sons, on a small pool of local labourers, and also on soldiers for seasonal work; the latter, like the prisoners in the eighteenth century, represented a cheap source of labour, recruited through the good offices of the Crown.[34] Ship's captains could only respond to this competition and get rid of their small cargoes by bringing in boys at appallingly low wages.[35] Later on, the hiring of Indians for domestic service would have a similar effect: the ratio of skilled workers among indentured immigrants decreased, and qualified persons had to be recruited on an individual basis and commanded top prices.[36]

Profile of the recruits

In the spring of 1653 Jerome LeRoyer de la Dauversière, a La Flèche tax collector and founding member of the Société de Notre-Dame, signed on 119 youths from the town and surrounding parishes. It was just after the Fronde. Only a few months had passed since the armies of the princes and royal mercenaries had devastated the area around Angers, and after the crisis of 1649–52 prices had begun to collapse.[37] He would have had no problems hiring under such circumstances. But as the overall situation improved between March and June 1653 (the sailing date from Nantes), almost half reneged on their promise, more confident about their prospects. The quotas were filled, on the eve of departure, with men hired on the waterfront. With a notary present, each was handed a chest and a few personal effects as an advance, and the contingent was carefully watched until the ship left its moorings. Of the 103 indentured servants counted at the outset, 8 apparently perished at sea.[38]

We can do no more than conjecture about the prior history of recruits who arrived before 1659, for only the passenger list has survived. They included families, marriageable girls, but only thirty indentured labourers. While the 1653 labourers had been recruited for the Société de Notre-Dame, these men came to serve the Sulpicians, the nuns who had travelled with them, and colonists who awaited them in Montreal. Some had been hired at La Flèche and others in Aunis, whence the vessel set sail.

All these men made similar commitments. They agreed to serve on the Island of Montreal, in their speciality or in any other capacity, for a fixed period, usually five years but occasionally three. The employers defrayed their fares and expenses for their maintenance in the colony. These were young men, twenty to twenty-five years old, and all but two were single or presumed to be.[39] In Montreal they would be set to clear the land to perform the ordinary run of agricultural tasks. Relying on the tasks they would perform both during and after their indentureships, I took the liberty of classifying three-quarters of these two shiploads of *engagés* as unskilled, irrespective of what they stated in their contracts. Up to a point their wages can be taken as an accurate gauge of their capabilities.

A fit labourer fetched 60 livres per year. Anyone who earned less was either too young or too frail.[40] Those in the second category, who earned 75 livres, cleared the soil like those in the first category, but also had another skill such as cobbler, hatter, paver, pit-sawyer, and so on. Some may have had proven prior experience; others, exploiting the recruiters' difficulties in meeting their quotas, negotiated for more favourable terms.

Besides four individuals either better educated or from a higher social class (singled out from the first), the third category included carpenters, joiners, masons, two millers, a gunsmith, and a locksmith, every one of whom would, once freed, basically make a living from his craft. One-fifth of the contingent consisted of journeymen of this sort who made 100 livres a year; a fair enough proportion, for no more were needed to dispense basic services.

Whatever their qualifications, the men had one thing in common: they had been destitute when they left France. The bit of cash and the clothing and shoes they received mortgaged a full year's wages, if not more. Their social origins remain obscure, for we are not told their parents' occupations.[41] Any hope of tracking down their antecedents in their place of birth appears very tenuous given their geographic dispersal.[42] Contemporary assessments are not helpful. In the seventeenth century few virtues were associated with the lower classes, and the boundaries between poverty, idleness, and vice were unclear. Submission was the key. These people must be ruled firmly for, "Canada contained several persons who had been driven from their homes by crime."[43] "These people are easy to govern," one intendant concluded, "for despite their varied origins and the fact that vice forced the majority to seek asylum in this country in order to evade prosecution, they are nevertheless rather docile and manage to live fairly peacefully."[44]

Are our impressions any sounder? The kin ties often found among these men or between them and families who had migrated

Table 3
Occupational distribution of the *engagés* recruited for Montreal in 1653 and 1659

Annual wages	In livres										Incomplete data	Total
	0	30	60	65	70	75	80	90	100	150		
1653	–	1	32	–	1	47	4	1	14	1	–	101
1659	2	–	7	1	3	3	2	–	4	–	8	30
Total	2	1	39	1	4	50	6	1	18	1	8	131
Reshuffled	42 Inexperi- enced			55 Hardy labourers			25 Crafts- men or higher status			1 Surgeon		

Source: E. Faillon, *Histoire de la colonie française au Canada* (Paris 1865–66), ii: 531–61; R.J. Auger, *La Grande recrue de 1653* (Montreal 1955); A. Godbout, *Les Passagers du Saint-André: La recrue de 1659* (Montreal 1964).

earlier point to cohesion in the family background.[45] The inheritance of tiny properties – a *journal* of land near La Flèche, a 341-livre house in La Rochelle, a pasture, a house, or some unspecified succession in France – also suggests modest or poor, if firmly rooted backgrounds.[46] The youth of these indentured labourers would argue against a protracted and demoralizing begging career. Emigration to far-off parts, to escape dire circumstances or some misdemeanour (should the intendant be right), displays an adventurous spirit not usually associated with pauperism. If any conclusion can be hazarded, it is that the social origins of indentured labourers would probably resemble those of the soldiers studied by André Corvisier: needy but not indigent, little schooling, yet responsible.[47] They shared with the soldiers who came to Canada the same plebian origins, and similar circumstances had spurred them to sign on.

If the following letter is at all representative, then there is no reason to doubt that most of these youths kept up ties with their homeland.[48]

My dear son, I am most astonished to have met people from your country and not to have received a letter from you. It is true that I find it strange to have a son whom I have cherished more than my own self but who has no thought for me. I thought I would have the happiness of seeing him within four or five years of his departure. My dear son, I beg of you to try to find a way of coming back to France and of spending two to three months in your native town of La Flèche. I swear to you that you are your mother's heir and should you come to La Flèche you would have over 800 livres. For it has not come to me, since the *coutume de Maine* does not let the father inherit. This is why I beg of you to come as soon as possible, since this affects you directly. I ask for nothing except that you show me the respect owed father and mother. Your father Leger Adverty, not forgetting Marie Lemoine, your mother. Your uncle Lucas sends you his best, as do your aunt, his wife, and all your good friends in this good land of Anjou, where white wine costs a sol. My son, I do not yet take my leave. I still hope, God willing, to see my eyes on you in La Flèche before I die. [in the margin] Florent Gaste, your cousin who married that late Michelle Vultte, has written this letter for me. [on the back] To be handed to the [Sieur] Maurice Adverty, resident in Canada.

Distribution

Three census lists indicated who employed this workforce. The 1666 and 1667 census returns show that more than one-quarter of indentured servants worked on the seigneurial domains. Saint-Sulpice and the other two religious communities on the island – the Hôtel Dieu and the Congregation de Notre-Dame – hired nearly half the hands. Two wealthy merchants, Lemoyne and Leber, employed five to nine men, while less important merchants hired three to five. Basically, only five farms besides the religious domains could boast of moderately large crews. A heterogeneous group including the garrison major, judicial officials, a dozen or so minor fur traders, and as many artisans kept one or two hands. These landowners rarely worked the land directly. Despite modest means, they depended on hired help to clear sections that would then be leased for revenue. In 1667 a dozen peasants among the oldest settlers also kept servants. But three-quarters of families could not afford assistance with the clearing. Only eight former *engagés* who had been in the colony since 1653 were able to declare a servant; three of them were artisans.

By 1681 indentured labour had seen its heyday. Only the religious communities and the richest merchants still supported some *engagés*. A native labour force replaced the immigrants, as colonists put their sons to the plough or relied on local youths for seasonal work. The mean age of servants born in Canada was fifteen, and these boys and girls were hired at very low wages by the notables for domestic service rather than for farm work.[49] New settlers continued to clear their land on their own. This distribution of *engagés* was not peculiar to Montreal, as the suits against servants by such as conseillers du roi, other civil and military officers, as well as merchants indicate.[50]

Table 4
Distribution of Montreal servants according to the 1666, 1667, and 1681 census returns

Year	House-holds	Servants born in Canada	Servants born in France	Households with engagés %	Households with servants %	Servants per household* 0	1	2	3–5	5+
1666	141	1	103	24.2	24.2	107	16	10	5	3
1667	143	1	124	28.7	28.7	102	23	11	2	5
1681	279	26	75	4.5	13.0	243	23	5	4	4

Source: AC, G1 460
*The three religious communities were counted as individual households.

There is no call, therefore, to maintain the myth of old and new *engagés* working shoulder to shoulder, breaking bread together, where newcomers merged into households with similar social origins.[51] Few of the ordinary settlers who declared a servant in the census could afford to keep him for three years. Indeed, whenever equality was likely to exist, the workforce was likely to be the most mobile. On the whole, masters formed a separate category, with distinct social origins and occupations. Most indentured labourers were employed in crews on larger farms overseen by vigilant foremen.[52] Masters with only one or two hands lived in the town and used these labourers to work properties located several leagues away in isolated spots with crude shacks for shelter. With few exceptions, the *engagé* began life in the colony in straitened circumstances that relegated him to the bottom of the social ladder.

Indentureship

An *engagé* was "a man obliged to go wherever and do whatever his master commanded like a slave during the time of his indentureship."[53] Contracts were followed to the letter, and until their full expiry, the *engagé* remained the absolute property of his owner.[54]

Table 5 presents an estimate of the expenditures in the hypothetical case of a man hired in France for a three-year service in Canada at 75 livres per year. Labour costs were inversely related to output. The Quebec councillors made no bones about the fact that in the first year the men were hardly worth half their wages.[55] They were a poor investment in the short run. The longer the contract and the more skilled they became, the higher the profit margin. This explains why Colbert's ordinances, which cut indentureships from

Table 5
Estimate of master's expenses for an *engagé* over three years

1st year	30 l.	Fare paid to the ship's captain
	70 l.	Advance handed the *engagé* and recruiting costs
	60 l.	One year's keep
	5 l.	Balance of *engagé's* wages
	30 l.	Other advances for clothing, wine, gun, etc.
2nd year	50 l.	Advances to *engagé*
	60 l.	Keep
3rd year	35 l.	Advances to *engagé*
	45 l.	Balance of wages
	60 l.	Keep
	30 l.	Cost of return trip
Total	475 l.	

Source: Various court cases where expenditures are quoted.

thirty-six to eighteen months, were rejected out of hand and had to be revoked.[56] It also accounts for the severity with which both masters and colonial courts treated breach of contract, a frequent enough occurrence at the close of the first year, when the investment finally started to pay off.

Absolute obedience to a master would hardly have disconcerted a seventeenth-century man. Serving as a valet to a noble or bourgeois household carried great prestige among the populace. Ill-treatment was not an issue either, for no servants entered an official complaint for cruelty.[57] There is evidence that the Sulpicians "thrashed" their servants, but such light corporal punishment was common practice in these times.[58]

Behaviour seemed on the whole humane, although never at the cost of profit. Should an indentured servant become debilitated, the master could nullify the contract, and the Montreal Seminary did not hesitate to break its commitment to a servant "given the ailment and disability of his eyesight, which render him useless."[59]

The indentured labourer faced no greater hardship than the land itself and the back-breaking labour it demanded. "Land-clearers" from La Flèche or Nantes, cobblers and masons trained in Rouen or Poitiers, were ill-prepared for their appointed tasks: cutting, squaring, and dragging trees (without adequate tools or often any traction), followed by speedy clearing of stumps and roots. This was debilitating work, performed partly in the exhausting heat of summer or during bitterly cold winters that strained vulnerable constitutions. What made it all the harder was that such strenuous activity came after months and perhaps years of quasi-idleness, unemployment having often prompted emigration. Land-clearance was far tougher than the range of agricultural tasks these peasants might have performed in France. It is true that natives of the more wooded regions of western France were familiar with clearing land. But these immigrants were young and relatively inexperienced men, and besides, they would never have been expected to repeat, day after day, for years on end, a chore that at home did not call for such a sustained effort.

Indentured labourers could specify in their contracts that they would only work at their trades. Some journeymen came only upon this condition, but there were few of them. Land-clearing spurred the demand for overseas labour, and land-clearing accounted for their presence.

One of the more despicable aspects of bondage involved the barter of indentured servants. Whether recruited personally or secured through a Rochelais outfitter, *engagés* often changed hands. Colonists and even religious communities willingly sold or leased their servants.[60]

Sometimes indentured labourers came as chattel to a property. The buyer refunded part of the seller's original investment and, if need be, answered all of the *engagé*'s debts to his previous owner – an amount he would then deduct from the balance of his wages.[61] Antoine Courtemanche, whom the Sulpician Souart hired for five years at 65 livres per annum, became the property of the garrison major upon landing. When the latter leased his lands a year later, he threw in his servant's four outstanding years for an extra 200 livres.[62]

Some Montrealers purchased indentured labourers from the Société de Notre-Dame or from the Quebec Seminary.[63] One of the Compagnie des Indes occidentales recruits, for example, served the governor of Trois-Rivières before being sold to a Montreal gunsmith who handed him in turn to a local farmer whose widow ceded him back to the gunsmith within a few months.[64]

There was little profit, however, in such individual deals, since the terms of transfer were bound by the original contract. They merely permitted the spreading of the cost of recruitment and the sea crossing, or the transfer of what had proved too costly an obligation. Colonial merchants must nevertheless have received some return, as did their Rochelais counterparts.[65] Why else would Boucher have recruited one hundred men whom he then sold to various inhabitants, or Charles Lemoyne have shipped men to Montreal "to be distributed there"?[66]

No record survives of casual labour performed by *engagés*. A master could make thirty sols a day by leasing his servant as a farm labourer in peak periods. He could thus recoup a man's annual wages in forty days.

Renting out an artisan was even more profitable. When the first intendant arrived in 1665 he noted that "most inhabitants had indentured craftsmen whom they only leased or lent for high wages, which explains why labour was so dear."[67] Even after the decline in the overall demand for indentured servants, these practices continued to be profitable in certain crafts, where workers were rare and dear. Thus individual recruitment never ceased completely. People took advantage of trips to France to handpick craftsmen who would not normally come to the colony. For example, a Montreal officer hired a Parisian wig-maker for three years at 35 écus annually, hoping to profit from the manufacture and sale of wigs.[68]

Potential settlers received a plot of land at the end of their indentureships.[69] Some may have obtained a "concession ticket" before the expiry of their contract, but such tickets did not provide full property title and, unless their masters allowed them time to start their own clearing, the lots had no value. As a bonded man the indentured labourer could not own land in the colony; he was not a habitant. Nor could he take part in the fur trade. There were some exceptions. At the Kente mission, the Sulpicians authorized men to barter with the Indians, for it allowed them to reduce wages. Despite pressures from the intendant, they were still doing so in 1682.[70] The authorities were more diligent inside the colony, where masters had no motive to tolerate such independent trading. Moreover, servants had so few means at their disposal that illegal activities were bound to be limited.

Indentured servants could not enter taverns, but this rule was easily violated. They were, of course, forbidden to marry. No official intervention proved necessary, for both masters and material conditions checked such a course. The Jesuits prosecuted one *engagé* for signing a marriage contract. The Council supported them and thwarted the young man's plans.[71]

Of the 130 or so recruits who arrived in 1653 and 1659, 47 eventually married, none of them during their indentureship, although 13 did so within weeks if not days of the expiry of their contract. The remaining alliances were contracted within the next seven years.

Punishments meted out for insubordination or desertion show the system at its worst. Since the culprits were destitute, sentences could only take the form of corporal punishment or extended service. But sentencing and enforcement fluctuated over time. They were harsh and on the whole strictly enforced until about 1676–77, or as long as there were relatively large numbers of *engagés*. In 1653 indentured servants made up half of Montreal's population. In 1666, 350 resided in the colony, representing over a quarter of the males over fifteen. Exemplary harsh penalties were necessary to hold them in check and to discourage them from bolting and ruining the settlers.

Flight was the most common and most serious offence, and it was initially met with preventative measures. Anyone leaving for Europe had to obtain a passport, and there was a move to extend this control to the fishing vessels that travelled to the Gulf of Saint Lawrence, or "the servants and labourers bonded to till the soil try to return to France without their masters' consent and embark at night in launches that convey them down river or elsewhere, where they meet French fishing boats." The decree provided for arbitrary fines and corporal punishment.[72]

Masters were obliged to declare when contracts expired. Such declarations were registered by the Council and served as passports.[73] At first the wilderness proved a better deterrent than official sanctions. The case of sixteen runaway soldiers who were said to have died of want, "eating one another," must have been instructive.[74] In 1665 three *engagés* captured while trying to leave the country were condemned, one to hang or serve as public executioner, another to be birched, and a third to a two-year extension of his contract.[75] In 1673 the Council stated once more that penalties for leaving a master would involve the pillory, the lash, or branding.[76]

Fines were usually meted out in cases of absenteeism or enticement away from a master. Compensation for the loss of a working day came to 4 livres in 1663, meaning than an indentured servant who was absent a single day and could not meet the fine had to work an additional twenty days at the rate fixed in the indentureship.[77] Other fines ranges from 10 to 20 livres for the enticed man, but rose to 100 livres for the colonist who had enticed him.[78]

Attenuating circumstances were taken into account. Settlers guilty of beguiling a servant pulled strings so that hefty fines were rarely inflicted. By and by the law softened, so that in 1673 a day's absence only cost 50 sols.[79] But penalties remained harsher for *engagés* than for servants born in the colony – a matter of initial outlay and, of course, of status. Absent eight days, carouser and insolent to boot, an indentured labourer had to beg forgiveness on his knees, pay 60 livres damages to his master, as well as see his five years through.[80] By contrast, given proper compensation, it was easy for the son of a colonist to cancel his indentureship contract.[81] Some shrewd *engagés* who tried to get their freedom without any penalties, simply by "annoying" their masters until the latter sent them packing, met with the resistance of courts that firmly intended to uphold the system. The judicial authorities replaced the worn-out master with a more resolute one for the duration of the contract.[82] There was an average of ten suits a year in the period of high immigration; they were usually instituted by the master and concluded in his favour. Some servants prosecuted for unpaid wages, but when their masters exhibited the bills covering advances, these complaints lost their sting.

On the whole this legislation resembled that in force in the English colonies and was subject to a similar evolution. Yet whereas the growing leniency towards whites in Maryland or Virginia was matched by the rise of the doctrines of black slavery, in Canada such repressive measures only extended to the soldiers who eventually replaced indentured workers.[83]

During his years of service the indentured servant became familiar with the country, made a few connections, and often secured his former master's protection. He could hardly have saved enough, however, to settle in the colony. Based on the hypothetical case presented above, *engagés* might end up with no more than 80 livres, a gun, and a few personal belongings after their three years' service. Every documented example confirms this. Antoine Chevassot, hired in 1653 for 50 livres a year, was released with a total of 90 livres after five years. His master had defrayed 52 livres on goods supplied at the time of his ocean crossing and an additional 158 livres to cover personal effects, a musket, shot, and so on.[84] Other accounts were even less favourable to the servants and they yield no information on possible outstanding debts to third parties. The indentured worker who owed his master money could be forced to extend his term until the debt had been settled.[85]

Since these men had practically nothing when they signed on, the first advances had to cover necessities both for the journey and for their arrival (including proper winter clothes and a musket). Since they were expected to pay for laundry and medicines, and since wine and brandy were expensive habits, and since the master deducted for lost tools and utensils, it is easy to see how 300 livres in wages, spread over five years, came to be fully pledged by the end of the contract.[86]

Six estate inventories of *engagés*, who died while still in service, have been found. They include a pine chest, some shirts, a coat, a hat, a pair of shoes, a pelt or two, a gun, snowshoes, and a claim for outstanding wages. The sale of these belongings brought just enough to cover funeral expenses once debts towards the master were settled.[87]

Those homeward-bound took back at the very least shoes and warm clothing. They returned hardened and more experienced but no richer. Several took advantage of the voyage home to visit their families and settle their affairs before returning to the colony, but lacking the 30 livres for the westward voyage, they had to sign on for another term or acknowledge some indebtedness.[88]

Some indentured servants chose to prolong their service at the expiry of the first contract. This was the case of ten out of the 131 men recruited in 1653 and 1659. They probably hoped that this would allow them to settle free of debt, and presumably they did indeed benefit from easier, if not more favourable, terms. For several others it was merely an avowal of failure, and glad of this security, they took no further risks. Older *engagés* were most likely to end their days in the employ of religious communities.

If seventeenth-century *engagés* who received relatively high pay could not manage to save, how could the youths who arrived for wages of a mere 25 livres (or three hundred pounds of sugar, that is, about ten livres a year) after the Treaty of Utrecht in 1713, without even a return ticket, ever have been expected to?[89] But the gap may not have been as wide if masters paid for their keep, which had certainly not been the case in the previous century.

Settling down or moving on

How many indentured servants decided to remain in Canada? Lists of recruits, official enumerations, and the work of genealogists provide part of the answer. (See Table 6.)[90] The incidence of death is strikingly high in an age group with a normally good life expectancy. Some perished while fighting the Iroquois, and others drowned accidentally through lack of experience of canoes and rapids.

Among the twenty-two who left no traces, five disappeared the moment their contract ended, while the rest lingered for a few years. Had they married in Canada, genealogists would not have failed to mention them. Their deaths might well have escaped registration, but it is unlikely that they took to the woods, for this was still a period when no one ventured alone beyond inhabited areas. The most likely hypothesis is that almost all made their way back to France. Of the survivors, 52 per cent settled in the colony, all but three on the Island of Montreal. Had the prematurely dead done as the living, 75 per cent of the 1653 and 1659 recruits would then have chosen Canada – a high percentage compared to the 1666–67 contingent. (See Table 7.)

However, the figures for the latter group are less certain. Whereas genealogists painstakingly traced Montreal's first recruits, the more amorphous group of 1666–67 servants has not benefited from such careful research. When Montreal contained only a handful of threatened inhabitants, a single death would not go unnoticed. Later, under-registration of fatalities became more common. The situation also changed: by 1681 the fur trade was in full swing, and those who did not marry but remained in America to search for some Eldorado might well have escaped notice.

Accounting for possible omissions in Tanguay's *Dictionnaire*, roughly 50 per cent of these indentured servants did not establish families in Canada, because they either died, stayed single, or returned home. They did not necessarily leave at the termination of their contract. Freed bondsmen swelled the ranks of "volunteers" of all stripes who sought their fortunes, espoused celibacy, and scorned agriculture. They were an intermediary group between servants and settlers, and timorous types compared them to Neapolitan bandits or to the buccaneers of Saint-Domingue.[91] They lived for a while on the fringes and then gradually drifted back into society. If their ventures proved successful, they would sooner or later reappear. The rest either perished or gave up and left the colony. It is unlikely that more than a tiny fraction could have led an anonymous existence in the wilderness.

If one-quarter of the first recruits, who had been more carefully selected and better treated, still returned to France, one can surmise that at least one-third of those who were selected more haphazardly, and rigorously compelled to do three years' labour, returned home.[92] Did Colbert not write in 1669: "Great care should be taken henceforth to ensure that fewer settlers return to the kingdom each year"?[93] But compared to the other colonies, Maryland or Martinique, the overall result is positive.[94] The majority of these young men,

Table 6
Ratio of settlers in the group of 1653 and 1659 *engagés*

	No.	%
Individuals tallied on arrival	124	100
Deaths prior to settlement	38	30
Enumerated in 1666 or 1667		
as servants	10	52
as settlers*	54	
Not enumerated in 1666–67 nor traced subsequently	22	18

*Includes those who died after marrying and whose families were enumerated.

Table 7
Ratio of settlers in the group of *engagés* enumerated in 1666 and 1667.

	No.	%
Individuals tallied on arrival*	143	100
Deaths prior to settlement	5	3
Enumerated in 1681**:		
as servants	3	
as settled in Montreal	32	40
as settled elsewhere in Çanada	23	
Not enumerated in 1681 nor traced subsequently	80	57

*Clearly identified by name and surname.
**Including those who died after marrying and whose families were enumerated.

having cleared someone else's land for three years, agreed to begin afresh on their own account.

The social position of the former engagé

The *engagé* who had served his term, staked some land, and taken a wife answered the administrators' hopes. He became a "habitant" and *a priori* his background carried no social stigma. If he had what it took to overcome his initial economic disadvantage, his origins were not an obstacle, and a modest achievement soon over-shadowed his past. Timing was of the essence.

Indentured servants who came to Montreal between 1642 and 1660 were treated as future colonists, whereas subsequent recruits were viewed primarily as servants. In 1666 and 1667 the census in-dicated servants' first and last names as well as their surnames. In the 1681 census they were a more anonymous group identified by their first name or sometimes by surname only. In the late seventeenth century it became more difficult for *engagés* to integrate rapidly into the existing framework and achieve a modest social ascension, compared to earlier recruits who had been expected, as it were, to create that framework. Those who fared better came from the latter group. Some might argue that, since they had been better recruited, they were more accomplished. Our response would be that every period brought a mixture of good and bad, and that it was the country that sorted them out, attracting or discouraging the best. What the mass of indentured servants had to bring to the colony mattered less in the end than what the colony had to offer them.

5 SINGLE WOMEN

Between 1646 and 1715, 178 French girls were married on the Island of Montreal. They represented 20 per cent of the overall permanent immigrants.[95]

The Société de Notre-Dame instructed the devout women who accompanied the governor to find young women, and from 1659 the Sulpicians were busy recruiting them in their own Parisian parish. Merchants brought over female servants. Later, the Compagnie des Indes occidentales included a number of women among its recruits. Nevertheless, in 1666 the colony still had 126 single men over twenty and no available brides. Yet it was wedlock that ensured that freed bondsmen or locally discharged soldiers would settle down in the colony.

The authorities therefore selected a few hundred girls from the Hôpital Général and La Pitié in Paris and entrusted the archbishop of Rouen with the duty of locating suitable Norman girls.[96] Official provisioning ceased in 1673, the colony relying on local girls reaching marriage age, women who emigrated voluntarily (usually in the footsteps of some relative), and a few servants recruited by French outfitters.

The importation of women was not a profitable operation, which is why it fell to the Crown and to those religious communities bent on increasing population. The women were not expected to repay their fares, and to stimulate speedy unions the government attached a 50-livre dowry to each female they transported.[97] The thirty-one girls who arrived in Montreal with the 1653 and 1659 recruits married within the year, some within weeks of landing.

The process was even more cursory in the case of the group known as the *filles du roi*, who found spouses on the Quebec waterfront.[98] Every single one was matched, even the most ill-favoured or the least commendable.[99] Attention was drawn to the fact that the girls from La Pitié could not withstand either the climate or farm labour.[100] "Experience shows," Marie de l'Incarnation wrote, "that those not raised in the countryside are not suited for this life and live in misery from which they cannot escape."[101] This situation prompted Colbert to ask the Archbishop of Paris to secure peasant girls from his diocese.

Health problems proved the major drawback. Habits and antecedents played a minor role. "Debauched" women, meaning those who arrived pregnant, were shipped home.[102] Recruiters had to ascertain that their girls were indeed single; as for the rest, the authorities relied on the husbands' authority – quite correctly, in fact, for no disorder accompanied this influx. These were very young women, and their pasts could not have been that shady.[103] Their circumstances had probably been more strained than those of their husbands. Whoever sent them, directors or hospices or parents unable to assume their responsibilities, they eventually landed on some isolated farm, in some wretched little cottage, with a man they barely knew. This was not the outcome they might have chosen for themselves, but it assured them of relative security. Although the *bailli* often had to settle squabbles among these women, their insults and slanders were confined to the present. Only once did anyone dare accuse a woman of having been branded in France, and it was a colonial girl who made the charge.[104]

To satisfy officers and more delicate souls, the Crown went to great expense to attract a limited number of ladies, the *demoiselles*, who were housed in convents for the duration of their courtships and had up to 600 livres of colonial bounty at their disposal.[105] Local merchants and clerics took advantage of this demand to summon young female relatives from France, and more than one impoverished cousin thus found herself a good match.

Contemporaries never confused the immigration of the ladies with the immigration of the others.

6 SOLDIERS AND OFFICERS

The men

W.J. Eccles has highlighted the importance of the military detachment in Canada and its impact on the society.[106] Its importance is even more striking in the case of Montreal. Five of the twenty-four companies sent to the colony in 1665 were stationed on the island,

and five more were sent to build forts nearby. The seigneury barely numbered a hundred families when the authorities issued the first order for the billeting of troops.[107]

The Ministry of War decided to use the Carignan-Salières regiment to people the colony but postponed informing the interested parties of this decision until after the crossing.[108] The companies decimated in Italian campaigns, had to be refurbished, and the regiment was moved from Lorraine, where it had begun reorganizing, to La Rochelle and Brouage, from where it was expected to set sail in the spring for a fifteen- to sixteen-month campaign against the Iroquois.[109] The recruiting captains spread havoc along the way. In January 1665 complaints intensified in the Orléans généralité.[110] When at the end of February not a single company was yet up to strength, the methods of recruiting were fierce enough to inflame the towns and villages of Aunis. One sergeant was murdered at Saint-Jean-d'Angély and guards had to be posted to rein in local resentment against the officers.[111] The regiment made up its strength the following year in Poitou and set off for three years in Canada along with four other detached companies.[112] When the troops returned to France in 1668, one-third of the soldiers stayed behind. These four hundred men represented no more than the number of indentured labourers recruited by the Compagnie des Indes occidentales in the same period.[113] The Crown relied on one other pseudo-military enlistment in 1669 to bring over some three hundred settlers.[114]

Thirty-one soldiers and non-commissioned officers discharged from the Carignan-Salières regiment were identified in the 1681 census of Montreal. Should a similar ratio of those demobilized around 1669 and 1670 have settled down, veterans would still have represented no more than one-fifth of the seigneury's households.[115]

Is there any difference between them and the mass of settlers who came as indentured servants? The last soldiers to enlist were likely to be the first discharged, which means that on the whole these men and the engagés were the same age, came from the same regions, and shared similar experiences.[116] Their social backgrounds were practically identical, but it is among the soldiers that we find the few exceptions: scions of merchant, notarial, or bourgeois families who would never have sunk to civil enlistment.[117] Thus we see three former soldiers of the Carignan regiment, of bourgeois extraction, listed as Montreal merchants in 1681.[118] The first military recruits that settled in the colony were granted better terms than the indentured labourers. They served no more than three years, and even less in the case of later arrivals. They had no debts to pay back, and were discharged with 100 livres for their establishment.[119]

Canada retained only a small garrison until the renewal of hostilities with the Iroquois and the outbreak of intercolonial warfare. The companies sent to the colony after 1683 came under the domain of the Ministry of Marine rather than of War.[120] Between 1685 and the end of the War of the League of Augsburg in 1697, military strength varied between 1,100 and 1,600 men, or some thirty companies more or less up to strength.[121] Two-thirds of these men were stationed near or on the Island of Montreal, and the presence of 600 to 800 soldiers among 1,500 to 2,000 civilians marked the next twenty or so years.[122] This force was reduced in the early eighteenth century, but no fewer than 300 men were still stationed in the immediate vicinity.[123]

The compagnies franches de la Marine were used in French ports and in the colonies. Unlike the army, their recruitment tended to be more regionally based and resembled the levies for indentured labour.[124] Did the men enlist as willingly? It seems highly unlikely, for the authorities turned a blind eye, giving the press gangs a free hand in wartime.[125] Men destined for the colonies were shipped to the Ile d'Oléron and were carefully watched until their departure.[126] There is no doubt that the quality of these naval recruits left much to be desired. In the past, trade companies, outfitters, and private individuals had selected healthy specimens capable of withstanding the voyage and of earning their wages, but this concern vanished once the Crown took over enrolment and assumed responsibility for deaths during the crossing as well as for illness and infirmity overseas. Governors and intendants tirelessly complained of the appalling quality of the recruits.[127]

Systematic demobilization in order to people the colony ground to a halt once the military situation began to deteriorate. Local administrators took the initiative by postponing discharges, which earned them an official reprimand in 1686.[128] They invoked the impending danger and the lack of new recruits to replace those who had settled (and who were thought to be, in any case, the better soldiers).[129] The minister bowed to these arguments, and service discharges were withheld until the end of hostilities, as can be gauged by the movement of the civil population in the same period.[130] Only a handful were allowed to marry while still serving in the ranks.[131] Montreal parish registers show that five soldiers married on the average each year between 1686 and 1689, practically none until 1696, followed by a rush of forty-four unions in the two years following the Peace of Ryswick in 1697. This would seem to confirm that marriages had not been authorized during the war. In the eighteenth century, however, the bishop would plead in favour of wedlock for soldiers, against their captain's wishes, on moral grounds and to reduce illegitimacy.[132] Perhaps the few marriages celebrated in wartime during the seventeenth century can be traced to the pressure exerted by curés.[133]

Although defence of the colony was always invoked to justify the need for a large and costly garrison, more telling interests were at stake. Most of the fighting was done by the Indians and the militia, for as the authorities themselves recognized, only 20 per cent of the soldiers were capable of following the natives through the wilderness.[134] The troops did perform some paramilitary services and were useful in keeping order, but the force stationed in the colony would have remained practically idle were it not for a system organized by the officers to take advantage of such inactivity.

It was quite common for soldiers in France to hire themselves out wherever they established winter quarters or happened to be garrisoned, but the institutionalization of this system was something peculiar to Canada, where it remained in force for nearly a century, despite its illegality.[135] With his captain's consent a soldier could be hired by a colonist for up to 12 livres a month plus his board. He could also work as a labourer for 15 sols a day.[136] He was authorized to do so by ceding his military pay to his captain, and there is even evidence that some officers tried also to pocket part of their men's wages.[137] A soldier's pay came to 6 sols, or 4 sols 6 deniers once his outfit was deducted. His food ration cost him 3 sols, which left a balance of 1 sol 6 deniers a day, or 33 sols a month.[138] Working for a colonist brought in five times as much. The captain who managed to withhold the pay of the fifty men in his company earned at least 1,350 livres a year, since some sort of agreement could be struck between him and the officials to split the value of the daily ration subsidized by the Crown.[139] The officials usually speculated on the men's uniforms, not a losing proposition, since soldiers who worked outside were not allowed to wear their uniform.[140]

Despite the bishop's fulminations and repeated warnings by the ministry, the governors, intendants, and captains found the practice too profitable to renounce. They argued that the wages held back in this way compensated colonists who mounted guard instead of the soldiers, but most frequently they turned a deaf ear and assured the minister that all was for the best, without mentioning the deduction, itself the bone of contention.

And so in the end the ministry opted for toleration, retaliating, no doubt, with cuts in the officers' bonuses. The system had grave economic repercussions: the overblown military expenditure was not transferred to more useful civil undertakings, and capital accumulated in the hands of a few officers, who, for the most part, eventually returned to France. This system mostly proved a drawback to immigration and settlement. Soldiers, discharged a few at a time, took the place of the old *engagés*. The colonists no longer had to pay for the crossings or keep their workers during the slack season, for the military provided the necessary workforce. While 50 per cent of indentured servants settled down in Canada, barely 20 per cent of the soldiers of the Marine who had entered the colony before 1715 stayed on.[141] And once discharges were postponed, these men proved too old for the good of the colony.[142]

In 1697 the intendant once more offered a bonus of one year's pay to any soldier who settled in the colony. The captains, however, proved a stumbling block, as did "the ardour with which most soldiers aspired to return to France, hoping for greater freedom."[143] The measure basically failed both then and during the War of the Spanish Succession (1701–14), even though the soldiers, who did not take part in the campaigns, could theoretically have been demobilized.[144] Yet the four hundred or so who opted to settle in Montreal between 1696 and 1715 (the bulk of all discharged soldiers in this period, it seems) represented the most important wave of colonists since its beginnings.

After the war the question of peopling the colony arose again. Some wished for a return to the system of indentureships, while others were satisfied with military recruitment. Councillor Ruette d'Auteuil proposed that the twenty-eight companies be immediately disbanded in the colony; the consequent demand for labour would then be filled with indentured labour.[145] He faced the combined opposition of administrators and officers. The companies were not demobilized and new recruits were brought over to fill the ranks. This policy, by definition, countermanded renewed orders to metropolitan outfitters to transport *engagés* to the colony.[146] The eighteenth century dawned with the military system still intact.

The officers

When Colbert dispatched the Carignan regiment to Canada in 1665, he exerted strong pressure on the officers to remain in the colony as an example to their men. "This would be the surest way for them to find grace in His Majesty's eyes."[147] Somewhat less than a third, thirty-three, to be exact, let themselves be cajoled, though eight later reneged on their decision.[148] Only three of the five who settled in Montreal finally remained, though not for lack of encouragement.[149] The intendant was free with seigneuries, and Montreal's seigneurs willingly carved out arrière-fiefs inside their domains.[150] Generosity did not end there. The Crown distributed hefty bonuses to put these men in a position to marry.[151] Any inclination to cultivate the land quickly merited additional subsidies.[152] Since well-born women were scarce, the authorities went to great lengths to send them to the colony and settled generous dowries on them. Although some returned to France to find brides and to see to their affairs, most discharged officers were in fact poor and depended on the king's bounty to round out their pensions and ensure their families' livelihoods after their death.[153] In return for such favours, they headed the militia, along with the local gentry. The two groups had much in common – good birth, for one, though both had a few members whose noble claims were based on doubtful titles. Following the edict that appeared in France in September 1664, requiring proof of nobility to benefit from tax exemption, about half found their names included on the tax rolls and began legal proceedings to revitalize their ill-established privileges.[154] The king was willing to oblige those who agreed to remain in Canada, and granted letters confirming their nobility "on the condition that [they] remain in our said land of New France."[155]

It is difficult to say how many officers of the troupes de la Marine came to Canada before 1715. A hundred accompanied the first thirty-five companies, and reinforcements came to fill later vacancies. Replacements were fairly quick. In 1691, for example, twelve of the eighty-four active officers died and fourteen left for France.[156] While fatalities were particularly heavy that year, the number of departures appears normal.[157] If we assume a minimum of eight openings a year (through death, leave, and promotion to the general staff), then two hundred and fifty commissions became available during a thirty-year span. Together with the initial contingent, this meant that some three hundred officers spent some time in Canada during this period.[158]

They were not given special subsidies nor granted any seigneuries to encourage them to stay.[159] Some married in Canada, but this did not stop them from heading back to France or to some other colony to pursue their careers, families in tow.[160] A few, however, chose to remain in the colony. The corps' high mobility helped their promotion to the general staff or to the command of some far outpost of empire, such advantages had a stabilizing influence.[161] At the end of the seventeenth century, seven officers of the troupes de la Marine, born in France, owned property on the island, and in 1715 fifteen were listed as tenants or as proprietors in the town.[162]

External recruitment of officers declined gradually, though a thin trickle continued to arrive from France. Vacant posts came to be allocated to local residents. The intendant, eager for retrenchment, began by calling upon the gentilshommes commanding the militia, in order to abolish the pensions and allowances that burdened his budget.[163] Another step in this direction was taken when sons of local nobles were sent to France for officer-training and later integrated into the regular troops. At the beginning of the eighteenth century about one-third of the officers who served in Canada were native-born. By 1740 the corps, recruited locally almost in its entirety, had solidified into a caste where commissions were handed from father to son.[164]

This method of officering the troupes de la Marine not only failed to encourage immigration; it did the very opposite. The troupes were unable to absorb the second and especially the third generation of officers produced by the local gentry, so they found themselves dispersed to the French ports and to other colonies.

7 MERCHANTS

By a contract signed in Paris on 29 March 1658, the son and daughter of a clerk of the Commissions extraordinaires du Conseil formed a partnership "to sell goods that they purchased in France and then shipped and carted onto the Island of Montreal near Quebec in Canada; and in which they each invested the sum of 1,000 livres tournois."[165]

The said Médéric Bourduceau, his wife, his sister, and his sister's husband reached Montreal a few months later. The men, aged about thirty, had already worked in Martinique as factors to a small tobacco-exporting company financed by Bourduceau senior and Gabriel Souart, a Parisian bourgeois who had joined the Seminary of Saint-Sulpice late in life and who had been sent in 1657 to organize the Ville-Marie Seminary.[166] The Bourduceaus followed in his wake. They brought with them their small capital, business acumen, and connections with the metropolitan circles engaged in colonial trade, as well as their ties to this local personage.

These were the four elements that characterized merchant immigration, but only the last three will serve to identify members of this group, since no one brought large sums in any case. Indeed, there was little difference between the man who crossed the seas with his bales of cloth and trinkets and the man who arrived without the wherewithal but assured of a position as clerk to some colonial merchant or as agent of metropolitan interests. The advantage did not necessarily lie with the first. Experience was more helpful, and the key to success was connections.

Montreal is not the best place to study this immigration. French merchants who transferred their operations to the colony, for however long, usually settled in Quebec. Montreal was still an interior outpost, a step beyond the overseas journey, and so did not attract the most important merchants.

Montreal merchants traced their origins to various metropolitan centres. Either they had been born to the trade or their fathers had been numbered among the notaries, clerks, bailiffs, tax collectors of every ilk, or bourgeois from Cognac, Bordeaux, La Rochelle, Paris, or Lyons: a middling group sandwiched between the lower classes and the upper bourgeoisie. They came also, though in smaller numbers, from the large villages of the Seine valley, sons of rural merchants, innkeepers, petty seigneurial officials.[167] Their families had turned their backs on manual labour for at least a generation, and in the event of failure, such men preferred to leave the colony rather than become mere peasants.[168]

They were not men of property. They had obviously had little opportunity to accumulate any in France, for any modest success was enough to bond them to the colony. Some came with their wives and children.[169] Others arrived alone and then returned to fetch their dependents. A number also married in Canada. Yet mobility remained very high, and family responsibilities proved no obstacle to departures.

Kinship was at the root of this immigration, and it was not unusual for whole families to relocate. Most of the hundred merchants who turned up in Montreal in the seventeenth century were related either to a previously established colonist or to a merchant who arrived almost at the same time. In some cases it is appropriate to speak of clans, but the complicated web of kinship, on both sides of the Atlantic, still needs to be elucidated. The Testard brothers from Normandy, related to the Godfroys of Trois-Rivières, are a perfect example; as are the Leber brothers, sisters, and cousins; the Messier and Lemoyne families, who rushed to the side of their first successful relations; the Hazeurs, new converts from Brouage who swarmed to the New World; the Perthuis d'Amboise, divided between Quebec and Montreal; the Lyonnais clan of the Patrons, two veteran officers and two merchants, uncle and nephews, who showed up in Montreal around 1675; the Arnaud brothers from Bordeaux; and so on.

Local kin enabled the merchant to get credit and to establish a clientele. His French relations helped him to locate suppliers. Participation in colonial trade required either a solid reputation in French mercantile circles or the sort of family network that might usefully replace it.[170] The Montreal merchants and their La Rochelle, Le Havre, or Bordeaux counterparts shared similar modest origins, bolstered by clannish tendencies, which they continued to cement through repeated intermarriage.[171]

Half the thirty-five merchants listed in Montreal in 1681 had originally come to trade. They belonged to the group described above. The other half consisted of a medley of immigrants: officers and gentilshommes for the most part, while four discharged soldiers and four indentured servants brought up the rear. These men acquired their experience in the colony. Thirty years hence their social origins would become irrelevant to the second generation. The number of incoming merchants dropped markedly, and newcomers without the benefit of exceptional connections found it hard to carve a place for themselves.[172]

8 ORIGINS

Montreal marriage records for the years 1643 to 1715 state the parents' residence, and this allows us to trace the birthplace of 616 male immigrants. Several historians and genealogists have attempted a similar reconstitution for the whole of the colony, and our own regional sample does not deviate significantly from the overall picture.[173] As one might expect, settlers came mostly from the regions surrounding the port of embarkation. A 1664 report vaunted the virtues of the natives of Normandy, Perche, Picardy, and the Parisian countryside, who were said to be docile, industrious, pious, and steadfast, better-fed, and hardier workers than people from farther south. The same source also vouched for the poor reputation of the men who set sail from La Rochelle, specimens "godless and unreliable, lazy, ... false, debauched, and blasphemous."[174] The commercial ties that Canada had forged with Normandy weakened after 1663, when La Rochelle became the major port of embarkation and trade. Most of the soldiers of the Carignan regiment and of the compagnies franches de la Marine, as well as the indentured labourers brought over by outfitters, were born in western France. This was especially true of Montreal immigrants. About two-thirds of the sample grew up in an area limited by the Garonne to the south and the Loire to the north. The Sulpicians usually chose their millers and other craftsmen from around Paris, and their steward maintained that the only decent cowherds, shepherds, and cheese-makers were found in Auvergne.[175] But it proved far easier to round up candidates for New France in Poitou.

Fully 65 per cent of this immigration was rural. It is fairly easy to distinguish rural from urban origins, since the urban contingent came from the bigger towns: Rouen, Paris, La Rochelle, Poitiers, and Bordeaux, in that order.[176] Only 10 per cent hailed from smaller localities with populations numbering ten thousand or less, which the Abbé Explilly classified as "towns."[177] Most, however, were born in the villages and hamlets of the *bocage*, where the forest still dominated, where habitation was often dispersed, the fallow irregular, and collective constraints weak or non-existent.[178] The open, overpopulated wheat belt of the north and east played no part in this overseas settlement, and despite official prejudices, settlers from these harsher western provinces peopled the Montreal countryside, while more urbanized northern immigrants preferred commercial or craft occupations.

Despite their diverse origins, people had few problems communicating. Local dialects gradually gave way, and early eighteenth-century observers were unanimous in praising the vernacular spoken in the colony. The women (mostly Parisian), the army, and the clergy, as well as the contacts occasioned by the fur trade, helped to homogenize patterns of speech.[179]

The analysis of signatures in immigrant marriage records shows a higher degree of literacy than one would expect from a population born in the less-developed regions south of a line drawn from Avranches to Geneva.[180] Over 38 per cent of the men were able to sign their names (out of 491 cases). The proportion of female signatories is equally high – 31.7 per cent – but the sample of 129 cases is too small to be conclusive. These percentages refer to the years 1647 to 1715, and therefore to men and women born between 1620 and 1690. The incidence of marriage and literacy was more or less evenly spread throughout the period.

Immigration is a selective process. Those who picked up and left were probably of harder mettle than those who bowed to difficult circumstances and stayed. More enterprising, capable of worthy initiatives as well as of dangerous ones, the immigrant was often out of tune with his own milieu.[181] The range of behaviour found in the New World was therefore broader than that prevailing in the Old. It took time for it to level off and settle into a new standard of conformity. While the influence of regional backgrounds cannot be dismissed, inherited characteristics should not be overstressed, not only because of their vagueness but because they soon merged in a new common experience.

CHAPTER THREE

Demographic Profile

1 POPULATION STRUCTURE

The enumerations carried out in 1666 and 1681 gave an indication of the age, sex, and origins of Montreal's population both during and after a period of heavy immigration.[1] In 1666, 56 per cent were newcomers, for the first generation born in New France had not yet reached adulthood. Fifteen years later the ratio of native-born had risen to two-thirds, a proportion that would gradually increase. Although French arrivals in the island were as numerous between 1690 and 1715 as they had been previously, they no longer stood out in the midst of an expanding indigenous population.[2]

The imbalance between genders was gradually corrected. The sex ratio stood at 163:100 in 1666, when few women had yet arrived: there were 131 bachelors of twenty years of age and over and no single women, except nuns. In 1681 the ratio of males had dropped to 133:100, but among the same age group one could still find ten bachelors for every unmarried woman. Censuses from 1681 to 1739 show that the point of equilibrium reached around 1695, with males accounting for 51.6 per cent of the population, was maintained artificially until 1710 through in-migration, predominantly male.[3] Later, the proportion of women increased, as would be expected, but the instability of the ratio is difficult to explain.

Strange anomalies in the sex distribution of those 15 years old and less appear when the population is broken down into three broad categories. The discrepancies are such that they shed doubt on the accuracy of the records. They show that males outnumbered females in that category up to 1710, followed by a sudden decrease in the number of boys. Since those under 15 represented about 40 per cent of the population, this drop, real or erroneous, skews the overall reversal in the sex ratio. Emigration of Canadian men, therefore, does not alone explain this phenomenon, although such an exodus could be partly responsible for the fluctuations in the ratio between single men and women of 15 years and over. For a higher male mortality cannot be the sole factor behind the preponderance of women in this group. The discrepancy is even greater than it looks, since, given their respective ages at marriage, girls aged 15 to 22 are linked to a broader group of young men aged 15 to 28. Definite departures to the west or to Louisiana would have had a visible impact circa 1713, 1719, and 1726–27. Although Montrealers proved particularly sensitive to the attraction of these new settlements, the drain should not be overestimated. What little inmigration there was sufficed to counteract it throughout the eighteenth century. Within the colony as a whole the proportion of men steadied to about 51 per cent from 1734 until the end of the century, irrespective of the fluctuations evidenced on the Island of Montreal.[4]

The ratio between married and widowed settlers of both sexes shows that widowers outnumbered widows more or less throughout. This is explained by the death of women in childbirth and the hard time widowers had in finding wives, even when there was a surplus of unmarried girls.[5]

The age structure in 1666 and 1681 reflects the migratory flow and attendant fluctuations in the number of marriages and births. The two smaller age groups, which divided the 1666 pyramid, have moved upward by 1681. Immigration had fleshed out the 30–34 age group but not the one directly beneath it. Since the average immigrant was 20–25 years old, this proves that the foreign-born were no more than marginal after 1671. As in 1666, the gap was slightly more pronounced on the male side. The narrowing of the pyramid at the 20–29 level is due both to the small number of baptisms prior to 1661 and to the halt in immigration. This interpretation contradicts that of H. Charbonneau, who, commenting on the age pyramid of the colony (which shows the same configuration), perceives a depletion due to the fur trade.[6]

In 1681 this population was still quite young. By the end of the century all of the pre-1671 immigrants had turned fifty, and there were too few newcomers to affect the ratios between the broad age categories used in the following census.[7] The figures point to a broad-based pyramid tapering off rapidly, reflecting a high rate of reproduction and a high rate of mortality.[8] (See Table 8.)

Table 8
Age distribution of the population on the Island of Montreal, 1681–1732

| | | % by age group | | |
Years	Pop. 100%	Aged 0–14	Aged 15–49	Aged 50 and over*
1666	659	46.6	53.9	4.5
1681	1,388	45.9	46.3	7.7
1692–1695	1,750 (average)	41.2	47.4	11.3
1714–1716	4,200 (average)	43.8	47.0	9.3
1730–1732	6,750 (average)	42.2	46.3	11.3

*The censuses include only men in this last category. Supposing an equal number of women, the percentages cited can therefore only be tentative and most likely underestimates.

2   MARRIAGES

The colony's crude marriage rates hovered between 185 and 210 per 10,000 inhabitants from the end of the seventeenth until the middle of the eighteenth century.[9] To attempt a similar calculation for the Island of Montreal is impossible given the small population, the importance of migratory movements, and the presence of soldiers not included in the censuses. But a broad overview of nuptiality can yield some valuable information.

Marriage fluctuations reflect the two major waves of immigration: the first, one-third female, prior to 1680; the second characterized by an influx of the military after the Treaty of Ryswick.[10] (See Table 9.) Since few people settled in the colony without marrying, these second-period newlyweds represent almost all the single immigrants, thus the total immigration, that of married couples being negligible by then. Since few native-born youths were either old enough or in a position to marry before 1690, it is not surprising that the newcomers claimed the colony's women. Apparently, Canadian men did not much care for French women, but this sample is too small to permit any conclusions. Geographic mobility among Canadians was practically non-existent at this time.

The second period (1690–1715) is more interesting, for it reveals unexpected behaviour patterns. One-third of single women and maybe two-fifths of all brides, if we include widows with unknown antecedents went on marrying immigrants.[11] Fully 62 per cent of the

Table 9

Distribution of marriages celebrated on the Island of Montreal, according to spouses' origins*

| | Origins of brides | | | | | | | |
| | Jurisdiction | | | | | | | |
Origins of husbands	France	Island of Montreal	Montreal	Trois-Rivières & Quebec	English colonies	Indians	Unknown	Total
1647–1689								
France	206	161	6	16	–	3	9	401
Island of Montreal	2	42	6	3	–	–	1	54
Montreal	–	–	–	–	–	–	–	–
Trois-Rivières & Quebec	2	8	–	1	–	–	–	11
English colonies	–	–	–	–	–	–	–	–
Indians	–	–	–	–	–	–	–	–
Unknown	–	2	–	–	–	1	11	14
Total	210	213	12	20	–	4	21	480
1690–1715								
France	14	169	33	68	6	1	52	343
Island of Montreal	–	223	13	15	2	–	14	267
Montreal	–	41	6	7	3	–	6	63
Trois-Rivières & Quebec	–	61	2	13	–	1	9	86
English colonies	1	3	–	–	4	1	–	8
Indians	–	1	–	–	–	1	1	3
Unknown	–	19	2	1	–	–	41	63
Total	15	517	56	104	15	3	123	833

Source: Montreal Island parish registers

*When the groom was registered as a soldier or ex-soldier he was treated as an immigrant even if he did not state his parents' residence. Spouses whose origins are unknown tended to be widowed. At least two-thirds of the women in this category were in fact born on the Island of Montreal.

brides' parents and only 32 per cent of the grooms' resided in the seigneury. It looks as if the women preferred foreigners, which makes no sense either financially or socially. Definite celibacy, often related to emigration, and a higher mortality among young men engaged in fighting and trading, provide the principal clues to this pattern at a time when relocation within the colony itself was apparently minimal.

Only 7 per cent of the men and women who tied the knot on the Island of Montreal came from seigneuries nearby (within a twenty-kilometer radius). A greater proportion came further afield, from Trois-Rivières and Quebec, and it would seem that women were as mobile if not more mobile than men. Yet the town was too small to support such a large contingent of female servants. The major attraction may have been that the girls might encounter soldiers by staying with a relative on the island. This assumption does not seem too far-fetched and certainly applies to the upper echelons. More than one daughter of a Quebec *conseiller* came to spend a season in Montreal in order to meet eligible officers.

Given the influx of immigrants, strict endogamy remained low on the island. Its rate stood at 16.7 per cent between 1690 and 1715. Meanwhile, in the small parish of Pointe-aux-Trembles it had already reached 50 per cent, heralding future local cohesion.[12]

Age at marriage

Jacques Henripin has established that in the eighteenth century the mean age at marriage among the Canadians was 26.8 for men and 21.9 for women. In Montreal between 1696 and 1715, the averages are 28.6 and 21.0 respectively.[13] Women married young, about three years earlier than in France, while their spouses tended to be older.[14] Early matrimony probably had more influence on the high fertility level of this population than all other factors combined.[15] While few of the colony's women remained single, Notre-Dame parish was an exception. Two religious orders attracted over a hundred nuns, including an important percentage of Montreal-born women.

The age of women at marriage probably increased over time. Thus there would be a correspondence between the mean age of 21 computed for Montreal in the period 1696 to 1715 and the 21.9 reached by Jacques Henripin for 1700–60. At first the scarcity of females instigated unusual proceedings.[16] Girls were married before they were nubile. The 1666 census shows very clearly that fourteen couples were joined before the wife could conceive and that the first births occurred only two to six years after the ceremony. If the wife were under twelve (the minimum required by canon law) and if this were to become public knowledge, then second nuptials would be celebrated.[17] Strengthened by casuist arguments (which held that a man could mate with a girl as soon as she reached puberty), the bishop, considering the demoiselle Carion well-endowed for her eleven years, sanctioned her marriage vows and their consummation, if the curé and the family had no objections.[18]

Such hasty arrangements sometimes failed. The widow Crevier sued Jacques Fournier for the 58 livres she had advanced him "while her daughter was left with him for three months in order to see if the marriage could be consummated."[19] If the girl were younger still, the parents might settle the terms of the future union at a notary's without proceeding to the altar. Thus eight-year old Marguerite Seigneuret entered a marriage contract with Louis Godefroy de Normanville. This was a most favourable match for the Seigneurets, who declared their future son-in-law their sole heir as long as he lived to consummate the marriage.[20] While these examples involved merchants and officers, we know of one case where a settler and his wife promised to *bailler par marriage*, that is, hand over their nine-year-old daughter as soon as she was ripe, until which time her suitor would reside with them and plough their fields.[21] In short, a few parents took advantage of the scarcity of women to satisfy social and economic ambitions.

The shortage soon ended, and despite official pressures, namely a royal decree that enjoined boys to marry at twenty and girls at sixteen,[22], women, on the whole, followed the normal pattern in this era. An even larger gulf yawned between the government's wishes and men's behaviour. To assess the latter it is necessary to set aside the 173 immigrants who married at the age of 30.6, a relatively low average considering that between 1696 and 1715 they were mainly demobilized soldiers. The mean age of Canadian-born grooms was 27.2.[23] One cannot but conclude that the colony's economic conditions were no more conducive to early marriage than were those prevailing in France.

Remarriage

Submerged in the exceptionally high number of marriages, remarriages may appear few, but the proportion shown in Table 10 (18.5 per cent of all unions) would be around 27 per cent as the population structure became normal.[24] This provides a clear indication that conjugal life was brief. In the seventeenth century women remarried more often than men: 15.7 per cent as compared to 4.3 per cent. This unusual situation, stemming from the greater availability of males, would be temporary, even if slow to disappear.[25] The economic position of the prematurely widowed settler, with unimproved land, was far from enviable. His chances of finding a wife were no better than a bachelor's and even worse if he happened to have children. Women had the advantage, and not merely because of the imbalance in the sexes.

Curés gave few details in the records of remarriage, so we only know the spouses' ages in 68 out of 186 unions involving widows and bachelors. (See Table 11.) The wife was older in 44 per cent of the cases, while in 23.5 per cent the partners were about the same age. The mean age of the brides was 34.5 years, while their mates were only 32.[26] Their first husband would have died around the age of 44, after fifteen years of marital life, leaving behind three or four children (the eldest not more than 12) and over twenty arpents of arable land, which remained at the second husband's disposal for a good dozen years before he need render accounts to the heirs. In 80 per cent of the cases, the groom was an immigrant who, by choosing a widow, saved himself fifteen years of hardship and backbreaking labour. There is every reason to believe that widows were sought after and that they turned their comparative advantages to good account by marrying young and unencumbered men. The occasional marriage between widows and widowers mainly involved partners 40 and over.[27] The widower of any age who chose an unmarried woman got himself a young bride, since most women were married by the age of 25.

Seasonal trends

Nearly two-thirds of the grooms were immigrants whose decision to stay in the colony was linked to marriage plans.[28] Young men had only one season, from April to November, to begin clearing their land and build a shelter, once they were freed from indentured or military service. In France the agricultural cycle provided a respite that translated into a peak of marriages in July. There was no such break for those who took an uncleared lot in Canada; they had to wait at least, until November, with the first snowfall and onset of winter, at which time future in-laws were ready to kill the fatted pig. Some brave souls put off their wedding bells until January or February, but who could know that his girl would still be waiting? On the whole these realities ordered the seasonal pattern of marriages and explain their remarkable clustering. (See Table 12.) For,

Table 10
Number of marriages according to prior marital
status, 1647–1715

	Women		
	Single	Widows	Both
Bachelors	1,071	186	1,257
	(81.5%)	(14.2%)	(95.7%)
Widowers	37	19	56
	(2.8%)	(1.5%)	(4.3%)
Both	1,108	205	1,313
	(84.3%)	(15.7%)	(100.0%)

Table 11
Age distribution of marriages between widows and bachelors in Notre-Dame
parish, 1658–1715

	Age of husbands						
Age of widows	–25	25–29	30–34	35–39	40–44	45 and over	Total
–25	1	3	2	1	–	–	7
25–29	4	3	3	3	2	–	15
30–34	5	3	5	2	–	–	15
35–39	1	5	2	–	5	–	13
40–44	–	1	2	1	1	1	6
45 and over	2	–	–	2	2	6	12
Total	13	15	14	9	10	7	68

Table 12
Monthly distribution of marriages on the Island of Montreal, 1646–1715

Month	1	2	3	4	5	6	7	8	9	10	11	12	Total
Total number	148	120	38	80	67	80	65	76	100	141	310	77	1,302
Daily number	4.7	4.3	1.2	2.6	2.1	2.6	2.0	2.6	3.3	3.4	10.3	2.4	42.6
Monthly index	1.32	1.21	0.33	0.74	0.59	0.73	0.57	0.73	0.92	1.26	2.90	0.68	12.0

leaving aside the abstentions of Lent and Advent prescribed by the Church, a 375 per cent gap separated the low count for spring and summer from the high point in November.

In the following century, when most grooms were born in Canada, the agricultural calendar would still exert an influence, with low points in August and September and a relatively less high peak in November. The population had become less prey to natural exigencies.[29]

It should be added that departures for the hinterland did not affect this shift: those who left in September or October returned the following spring, and summer traders were back by late August. No correlation between trading and the month of marriage can be shown, and there is every reason to suppose that young men did not take off during the courtship period or on the morrow of the ceremony.

3 BIRTHS

In the eighteenth century, the colonial birthrate oscillated between 53 and 57 per thousand.[30] Similar rates could be found in Montreal before 1686, but thereafter, and for the following two decades, the number of marriages and births suddenly shot up, a movement that is not reflected in the population figures. For this reason birth rates for Montreal were not calculated. Why should these rates have been so much higher than the colony's already exuberant showing? The baptisms of children born to South Shore families who took refuge in Montreal during the war, mainly around 1690–92, have been considered. However, the increase in the number of births both preceded and outlasted these events.[31] A more significant point may be that Montreal had been peopled almost at one stroke twenty-five years earlier, so that practically all the immigrants' daughters reached the age of marriage and the period of highest fertility at the same time. The correlation one finds between marriages and births agrees with this hypothesis. The repeated virulent epidemics of this period might be an additional factor. The death of large number of infants would have reduced the inter-birth intervals (which would normally be twenty-three months as calculated in the eighteenth century) and caused an increase in births after each crisis.

Dividing legitimate births by the number of marriages between 1647 and 1715 yields a quotient of 5.0.[32] Henripin found an average of 5.6 children in the eighteenth century, taking complete and incomplete families together. It is not surprising that the data from the parish registers would include fewer complete families than the genealogical dictionary on which this demographer relied for his work. Although some young couples moved out of the seigneury, this loss was compensated for by offspring born to couples who sought refuge in the town. The averages I found are identical to those cited by Pierre Goubert for twenty seventeenth-century Beauvaisis parishes (reached by similar crude methods) and recall the ratios generally found in France during the Ancien Régime. When this figure is placed side by side with the high fertility levels of the Canadian population and the mean age of women at marriage (still uncommonly low at this time), it is quite obvious that "complete" families were relatively few.[33]

"After methodically visiting every Canadian farm," one intendant reported in 1684, "I found that all contained large families. Couples frequently have ten to twelve children and even fifteen, sixteen, or seventeen. When I asked how many had died, most replied none, while several mentioned a number of drownings, for more die in this fashion than from natural causes."[34] Seventeenth-century officials were famous for such observations, which delighted the Court. Yet the 300- to 400-livre pension to families with ten to twelve surviving children (excluding those in convents) certainly put no strain on the colonial budget.[35]

If this issue cannot be mastered without family reconstitution, none the less the overall impression is that households with ten to thirteen children were more common in the seventeenth than in the eighteenth century.[36] This accords with the fact that women initially married much younger. According to the 1681 enumeration, four Montreal families were eligible for the large-family pensions. The wives had given birth to their first child between the ages of thirteen and eighteen; the couple had survived until the end of fertility, and their children had shown extraordinary resilience. Two of the fathers in these four families had artisanal occupations while the other two were notables, and it is obviously this last group who stood a better chance of setting a record.[37] Yet it is worth stressing that the birth intervals among them were no closer than the average and that people only resorted to wet-nursing if the mother died.

The seasonal distribution of conceptions and births establishes that most children were conceived in the spring. (See Table 13.)[38] May had the highest aggregates, followed by June, with above-average showings in April and July. For the whole Canadian population in the eighteenth century, conceptions peaked in June.[39] But spring arrived three weeks earlier in Montreal than in Quebec, so conceptions on the island peaked in May. Is there better proof that nature influenced the rhythms of life?[40] The second surge of concep-

Table 13
Monthly distribution of conceptions and births in Montreal, 1646–1715

Presumed month of conception	Month of birth	Total number	Daily number	Monthly index
4	1	590	19.32	1.04
5	2	628	23.14	1.25
6	3	648	20.90	1.13
7	4	559	18.63	1.04
8	5	541	17.45	0.94
9	6	505	16.83	0.91
10	7	467	15.06	0.81
11	8	569	18.38	0.99
12	9	597	19.90	1.07
1	10	581	19.00	1.03
2	11	501	16.70	0.91
3	12	498	16.00	0.86
Total		6,684	221.31	12

tions in December accentuated a rise already detectable a month earlier and reflects the incidence of first conceptions, whose pattern could not be isolated. Had this been possible, the increase in the mild season would have been even more apparent.

The fact that most children were conceived between April and August invalidates the widespread belief that settlers abandoned their farms to run to the woods. Trips up-country did extend from May to August, in the very period when most husbands were apparently quite attentive to their wives.

Montreal's illegitimacy rate of 1.87 per cent was higher than that of the rest of the colony. In French rural parishes, rates fluctuated around 1 per cent. Tanguay estimated that the Canadian rate rose from 0.2 to 1.2 per cent between 1700 and 1760. Montreal's status of garrison town granted it a practical monopoly of such cases. Unwed mothers from the countryside abandoned their infants in the town, for there are a fair number of foundlings among the 125 cases of illegitimacy recorded.[41]

Christenings were performed the day after if not on the very day of delivery. The Sulpicians must have been responsible for such strict observance of the regulations, for it appears that elsewhere in New France, in the remoter rural areas, for example, the parents held emergency baptisms in their homes to save the trip to the church. The bishop's pastoral letters on the matter, first in 1664 and then in 1667, threatening the parents with excommunication, suggest that this custom was widespread.[42] Montreal was the exception.

Registers also include baptisms of other categories of people with European backgrounds: freshly converted soldiers, prisoners from New England, and French children born during their parents' stay in the English colonies. Some of these tardy baptisms could point to Huguenot resettlement in America, following the revocation of the Edict of Nantes in 1685.

4 DEATHS

Canadian tradition has it that the local population was thriving, and that the mortality crises and precarious equilibrium described in the best French monographs or the INED's demographic studies have no local resonance. In Canada, we are told, girls were fiery, children abundant, times good, and death kept at bay.

"This country has such fresh air," rejoiced Marie de l'Incarnation, "that few babies die in the cradle."[43] We have already had occasion to note that officials waxed even more enthusiastic: "Parents take such good care of their progeny that they only lose them by accident and almost never through illness."[44] Marguerite Bourgeois, who had come to Montreal to teach school, was disappointed without losing heart. "For the first eight years we were unable to keep any of our children," she admitted, "yet God's gathering of the first-born instilled us with hope."[45]

Demographers have begun to take a closer look at mortality levels, following Jacques Henripin, who estimated that infant mortality stood at 245.8 per thousand in the eighteenth century. Yet he accepted unquestioningly total death rates of 17 to 18 per thousand before 1700 and of 24 to 25 per thousand between 1700 and 1740.[46] This low mortality was due, he argued, to the youthfulness of the population and the near-absence of the elderly, and he conjectured that the level increased once the age structure became normal, that is, around 1730.[47]

This explanation is unsatisfactory. The high birthrate and broad-based pyramid should rather have spelled vulnerability. Could conditions have been so much more favourable in the seventeenth century than a hundred years later, when mortality reached 34.5 per thousand in the 1770s, a period of relative prosperity? It does not seem likely, and an important aspect of this early colonial society would be lost without a crude attempt to gauge the impact of death.

Hubert Charbonneau has ascertained the under-registration of deaths by comparing census data and the entries in the colony's parish registers between 1665 and 1668.[48] One might have supposed that such omissions would diminish once parish organization improved, yet they did not, at least where infant mortality was concerned, for one can assume that one-quarter of children died within the first year of their lives in the seventeenth as they did in the eighteenth century. The total mortality rates calculated after this correction still presume that the deaths of individuals over one year old were faithfully recorded – which remains far from certain. It is not impossible that unidentified soldiers may have been reckoned among the civil dead, but this error is compensated for by the absence of burials of young men engaged in the militia or fur trading who died far from their parishes. Finally, would curés who so easily ignored infants before the age of one have paid more attention to those slightly older? Thus the rates presented in Table 14 might well be underestimates, especially in the first decade. The abrupt changes in the population figures between 1695 and 1705 seriously limit the value of the calculations, and one can only hope that demographers will re-examine this fundamental question.

5 HARD TIMES

The ordeals at the end of the seventeenth century are clearly expressed in Graph 5,[49] which reproduces the data from the parish registers: five high peaks of mortality in thirty years. In examining the more severe crises of 1687 and 1703, we should not forget that better registration would add ten to fifteen burials a year or three to four each quarter.[50] But numbers matter less here than the nature of the crises and their effect on the numbers of marriages and conceptions.

Between 1687 and 1693 war, disease, and death fell upon Montreal. As one priest put it: "The destruction of the Lachine parish had been preceded by a form of plague or contagious disease that in 1687 killed 1,400 persons in Canada, and it was followed by many years of famine."[51] In September 1687 the boats had brought a measles epidemic, which claimed ten times as many lives as usual in the three months it raged, before disappearing as suddenly as it had come.[52] Deaths more than cancelled out that year's births. In Montreal 6 per cent of the civilian population died from the outbreak, and it also took a heavy toll of Indians and soldiers, who are not included in our data. Between 1688 and 1694 the Iroquois wreaked havoc in the countryside, and three consecutive crop failures topped this series of calamities. The price of grain may have been high and poverty widespread, but there is not the slightest

Table 14
Infant mortality and total mortality on the Island of Montreal, 1676–1715*

Period	1676–1685	1686–1695	1696–1705	1706–1715
Population at middle of period	1,375	1,360	2,700	3,750
Mean annual burials age 1 and over	15	39	52	68
Mean annual burials before age 1	7	19	30	38
Mean annual births	72	109	186	212
Infant mortality rates according to registered burials	9.8%	17.2%	10.9%	18.0%
Calculated annual deaths before age 1 with rate of 24.6 per cent	18	27	46	52
Corrected mean annual deaths, all ages	33	66	98	120
Total death rates	2.4%	4.85%	3.6%	3.2%

*Before 1676, the age at death is too often missing.

indication of an "old-style" crisis[53]: conceptions and marriages remained unaffected.

Although the island was not under attack between 1699 and 1714, it had not seen the last of its woes. A fever broke out in the spring of 1699 and lasted throughout the summer. Then a *maladie de petite vérolle pourpre et flux de sang*, or smallpox, struck in January 1703, reached its peak in April, and dragged on until July, claiming 1,000 to 1,200 victims in the colony among the French and local Indians.[54] In Montreal mortality was twelve times the usual during the first six months of 1703, and 8 per cent of the European population succumbed. This time, however, the number of conceptions clearly dropped in April, when they customarily began their seasonal climb. But the recovery was immediate. The two years of grain shortage that intervened between these epidemics had no repercussions on the three demographic curves, despite many complaints of hard times.[55]

Thus for a quarter of a century the population suffered a sequence of poor crops and epidemics.[56] One missionary reported that smallpox hit the local population, white and Indian, more severely than it did immigrants,[57] which is clearly correct for the Indians but needs to be verified in the case of Canadian-born colonists. As to the demographic unresponsiveness to food shortages, it may not be as total as it seems. The egalitarian agrarian structure and the additional food supply gathered by hunting and fishing quite likely softened the impact of such shortages, but the population was often forced to rely on poor-quality grain, pea soup, and oaten bread. The inadequacy of the diet, intensified by vitamin deficiency during the long winters, made the population more vulnerable to epidemics. Yet despite their frequency, their toll was limited, for the colonists had the great advantage of not being overcrowded.

In normal circumstances burials were more or less evenly distributed, with a barely perceptible rise in the fall.[58] Priests rarely mentioned the cause of death, only sporadically noting violent ends, especially by drowning. Fuller details can be found in the Lachine parish records, which list the causes of death as "persistent dizziness," dropsy, burst internal abscesses, diarrhoea, pleurisy, paralysis, and suffocation and dysentery, which mainly afflicted children. To the minister inquiring into the illnesses current in the colony, the governor sent the following list, in this order: scrofula among Indians and a few settlers, worms, the "runs," and other intestinal afflictions, "cold sweats from having fallen in the water in winter," and "fallen bowels."[59] The western outposts in particular were affected by scurvy, which decimated the garrisons in 1688 and 1689.[60]

The fanciful nomenclature points to deficiencies in the diet and poor sanitary conditions. Take the case of meat frozen in early winter, stored unsalted in attics, and then probably consumed even though a series of thaws had spoilt it.[61] There were no doctors in Montreal, only midwives and surgeons. According to the governor, the latter could not even reset dislocated limbs, and this accounted for the great number of cripples.[62]

However gloomy, the picture was not nearly as tragic as that found in France under Louis XIV.

6 CONCLUSION

Over one hundred years the Montreal population developed with approximately the same rhythm as that of the whole colony.[63] The trend can only be interpreted over a long period. It began harmoniously. A high natural increase prolonged the momentum created by immigration, yielding an annual population growth rate of 8.5 per cent in the early period of settlement (1650–86). The next ten years witnessed losses that weighed more heavily on Montreal than on the rest of Canada. War and disease brought a sharp drop. Men died in the militia and in the western forts, and many drafted for distant campaigns chose not to return.

In the course of the eighteenth century the colonial population grew at the even rate of 2.5 per cent per annum. The Island of

Montreal recouped its losses and immigration stimulated a rapid recovery, so that the island was then temporarily in alignment with the rest of the colony, but from 1725 up to the end of the century its growth levelled off to 0.7 per cent a year. As it is unlikely that natural increase was lower than elsewhere, only out-migration can account for this slower growth.

It is difficult to explain these trends without isolating the urban population – which the censuses fail to do. The rough estimates shown on Graph 1 are fairly accurate for the eighteenth century but more tentative for the earlier period.[64] Montreal developed independently from the countryside, essentially as a fur-trading post. Initially all the population lived in *le lieu designé pour la ville*, an area of 120 arpents circumscribed by a palisade. Cultivation was limited to small plots within or just outside the enclosure. By 1665 people began to spread out. The new, essentially agrarian settlements grew at first much faster than did the urban nucleus. Over the next forty years, the rural component represented about two-thirds of the island's population, after which it did not increase, while the urban population continued to develop. By 1715–30 the urban proportion had reached 45 per cent.

These movements point to the two secular characteristics of the colonial economy. First, the lack of industry impeded any real sustained urban growth. Substantial in-migration and warfare (when refugees streamed in from the *côtes*, as in 1690 or 1696) swelled the town population, but in the long run the town proved incapable of absorbing either outsiders or even its own natural surplus. The farmland that developed in the seigneury would soon support a larger number of people. Yet, as we shall see, the agricultural system itself stifled population growth. It is this second factor that accounts for the migratory deficit in the eighteenth century. Second- and third-generation Montrealers cleared lands beyond the island, in the plain that stretched from the Laurentian terraces to the South Shore seigneuries. After the opening of Louisiana, the establishment of permanent outposts in Detroit, Michilimakinac, and Illinois attracted many urban and rural Montrealers, especially after 1725. This little town, with its bent for trade and its endemic unemployment, could hardly have hoped to keep them.

PART TWO

Trade

The traditional histories of New France centre on external or peripheral factors affecting the colony rather than on its internal composition. While historians have showered boundless attention on the fur trade and territorial expansion, they have usually compressed the process of colonization into a single chapter, where they treat it from an institutional perspective. It was very tempting, therefore, to try to redress the balance and do justice to the neglected social formation by applying the methodology devised by French regional historians to capture the interrelationships between production, distribution of wealth, and social roles.

With this model in mind, it seemed natural to turn to the rural context once I had dealt with the population. But this would have led me astray. "Since France was a nation of peasants," wrote Pierre Goubert in *Beauvais et le Beauvaisis*, "I made them my primary focus. In towns dominated by the "mechanical arts" and "common people," I could not restrict my research to the circle of merchants." The corollary applies: in a trading colony the emphasis must rest on the merchants. A regional economy moulded by external developments cannot be grasped through study of embryonic internal forces alone. The desire to break new ground and part with tradition would merely have led to confusion.

There were two types of production. Furs, the object of the oldest and most important of the two, were only traded, not produced in Montreal. The network between native producers and merchants had been operating for well over a century when the first wheat-field ripened on the Island of Montreal. The starting point, therefore, is trade, with its various components – goods and furs, credit, exchange operations, profits, and capital – which shaped the first social organization.

CHAPTER FOUR

The Basic Features
of the Trade

1 MONTREAL'S LOCATION

The Island of Montreal lies at the junction of important waterways. Taking the *grande rivière*,[1] the trader reached Lake Ontario and the huge network of waters that gradually drew him deeper into the interior. A voyageur heading for Lake Michigan, the Lower Mississippi, Lake Superior, and the "Western Sea,"[2] if he wished to avoid a southern detour, would have to follow the Ottawa River, the Mattawa, and Lake Nipissing on to the northern shore of Lake Huron. This route was safer, sheltered from Iroquois and English attacks. The trading station at Michilimakinac soon formed the heart of the inland trade. Besides the two routes to the west winding through countless tributaries, the Richelieu River linked Montreal south to the Hudson, the Dutch merchants at Albany, and the port of Manhattan, 550 kilometers away. And finally there was the St Lawrence, gateway to the Atlantic – an inlet rather than a river, for the tide still ebbed and flowed 50 kilometers below Montreal. Quebec was about two months' remove from France, and France only about one month's sailing from Quebec.[3]

Montreal was not merely a stopover on the route to the interior but a point of trans-shipment. Here free sailing ended and portages began. Upstream the river spread and cascaded into rapids, as did the Ottawa and the Rivière des Prairies, north of Montreal. This young hydrological network was still searching for its former bed in the glacial deposits and digging through the soft layers to the next rocky outcrop interrupting its course. Thus checked, the waters ground their way, spread to form lakes, and then narrowed and bounded into rapids known as saults. Sault-Saint-Louis, a thirteen-meter drop, followed by another gentler rapid, barred Lake Saint-

Louis (at the western end of the island) from the navigable stretch to the east.[4] This obstruction caused a thirteen-kilometer portage. The boats were not towed down but had to be left at the head of the falls and the cargo lugged to town. Supplies for the west were conveyed from the urban shops to the embarkation point above Sault-Saint-Louis, known locally as Lachine in mock tribute to the days when explorers paddled off to discover Cathay. There was no better way to transport bales of cloth, barrels, and hardware boxes on their way inland than in the light and flexible Algonkian bark canoes. Montreal's fortune was therefore secured through a navigational quirk that transformed it from a mere trading post into a major transit and distribution centre stocking merchandise and pelts between ocean and hinterland.

The journey upstream from Quebec to Montreal might take four to six days, including overnight stops.[5] While some of the sloops and barks that plied the route could carry about eighty tons, most craft were much smaller.[6] As Montreal lacked quays for proper mooring, the unloading of trans-Atlantic vessels continued to take place in Quebec until the nineteenth century, although there was no real obstacle to navigation. The first road linking the two towns, punctuated by countless river crossings (part forded, part ferried), was not completed until 1735. The river, therefore, was the only viable trade route – interrupted, however, by ice for five months of the year.

The roads on the Island of Montreal proved so unmanageable that the inhabitants put off carting grains and wood until the winter. But supplies for the west had to leave Lake Saint-Louis in the spring, so oxen and carts were forced through a thirteen-kilometer course of potholes, where they inevitably got stuck. It is no wonder that a project to canalize the small Saint-Pierre River was entertained as early as 1679, for it would allow loading of canoes closer to town and reduce cartage costs. All that was entailed was broadening the waterway to channel a passage twelve feet wide and four feet deep. Despite the initiative taken by the Sulpicians, the project fell through, only to be revived under the direction of a royal engineer in 1700, before being abandoned once more. It proved impossible to dig through the layers of sandstone and limestone extending from the outcrops that formed the rapids and hampered the flow of water into the canal when the river receded.[7]

It took two months to reach Michilimakinac by the northern route, and the trip called for thirty portages between Lachine and Lake Huron, not counting the unloadings so that the lightened boats could be hauled up or run down the rapids. The canoes were carried during portages, which were less frequent on the return journey. The whole process might involve unloading and reloading as many as fifty times.[8]

At first, canoes with three-member crews hauled about a thousand pounds of freight. By 1715 thirty- to forty-foot-long canoes, manned by four or five men, carried up to three thousand pounds.[9] To give the paddlers a break, a sail would be raised whenever possible. Although a few sloops were used on the Great Lakes – mostly for military purposes – the canoe remained the fastest and most suitable means of transport up to the middle of the nineteenth century. Once the dangerous spring waters and ice jams subsided, around May, navigation could last to early December.

Canoes also conveyed passengers to Quebec in half the time it took the sloops.[10] In winter travellers made the journey in sleds along the banks and on the frozen river. Given enough halts, a good dog-team could pull up to four people.[11] Travel conditions improved once the colony acquired more horses, which could pull sleighs that were set higher off the runners and thus better protected.[12]

Isolated and often difficult to reach, Montreal remained subservient to Quebec, which controlled relations with France. Nothing, however, interfered with Montreal's control over its immense hinterland.

2 THE MONETARY SYSTEM

Currency and credit

From the outset, specie (or coined money) circulating in the colony was worth 133 per cent of its French value.[13] The discrepancy corresponding to the devaluation of the colonial money of account, or nominal money, was maintained until 1717. The devaluation was less the effect of a shortage of coin and more of a cover for a profitable exchange operation. The first trading companies were entitled to raise a number of taxes in the colony, the most important being a 25 per cent duty on beaver exports.[14] In return the companies became responsible for administrative salaries in the colony. These salaries, generally expended on merchandise, were based on the colonial currency, where 1 écu was worth 4 livres (not 3, as in France). A 120-livre salary would therefore only cost the company 30 écus. Altogether, the price of imported goods supported first a mark-up of about 50 per cent to cover transportation and sundry profits, and another 33.3 per cent due to the nominal increase in the value of the livre against the écu.

The system was denounced by those individuals and religious communities entitled to a share of the colonial budget, but remained sanctioned by a number of regulations issued between 1654 and 1672.[15] Once fur-trading in the interior became free (as of 1664), the fiction was kept alive by merchants who sold French products at the colonial rate but demanded payment in beaver on par with the livre tournois.[16] Thus, a pound of beaver set at 110 sols in Canadian currency, subject to the 25 per cent export duty (or 27 sols 6 deniers), was accepted by merchants for 82 sols 6 deniers, while they in turn received a bill of exchange for the same amount drawn on the metropolitan *fermier*. The burden of the export tax had to all intents and purposes been shifted on to the middlemen who supplied the furs.[17]

Of course, the increase in the nominal value of money had no positive effect on purchasing power, since all prices were accordingly inflated. There were neither winners nor losers when local products were exchanged for imports, and the additional 33.3 per cent profit evaporated whenever the imports were purchased with cash. But such transactions were few in the seventeenth century compared to those in the fur trade, which was, in fact, at the basis of the monetary system. Given the general price increase, can one trust the good faith of officials who claimed that the appreciation of the coinage would draw it to the colony and keep it there?[18]

The debate on these matters had divided the financiers of the *ferme du Canada* and the clerks of the *contrôle général* in the 1670s and was revived in the early eighteenth century, when beaver prices crumbled and metropolitan finances entered a period of crisis.[19] In 1717 the Marine Council had no difficulty abrogating the distinction between the money of Canada and the money of France, for it had become pointless once the 25 per cent duty was no longer collected on depreciated furs.[20] Parity, however, did not signal a drop in the nominal prices of imports.[21] The profits, formerly hidden in the debasement of the colonial livre, were now openly displayed: they formed the Canadian retailer's margin. But the overstock and therefore depreciation of beaver increased the price of imports. Only the value of colonial commodities appeared to drop temporarily.

Specie was scarce everywhere in this period, but the colonies were especially hard hit. Prior to 1689 part of the colony's funds were sometimes remitted from France in coin.[22] Religious communities with metropolitan revenues procured some as well.[23] The odd merchant probably converted a small portion of his bills of exchange, drawn on the *bureau du castor*, into cash, but the bulk was usually reinvested in return cargoes. The real problem was shortage of incoming coin rather than its flight, attributed to an unfavourable balance of trade. The colony lived frugally, was under-equipped, and the merchants gave bills of exchange in advance for supplies obtained in La Rochelle. Although not altogether absent, hard currency represented merely one of several alternative methods of payment. The coins listed in merchants' post-mortem inventories, or counted at a notary's to cover dowries, land acquisitions, or loans for "trips to the old country," were gold and silver, and nearly always of French origin.[24] We find no trace of the bullion produced for the colonies.[25] Sols marqués and liards, on the other hand, had a wide circulation.

Payment of seigneurial dues, taxes, and rents was rendered in kind or in labour. In some contracts before 1665 one can find exchanges of wheat, furs, land, and cattle, without reference to their monetary value. Stable prices, resulting from chronic scarcity and the Council's control of wheat prices, encouraged this sort of practice. Beaver began to fall in value around 1664, and wheat, freed in 1665, soon followed suit.[26] This spelled the end of barter in the agricultural sector. Since the myriad of payments in kind, such as in corn, furs, or imported goods, were from then on all expressed in livres, they ought not to be confused with barter. This brand of payments in kind gradually disappeared from real estate transactions once the long-term drop in the price of grain reduced its appeal and once fur-trading ceased to be a common activity. Cash, transfers, and especially private and public notes took their place.[27]

When the governor reported to the minister that beaver was used as the local currency and carefully hoarded, he was merely trying to stop the agents of the Compangie des Indes occidentales from searching the homes and warehouses of merchants, including his own associates, for the furs they smuggled back to Europe. Not a hint of hoarding appears in the three hundred post-mortem inventories analysed for this study. Such practices, which historians have viewed as typical of this society, must therefore be dismissed for lack of evidence.[28]

The shortage of coin did not impede the commercial sector to the same extent, for it rested on a double exchange of furs and trade goods: one between Indians and traders, where goods were valued according to a "beaver standard," irrespective of the value of furs on European markets;[29] and another between merchants and traders, where the latter "paid" in pelts for the supplies they had received, according to market value of the pelts in the metropolis – that is, using a monetary yardstick.[30]

Local monetary fluctuations did not affect the price of furs, and one sometimes gets the impression that this trade was above and separate from any trading in the settlement evolving alongside. Yet it was definitely linked to it by a complex web of credit that spread through every layer of the population, even if this link was somewhat inelastic. There is no doubt, however, that the merchant who wished to direct some of his profits away from the fur trade and diversify his investments would be hampered by the chronic and often severe shortage of specie.

Public finances

When the intendant first resorted to "card money" in 1685, he did not envision it as an economic measure to speed up circulation, to provide the population with the means of meeting small internal payments, or to ward off a recession occasioned by the shortage of coin.[31] It was a mere expedient to settle administrative debts, pay the troops, and satisfy various tradesmen and craftsmen. France was entering a period of financial distress, so that the 300,000 livres earmarked annually for the colony reached it only sporadically. By the end of the century nothing was coming through – neither money nor merchandise. The intendant, who somehow managed to cover the first issues, continued to produce cards whenever needed. This tender was not secured by land or fiscal revenues but by the expectation that the government would one day meet its obligations.[32] Given the small scale of the economy, a public debt that reached 2 million livres by 1714 could only produce spiralling inflation. This debt represented about 100 livres' worth of paper currency per person and perhaps as much as half of the colonial assets at the time.

This paper money was in small denominations, and soldiers and fortification builders helped to scatter the bills through town and country, although they inevitably ended up in the merchants' coffers.[33] The merchants then took them to the intendant, who initially exchanged them for money, merchandise, or bills drawn on the fermier du castor and later replaced them with bills of exchange drawn on the treasurer of the Marine. There was little confidence in the cards. In 1689 the first of a series of ordinances compelled merchants to accept the cards at their nominal value or face a 100-livre fine. Yet in 1690 Montreal merchants were still taking them at half their value, while some creditors refused them altogether. New threats followed,[34] but the only possible response was to adjust prices upward, irrespective of the form of payment. Prices began to spiral. Treasury notes and bills of exchange – given in lieu of the cards – were rarely redeemed on time, and merchants took them only "with the greatest reluctance."[35] From 1691 to 1709 merchants occasionally delved into their purses to advance the intendant their available cash, in return for the 33.3 per cent profit on exchange rates and the assurance that their debts would get preferential treatment. But when these special bills of exchange ceased to be honoured, sharing the fate of bills issued in lieu of cards, merchants stopped all funding, and the intendant had no choice but to issue cards for all his expenditures.[36]

La Rochelle correspondents and suppliers demanded that Canadian merchants personally guarantee the government bills. Yet despite these drawbacks the merchants could hardly deny access to their shops to the card-bearers or forgo advantageous supply contracts afforded by the intendant, especially at a time when beaver prices were toppling. The discredited bills of exchange were openly traded. The governor himself was said to discount them at 8 per cent.[37]. When the French treasury began to replace them with bills, which added to the flood of government notes circulating in the kingdom, the merchants flatly refused to accept them and banked instead on the cards, which at least had the advantage of not maturing at a fixed date.[35] The cards changed hands incredibly quickly. Property transactions multiplied as debtors rushed to retire their loans, and creditors, forced to accept the repayment, searched far and wide for new borrowers.[39] The colonial treasurer wrote that the "merchants had done everything in their power to get rid of their card money, both this year [1714] and last, by investing it in fishing, housing, and shipbuilding, in squared and sawn timber, in masts."[40] It was at this point that the undeveloped seigneuries around Montreal began to acquire large-scale facilities such as mills.

The price of French manufactured goods fluctuated irregularly, sporadically, and excessively after 1690 as a result of the depreciation of the cards, the beaver slump, and the diminution of shipments due to an inability to pay suppliers. All these difficulties were compounded by the financial difficulties experienced in France. Foodstuffs remained unaffected for the moment, illustrating the gulf between merchants' activities and agriculture, then undergoing a long-term decline in prices, punctuated by cyclical crises.

In 1712 the Marine department considered the various means of retiring the cards and of disposing of this 2 million-livre liability (though a mere drop in the bucket of the overall national debt of 2.5 billion livres). It soon found a solution: the bearers would exchange their cards for rentes (annuities) on the Hôtel-de-Ville and French généralités.[41] Yet despite "pressures that his Majesty deemed fit to apply," the Canadians found the annuities quite useless and demanded cash payments.[42] They suggested an alternative that was duly passed on and finally agreed to in 1714: the cards would be reimbursed in coin, at half their face value. As one of them wrote, "the pitiful hope that they might lose only half, after fearing losing all, made the merchants quite sanguine."[43] In fact prices had already risen in anticipation of such a devaluation. Prices, embracing even local produce and wages, doubled as soon as news of the Marine Department's consent reached the colony.[44] The price of imports sky-rocketed.

The five-year scheme to redeem the cards immediately ran into difficulties. Unable to pay for the first allotment of cards in coin, the Controller General offered the bearers treasury bills, which were discounted to 60 per cent of their face value when the treasurer of the Marine failed to meet his payments.[45] La Rochelle merchants kept the bills, subpoenaed the treasurer-general, and sent no supplies. The Canadian merchants retaliated by holding on to the proscribed cards and threatening to rely solely on "the barter of pelts."[46] Despite endless postponements, the cards were eventually redeemed in banknotes from the bank begun by John Law.[47]

Small merchants had united to face the crisis in public finances and skilfully turned a possible catastrophe to their advantage. It is far harder to gauge the effects on the rest of the population. The intendant stressed the pitiful lot of government employees – a natural reaction from one of their kind – yet given their commercial activities, one cannot help but surmise that they escaped un-scathed.[48] The negative effect on religious communities, which held numerous mortgages, cannot be doubted, however. Many peasants used the cards, which circulated in the countryside, to repay their debts. There were few creditors in rural areas, and certainly no hoarders.[49] Inflation had intensified the gap between the peasants' agricultural output and the imports they could not do without, and so could well have encouraged them to be more self-sufficient, but it did not trigger such a trend.

3 THE FURS

Beaver: prices and monopoly

In the seventeenth century the major Canadian export was fur, with beaver filling about four-fifths of the cargoes. Table 15 summarizes the fluctuations in prices and volume. There are no exact figures available for the period prior to 1659. Montreal had barely been founded and counted only eight "habitants" when the Compagnie des Cent Associés farmed out its trading rights to a group of colo-

Table 15
Price of a pound of beaver pelt (1659–1725), and approximate volume of beaver exports to France

	Canadian market price	Export duty %	Official Canadian price	Sale price in France	Volume of annual exports to France (in pounds)
1647–53		50			30 to 40,000
1653–58		25			
1659–64	210 s (coat) 90 s (parchment)	25	280 s (coat) 120 s (parchment)		50 to 60,000
1664–74	135 s (coat) and gradual decrease	25			70 to 80,000
1675–77	67 s 6 d all types	25	90 s all types	170 s in Paris	100 to 160,000
1677–96	82 s 6 d (coat) 52 s 6 d (parchment)	25	110 s (coat) 70 s (parchment)	226 s (coat) 110 s (parchment)	
1696–1706	78 s 9 d (coat) 40 s (parchment)				(200,000)
1706–10	[20 s] (coat) 30 s (parchment)		same as market		60 to 70,000
1710–14	30–40 s (coat) 30 s (parchment)		same as market		rising
1715–19	57–80 s (coat) 28–32 s (parchment)		60 s (coat)		rising
1720–22	70–76 s (coat) 34–38 s (parchment)	5 plus 15 when entering Paris	80 s (coat) 40 s (parchment)		rising
1722–25	76 s (coat) 38 s (parchment)	5		90–100 s (coat) 60 s (parchment) (in La Rochelle)	140,000 and more

Sources: Series C11A of the colonial archives provides all the prices from 1675. There were sharp fluctuations after 1710, and for greater clarity only the extremes were chosen for each period. The table in fact summarizes the findings scattered in H.A. Innis, *the Fur Trade in Canada*. Some French sale prices are available through the account books of the *fermiers du Domaine d'Occident* (A.N. France, G7, 1312, item 91). La Rochelle prices can be found in Lunn, "Economic Development in New France, 1713–1760." These were always lower than in Paris, where the beaver was sold. The Canadian market price represented the official price agreed upon by the Crown and the *fermier*, less the export duty. That was the price assigned to beaver in inventories and when it circulated in the colony.

nial merchants who gained complete control over trade with the Indians and over exports to the metropolis.[50] This "Communauté des Habitants" was a type of joint-stock company that divided the colonists into three groups, based on their investment.[51] The sponsors were to receive dividends but had no right to trade on their own.[52] The furs were supplied both by the Indians and those company agents who fetched them from beyond the confines of the settlements. As early as 1647 the company officers had been compelled to relax these restrictions in order to increase their turnover and curtail the smuggling that the measures incited. The colonists were then authorized to act as middlemen. The company advanced the necessary supplies and bought the beaver pelts, on which they levied a 50 per cent duty, in kind.[53] To compensate for the low price the company offered for pelts, traders could try to charge the Indians more for supplies. However, as native people grew more familiar with European products the terms of trade grew less and less favourable for the colonists, and the Communauté had to give better terms to ensure co-operation and prevent the colonists from taking their furs to the Dutch. The duty dropped to 25 per cent in 1653, and beaver prices were quoted on par with those current at the company's *bureau du castor*, that is, 10 livres and 10 sols (or 210 sols) for top-quality pelts in 1659 – a price that apparently did not change for the next five years.[54] Interior trade remained restricted, for only the company's stores were entitled to import the trade goods.[55] Nevertheless, the ease with which private supplies entered the colony makes it plain that the major stockholders were the first to break the rules. The company experienced setbacks, especially during the Iroquois wars, which interrupted large shipments of furs. It could not meet the colony's administrative expenses, and its directors and sponsors let it drift towards semi-bankruptcy, while individually trying to keep afloat. This situation provoked the gradual freeing of interior and exterior trade, enticed Rochelais exporters to Quebec, and heralded the rise of independent colonial merchants.[56]

Around 1664 the price of beaver suddenly declined on European markets and continued to fall until 1675. The Compagnie des Indes occidentales took over from the Cent Associés and the Communauté des Habitants ceased to exist. The new order allowed freedom of internal trade and, in 1666, extended it to external trade. The Compagnie des Indes occidentales and its sublessors abandoned the import of trade goods and export of furs to France in favour of metropolitan and colonial merchants, and held on only to the 25 per cent export duty on beaver and 10 per cent on moose hides.[57] After the decade that saw beaver prices drop by about two thirds the Canadians willingly renounced part of this privilege, which entailed so much insecurity. In 1674 the Crown leased the revenues of the Western Domain (including those taxes levied in Canada) to a group of financiers, who also obtained the exclusive privilege of exporting beaver to France. The terms were highly favourable to the colonials, since the financiers committed themselves to buying every pelt supplied at a pre-set rate, which, after a slight adjustment in 1677, remained stable until the end of the century. The Canadians were thus assured of a permanent outlet, safe from market fluctuations, and could devote their energies to increasing output.[58]

The beaver glut at the end of the century triggered a slump, and as prices collapsed on European markets, the *fermiers* tried to push down their own purchase price. On 1 October 1699 colonial merchants formed a company to exploit the Canadian rights and privileges attached to the Western Domain. With lower profit margins, the thinking went, there was no room for middlemen. Selling furs in France and eliminating competition in the colony would concentrate all the profits in a single hand. Lowered costs would mitigate the effect of the drop in prices. Parisian financiers lent up to 1 million livres to the enterprise, corresponding to the value of unsold furs acquired by the company.[59] The colonists had to invest amounts proportional to their means and their position in the company's structure. Only shareholders were to participate in the fur trade, as agents of the company.[60]

Confusion reigned as market conditions continued to deteriorate. The interior monopoly was violated, and each struggled to save his own skin. As debts and lawsuits mounted in Paris, the consequences of overproduction, obscured a while by this bold venture, came crashing down on the merchants. The Parisian financiers who took over from the colonial company in 1706 bought beaver at half its former value and imposed quotas on production. Business was slow. The London fur market was also affected, but less severely, so that Canadians got better value for their furs in Albany. Smuggling reached such proportions that in 1706 a pound of beaver fetched 1 livre in Montreal; the Quebec agent refused to trade at any price. It had risen to 4 livres by 1715, when it was still officially quoted at 3 livres.[61]

The market slowly recovered. The authorities did all in their power to hasten the price rise and attract traders back to Quebec, along with their Indian suppliers, who might well slip away to the English. In 1717 beaver exports were handled by the Compagnie d'Occident, followed by the Compagnie des Indes, which reserved the right to alter the purchase price annually if need be.[62]

Beaver finally recovered its nominal 1677–86 value by the middle of the eighteenth century. Although frequent, the fluctuations were not pronounced. The 25 per cent duty had vanished in the fray. Rather than burden already reduced profit margins – and thus encourage smuggling – the government decided to tax the furs at source through the sale of trade permits and the lease of its western outposts. This income was collected directly.[63] The Canadian dues devolving to the Western Domain became so paltry that its *fermiers* relinquished them to the Ministry of the Marine in 1732.[64]

Hides and furs

The sale of other furs, insignificant at first, increased when that of beaver fell. Except for a 10 per cent tax on moose hides, these exports were not subject to duties, quotas, or monopolies. While beaver was primarily aimed at the highly concentrated hat industry, other pelts wound their way to tiny workshops or were re-exported to various parts, and eluded sudden fluctuations. The occasional prices to come our way indicate that their nominal value did not waver much between 1660 and 1725, but the price of certain items did increase.[65] Not only did the volume of other furs increase, it took a growing share of the overall value of exports: up to 75 per cent between 1706 and 1720, when beaver was low.[66] Those merchants who invested in this bullish sector salvaged their affairs and kept the export of hides and furs a going concern once the trade recovered.[67]

The reference to "hides" as such, with no qualifier, denotes moose (*orignal*), the most expensive and most sought-after hides.[68] Elk and deer, smaller and more fragile, came next. There were fewer caribou hides, and prairie buffalo hides would only be exported in bulk after 1715.[69] Inventories mention raw or parchment hides as well as partially dressed skins.[70] Other varieties included harp seals, porpoises, and "sea cows" or seals, which were tanned and shipped out. Quebec craftsmen also fashioned them into straps and harnesses that found a partial outlet in the colony.[71] A small manufacturing industry thus developed around the trade in hides.

By the term *pelleterie* the merchants meant skins worn as furs, unlike beaver sought after for felt, as hides were for leather. Peltries of this sort represented a small fraction of the value and volume of stocks, with marten, raccoon, otter, and bear favoured in that order. (See Table 16.)

Table 16
Furs received by Chartier and Lesperance as evaluated by Lamarque, Maillot, and
Gamelin. Montreal, 11 August 1724

Types of fur	Quantity		Unit price (livres)	Value (livres)	Percentage of value
Coat beaver	1,122	pounds	4	4,488	
Coat beaver (summer)	20	pounds	2.10	50	
Parchment beaver	220	pounds	1.18	411	
Parchment beaver (summer)	62	pounds	1	62	
Total beaver	1,424	pounds		5,011	
	or 950	pelts			57
Moose	48	pelts	16	688	
Dressed moose	2	pelts	8.10	17	
Elk	4	pelts	10	40	
Deer	53/4	pounds	1.15	10.3	
Total hides	57	pelts		755.3	8
Marten top quality	620	pelts	3	1,860	
2nd quality	30	pelts	2.5	74.5	
3rd quality	41	pelts	1	41	
Otter top quality	51	pelts	2.10	127.10	
2nd quality	46	pelts	1	46	
Bear large	60	pelts	4	240	
medium	8	pelts	3	24	
Bear cub large	22	pelts	2	44	
small	14	pelts	1.5	17.10	
Fisher	86	pelts	3	258	
Lynx	3	pelts	16	48	
Lynx (poor)	1	pelts	8	8	
Southern bobcat	3	pelts	2	6	
Red fox	17	pelts	3	51	
Wolf	4	pelts	2.10	10	
Raccoon	177	for 160 pelts	.18	144	
Total small furs	1,183	pelts		2,999.5	35
Total valuation				8,765.8	100

Source: A. Monière's account book, NA, M-847. In this example, chosen for its variety, hides were less numerous than usual. Moose was generally better represented, and there were fewer small furs.

The bundles of beaver consigned to the merchants were quickly inspected, given the guaranteed sales to the *fermier*. Hides and furs underwent closer scrutiny.[72] Tainted pieces were either rejected or taken at a rebate, expressed by a reduction in the volume of these articles and not in their market price, which the body of merchants fixed annually in an unspoken but widely respected agreement.[73] Such furs tended to fall into the hands of a few major colonial merchants who shipped them back to France on their own account or sold them to their French counterparts, who were avid for returns.

4 EUROPEAN GOODS

Colonial and native consumption patterns

Most European goods were at first absorbed by the native market, so the changes in the merchants' stocks between the initial period and the later one (Table 17) reflect mainly modifications in native consumption patterns. Decorative items fell behind functional articles, revealing the gradual adaptation to European material culture. The trend governing imports of clothing, however, also reflected the development of a small-scale local industry. The colony soon provided for its subsistence but continued to depend on France for a whole range of finished products, iron, and salt. Graph 11, based on the retail sales of one merchant during the years 1715 to 1724, gives a good idea of the consumer habits of the Indian and colonial populations.[74] Further understanding of the trade can be gained by considering the various categories of merchandise.[75]

The principal import was finished fabrics. Domestic manufacture developed towards the end of the seventeenth century and drew primarily on local raw materials, mainly wool. A handful of sheep-owners produced a rough cloth, *drap du pays*, for which they found their own outlets. This was the case, for instance, of the merchant Leber, who stocked a few blue and red pieces.[76] It is quite likely that the colony's largest flock-owners, the seigneurs of Montreal, lost no time in organizing the manufacture and sale of their wool. Yet these were isolated cases. When the peasants began to grow flax and hemp, or to keep a few sheep in the early eighteenth century, their production was primarily intended for their own needs; this kept a few weavers busy, but no merchants were involved.[77] One can hazard a guess that no more than 5 per cent of the textiles sold in Montreal in this period were manufactured locally. There was no

Table 17
Various types of goods stored by Montreal merchants, 1650–1720, as proportion of
total value of stocks

Type of goods	before 1664	1680–1720
Woollens, linens, and haberdashery	10	40
Blankets	–	2
Clothing		
a. French-made	20	–
b. French or colonial	–	11
Tools, nails	20	4
Iron	–	3
Musket, powder, shot, etc.	20	12
Iron, pewter, and copper implements; earthenware, etc.	8	6
Glass beads, bells, mirrors, rings, needles, combs, dyes, and other trinkets	20	5
Wine and brandy	–	8
Imported foodstuffs and tobacco	–	4
Shoes and clogs	–	2
Miscellaneous	2	3
Total	100	100

Source: Notarial records, that is, ten inventories for the period before 1664 and twenty-seven
between 1680 and 1720.

market-oriented production of fabrics and, understandably, no import of raw materials.

Woollens, the principal trade good, made up 80 to 90 per cent of imported fabrics. One cannot be very specific about the varieties shipped up-country: they figure simply as "woollens," "Iroquois cloth," and écarlatines (scarlets), and, in more detailed lists, as Limbourg, Tarascon, Carcassonne, or Montauban woollens; more rarely, they came from Poitou and Normandy. Lighter and cheaper revesches or rough cloths, coarse muslins, flannels, and serges complemented the assortment of heavy and expensive pieces.[78] This heavy material was cut up into blankets or couvertes, which the Indians preferred to their traditional – warmer perhaps but slower-to-dry – leather clothing.[79]

Seventeenth-century stocks also included a small number of wool blankets from Normandy or Paris, apparently restricted to the colonial market. The English introduced a type of blanket that the Canadians spread illegally within their own native markets when trade with France was interrupted at the turn of the century.[80] A decade later, the Indians would reject the blankets that the French had always fashioned from scarlet woollens as shabby imitations of the article they now preferred. Desperate to keep their clients and to stem the smuggling, the Compagnie des Indes obtained leave to import the English cloth through La Rochelle until the Montpellier workshops managed to produce a decent copy. This question long engaged the ministry's attention, since it affected French trade and industry (without, however, altering colonial revenues).[81]

The Indian market also absorbed coats, shirts, *manches sauvages* or sleeves, and leggings. After 1680 the merchants had them sewn up in the colony, thus increasing their profits: coats and sleeves were pieced together from common serge, while the shirts were made from unbleached "trade" linen.[82] They came in three sizes for men, two for women, and one for children. Two-thirds of the European goods acquired by the Indians consisted of such clothes, blankets, and unfashioned cloth.[83]

A far wider range of textiles was retailed in the colony, though one would be less likely to find high-quality southern woollens than an array of rough cloths and stuffs such as flannels, crapes, coarse muslins, camlets, Aumale serges, linsey-woolsey, druggets, and so forth.[84] After 1700 peasants used a locally produced drugget, warmer than most imported varieties, but they continued to buy linen, and its sales accounted for half of all retail trade. They mostly purchased the sort of linen cloth destined for the fur trade: grey, yellow, or white hemp, and *mélis*,[85] as well as bleached linen and lesser amounts of the finer linens manufactured in Roux, Morlaix, Rouen, Paris, Beaufort, Laval, Holland, and elsewhere. Small stocks of fine linens, taffeta, brocade, muslins, cottons, real or imitation prints, and silks completed the assortment in the best merchants' shops, catering to an exclusive clientele. There one would also find high-quality accessories, braids, ribbons, buttons, silver and gold thread, lace, and embroidery.

The colonists could also buy hosiery from western France – above all, common Poitou and fancier Saint-Maixent stockings[86] – and gloves and caps. The merchants' inventories did not include locally produced stockings, such as those manufactured by the brothers of the Hôpital général, which the population purchased directly from the artisans. Montreal merchants initially ordered various items of clothing from France or from Quebec, but after 1680 they stocked only hosiery along with some handkerchiefs, taffeta scarves, and a negligible quantity of felt hats and silk stockings.

Guns, shot, bullets, and powder invariably represented about 15 per cent of the total value of cargoes for the west.[87] The most valuable

and bulkiest of these items were the dozen or so fifty-pound powder kegs taken on each voyage. The colonial authorities ensured that
their allies were properly armed, and this feature of the trade
acquired a semi-official character. Powder normally arrived on royal
ships and was distributed through the royal stores. This more or
less guaranteed state control over pricing.

Colonial gunsmiths put together a standard "trade gun." By the
1680s western outposts began to retain the services of blacksmiths,
or *arquebusiers*, to repair firearms, manufacture bullets, and perform
other duties that reduced their dependence on merchant consignments. The governor frequently gratified his allies with free gifts of
arms and munitions.[88] The Indians used them primarily as weapons
and not for hunting, where traditional methods continued.

In the early days of settlement, merchants had shared in the arms
trade with the colonists, but gunsmiths had later cornered the
market. They imported and assembled ordinary guns, turned the
lead into bullets, and bought back scrap iron for grapeshot. By the
end of the century the merchants' supplies had dwindled to a few
better-quality guns and pistols, although they still included shot.[89]
Until the end of the War of the Grand Alliance, the authorities, who
insisted that all the settlers be armed, intervened on several occasions to compel merchants to accept wheat – at a fixed rate – in
return for guns.[90] The intendant resorted to importing ordinary guns
that the king's stores either sold at cost or loaned to those who
could not afford them. This accounts for the low incidence of sales
by merchants. Even shipments of arms out west often seemed to be
based on strategic considerations rather than those of profitability.

One item was worth 4 to 5 per cent of the merchants' stocks: the
kettle, or, more accurately, the easily transportable large copper
cauldron that changed traditional cooking methods the moment the
natives came into contact with the Europeans.[91] Indians also acquired large and varied stores of knives, scissors and awls, arrow-
heads, sword blades, and quantities of axes, tomahawks, chisels, and
scrapers. All but the last four somewhat cruder articles (which
began to be locally made around 1660) were imported from France.
Merchants sold iron and steel, although some artisans obtained their
raw materials directly from France.[92] By 1720 Montreal outfitters
would be able to buy all the axes and iron tools they sent to the
interior from colonial blacksmiths.

Local craftsmen also supplied the basic carpentry and agricultural
tools as well as the majority of utensils used by the settlers.[93] Nails,
fancier kitchenware, and ordinary pewter dishes and cutlery (sold

by the pound) remained the domain of the merchants.[94] Since artisans melted down and refashioned used pewter, there was only a limited market for imported ready-made goods.[95] By around 1700 local earthenware was more widespread than French pottery.

The settlers' meagre resources and local craft production tended to limit massive imports of such basic finished products. This did not interfere, however, with the limited import of finer articles and luxury items, such as glassware, porcelain, and china, which the best shops continued to stock in small quantities.

A missionary who exposed the ill effects of brandy on the natives and had no cause to downplay its extent estimated that about forty kegs (*barriques*) a year were dispatched up-country by the end of the seventeenth century.[96] There was little profit in it for the merchants, and indeed Monière's accounts, two decades later, show that brandy amounted to no more than 4 to 5 per cent of the value of shipments.[97] The brandy that arrived in the interior had theoretically been sent to the outlying garrisons or earmarked for the voyageurs' private use, since outright sale to the Indians was prohibited. But brandy did in fact play a major role in the trade, more as a token of goodwill than as a commodity: it served to cement mutual agreements, moisten the send-offs to the hunt, and toast successful returns as all voiced their hopes for the following season. On such occasions the traders let the liquor flow freely and reckoned these gestures as part of their overhead costs. Meanwhile, coureurs de bois could make a huge profit by selling a single bottle of watered-down brandy in outposts where demand inevitably outlasted supply.[98] Such abuses cannot be measured either for brandy or for rum bought illegally from the English. The unruliness displayed during this period can be attributed mostly to greedy small traders, who were not backed by the merchants and who had little else to offer the Indians.[99] The trader who wanted to secure a faithful clientele and convince the Indians to hunt on his behalf, in order to secure steady returns, did not turn brandy into a major item for sale.

Importers made more consistent profits because they rarely dealt face to face with the Indians and retailed brandy to the traders on the same terms as the rest of the settlers. Montreal's principal innkeepers and taverners ordered their supplies directly from France or got them from Quebec merchants. They had to contend with competition from merchants who were also entitled to sell brandy by the pint[100]; this is how settlers obtained whatever brandy they bartered to resident or visiting Indians.

Twice as much wine was sold within the colony as brandy.

Turnover was quick, which explains why so little figures in inventories. There were some attempts to fix retail prices, but these continued to be dictated by the arrival of shipments.[101] Most imported wines came from Bordeaux, the reds especially, and occasionally from Spain. Brandy appears to have originated exclusively from the Charente and Aunis.[102]

Multi-coloured glass beads (known as *rasade* and sold by the pound), porcelain beads, rings set with imitation stones, small bells, tinplate mirrors, boxwood and ivory combs figured in every cargo, though their relative value diminished over the second half of the seventeenth century.[103] By 1720 the value of these trinkets had fallen to 3 per cent of overall sales to the Indians. Vermilion powder, included in this assortment, found a steady if not very extensive market. Most of the tobacco used in the fur trade was the black Brazilian variety, imported from La Rochelle, rather than the white home-grown variety.

It was not until the middle of the eighteenth century that an attempt was made to establish salt works in Canada.[104] Salt shortages were therefore endemic in the period of this study, and imports were rigorously controlled. Most of the salt went to the Gulf fisheries and the preservation of eel.[105] The Crown named a *garde-sel*, who oversaw its distribution and forbade the merchants to stockpile it.[106] Although the Conseil and the intendants desired every ship bound for New France to carry salt as ballast, these demands could hardly be met as long as outbound cargoes remained fuller than those homeward-bound.[107] Official imports of salt, as well as the imposition of price controls whenever stocks dwindled, checked merchant profits on this product.[108]

Montrealers appear to have done little salting, relying instead on the long frost to preserve their food. Still, existing production of salted butter and meat for the local market, the western outposts, and export suffered from the shortage of salt and its usually high price.[109]

The town's best merchants provided a select clientele with a range of fancy foodstuffs such as vinegar, olive oil, pepper and spices, brandy plums, raisins, rice, coffee, and Dutch cheese. None of these found their way to the average settler's post-mortem inventories. White and brown sugar were rarely imported in the seventeenth century. Local production from maple sap was as yet undeveloped; sweeteners were not a part of the ordinary diet.[110]

Alum, practically insignificant at first, began to figure in every stock at the end of the century, paralleling the growth of the tanning industry, for which it was primarily destined, and that of domestic cloth production. The settlers made their own soap, but the merchants continued to import a finer variety for the urban market.

Among these various other imports, paper was the most important item, and included reading primers. Window panes, razors, and other sundry articles with a small turnover round out the list.

Prices

The normal differential overall between the metropolitan cost price and the Montreal retail price was 100 per cent.[111] The inelasticity noted in the prices of metropolitan manufactures was perhaps even more pronounced in the colony, where the profit margin was sufficient to offset any slight fluctuation.[112] Salt and wine were far more exposed to changing circumstances and therefore were regulated again and again. But with the exception of those years prior to 1666 when trading companies monopolized imports, other commodities were not affected by price regulations, except in so far as the merchants tacitly agreed to set a seasonal rate. Any attempt by itinerant merchants to undercut the established rates caused the established merchants to appeal to the Sovereign Council, which then promulgated its price list.[113]

Post-mortem inventories, with their vague reference to volume and quality, are a poor guide to the movement in prices.[114] The chaotic monetary situation compounds the difficulties. Even if we were to set aside the interlude of the card money (1690–1720), it would still be necessary to push forward into the eighteenth century to determine whether the high prices recorded in Monière's ledgers and some inventories dating from 1722–25 merely reflect the inflation of metropolitan prices or represent an additional increase for the colony.[115] From the time of Colbert's ministry to 1721–25, there was an important increase in the nominal price of imports, which did not affect all goods equally but never fell under 20 per cent.[116] Whatever the origins of these price increases, the population was affected, since the price of wheat used in payment for these European goods had fallen by 30 per cent during the same period, and wages had not risen.

5   COSTS AND PROFITS

"The trade in goods usually brings in a 700 per cent profit," Lahontan reported in 1690, "for the Indians get skinned."[117] He was right, but his figure makes no sense until we isolate net profits and break them down into various components. Trading involved two separate transactions: the exchange of European goods for furs, and the exchange of furs in France for money. Table 18 describes the process through a concrete example. Each step has been demarcated from the next, for simplicity's sake, but it should be evident that an individual could act in more than one capacity.

The first transaction – the exchange of goods for furs – generated the greatest returns. Had Canada remained a trading post like that of the Hudson's Bay Company, these would have landed in one single pocket, but colonization set in motion forces that defeated companies' attempts at monopoly, so that profits were shared among several intermediaries. This example starts with, say, five pounds of shot, worth 15 sols in La Rochelle and 30 sols retail in Montreal. The 50 per cent margin left enough for the importer in Quebec to cover shipping costs, and in the best of times (when costs approximated those of Table 18) the importer could clear a 15 per cent net profit. But a string of catastrophes – war, seizure, shipwreck, or damage at sea – combined with capital depreciation, periodic slumps and defaults, could lower the average return to 10 per cent, which was, in fact, the norm for overseas trade in this period.[118] Transport to Montreal, handling, and the measures required to put together a shipment to the interior took up another 30 to 40 per cent. Losses and delays engendered by the Indian wars or by the shortages in agriculture and consequent insolvency gnawed away at profits. Given the risks, it is unlikely that the outfitter could get more than an average 10 per cent return on such retail sales over the years. Importers and retailers could not let their ventures fall below a certain minimum size and profit without either abandoning the trade or attempting to combine both functions.[119] This latter course required, however, both solid connections in La Rochelle and an extensive knowledge of the colonial clientele: a double prerequisite that spawned many a partnership.

The five pounds of shot were next exchanged for a pound of beaver. The value of the pelts depended on the goods offered in return. Although not altogether absolved from the constraints of time and space, their worth gravitated towards a local standard, from which it hardly moved. E.E. Rich and Abraham Rotstein, who looked at the Hudson's Bay Company books, note that the terms of exchange remained practically the same throughout the eighteenth century.[120] They had probably been far more favourable to the Europeans in the early seventeenth century, when contacts were still occasional and the traders fleeced the natives for a handful of trinkets. However, as the Indians became essential suppliers who

Table 18

Approximate margins of profits in the beaver trade during the last quarter of the seventeenth century (a)

Steps	Purchase price	Mean costs	Cost price	Sale price	Max. net profit	
					sols	%
For the importer	Goods in France 15 sols	Freight, import duties, handling, storage, etc. 30% or 4.5 s (b)	19.5 s	To the outfitter 22.5 s	3 s	15
For the outfitter (retailer)	Goods in Quebec 22.5 s	Transport to Montreal, wastage, handling, storage, etc. 13% or 3 s (c)	25.5 s	To the voyageur 30 s	4.5 s	18
For the voyageur	Goods in Montreal 30 s	Purchase of permit, wages, canoes, provisions, other expenses 100% or 30 s (d)	60 s	To the Indian. Exchanged for 1 pound of beaver at 67 s	7 s	12
For the outfitter	1 pound of beaver worth 67s in Montreal 67 s	Storage, transport to Quebec, etc. 22 s (e)	69 s	To the exporter. 25% export duty being deducted from the official price of 90 s) 67 s	-2 s	-3
For the exporter (lessee of the Western Domain)	1 pound of beaver worth 67 s in Quebec 67 s	Freight, insurance, handling, commissions, transport La Rochelle – Paris, wastage, cost of lease, general expenses, capital tied up, depreciation 100% or 67 s (f)	134 s	To the Parisian hatters 168 s	34 s	25

Table 18 continued

(a) These are the exact prices. Inventories and account books provide the mark-up between invoices and sale prices at each step. The margin, 50 per cent upon entry and 33.3 per cent at the retail level (30-40 per cent from 1715 to 1725), remained stable throughout the period under consideraton and apply to all dry goods. The beaver price quoted here represents the arithmetical mean of the value of one pound of coat beaver and one pound of parchment beaver (see Table 15). The cost evaluation is tentative, however. Supporting evidence appears below.

(b) In the seventeenth century the *ad valorem* freightage rate for dry goods ranged between 8 per cent and 10 per cent in peacetime. This came to 50 to 80 livres per measured ton and seems to have stayed within those limits until the middle of the eighteenth century. Freightage was higher on wine and brandy. See AC, C11A12, fol. 76; minutes of 10 June 1664, JDCS, vol. I; A.J.E. Lunn, *Economic Development in New France, 1713–1760*, p. 380. In wartime, as in 1692, freightage might rise to 120 livres per ton: AC, C11A12, fol. 10. In the seventeenth century maritime insurance premiums fell slightly below 10 per cent. Some shipments were insured at three-quarters of their value, and others not at all. The rate could easily climb to 20 per cent in wartime.

Wine and brandy paid 10 per cent import duties, tobacco 5 sols per pound, but goods bound for the colonies were not liable to French export taxes. AC, C11A10, fols. 171–4. It is more difficult to assess other miscellaneous expenditures, but it seems reasonable to presume that these costs amounted altogether to 30 per cent of the value of the merchandise at the embarkation point.

(c) Freightage between Quebec and Montreal would not exceed 3 per cent *ad valorem* (see, for example, J.B. Beauvais' inventory. Not. rec. 17 Apr. 1705, A. Adhémar). Goods do not appear to have been insured for this part of the voyage. Even if the merchant could sue the captain of the boat, losses and waste consistently cut into his profits. Merchants also paid for cartage on the island and they kept other costs to a minimum by storing and selling the goods from their homes. In the best of times, total cost would amount to 13 per cent.

(d) The 1,000-livre permit represented 33 per cent of the value of one canoe-load of merchandise. On the basis of Alexis Monière's books, the expenses of twelve-to eighteen-month trips to the interior, including the permit, could well have equalled the value of the trade goods. The notion of diminishing costs does not, of course, apply to such ventures.

(e) In the eighteenth century the exporter received the furs in Montreal, which eliminated this extra expense for the merchants.

(f) Basing his analysis on an eighteenth-century report (AC, C11A, 37, fol. 494), H.A. Innis estimated the cost of transport between Quebec and Paris at 10 sols per pound of beaver. Given higher freight and insurance rates in the seventeenth century as well as the commissions paid along the way, and the barriers to internal circulation, this estimate was doubled. The lessees of the Western Domain reported that wastage came to 10 per cent. AC, C11A12, fols. 174–9vol. They paid 350,000 livres annually for the lease but this included other privileges, as in the sugar trade, and we have no way of isolating these various items in their accounts. By positing 100% for all costs, the margin of profit remains large enough to give credibility to such estimates.

also distributed European goods in the interior, new commercial relations arose which were less advantageous to the French. The gradual extension of the networks also eventually extinguished regional disparities.

The value accorded to the furs over a large area had little to do with supply and demand. Nor did it reflect Anglo-French rivalry or internal competition. Traders attracted and retained their clientele through treaties involving a complex interplay of alliances, tributes, and lavish distributions of powder, necklaces, tobacco, and liquor, as well as by manifesting their trustworthiness, personal valour, and dexterity, and, of course, by providing quality goods. With a rifle worth five beavers, anyone hoping for better terms had to search further afield, beyond the purview of the middlemen, but this automatically raised travel costs. And then it was only a matter of time before the standard spread throughout the further zone.[121] Competition from English goods shipped inland from New York or Hudson Bay could not be stemmed simply by extending networks. The French had to adjust their rates and deliver goods on the same basis as their rivals, despite the difference in the original purchase price, which gradually worked in favour of the English and forced Canadians to increase exports to offset their lowered profit margins.

Although there is little information on the terms of exchange governing transactions between Indians and Frenchmen, rough estimates are nevertheless possible, thanks to the Hudson's Bay Company records.[122] The piecemeal evidence available in our own records allowed some cross-checking that justified the use of this data.[123] The price of beaver traded for powder, shot, blankets, or copper kettles came to about 30 sols a pound but was less in exchange for vermilion, tinplate mirrors, gunflint, or ramrods, in which case the Indians received goods worth 6 to 20 sols per pound of beaver. It was more valuable, however, in return for clothing. Traders had to provide a whole range of articles, some not very profitable, but since cloth, copper, and munitions made up two-thirds of the exchanges, it is legitimate to suppose that at the end of the seventeenth century a pound of beaver was worth an average of 30 sols within the established network.[124]

The beaver pelts taken back to Montreal by the voyageur served to pay off supplies according to a market value of 67 sols per pound.[125] From his remaining 37 sols the trader had to deduct the costs of the voyage, food, wages of his men, if any, plus the cost of trade permits; this would leave a 10 to 15 per cent return on his investment.[126] Trade in the furthest reaches required at least three participants, whose net profit was consequently lower than that of the merchant advancing the goods – otherwise, opportunity costs would hardly justify the existence of a body of outfitters. Still, the margin was a narrow one, and in over half the cases these merchants also had a stake in the returns. They either bought the permits and received half the surplus, without sharing other expenses with the *voyageurs*[127] or else they split the cost of the permits with the latter, bore part of the costs, and received only a fraction of the surplus, proportional to their investment.[128] And so it came about that over the eighteenth century the outfitter went into fuller partnership, and the voyageur stopped being a customer and turned into a "wintering partner."

The merchant took the beaver pelts to the *bureau du fermier* – an operation in which he made no profits since he received the same amount (in bills of exchange) as he had already dispensed to the voyageurs. The way to increase his means of payment overseas and gradually to extend his operations was to collect more furs and generate more revenue than had been expended that year.[129]

We have reached the ultimate step, when the holder of the beaver monopoly collected the final profit on sales in France. Even obvious expenditures still left him a handsome margin of profits. Yet it was prey to a number of imponderables, be they slumps or the vagaries of hat-making, and could only be sustained by an organization with sizable reserves.[130] The lessees of the Western Domain were unable to keep up the profits estimated in Table 18, and it is unlikely that their predecessor, the Compagnie des Indes occidentales, fared any better than the rest of these large-scale enterprises, and cleared more than 10 to 15 per cent. Small merchants in the colony, who could ill afford the shipping costs and the immobilization of their capital, had to forgo the profits reaped from the overseas sale of hides and small furs.[131] The more important merchants did play a role in this export trade, and in the one specific and perhaps exceptional case I encountered, received a net return of 21 per cent on one shipment.[132]

Isolated accounts of fabulous profits, or the concern about the catastrophes of the early eighteenth century, which figure in official correspondence and are therefore emphasized by historians who dwell on these records, should not overshadow the normal yields of this trade, distributed on both sides of the Atlantic. The nature of the product itself checked any real expansion entailing heavy investments. The colony developed on a scale commensurate to this small staple production.

CHAPTER FIVE

Trade Relations

The ties linking the various participants in the fur trade remained hazy and tenuous as long as the economy lacked a well-defined structure. As this structure only came into being in the eighteenth century, the agitation of the preceding period was in fact a series of adjustments to external change – quick and choppy adaptations. Since the major fluctuations have already been described, it is easier to follow the phases in the development of commercial practices and the inner logic of this process.

1 THE EVOLUTION OF COMMERCIAL FUNCTIONS

1642–68: Participation by the local population

"I should inform you that the Iroquois and Sanontouais are wintering in Montreal and that I have furnished them with the means to go hunting," one woman wrote to her Quebec supplier.[1] Colonists could easily obtain furs from no farther away than their front doors. As soon as the Communauté des habitants relaxed its monopoly, settlers hastened to trade directly with resident or visiting Indians, whom they in turn attracted, exasperated, and feared. Waiting for dividends that would never materialize, the colonists availed themselves of the then favourable terms of trade, which afforded them sizable returns despite the company's substantial levies. Settlers had plenty of opportunities to barter away a few knives or awls.[2] This was the bait that lured indentured servants to remain in the colony and bound the free man to the trading post more surely than the servant not privy to these benefits.

Protected by its isolation from the rest of the colony and by its precarious situation, Montreal could easily intercept occasional shipments from the west, while still relying on the furs regularly supplied by local Indians.[3] In 1662, when Pierre Pigeon began homesteading, he owned 1,200 livres in fur and trade goods. From then on his activities were confined to improving his land. When he died sixteen years later, his total assets amounted to little more than what he had amassed during his two years' experience as a trader.[4] If an ambitious young man was unlikely to make his way quickly to the ranks of Quebec's merchant elite, the path remained wide open in Montreal. Charles Lemoyne, an innkeeper's son from Dieppe who had worked as an interpreter and servant of the Jesuits, arrived early enough to grab the lion's share. Others followed from Paris, Rouen, or La Rochelle, and they slowly multiplied, return upon return, their original investment of a few hundred livres.

Ingratiating small merchants, protected from above, and well-connected gentlemen-soldiers ordered their goods from France and soon concentrated all the profits, gradually edging out the ordinary inhabitants. Progressively larger advances, coupled with the support of the missionaries, assured a few merchants a monopoly over local Indian output, while their choice location allowed them to corner the shipments brought by visitors to the August fair. What else could the settlers who wanted to gather up a few crumbs do but entice these wayfarers to their homes and intoxicate and despoil them?

The slump in beaver prices hastened the movement towards concentration, which would spell the gradual retreat of the bulk of the population from an activity that had once been an important source of income during the difficult early years of land clearance.

1668–81: Chaos

Propelled by the fall in beaver prices, men and merchandise suddenly rushed west, beginning in the latter half of the 1660s. The peace treaty with the Five Nations reduced the dangers of the journey at the very time when three thousand soldiers and indentured servants set foot in the colony. The Ottawas, who supplied the French, bypassed Lake Superior with traders in tow and found tribes ready to barter their furs for a pittance. The colony went wild. The time was ripe to relocate the trade, and although the fair survived until the end of the century, it received fewer furs.

Trade became the preserve of professionals, but the role of the various participants remained ill defined. At the top, governors and other officials, principal if shady players, protected their private interests through a well-orchestrated medley of decrees, ordinances, denunciations, and exemplary sentences to stop illicit trade that was carried on under cover of defensive operations "deep in the woods." It comes as no surprise that no notarial records or accounts have survived to indicate the extent of this collusion.[5]

The lower ranks were filled by merchants of every stripe. Montreal had 39 merchants in 1681 out of a total population of 1,350 (270 householders): a telling statistic, as significant as the rapid turnover among a group depleted by ill-luck, bankruptcy, departures, or withdrawal to less risky occupations. Two individuals stand out. The fortunes built up by Lemoyne and his brother-in-law Leber during this unsettled period rank among the most solid the colony would ever see. Five other importers transferred operations to Montreal.[6] A number of Montrealers managed to rise above the mass of small shopkeepers. Firmly established merchants continued to trade with nearby Indians and with the fair's customers, whom they shrewdly met at the island crossing.[7] Post-mortem inventories in this period show the continued importance of such transactions, where proceeds were neither shared nor liable to expenses.[8] Such merchants might also advance supplies to coureurs de bois, who fetched the furs at source, in defiance of regulations. This illicit trade was at first mainly handled by marchands-forains, merchants without resident status in Montreal.[9] As long as shipments still came down, those to whom they were destined by right shied away from becoming lenders, given the greater risks and lesser returns. Until the shortage of furs compelled them to resort to adventurers, they remained content to inform on the threat posed by the outlaws and their suppliers.[10] But 33 per cent interest on thousands of livres proved more alluring than 150 per cent profit on fewer and fewer shipments, and legitimized this precarious trade based on trust and the ability to secure high-placed protectors. Sound judgment of men, entrusted with valuable cargoes, was also essential, since there was no possible legal recourse.

The intendant's claim that some five to eight hundred men were off in the woods in 1680 far exceeds what one might expect from the volume of exports.[11] Even if officials were correct in their estimate of illegal activities, it is unlikely that more than a hundred of these coureurs de bois worked for merchants, setting off with cargoes worth 1,000 to 2,000 livres and dispatching furs back to the colony in some roundabout way. A specialized workforce was being created from a few soldiers employed by their commanders and a majority of native-born youths who had been trained when fur-trading was still a common occupation and who did not accept their exclusion as readily as their elders.

Some former soldiers and indentured servants also joined the trade. No sooner were they freed than they took off to the woods trundling small bundles of wares advanced by some foolhardy merchant.[12] They scattered inland, living off the Indians, selling a few furs to those who could take them back to the colony, and sometimes accompanying their hosts to the English settlements.[13] With neither family nor connections to protect them, they risked the rope.[14] This is why, weary of this unprofitable existence, they seized on periodic amnesties to take the boat home or to take up some land in the colony. Many died without leaving a trace. A minority, proving their skill and honesty, joined the ranks of coureurs de bois employed by the merchants. In 1684 the merchant Auber felt he could rely on some two hundred coureurs de bois to fight against the Iroquois.[15] The body of outlaws was shrinking, and a new group of middlemen was emerging.

1681–1700: Setting up a system

Officials were conscious of the dangers of disorder, however profitable it may have been for them. The lessee of the Western Domain had good reason to complain, for, threatened by fines, traders smuggled the furs to Albany, evading also the export duties.[16] Its agent put pressure on the Council to prosecute offenders. Favouritism had given rise to secret associations denounced by the excluded merchants and officers.[17] The semi-official recognition of fraud was an open invitation to disobedience. In Montreal young men armed with clubs contested the ordinances, while the notables, fearing the worst, closed ranks.[18] The unsecured loans that underpinned the illegal trade gave the merchants pause, and the intendant expressed a general concern when he suggested that fur traders should maintain ties with the colony "in order to secure their debts."[19]

Twenty-five permits, or congés, were issued annually as of 1681 in order to stem the lawlessness and legalize departures. This system allowed merchants an added share of the profits, above and beyond the interest they charged on their advances, and enabled the Crown to use these congés in lieu of pensions and bonuses. Thus, each year twenty-five recipients from among the impoverished nobility, deserving officers, and religious communities were entitled to ship one cargo out west.

The 1682 list contained sixteen active or retired officers, two officers' widows, three noblemen and seigneurs, and two congés to the Notre-Dame vestry.[20] This privileged contingent, handed these permits gratis, either turned each over to three traders in return for a share of the profits or else sold them outright to a merchant. Through various transfers and combinations, the outfitters came to ultimately control the situation.[21] The intendant often sold *congés* to the biggest among them in recognition of their knowledge of the crews, their lower propensity for smuggling, and their willingness to adapt to military circumstances and put off return shipments if so ordered, once conflict with the Iroquois and their allies broke out anew.[22]

Yet far more than twenty-five canoes circulated in the upper country. The intendant increased the number of *congés*, and the holders applied them to two or more trips, thereby effectively putting an end to fur-trading within the settlement.[23]

An organization was taking shape. The number of local merchants fell gradually, to twenty or so at the end of the century, and half of these imported their goods directly from France.[24] While the majority of the latter had been active in the previous period, the lower rungs were filled with newcomers from France and from the Quebec and Trois-Rivières regions. All were now essentially outfitters, for the fair was dying and the mission Indians, decimated by illness or called on to fight, did little trapping. Some bought their supplies from Quebec importers and acted at times as their agents. There were no wholesalers in Montreal. Local importers sold the goods retail or advanced them to other merchants at the market price.

A new group of fur traders came to the fore: the voyageurs. From 1680 this was the title favoured by former coureurs de bois trusted by merchants for their experience and for their good relations with inland tribes. This group included a number of small merchants who found themselves excluded from the new, more complex organization. Officers and rich merchants had their sons apprenticed to these former coureurs de bois. Voyageurs always worked with two or three associates, and their partnerships and debt acknowledgments began to figure in notarial records.[25] They had become professionals. By the end of the century the merchants could well rejoice: they had secured the core of the debt; the voyageurs were investing in land and would, when they retired, style themselves "*bourgeois* of this town."

The population at large had long since ceased to depend on the fur trade for supplementary income. Voyageurs had to be experienced and good credit risks, so that country boys who chose such occupations tended to make them lifelong.[26] Meanwhile, a new type of involvement emerged: fur-trade indentureships. A number of post commanders, who had a monopoly over furs trapped by

Indians on their territories, hired crews to bring up supplies and haul back the pelts; they were forbidden, however, to trade independently.[27] This system provided seasonal employment to a few peasants' sons. In this period, the annual west-bound contingents averaged one hundred men and included only a few of these *engagés*. Since voyageurs often spent more than a year inland, there were at any given time, up to two hundred of them around the Great Lakes, not counting the garrisons.

1700–25: Gradual consolidation

The movement west increased when the trade devolved to the Colony Company in the early eighteenth century. Relying heavily on *engagés*, up to 1705 the company dispatched some sixty men each year to Detroit at the end of Lake Erie for modest wages.[28] An equal number of independent voyageurs wound their way inland, despite the company's attempts to corner all exchanges, and ventured beyond its trading posts. The opening of Louisiana in 1699 encouraged these moves, and, if the sixty Canadians who settled with d'Iberville in Mobile had travelled by sea, more came down the Mississippi to join them.[29] Enterprises sponsored by the Jesuits, the Séminaire des Missions étrangères, Le Sueur, or Juchereau may have scattered in all directions, but they created so many way-stations and shelters that many of these journeys were one-way. Formerly coureurs de bois had to return sooner or later to the colony, but now there were other options: voyageurs who had squandered their credit in Montreal could make a new start in Louisiana.

Then, for the second time in fifty years, beaver prices plummeted, and this crisis would have lasting effects upon the emerging trade organization. Between 1706 and 1712 imports declined, reducing the number of obligations signed by voyageurs and the hiring of *engagés*. The number of outfitters reached a ceiling.[30] While it is impossible to gauge the extent of illegal trading, it provided a measure of relief that kept the commercial structure afloat.

Although trade revived eventually, its practitioners had to make do with reduced profit margins. This would lead to gradual concentration. As the volume of exports increased, indentureships for the fur trade were reintroduced on a vast scale by voyageurs, who no longer sought partners but hired canoemen instead. Technical progress also fostered such changes. Canoes, which had previously held three men, required crews of five by 1725, and six or more after 1740. The outposts became better provisioned.[31] The workforce was enlarged to keep pace with the output and the increasing remoteness of the source of pelts. The number of voyageurs remained steady. Joined in various partnerships, they controlled regular brigades that plied the route between Montreal and the outposts. In 1717, 61 of the 151 men who set off west were *engagés*. Their number would reach 146 by 1727, and 300 a decade later.[32] This trend towards concentration in the early eighteenth century was no temporary phenomenon but presaged the gradual proletarianization of the men employed in the fur trade, as later data indicate. Some of the hundred or so voyageurs who set off annually were recruited internally, while others were drawn from merchant and officer families. Relations between the latter and the traders, who now called themselves marchands-voyageurs, grew closer. The profession was sealing itself off from below.

There seems to have been no such concentration among outfitters.[33] While death had claimed the seventeenth-century leaders, the crisis brought forth a renewed and broader contingent composed mainly of middling merchants who scrambled to occupy the vacant places. By 1720 their number had once more fallen to twenty: mainly native-born survivors of the fray, members of Montreal, Quebec, and Trois-Rivières merchant families. Four recent arrivals made their mark. One, Pierre de Lestage, immediately rose to the first ranks.[34]

Military officers had always had a finger in the trade, but their involvement became more conspicuous after 1700.[35] The issue and sale of permits to supply the western garrisons assured them a share of the traders' profits.[36] Furthermore, the Crown's decision to farm out fur-trade revenues in a particular territory to its area commander sanctioned their direct involvement. Ties between merchants and the petty nobility, which had been quite loose in the seventeenth century, tended to solidify as the two groups' interests increasingly converged. The officer needed credit to capitalize on his privileges, and the merchant needed the officer's permission to enter his territory. By the second quarter of the eighteenth century, the officer corps had become fully involved in commerce. This was a highly significant social phenomenon.[37]

2 CREDIT FORGES NETWORKS

Agriculture grew at a different pace from commerce. The wherewithal for the earliest land clearance had come from the proceeds of the fur trade, and there was more than one disillusioned trader among the peasants and many of their sons among these canoemen recruited by the merchants. Commodities and men moved easily from one sector to the other. Yet the distribution of land-ownership, the usual gauge of urban-rural interdependence, points to a complete separation between commerce and agriculture. This is an exaggeration, however, and we must look elsewhere, in merchants' account books, for a truer picture of the nature and extent of the actual links between the two sectors.

Means of payment

Montreal merchants were above all fur merchants. There is no evidence that they began by selling or peddling cloth and nails to the settlers only to become outfitters once business improved. It normally worked the other way round. A merchant who did well in the fur trade built up a local clientele, which, however slight, supported and sustained his primary activities. The process is illustrated in one merchant's account books. (See Table 19.)

All of Alexis Monière's business centred, in fact, on the twenty-two individuals to whom he regularly advanced supplies (worth 2,000 to 9,000 livres) in the course of that decade. The son of a small Trois-Rivières merchant, Monière had spent ten years as a voyageur. By the time he was thirty, in 1715, he was already supplying his former companions, even though he still occasionally went west with them. His wife managed the store in his absence, but in the early days local custom hardly amounted to more than 10 per cent of his turnover. His clientele gradually increased thanks to Monière's fur-trade connections, which included former *engagés* now settled on the land, voyageurs' dependents living in town, and artisans and peasants who provided goods and services for the outward journey. The five thousand residents on Montreal Island, however, only represented a secondary market.

The methods of payment, illustrated in Graph 12, highlight the personal nature of this activity, its frailties, as well as its base in the colony.[38] Voyageurs repaid their advances with furs. The predominance of hides and small furs was peculiar to this period, for at all other times beaver outnumbered them. Occasionally, the shipments fell short of the debt and merchants took money (cards or cash) or negotiable notes or else recouped some of their supplies. Voyageurs usually paid *engagés* with beaver, which is how they in turn refunded the outfitters' modest advances of brandy, guns, shoes, or the occasional small pack of goods.

The inhabitants' payments bore a more interesting character. Once the card money was retired, hard currency reappeared and, curiously enough, remained the favourite form of payment.[39] Arti-

Table 19
Distribution of a merchant's customers and value of sales in each category,
1715–1724

Customers			
Categories	Number	Sales (livres tournois)	%
Voyageurs outfitted by the merchant	22	60,000	60
Engagés and other voyageurs who made occasional purchases	34	11,470	11
Military officers and their families	26		
Artisans who paid with their labour	10		
Artisans who paid with goods they had made	19	28,495	29
Merchant's creditors	12		
Other urban and rural clients	148		
Total	261	99,965	100
Other merchants in transactions that brought in little or no returns	13	5,293	

Source: Account books of Alexis Monière, PAC, M-847 and M-848.

sans, and especially officers, tended to purchase their goods with pelts. The officers provided Monière with their trade permits, which he would credit to their accounts at market value. In this decade Monière rented and then purchased a house. When he lost his wife, he sent his youngest children to a wet nurse and the eldest girls to a convent. To fulfil these obligations he granted his new creditors a line of credit and supplied them with whatever they needed. The same pattern applied to trade-related services such as cartage or his men's board at an inn. The peasants paid with grain, meat, butter, eggs, or wood, which they might bring to another customer rather than the merchant. His shop thus acted as a small redistribution centre. For example, Jean might order flour from Monière, who had it delivered by Jacques. Or Jean might request that Jacques, who owed him money, turn over his wheat to Monière, who in turn asked Jacques to deliver it directly to Pierre. Debts were thus cancelled on the books without the goods' actually being stored under the merchant's roof. The one way to increase profits was to extend the network of exchange, for each new creditor might prove an outlet for imported products.

Such accounts suggest that merchants had no control whatsoever over artisanal production. Blacksmiths, tanners, coopers, or joiners might pay for their purchases with articles they made, but these did not circulate as well as country produce.[40] Most of these articles were included in westward cargoes at eastern prices – that is, without any mark-up. In two instances only did blacksmiths, who owed money to Monière, accept his terms and work the iron he provided into a specific set of sickles, axes, or currycombs on which the merchant then added a mark-up. They repaid their debts within a year and recovered their independence. There is no better illustration of the separation between merchant capital and local manufacture.[41] Monière did, however, hire seamstresses: he pocketed the surplus value on the shirts and greatcoats they fashioned for him and sold these articles to the voyageurs at a 10 to 15 per cent profit. Although wages were low, this feminine labour force was plentiful, for there was little other work available for widows or wives of absent men.[42]

For the most part, payments in kind filled out western cargoes: flour was turned into biscuit, and barrelled pork fed the voyageurs; boxes and barrels were used in packing; axes, scrapers, and other tools were for the Indian market, along with some of the local white tobacco. Once he had taken care of the handling costs, the merchant made little or no profit from the resale of such goods.[43] In short, anyone could set up shop, sell sundry articles, collect furs, receive bills of exchange in return, and begin the cycle again. It was perhaps easier to obtain initial backing from metropolitan suppliers than to win the trust of skilful and honest voyageurs, but the merchant who wished to attract and keep the custom of the men who ensured his prosperity had to provide all the necessary services: hiring the crews, finding them lodgings before their departure, organizing the cartage, buying and repairing canoes, gathering the provisions, and securing the necessary permits.[44] He held on to this clientele by his ability to perform these functions smoothly. If he skimped or overcharged for goods that the traders could acquire more cheaply from habitants and artisans, he would be condemned to deal with adventurers who might never refund his advances.

This leaves the last item on Table 19: dealings with other merchants. Monière frequently resorted to other merchants for deliveries.[45] If his stocks were low or he ran out of an article, he would borrow a neighbour's, and vice versa. Such transactions had no effect on retailers' profit margins, since they exchanged the commodities at cost. Retail prices were uniform in Montreal, and merchants worked side by side, apparently without competing. Yet if there were no price wars, competition in the services described above could be harsh, going as far as the denunciation of rivals to the authorities.[46]

We should not forget that merchants made all their money from the sale of imported products and were therefore, by definition, indifferent if not opposed to the development of local industry, which would eventually reduce the value of their wares. Potentially cheaper Canadian products would not generate the sort of profits secured through European imports even if the merchant were to produce them himself, for he would still have to pare down his prices to match those of other merchants. The activities of this small merchant therefore sum up perfectly the fundamental contradiction at the heart of the country's development.

Short-term credit

Accounting methods were rudimentary, and this seems to remain a characteristic of small businesses managed individually or in partnership by Canadians and, later, British merchants until the end of the eighteenth century.[47] A merchant of Monière's station did not rely on double entry, capital accounts, or inventories but stuck to his daybook, where every page was numbered and initialled (according to regulation), and to his indexed current-account books.[48] Direct dealings with the Indians always figured in separate registers; so did the accounts of the voyageurs and transactions with suppliers, as is shown by the descriptions of these accounts in seventeenth-century post-mortem inventories. Promissory notes were credited to customers' accounts and bundled together. Every partial payment was then noted on the back.[49]

Do such practices demonstrate a general ignorance of proper accounting among these merchants, which could have compromised their businesses? One would think not, for the trade did not demand sophisticated techniques, and whenever accounts had to be settled between associates they refined their methods, introducing regular stock inventories and balance sheets for their joint enterprises.[50] Merchants who began as factors of metropolitan interests had a broader technical expertise, and several colonials had their sons apprenticed in France. Monière could be numbered among those who learned the business in the wilds, as it were. His accounts may therefore be particularly crude: the handwriting and spelling are atrocious, but he knew how to count and could manage even the most complex and indeed vital currency exchanges.

These account books show the flexibility of the credit system. Besides third-party buying and selling, there were many entries that did not reflect any actual movement of goods, furs, or cash: a customer's account would be credited by his debtor, while the latter's account was debited the same amount.[51]

In the period when merchants were strictly forbidden to outfit coureurs de bois, advances were handled by means of private accounts, daybooks, and promissory notes, which were clearly inadequate. Even when the merchant could prove advances without risking penal sanctions by seeking an injunction, he was often hard put to validate claims made in his own handwriting when some illiterate debtor had been unable to sign his name.[52] Besides, it was easy to lose the claims that were taken deep into the wilderness for collection.

The moment the issue of congés legalized fur-trade advances, transactions were recorded by notaries. Promissory notes became no more than a form of consumer loan, a guarantee of outstanding debt, or, above all, a transaction between merchants. Since cancelled notes were returned to the debtor, who usually destroyed them, the only glimpses we have of the financial dealings between Montreal merchants and their suppliers are provided by the lists of debts in post-mortem inventories.

As of 1685, advances to voyageurs were transformed into notarized obligations. The fur trade came to depend on this financial instrument, and plotting its frequency in the notarial records provides a good indication of the overall state of the trade, the number of voyageurs supplied each year, and the turnover in merchandise. Such obligations filled the drawers of notaries who worked for merchants, while those serving the countryside hardly drew up any.[53] The wording was always the same: two or three voyageurs bound themselves to refund a cargo valued at so many livres advanced prior to the contract for an up-coming trip. They would repay such sums upon their return with beaver at the official price and small furs at the current price at time of delivery, or else incur costs and damages. The debt was guaranteed by their present and future assets, movables and immovables, and especially by the furs they were to bring back to Montreal.[54] The parties elected domicile in the town.[55] Advances of this sort, which could rise as high as 5,000 to 10,000 livres, were seldom granted to a single individual; partnerships were preferred.[56] The merchant would then recover his entire loan, even if one of the members defaulted, and it was up to the members to seek redress among themselves.[57] Loans lasted an average of eighteen months: goods sold in the spring were paid for at the end of the following year. Voyageurs were bound to take the furs directly to the outfitter, who was the preferred creditor once the *engagés* had received their wages.[58] The merchant also advanced the voyageurs and their men smaller sums ranging from 30 to 400 livres. This was their private reserve, to use as they saw fit. The voyageurs generally guaranteed their crews' loans, and wages were paid only when merchants had been reimbursed.[59]

The cumulative credit and debit curve charted from Monière's books shows that furs came in on a regular basis, the fall arrivals being within a reasonable range of the expected eighteen months.[60] But Monière was a cautious man, and between 1717 and 1724 trade was reviving. There were plenty of instances where drawn-out immobilization of capital or defaults drove merchants to bankruptcy.[61] Debts often exceeded all present and future assets: for example, Maricourt's heirs had long since given up on Joseph Lorrain, "who had gone missing in Mississipi seven years earlier," except for an eventual claim on his share of an inheritance, which would fall far short of the 5,000 livres he still owed.[62] Such risks declined once the fur trade personnel became professionalized, but for a long time merchants had to contend with the possibility of desertion and with long delays, especially whenever wars broke out and Montreal was cut off from its hinterland.

The low incidence of legal seizures of debtors' assets shows how little they yielded. Patience was the key. The merchant entered a plea soon after the maturity date in order to collect interest, and his debtor was duly sentenced. Given the thirty-year statute of limitation, the merchant waited until his debtor's situation improved. If the latter abandoned the fur trade for the land, he would, sooner or later, gather some assets. The merchant would then be able to turn the obligation into an annuity. He sometimes hastened the process by loaning the necessary capital in return for such a *rente*, which incorporated both the old and the new debt.[63] In the case of a professional voyageur temporarily out of funds, the merchants would sanction a new advance if he was not too heavily in debt, and would even cancel the seizure of his goods, as long as he could make the trip west and rekindle his activities.[64] The conversion of the blanket mortgage into one secured by a specific property offered a better guarantee to those merchants who could afford to wait and who dealt with traders well established in the colony. It was not unusual in this period to see, for example, an obligation, signed in 1693, claimed and pursued for default fifteen months later and eventually redeemed in 1699.[65] What may at first glance appear sloppy accounting practice proved in fact quite shrewd, for by rushing things the merchant could discourage debtors and lose everything.

Bailliage records contain relatively few sentences against voyageurs. While creditors waited to be paid, all these notes and obligations were put into circulation.[66]

The most common bills of exchange, known locally as *lettres de castor* (beaver bills), were drawn on the lessees of the Western Domain in France for the beaver received in their Quebec bureau. These bills rarely circulated in Montreal. Merchants passed them on to their Rochelais correspondents, or to local suppliers, but these transactions were not recorded by Montreal notaries. More often we find Quebec bills of exchange created by the Crown or by individuals, drawn on France, Quebec, or on Montreal.[67] The first were sometimes discounted. The bearers endorsed them and used them as payments inside the colony. If they matured late, the taker charged interest until the debt had been met.[68] Drafts on colonial or metropolitan residents were less common, except for those on religious communities, which used them regularly to transfer funds.[69] Bills of exchange played a minor role in dealings among merchants, in contrast with the plethora of promissory notes.[70] If the drawee, Crown, or beaver lessee was in financial trouble, the colonial merchant had to offer additional collateral to his metropolitan suppliers.[71]

Post-mortem inventories do not mention cashbooks, and it appears that cash payments were exceptional. The usual practice was to pay outstanding bills within three months, after which the merchant refused to sell goods to customers who had not yet settled at least part of their debts. These were, in fact, usually repaid in several instalments, and the merchant made sure that peasants did not run up an account of more than 30 or 40 livres at a time.[72] Buying took place in November, at the end of the agricultural cycle.[73] Most of the habitants' purchases consisted of material that the women fashioned during the winter months, nails for carpentry projects, and so on. A few items would be bought over the winter, but none during the summer. Debts were gradually paid off until March with provisions of wheat, pork, or firewood. About three-quarters of outstanding accounts were settled on time.[74] If a debt had not been repaid by April, it was carried over to the fall and tallied a year after its original creation.[75] Should the interested party pay the balance, he would be allowed to stock up for the winter. Otherwise he signed an obligation – a promissory note sufficed for small sums – and received no more goods until he had repaid the outstanding amount. This could take some time.

The seasonal movement of incoming and outgoing stocks reflects the harmonious relationship between local commerce and the fur trade. In winter the merchant would stock up with foodstuffs and other local goods; come fall and early spring he would receive French imports, and in May the voyageurs would take the lot away. His summers might then be occupied with receiving his furs, and preparing a few canoe-loads for September, after which he took the furs to Quebec, settled his accounts, and replenished his stocks for the November sales.

The habitants' debts were sometimes transformed into an obligation, which included, apart from a specific mortgage on their farm, a special clause specifying that the loan could be called "whenever it suited the creditor."[76] Such obligations were either meant to secure debts to the merchant or a third party who had passed them on to him, or else to cover new loans, most likely for land purchases.[77] These barely cleared properties were usually not very valuable and could hardly support a *rente*. How could the settlers then be expected to refund the loan on demand? But the merchant's calculations make sense: the obligation began to bear interest whenever he called for the principal, and from then on he could afford to wait. Pawnbroking was also practised, although rarely.[78]

Special annuities

The habitants, however, preferred raising money by means of *rentes constituées*; the interest on these loans would be paid annually, but the lender could not demand the principal. The borrower could repay it under certain conditions. Lenders did not abound, however, if we go by merchants' portfolios, where such loans rarely appeared. These loans, the primary vehicle of non-commercial credit in seventeenth-century France, could hardly flourish in Canada, where ground rent remained weak and the usual body of rentiers – judicial officers, tax farmers, or big merchants at the peak of their career – was severely under-represented.[79] Merchants could not easily disengage their assets from trade, and if they succeeded, they were left with the problem of finding solid borrowers, with good land, to whom they might safely entrust their savings.

Vestries and religious communities (the Sulpicians above all) provided such *rentes constituées*, as did a few retired bourgeois, notaries, and widows, or guardians who had money on hand. The practice had been more common in the early days of settlement and merchants figured among the lenders. Around 1675–80 *rentes* creations had sunk to a mere 2 to 3 per cent of notarial deeds, and merchants hardly ever used them.[80] As land value collapsed and agriculture entered a recession, such investment lost its appeal. The *rentes*, often payable in wheat, proved a sorry prospect once 3,000-livre loans became guaranteed by properties worth half as much.

The monetary troubles of the early eighteenth century reactivated this instrument of credit. The circulation of card money encouraged borrowers to refund the principal, and the unwilling recipients looked for new annuity-payers on whom to unload the currency.[81] The lenders then tried to protect themselves by stipulating that the sum could not be reimbursed before two or three years.[82] This turbulent period saw the retirement of many of the mortgages burdening the island's oldest and finest land.

Canadian *rentes* were no different from their metropolitan counterparts. They bore 5 per cent interest, and the modalities of repayment were clearly specified. They were secured by blanket as well as specific mortgages, and except in the earliest period, annuities were paid in cash. The typical loan-seeker was a habitant who bought a farm with a solid return or the purchaser of an urban dwelling. The seller was rarely the lender, however. A third party came forward with the requisite sum before a notary and made his investment. These *rentes* were also handy for taking care of debts that had to be met on the spot: an overdue obligation, or countless small debts that the lender would then settle. In such cases *rentes* were quickly redeemed or transferred.[83]

Since *rentes constituées* were far less common than in France, they cannot be used to assess urban dominance over the countryside. They were simply among the most secure of the many available credit options, and their relative scarcity in this shaky economy should come as no surprise.

Interest and usury

Since charging interest on money or merchandise was considered usury, we can say that it was commonly practised in Canada, and openly so. Bottomry loans at 33.3 per cent accepted by voyageurs have already been mentioned. The bishop roundly condemned them as illegal and usurious, as he did the livestock leases that made the lessee solely responsible for animal losses. The link was justified by a similar absence of risk to the lender.[84] The merchant incorporated his 5 per cent interest in the notes and obligations signed over by people who came to square their accounts.[85] The official rate of interest, added on annually as soon as a claim was entered, also amounted to 5 per cent and, as far as we can see, was not compounded. A 5 to 10 per cent interest rate figured openly in the wording of private agreements.[86] Claims transferred as security for loans were often discounted at hefty rates.[87] Colonials seem to have had no qualms about such procedures, and they tried to muster as high a return as possible on their advances without bothering to disguise the profits as currency exchanges or annuities.

Transfer of claims

All these notes claiming a debt of some kind circulated freely. Most payments entailed a transfer of claims, with no exchange of funds or commodities. Cash payments were exceptional, and if we set aside returns from the fur trade and focus for a moment on the rural economy, it seems clear that payments in kind trailed far behind transfers of notes, *rentes*, obligations, and a variety of other claims. They appear to have had a far wider circulation than in the Auvergne studied by Abel Poitrineau or the rural southeast examined by Pierre Guichard.[88] The borrower passed on a note guaranteed by his own debtors, and the various liabilities were set off against one another. We can see this in the promissory notes made out to a given creditor, which lay among the transferee's papers at the time of his post-mortem inventory. Sometimes the sundry claims on colonists were used only as collateral for fairly sizable short-term loans.[89] In most cases, however, a real transfer took place, followed by due notice to the interested parties. When two merchants were involved, the assignor guaranteed the repayment, either by pledging to *fournir et faire valloir* (meaning that the taker could prosecute him if the debtor defaulted) or by guaranteeing the future repayment without due process or the expenses this might entail.[90] Merchants or peasants transferring small sums to each other usually resorted to straightforward subrogation without guarantee.[91]

These notes would gradually fall into the merchant's hands, and such complicated transactions confuse the issue of indebtedness. When a 300-livre obligation bearing a habitant's signature suddenly crops up among a merchant's papers, we might be tempted to conclude that peasants overextended themselves in buying consumer goods. The habitant had, in fact, signed over this note to discharge a number of farm and family debts, and his creditor had then transferred it to the merchant. The peasant had never had direct recourse to the merchant himself.[92] Lastly, we cannot estimate the duration of loans because of this continual restructuring of old debts into new forms.

Inheritance claims were also negotiated, being as they were the only collateral most young men could provide when buying land or seeking fur-trade advances. Claims were sold before any actual inheritance, despite the fact that the *coutume de Paris* reproved such unseemly and improper behaviour.[93] Even when the buyer was a co-inheritor, these claims could eventually be transferred to a merchant, who would be present at the division of the estate. Merchants might acquire claims to French successions, mainly from officers but sometimes from mere soldiers; through a similar series of transfers, La Rochelle merchants held rights of inheritance in the colony.[94] Everything was negotiable, including the damages that the heirs could claim against their father's murderer, a lieutenant in the troupes de la Marine who had gone back to France and been sentenced in absentia.[95] On this varied credit base colonial merchants, and, to a large extent, their metropolitan suppliers, built their fortunes.

Merchants' account books and commercial techniques reveal two things: how easy it was for the fur traders to obtain credit, and how difficult it was for the settlers to do the same. The analysis of post-mortem peasant inventories will take this further, but it has already become apparent that the countryside could hardly depend on the merchants and that, except in periods of galloping inflation, loans were quite restricted.

Despite strong reservations about rural investments, merchants had to contend with the fact that the movement of men between farming and trade (as voyageurs invested in land and country boys hired themselves out as crew members), combined with the circulation of claims, changed some of their commercial advances into rural debts. Whatever the process, funds were immobilized and inevitably invested in agricultural production, despite the merchants' reluctance to part with even a fraction of their working capital. The narrow and fragile agricultural base thus came to support commercial loans, and this in some measure linked commercial expansion to the agricultural sector.

3 THE MERCHANTS AND THEIR CAPITAL

Table 20 shows the distribution of commercial assets from twenty-one merchant inventories.[96] It would have been pointless to average

Table 20
Breakdown of the circulating capital found in 21 merchant inventories, 1679–1712

Numbered columns:

1 = Total gross assets*
2 = Liabilities
3 = Cash
4 = Card money
5 = Furs
6 = Bills of exchange
7 = Stocked goods
8 = Cargoed goods
9 = French accounts
10 = Indian accounts
11 = Claims in notes
12 = Obligations
13 = Total short-term claims in the colony
14 = Annuities (rentes constituées)
15 = Shares
16 = Miscellaneous

Date	Name	1 (100%)	2	3 (%)	4 (%)	5 (%)	6 (%)	7 (%)	8 (%)	9 (%)	10 (%)	11 (%)	12 (%)	13 (%)	14 (%)	15 (%)	16 (%)
1686	C. de Couagne	64,917	32,900	0.08		5.9		24.9		63.6		3.1	2.2	68.9			
1706	C. de Couagne	224,058	53,256					0.05		8.2		5.4	64.4	78.0	22.1		
1685	C. Lemoyne	85,754	8,755	3.3		2.8	6.3	40.0	3.2	23.3	5.8	1.2	0.7	31.0		5.1	ship: 8.1
1691	Lemoyne's widow	98,932		0.5		1.6	26.5		21.3	38.9				38.9		11.0	
1693	J. Leber	303,895	48,923	1.9	2.5	8.6	34.8	13.3		9.0	2.2	5.4	12.9	35.8	0.3		
1706	J. Leber	176,250	21,541	3.8	0.4	12.2	31.7	6.0		26.8	2.8	21.5	17.5	47.9			ship: 3.3
1697	Veuve Leguay	34,747	1,248	0.9	1.3	2.3		41.1	0.4	13.3		25.1		52.3			in France: 24.6
1712	J.-B. Charly	32,000	1,000		0.4	23.4	47.5	3.3		25.1				25.1			
1708	J.J. Lebé	25,370	15,200		0.3	7.2		20.1		28.0		15.5	28.4	71.9			
1691	J. Lemoyne	22,428	1,120	2.9	0.1	3.1			1.7	4.4		73.2	3.1	80.7		7.1	
1687	J. Maiihot	21,436	10,741	0.6		0.7		36.6		26.2	2.3		33.4	61.9			
1697	J. Maiihot	15,696	1,276	0.6	0.9	2.8		10.4		6.8		4.2	74.0	85.0			
1691	F. Pougnet	13,821	5,360					72.1		25.6				25.6			
1705	J.-B. Bauvais	12,896	5,140				18.9	9.1		11.3	35.1	12.0	13.4	71.8			
1679	P. Picoté	11,432	6,580			2.9		41.6		18.5	36.8			55.3	1.6		

Year	Name										
1683	P. Carion	11,980		3.0	2.0	47.0	—48.0—			48.0	
1685	J.-F. Hazeur	6,042	2,493	2.8	0.8	93.4	3.0			3.0	
1689	D. Sabourin	6,176	482		1.7	67.8	3.7	2.2	20.0	25.9	
1691	J. Patron	10,635	2,915			0.4		9.4	90.2	99.6	
1704	C. Juchereau	14,626	12,701				—68.0—	10.7		78.7	21.1
1705	B. Arnaud	12,078	15,944			13.2	7.6	52.0	27.1	86.7	

Source: Not. Rec. Basset: 27 March 1685, 6 Feb. 1691, 16 March 1691, 25 Sept. 1691, 1 Dec. 1693; Maugue: 13 March 1679, 21 Dec. 1683, 7 Aug. 1686, 4 Jan. 1687; Bourgine: 25 Nov. 1685; M. Le Pailleur: 24 May 1697, 14 April 1716; A. Adhémar: 24 Nov. 1689, 1 Oct. 1691, 24 May 1697, 4 July 1697, 2 Sept. 1704, 17 April 1705, 18 May 1705, 28 Aug. 1706; Raimbault: 1 Dec. 1706. Values are in local currency: 1 livre = 15 sols tournois

*excluding household possessions and real estate.

the data with such a limited and disparate sample; but some common features do nevertheless emerge.

If the wealthiest merchants owned little cash, the rest often had none at all. The best-endowed, Jacques Leber, left behind 5,077 livres in gold louis and écus and silver coins, equivalent to about one-twelfth of his accounts receivable.[97] He was an exception, and other cases show no more than 2,000 to 3,000 livres saved for an unforeseen personal expense such as a dowry or a trip to France. Money was not hoarded as such, and as we noted earlier, the ease with which colonial merchants agreed to advance the intendant ready cash (as long as they were sure to get it back in one way or another) seems to indicate that they could do without it. Merchants kept very little card money and would, we recall, get rid of it as soon as they received it.

The stock of furs fluctuated over the year. Bills of exchange usually covered furs from the previous season. These items, along with his stock of goods and expected shipments, made up the merchant's tangible assets, the apparent value of his estate. The value of the furs, bills of exchange (representing previous profits), and supplies (representing current profits) in the hands of any active merchant could not fall below half or, better still, two-thirds of his total assets. Based on this criterion, half of the businesses included in the sample are sound, irrespective of their turnover. Mailhot's inventories are a good example of worsening conditions: the value of his stocks fell from 37 to 13 per cent in one decade. He had repaid his creditors by 1697, but his credit was in a shambles. He no longer outfitted fur traders and eventually joined their ranks. Other merchants (Beauvais, Lebé, Patron, Juchereau, and Arnaud) were either assailed by their creditors or already insolvent. The balance between assets with a quick turnover and the sluggish mass of claims reveals more about the viability of any business than the ratio of assets to liabilities. The danger was not getting into debt, since they paid for their supplies in advance, but immobilizing funds in unsound loans, which led to desperate borrowing, to a transfer of claims that could not be capitalized, and ultimately to repossession.

In the post-mortem inventory drawn up at the death of his wife in 1714, J.-B. Charly declared that his sound claims amounted to 4,968 livres, bad claims came to 3,378 livres, and doubtful ones to 3,086 livres.[98] If we grant that half of these last were eventually recovered, then in all likelihood about 40 per cent of the merchants' claims consisted of bad loans. The merchant who only immobilized a third of his capital in commercial loans would end up losing 15 per cent, whereas the one who immobilized two-thirds would probably lose 25 to 30 per cent of his advances.

The careers of the merchants Leber and Couagne present interesting contrasts. Both died in 1706, already well on in years. They had amassed sizable fortunes by colonial standards, primarily in the form of movables that were still circulating, a typical feature of this period's estates. It seems to have been difficult to retire from business altogether.[99] Neither man's liabilities gave cause for concern, but there are no further similarities. Leber had held to the early business methods.[100] Advances to fur traders – some 48,000 livres – had simply been registered in his ledgers. Exchanges with local Indians accounted for 4,400 livres, while bills and obligations came to 32,400 livres. It is legitimate to assume that his current-account debts were of recent origin.[101] Two-thirds of the claims secured by notes and obligations had been granted that same year. Doubtful current claims therefore made up no more than 15 per cent of his colonial loans, which altogether accounted for less than half of the working capital.

Couagne's activities were quite different. A latecomer to trade, he moved full steam ahead from the start,[102] but an illness that lasted at least a year caused his affairs to go unattended, piling up 18,500 livres in current claims, 144,800 livres in notes and obligations, and 48,700 livres in *rentes constituées*. Forgetting the last two years before his death, we reckon that 75 per cent of his commercial loans could be dismissed as doubtful. How can we account for this merchant's behaviour? Especially, how could he have kept up this frenetic pace and advanced as much as 60,000 livres' worth of goods in a single season (despite slow returns, which would only worsen after 1696) without being literally run to the ground by his creditors? They pursued their claims closely, of course, but made no attempt to seize his assets.[103] The claims travelled back and forth across the ocean, and his heirs pulled through in the end. This demonstrates that the trade was far more elastic than one would have supposed.

It is easy to see how Couagne fell into such straits. His major problem was not delayed payments from voyageurs and settlers as much as it was munificent advances to merchants or to fort commanders.[104] He attempted to branch out into wholesale possibly by making some sort of deal with the directorate of the Colony Company.[105] By doing business with the poorer strata of merchants always on the brink of bankruptcy or with officers who were notoriously bad risks, he foundered just as wiser merchants, realizing the impending collapse of the beaver market, tightened their credit and pulled back until the end of the crisis. Part of his fortune was nevertheless safely invested in real estate, and the annuities alone brought in a revenue of 3,000 livres in the last, difficult period of his life.

Although on a smaller scale, other inventories display a similar mixture of stable and shaky components. The widow Leguay headed, from 1691, a small but sound concern, and in her twelve years of activity unredeemed or doubtful loans never exceeded 12 per cent of her advances.[106] Yet it was more common to see rash and foolhardy ventures, capitalized by what would prove to be unreclaimable debts. Between 1642 and 1725 only ten or so merchants had a working capital of over 50,000 livres. Only three, Jean Soumande, Pierre de Lestage, and Antoine Pacaud, were in the same league as Leber, Lemoyne, and Couagne.[107] For as the exhilarating returns of the early era paled into memory, it became more and more difficult to bridge the gap between the handful of large outfitters and the scores of small businesses with a modest capital of 10,000 to 30,000 livres. With net annual profits hovering around 10 per cent, it took twenty-five years to raise a 5,000-livre investment to 50,000, assuming that profits were systematically reinvested in new supplies. Yet the merchant had to use some of his initial returns for his personal ends, and as long as the revenues from property or annuities were too meagre to cover his private expenses, he continued to draw on his commercial profits. Few, therefore, were in a position to rise to the top, and the likelihood of becoming an outfitter without prior means was considerably reduced over time. After ten years, for example, Alexis Monière had a turnover of 19,000 livres; he ploughed back almost everything into trade by spreading payments for personal expenditures over a number of years.[108]

On occasion, these individual businesses were backed by outside investors, bringing in beaver, trade goods, or even redeemable claims. The return was 5 per cent when the loan was secured by a *rente constituée* and slightly more otherwise.[109] The funds usually came from estates under guardianship, and the squaring of these accounts often gave rise to bitter and intricate lawsuits.[110]

The nature and the limited value of these merchants' assets account for the scarcity of *rentes constituées* in their portfolios, for few could afford to pull capital away from the trade. Only two merchants owned any assets outside Montreal.[111] Although Quebec had begun to diversify beyond the fur trade, Montreal remained bound by its hinterland and bundles of beaver.

The balance sheets shown in Table 21, the only documents of this kind that could be found, may serve as a conclusion. When the Widow Lemoyne lost her husband, she put a Montreal and La Rochelle merchant, Antoine Pacaud, in charge of her business in a typical merger of capital and labour. The Lemoynes provided the wherewithal, merchandise, furs, and bills of exchange, along with a certain number of redeemable claims. The partnership was drawn up for three years. The participants were to share the profits after the initial capital had been deducted, with the investor receiving two thirds. Should there be any losses, the same ratio would apply.

The company made 33,182 livres over three years, and so the Lemoynes' capital produced, on paper at least, an annual return of 11.3 per cent. Given how difficult it proved to recover some claims, the actual return was more in the order of 7.5 to 9 per cent. This accords with our overall findings.

4 MARCHANDS-FORAINS AND COLONISTS

Upon the appeal of Montreal's leading inhabitants stating that His Majesty had seen fit to grant to the true and sole habitants of this country the right and privilege of trading with the Indians, to the exclusion of the *marchands forains* coming from France with goods that they sell more cheaply than the aforesaid habitants who buy these goods from them, and thereby deprive them of all the profit they might make from the fur trade ... because the above merchants trade with the Indians by various illegal means such as buying worthless properties with no intention of improving them, or else by forming partnerships with local habitants and trading in their name, despite the prohibitions ...[112]

Petitions of this sort presume a clear-cut opposition between colonists and metropolitans that the evidence simply will not support. The initial capital or extension of credit came from France, whereas local capital accumulation rested on Indian labour. The boundaries of imperialism lay to the west of Montreal. There could be no basis for a real confrontation as long as the settlement generated fewer profits than those of the fur trade and as long as the local population siphoned off part of the fur trade's returns. What did exist was a grey area where private interests and temporary associations merged or collided in a joint process of appropriation.[113]

Once the Compagnie des habitants started to issue permits in 1650, French merchants and shippers, mostly from La Rochelle, began to trade regularly with Canada. Delafosse has identified an initial group of about half a dozen individuals. This was a secondary trade, less attractive and, for this reason, safer than West Indian ventures. The participants were relatively small merchants who depended for capital on the Rochelais or Parisian mercantile and

Table 21
Assets invested in the partnership between the Widow Lemoyne and Antoine Pacaud, 1687–1690, including returns to 1695 (in livres tournois)

Capital invested by the Widow Lemoyne in September 1687

Claims (102) on colonists	5,318
Trade goods, furs, bills of exchange drawn on the lessee of the Western Domain	44,441
Shares in the Société de la Baie d'Hudson	8,456
Original investment	58,215
Returns	
Two-thirds to the Lemoyne family	22,121
One-third to Antoine Pacaud	11,061
Total	91,397

Assets on 31 December 1690

Accounts receivable antidating the partnership	5,297
Accounts receivable of the partnership	8,683
Dry cod sent to France	1,898
Cargoes (4) of merchandise for Canada	13,929
Furs stocked in Montreal	1,200
Bills of exchange (15) drawn on the lessee of the Western Domain	18,577
Bills on the treasurers general of the Marine	1,087
Shares in the Société de la Baie d'Hudson	8,193
Advances to the Widow Lemoyne	5,406
Goods advances to a Lemoyne son, acting as guardian to his brothers and sisters	25,854
Interest due on these advances	833
Cash reserves	440
Total	91,397

Table 21 continued

Statement of Returns (1695)

Accounts receivable antidating the partnership	180
Accounts receivable of the partnership	5,586
Proceeds from the sale of cod	1,854
Value on arrival of the 4 cargoes (losses at sea partly covered by insurance)	13,313
Proceeds from the sale of furs	2,177
Bills of exchange drawn on the lessee of the Western Domain	18,577
Bills on the treasurers general of the Marine	1,087
Shares in the Société de la Baie d'Hudson	2,030
Advances to the Widow Lemoyne	5,406
Goods advanced to a Lemoyne son, acting as guardian to his brothers and sisters	25,854
Interest due on these advances	833
Cash reserves	440
Total	77,337
Unrecovered claims	8,214
Losses	6,823
	15,037
	92,374
Profits not accounted for in 1690	977
	91,397

Source: Not. Rec. 6 Feb. 1691, 14 July and 5 Dec. 1695, Basset.

banking elite, and showed an unwavering commitment to the Canada trade.[114] By 1715 half a century of uninterrupted contacts, punctuated by lengthy stays in the colony, had nurtured real clans whose members worked interchangeably on either side of the ocean. The wealth displayed in the Rochelais post-mortem inventories analysed by Delafosse are of a level with those of their Canadian relatives – that is, between fifty thousand and several hundred thousand livres. Claims on La Rochelle held by partners in Canada were probably as numerous as those on Montreal owned by their Rochelais suppliers.[115] Vertical relations tied this group of Franco-Canadian families to metropolitan merchants who financed their operations, and to their colonial clients.[116] As long as merchants' assets were tied up in the trade, there was a limit to the oft-mentioned "flight of capital."[117] Capital would take on a French or a colonial colouring when these merchants retired or died, depending on their heirs' residence and on whether or not they pursued the family business.[118]

Besides these Rochelais-Canadian firms, a sizable body of small merchants resided in the colony, while a number, armed with bottomry loans, came over to try their luck, only to return home at the first hint of trouble.[119] These three groups made endless attempts to seize, hold on to, or undermine each others' positions.

These positions are all represented in Montreal between 1670 and 1685. Lemoyne and Leber dominated the trade, imported goods, traded directly with the Indians, outfitted voyageurs, and occasionally supplied other merchants without becoming wholesalers. This left enough room for some thirty minor figures who ordered their supplies from France or obtained them from the Rochelais in Quebec. Relations were peaceful as long as the latter did not invade Montreal's retail trade. The town's leading merchants had no wish to share their territory, and middlemen quite rightly dreaded such unfair competition. The French adventurers who turned up each summer to sell their small wares were a lesser menace, but they took a share of the small merchants' business. Thus the support given by the resident merchants to the ordinance dictating that anyone who wished to sell goods to the Indians had to own at least 1,000 livre's worth of property in the colony and had to have resided there for two years.

Quebec importers threatened the Montrealers' territorial control as much as the *marchands-forains*, but the prerequisites spelled out in the ordinances did not deter them from trading or outfitting coureurs de bois even when property requirements were raised to 2,000 livres.[120] The Charrons, Hazeurs, Simon Baston, Moyse and Gédéon

Petit and their father Alexandre, Simon Mars, Jean Gitton, Charles Aubert, and Guillaume Changeon could well afford to buy land in the seigneury where they came every summer to man their stall at the fur-trading fair.[121] If their presence helped to deprive occasional traders of their shares of the seasonal profits, this competition did not threaten the solid positions of Lemoyne and Leber, and with time all these importers forged close commercial and familial bonds.[122] The small *marchands-forains* alone were forbidden to trade in Montreal between 1 June and 31 October, and this left them no option except to offer their service to well-established merchants as coureurs de bois or go back to France.[123]

Little of this changed before the second quarter of the eighteenth century. Every now and then, those with large interests in the colony would seek the support of all retailers to crush new competitors.[124] However, should one of the established figures, native or immigrant, succeed in drawing more than his just share by striking some lucky deal with his Parisian bankers, the others would immediately unite to censure the monopolizer.[125]

In short, exclusivity would only be tolerated if it involved a large enough segment of colonial and metropolitan interests, so that the only long-standing conflict was the one that pitted the weak against the mighty. A regulated merchant guild was doomed to failure, for it was constantly undermined by individual ambitions that only coalesced in the face of external threats.[126]

5 THE VOYAGEURS AND FUR-TRADE *ENGAGÉS*

The practice of recording all transactions touching the fur trade (such as partnerships, obligations, and hiring) in notarized contracts had become so entrenched by the beginning of the eighteenth century that notarial records can be used to quantify voyages to the west. Historians of New France tend to take a widespread popular participation in such activities for granted and then go on to deduce a number of typical behaviour patterns, including neglect of the land, poor husbandry, insubordination, immorality, and so on.[127] It seems pointless to discuss such issues before gauging what sort of impact the fur trade had on the settlers, by tracing those who took part in this activity between 1708 and 1717. The sample that includes 668 men who made one or more voyages inland in this period (see Table 22) should suffice to draw a portrait of the voyageurs.[128]

Table 22
Number of individuals involved in the fur trade
between 1708 and 1717, classified according to their
activities

Category	Number
Merchant outfitters	68
Military officers	29
Voyageurs (traders)	(448)
Engagés	(220)

Departures west

A total of 1,120 departures to the upper country were registered in
that decade, and most took place between 1713 and 1717.[129] The
length of the journey partly explains the prominent annual fluctuations. A smoother curve would have been obtained by using 24-
instead of 12-month periods. About the same number of traders or
voyageurs, who still formed the bulk of the contingents, left in the
spring (April–May) as in the autumn (October–early November).
They were back in Montreal the next August or September, and so
spent every second winter in the colony. Most of the engagés, however, took off in the spring and returned in late summer, having
spent four months going to Michilimakinac or Detroit and back.
Since they were novices, their owners saw no reason to pay for
extended stays in the outposts and used them mainly to man the
canoes. (See Table 23.)

Although the number of departures increased over the decade
(see Table 24), this only signified a recovery from the 1705–11
depression. A longer time-frame, say from 1685 to 1750, would
exhibit quite clearly a return to a pre-crisis level. The volume of furs
and the size of the crews would not rise dramatically until the
second quarter of the eighteenth century.[130]

We can get a better idea of the frequency of individual trips west
by focusing on the men who appeared in the first part of the same
period. For about one hundred of them, fur-trading was a full-time
occupation. These voyageurs were the backbone of commerce in the
interior. For the others, it was no more than a temporary or occasional activity.[131]

The men

In the early eighteenth century the percentage of men who travelled
inland each year oscillated around 2 per cent of the overall adult

Table 23
Incidence of departures west, 1708–17

Category	Spring departures	Fall departures	Total	Number of departures per person		Total
				One	More than one	
Voyageurs	453	400	853	472	381	853
	(53.2%)	(46.8%)		(55.4%)	(44.6%)	
Engagés	167	100	267	198	69	267
	(62.6%)	(37.4%)		(74.2%)	(25.8%)	
Total	620	500	1,120	670	450	1,120

Table 24
Frequency of fur trade voyages

Number of those who went west once or more between 1708 and 1713 (incl)	373
Among them, those who travelled once between 1708 and 1717	179
those who travelled twice between 1708 and 1717	82
those who travelled three times between 1708 and 1717	64
those who travelled more than three times between 1708 and 1717	48
	373

male population. Calculated over a decade, the proportion of those who went west for varying lengths of time reached 12 per cent, but their regional distribution was uneven.[132] More than half – 337 – came from the Island of Montreal, meaning that a quarter of local males participated in this activity; in terms of numbers, they came second to those in agriculture.

Some regions supplied even more men in relation to their population. Trois-Rivières took the lead, for 54 per cent of its men had gone trading at least once, and in the nearby seigneuries participation amounted to 30 per cent.[133] The seigneuries lying between Varennes and Châteauguay, south of Montreal, sent out a strong contingent of 108 voyageurs with percentages of their populations varying from 21 to 30.[134]

The percentages were much lower in other parts of the colony: 5 per cent in the Lower Richelieu; 6 per cent in seigneuries north of Montreal; 5 per cent in the town of Quebec; and 1 to 2.5 per cent in the more densely populated countryside around Quebec. None of the men in this sample came from the seigneuries in the Lower St

Lawrence. This means that fur-trading was not a common or normal occupation for a good two-thirds of the colonial population. Only the odd peasant from the Ile d'Orléans or the côte de Beaupré ever went west, and in many of the more distant *côtes* the procedure remained completely unknown. The argument that fur-trading shaped the people's character, therefore, becomes more than tenuous.[135]

Most of the voyageurs were native-born Canadians. New arrivals at the end of the seventeenth century turn out to be relatively under-represented in the figures in Table 25. It was they who married, while country youths put off settling down unless they gave it up altogether. The different behaviour patterns may be traceable in part to the easier credit terms granted the sons of habitants. The French-born in this sample were either soldiers or former soldiers married in the colony.

Voyageurs recruited their kin, so the regional concentration noted earlier may be due to the importance of family bonds. Brothers followed in each other's footsteps. They either signed on together or formed partnerships to take advantage of trading permits. I was able to trace twenty-five kin groups who dispatched as many as 137 voyageurs in that decade. (See Table 26.) Families like the Cardinals in Montreal or the Rivards from Batiscan specialized in the fur trade generation after generation.[136]

If a quarter of the men came from such "professional" fur-trading families there were obviously other major sources of recruitment.[137] A sizable contingent came from the town – from artisanal backgrounds in particular. There were two reasons for this: the Crown, for example, hired carpenters to work on western posts, and merchants often required the services of surgeons, blacksmiths, and gunsmiths.[138] These men, who journeyed regularly to the west and spent months in the upper country, began to trade on the side. The fur trade proved a partial palliative to seasonal unemployment in the building trades, in particular.

Other recruits came from mercantile circles. A number had been unable to withstand the competition and were moved to subordinate positions. Only a thin line separated the voyageurs from small merchants who outfitted only one or two parties a year, and it was not unusual for such persons to figure in one capacity one year and another the next, until they either made a success of their business or gave it up altogether and became full-time fur traders. All categories of merchants sent their sons on these trips, and it became a regular feature of their apprenticeship. Their fathers' positions allowed them to start very young, guided by experienced voyageurs. They were barely twenty by the time they signed their first con-

Table 25
Generational recruitment of voyageurs
and fur trade engagés, 1708–17.

Immigrants	39
Second generation	470
Third generation	116
Indians	5
Unknown	38
Total	668

Table 26
Family recruitment of voyageurs and fur trade *engagés*, 1708–17

Number of families	Number of voyageurs
206 (nuclear) who sent out one man	206
78 (nuclear) who sent out two men	156
29 (nuclear) who sent out three men	87
16 (kin groups) who sent out four men	64
4 (kin groups) who sent out five men	20
5 (kin groups) who sent out more than five men	53
338 Total	586

tracts, although they had probably made a number of unrecorded trips by then.[139] They perfected their training in either a colonial or a Rochelais shop. Many officers' sons followed much the same path; they started out as voyageurs and pursued this calling until their appointments as cadets or ensigns, for which there was a long waiting list. Meanwhile, they traded. The children of court clerks, notaries, or innkeepers, who thought themselves a cut above the peasants, did not disdain this occupation, for it allowed them to maintain their station while waiting to succeed their fathers or to obtain some other commission.

There was, of course, a large contingent of peasants' sons, especially among the fur-trade *engagés*. Yet given that about 80 per cent of the population lived in the country, rural recruits were considerably under-represented. Except for regions where recruitment engendered recruitment, the fact that trading took place at the height of the agricultural cycle seems to have prevented many habitants from seeking such supplementary revenue.

The age and marital status of these voyageurs should clarify certain matters. (See Table 27.)[140] The modal age at first departure was twenty-two for the whole sample and twenty-one for the engagés.[141] A little over half the men were between twenty and thirty years old. This was difficult work, unsuited to the very young, and the income was unlikely to encourage early retirement. Those who chose this profession kept going until they were fifty or even sixty years old – their whole working lives. The 217 who married did so on average at the age of 28.7, which turns out to be the average age of spouses in Notre-Dame parish in this period. The large proportion of Montrealers from that parish within our sample surely has some bearing on the coincidence.

The normal procedure was for professional fur traders to marry and leave their families behind in Montreal, although later on some families would move to the outposts to avoid lengthy separations. Since most voyageurs belonged to the premarital age-groups, it comes as no surprise that most were single. One might well wonder, however, why so few married subsequently. There are four possible explanations: the genealogists failed to trace their unions; they died before the usual age of wedlock; they remained single; or they left the colony. Although it proved impossible to verify the omissions in Tanguay's genealogical dictionary, these could not have been numerous enough to account for the phenomenon. If the significant variable was celibacy, then all age groups would be proportionately represented among those "whose fate is unknown," but this is not the case. We should not discount the heavy casualty rate, not only on the perilous journey but also during military campaigns, for these young men were called up for militia duty more often than others. But even if we assume three or even ten times the normal death rate for these age groups, there would still be quite a few puzzling disappearances.[142] The only likely explanation is that about 150 to 200 of these young men left the colony in this decade or shortly thereafter and headed for the Mississippi. Each trip had meant a further step towards a destination from which they would never return.

Conditions on the journey

Trips to the wilderness suited "the sort of person who thought nothing of covering five to six hundred leagues by canoe, paddle in hand, or of living off corn and bear fat for twelve to eighteen months, or of sleeping in bark or branch cabins," as one Jesuit reported.[143] The catalogue of hardships could go on forever. The

Table 27
Marital status of the voyageurs and fur trade *engagés*, 1708–17

Category	Number		
Known date of birth	512		
Men who married before 1718		147	
Men who married (date of marriage unknown)		29	
Bachelors up to 1718, of whom:		336	
those who married later			70
those whose fate is unknown			266
Date of birth unknown	156		
Total	668		

men had to carry two bundles weighing together almost two hundred pounds (held by a tumpline or a head strap), both on portages and along dry river beds, sometimes for days on end. Mosquitoes would drive even the old hands wild in May and June. There was the ever-present danger of drowning or injury if the canoes tipped over the rapids. The toughest part could well have been the isolation of these three or four men who had to rely on each other for two months, whatever their character differences – which alcohol would only exacerbate.[144] Choosing suitable companions thus became a primary concern, and this explains the preference for kinsmen and the constancy of certain crews. Partnerships were usually limited to one trip, but if the experience proved positive, the parties would renew them time and again. A voyageur who was satisfied with one *engagé* would be likely to hire another from the same family. A whole network of solidarities bound the men in the interior.

Although their revenues fluctuated, the voyageurs made enough to attract them back year after year.[145] *Engagés'* wages varied depending on their experience.[146] At the end of the seventeenth century officers in the trading posts paid them 150 to 200 livres' worth of beaver a year. It made no difference whether these payments were stipulated as being in cash or pelts, since they were always met with merchandise that the merchant either advanced to the *engagé* (and which he then passed on to his family or creditors) or handed him when he returned, unless he had used up his credit.[147] *Engagés* might earn 300 to 400 livres for trips lasting twelve to eighteen months. Their food was provided free, and they could take along clothing, a gun, a blanket, and other personal effects, which were then fully detailed in the contract. They were allowed to barter these effects and bring back as well a bundle of pelts worth 50 to 75 livres.[148]

The Compagnie de la Colonie dictated harsher terms between 1701 and 1706. Their numerous recruits were paid with cards whose purchasing power did not exceed 150 livres. They were forbidden from trading on the side, and those who "manifested any spite, laziness, or ill-will" had fines deducted from their wages.[149] In 1708–17 the employers were voyageurs and merchants who were beginning to hire canoemen. Once the value of the cards is deflated by three-eighths, wage levels proved no different from those that prevailed earlier, although the men still did enjoy a few bonuses such as shoes, leggings, or brandy and recovered the privilege of trading a few personal effects. But they only earned 30 or 40 livres more for a year's trip than they received for the five-month journey to Michilimakinac and back.[150]

This could only mean that there was no work for them in the colony in the off-season. By going off they were at least assured some sort of shelter and free food. These trips basically brought them about twice as much as they would have earned as year-round labourers back in the colony.[151] The supply of labour continued to exceed demand, if the steady wages and geographically restricted recruitment are anything to go by. This put the professional voyageurs in a position to reduce to the status of wage-earners those who were looking for escape or for the means to start a farm.

6 CONCLUSION

The staple theory, which has dominated Canadian historiography since H.A. Innis, relates the development of this country to the successive exploitation of certain raw materials, each of which ruled the economy in turn.[152] Profits from the staple trade were theoretically used to broaden the resource base and establish a network of communications. In the following phase they would be invested in the partial transformation of the export commodity. The entire economy was therefore seized by external demand, and as luck would have it, as soon as one staple ran out, another would emerge that proved just as suited to meet foreign needs. Yet economists also agree that instead of crucial reallocations from the staple sector to the rest of the economy and a harmonious interplay between old and new leading sectors, the process was marked by dislocation, violent tremors, and an overall vulnerability that still echoes today.

The seventeenth century was characterized by a quasi-feudal trading venture based on the export of a limited amount of goods, a tension between two civilizations, and a succession of monopolies. The small commercial sector proved rather sturdy. It adapted quickly to circumstances and bounced back after each crisis. The social distribution of capital was not extreme, and it seems unlikely that a greater concentration of capital would have altered the nature of the investments. In this period as well as in the following centuries, merchant capital did not act as a motive force. The development of an internal market depended on the number of men and on their labour; returns from the export trade had to drop dramatically before merchants were ready to invest in local industries.[153] In this isolated and underpopulated seventeenth-century colony, one could hardly expect any spontaneous diversification or important reallocation of capital from the fur trade to agriculture.

It was necessary to demonstrate this unconnectedness before examining the rural settlements, which evaded capitalist expropriation and developed somewhat outside the market economy.

PART THREE

Agriculture

CHAPTER SIX

The Physical Setting

Montreal island covers 49,773 hectares. It is 51.48 kilometers long and measures 17.7 kilometers at its widest point. Two smaller islands that nestle within the curved shoreline of the Rivière des Prairies give it a diamond shape, with a southwest-northeast tilt. Aside from Mont Royal, an extinct volcano that rises 230 meters, the island is practically flat and does not stand out from the surrounding countryside. This open landscape unfolds as a series of small valleys and low morainal ridges. Altitudes range on average between 25 and 58 meters, or 17 to 50 meters above the level of the river. Both the northeastern tip of the island and the strip of land known as Pointe Saint-Charles, where the founders first landed, lie even lower. In most places meadows slope down towards the river.

The region, subject to glaciation in the Pleistocene era, still bears reminders of this in morainic ridges, mostly made up of limestone and some schist. Later, this peneplain was submerged by the Champlain Sea. Its subsequent recession, occasioned by a gradual rise of the land, left clay deposits in the midst of the glacial till ridges as well as some sandy areas. Many of the region's characteristics result from the double action of glaciation and submersion.[1]

The soil on the island ranks among the best in eastern Canada. Fully 72 per cent lies directly on the limestone tills or above a middle layer of alluvium that is humus-bearing with a strong calcium content. It includes a whole variety of loams, some stony and better drained, others finer and less porous. Another 20 per cent lies above a bed of clay or alluvial deposits containing varying build-ups of sand and silt, among which figures the heaviest and least permeable soils. Black soil composed of organic deposits over marshland represents 7 per cent of the total territory.[2] Except for these black soils, scattered about the middle of the island and the lower reaches of Pointe Saint-Charles, and a number of poor, sandy parcels in the southwest, this land was perfectly suited to grain production and grazing. The Island of Montreal was clearly better off than the southern plain, where drainage problems proved more severe, or the settlements downstream, where the soil was often of poorer quality.[3] Still, most of this land required heavy ploughs and costly drainage.

The elevation, however slight, allowed drainage here and there, especially along the lower flanks of the mountain, which attracted the first settlers. The town itself was built along a narrow terrace 13 to 15 meters above the river and separated from it by a ravine where the small Saint-Martin creek made its bed. Beyond this gently rising terrace, the terrain rises abruptly to a second plateau 45 meters high leading to the three summits of Mount Royal, which covers 3.8 square kilometers. Although it had no natural defences, the site provided easy access to the St Lawrence without danger of spring flooding. The first crops were grown on these two terraces, on the surrounding hillside, and within the town itself. Farms that spread east and west faced drainage problems. There are several streams on the island, but their flow is uneven. During the spring and after heavy rains they swell, but are swampy gullies the rest of the time. The slightest depression turns into a large pond that the inhabitants called "lakes," while beaver dams here and there also held back the waters. Eventually settlers would try to restore some grass to these wettish declivities.[4] The Saint-Pierre, a small stream which flows northeasterly from Lachine, meeting Saint-Martin Creek along its way, was of some use despite its seasonal variations. Although a projected canal was never built, the enlarged riverbed afforded better drainage for the riverside farms and permitted the construction of two mills. On the whole, however, the town did not draw much power from the waters that either crissed-crossed it too slowly or raged beyond it, and relied rather on the windmills erected in the parishes of Lachine, Pointe-aux-Trembles, Rivière-des-Prairies, and Sainte-Anne.[5] Until the seigneurs managed to dike the des Prairies River and to harness the Saint-Pierre in the eighteenth century, the water mills, which functioned neither winter nor summer, proved poor investments.

The Island of Montreal is located at a longitude of 74° to 73°30′ west and a latitude of 45°25′ to 45°40′ north, giving it a better climate than the rest of the colony, although the expenses and problems caused by the intense variations in temperature proved as severe here as elsewhere. Rather than adopting the four European seasons some Quebec geographers identify only three – frigid, growing, and transitional – each of which would extend over four months in Montreal.[6] Winter lasts from December to March; the temperature averages –17°C but can also drop suddenly. The climate is dry and on the whole bearable given proper clothing, housing, and nourishment. French rural architecture was eventually modified to suit these harsh conditions, but only after a long period of trial and error compounded by the settlers' initial poverty. Their dwellings and even those of the religious communities and wealthier inhabitants offered little protection against the cold at first.[7] Animals were kept in barns until the end of April, the critical month when changes in temperature could have serious repercussions both on the harvest and on the dwellings. The damage was somewhat mitigated if an early snowfall had preceded the big cold: the ground only would have frozen on the surface and could then absorb a sudden thaw and store moisture for the dry season. Late snowfalls could mean frosts over a meter deep and so poor drainage, which flooded the countryside, rotted the wooden buildings even more, shook the most solid foundations, and transformed the roads into a succession of bumps and mud-pits.

Buildings had a short lifespan. The few houses, cellars, or fireplaces built from local quarries using a black, compact, high-quality limestone soon showed signs of wear, while all wooden buildings, barns, sheds, and houses were described as either "in ruins" or as "falling apart." The most expensive "new houses" had probably not faced their first thaw. Streets were poorly drained, and oxen got stuck on the rural roads, built and kept up by statute labour, which remained practically impassable to carts.[8] Carting was therefore usually put off until wintertime. At other times of the year, and wherever the rapids did not present an insurmountable obstacle, grain and fodder destined for the town were transported on boats that hugged the shore. All these seasonal disruptions involved unproductive expenditures in money and time that these young communities could ill afford.[9]

Winter lasted until the end of March. The settlers began to sow peas towards the middle of April, followed by wheat a fortnight later.[10] Frost could no longer harm the major crops.[11] Summer arrived heralded by swarms of mosquitoes bewailed by every contemporary observer. With its forests, ponds, and nearly stagnant streams, the island proved a perfect breeding ground and quickly became mosquito-ridden.[12] The habitants, as well as the coureurs de bois, had no doubt learned from Indians how to protect themselves with bear fat. The settlers' dwellings had few if any openings, and those that did were covered either with paper or pieces of parchment leather, which allowed only a weak yellow light to filter through but provided protection from insects.[13]

There followed four months of warm weather, with even tropical bouts of debilitating heat and long dry spells. The water would evaporate, and while this may have partially solved drainage problems, the damage to the crops could be quite severe. Plants ripened quickly. Hay was cut in July, and the harvest proper began in late August or even sooner. Only the autumn months would remind these men from western France of the mild weather, the persistent, light rainfall and temperate climate of their native land.

The island was covered with a lush array of deciduous trees that amazed and enchanted travellers who had encountered only boreal or mixed, though mainly coniferous, forests on their journey up-river. Oaks shaded the hillsides around the mountain along with wild cherry, elm, and walnut trees. The settlers used these trees for building and carpentry. At first they relied on squared logs made from oak or wild cherry.[14] They also cut boards and beams out of the tall pines that proliferated on dry ground and whose straight, smooth trunks rose some twenty meters to their branchy tops. Maple, poplar, beech, and birch, although timber material, served mainly as fuel, as did larch, ash, fir, and spruce. The thuja, known locally as cedar, which grew on humid soil, provided the stakes for the palisades.[15] This was no wilderness: there was little undergrowth and the woods were easy to cross. But the settlers had to manage timber reserves carefully, even from the first, for an endless expanse of trees would provide little comfort once nearby resources had been depleted.

The natural meadows on the river banks or those in low-lying areas in the interior provided some kinds of grasses, mixed in with rushes and horsetail. These may well have provided adequate nourishment for the animals in summer, at least as good as wild oats or stubble, but they gave very poor hay. Most of the drainage efforts were directed towards improving such lands, but they also proved too small, and soon the habitants had to create new meadows out of their arable land.

Wherever the forest receded, wild berries grew in profusion.[16] Although there were fish in the river, a few years after the founding of the town Montrealers were importing salt eel from Quebec, leading one to suspect that the supply proved insufficient. All the settlers hunted, but even in the first years game could not stave off food shortages, and this would become even more evident once the island population increased. "There seem to be less [fish and game] around," a nun noted in 1697.[17] Yet the real cause was the seasonal nature of hunting, and except for the period of major migration, local fauna proved neither plentiful nor easy to hunt. Come spring and fall, ducks, teal, larks, and plover covered the banks and small islands nearby. Thousands of turtledoves filled the beech groves in early summer. In wintertime, however, partridges cost more than poultry, and elk as much as beef. A court battle between hunters over the possession of the hide and meat of a moose that they had flushed but which had been killed by two other hunters shows that such big game did not abound around the settlements.[18] Nevertheless, if at times the forest offered little to eat, in a good season it put meat on the table, particularly at the time when the previous years' harvest had been consumed. For these bread eaters, however, this was just an unreliable substitute that could not dissipate the fear of hunger whenever the harvest was short.

Such was the initial state of the country. The people who had occupied this land in previous centuries had left no other traces than the large clearing Champlain observed decades earlier. It was already overrun by new growths of alder and aspen by the time the French came to settle.[19]

CHAPTER SEVEN

Land Ownership

A bird's-eye view of present-day Quebec reveals a striking pattern of similarly aligned and similarly shaped fields. These elongated, parallel plots stretch, one next to the other, in a monotonous array of shoestring villages that bear little resemblance to the anarchic organization of the French rural landscape. Eighteenth-century Canadian seigneurial records convey the same impression: large parcels, clear cut legal title to land, dispersed habitat, and agrarian individualism. At three centuries' remove, the basic features of the old landscape can still be discerned in those places left untouched by urbanization. With the past still in evidence, it proved easy to reconstruct the early years of the settlement.

By looking first at the countryside from a legal standpoint, I do not mean to overemphasize this aspect to the detriment of material conditions, which remain my primary concern. In Canada, however, the seigneury antedated settlement. When the Société de Notre-Dame was handed the Island of Montreal in 1640, in return for homage and fealty, the property bore the full judicial and seigneurial prerogatives recognized by the coutume de Paris.[1] The first settlers did not arrive until two years later. Since Montreal was an island, settlement and seigneurial boundaries coincided. This was purely fortuitous in a colony where the pattern of occupation tended to ignore the legal frontiers and follow closely the contours of the land.[2]

1 LAND GRANTS

Land was granted in Montreal, as in the rest of the colony, in the form of *acensements*.[3] The governor of Montreal, who represented the owners, carved out 111 parcels of land outside the town and thirty-odd lots in the "area defined as the town" between 1648 and 1666.[4] Even the slow pace of settlement cannot account for such parsimony. It would appear that the Société was reluctant to dismember its domain. Its members had little knowledge of the real situation in the colony and overestimated both their financial resources and the appeal for immigrants of this island afloat in the wilderness. Did they hope to create in Canada some vast domain with only minimal subinfeudation so as not to discourage the settlers? Did they plan to rely on Indian labour at some future date? Their intentions, whatever they were, would not be realized, for the Société de Notre-Dame, tired of this undertaking and in debt, ceded its Canadian holdings to the superior-general of the Saint-Sulpice Seminary in Paris, who had a more realistic outlook.[5] The tergiversations of this period nevertheless left a most confused legacy.

Up to 1653 Montreal did not produce enough to feed itself. The residents, fearing Iroquois attacks, locked themselves inside the fort, and preferred fur trading to farming. To ensure the development of the seigneury the governor resorted to collective land clearance, which would confound the issue of land ownership in years to come. He struck the following deal with the indentured labourers hired in 1653 and following years: they were to clear and sow a number of acres on the domain and keep the produce as their wages, as long as they were not given by the seigneur similar amounts of land, in the same state of cultivation, elsewhere.[6] This policy yielded two hundred arpents of arable land within five years, and in 1662–63, he reached similar arrangements to clear another four hundred.[7] Some early settlers, among the few who received regular land grants, made similar arrangements. But these individuals were more prudent than the governor and their leases stated that the servant would enjoy the returns from the cleared property only for a fixed term, without any other compensation.[8] The system clearly suited seigneurs and landowners, who disbursed not a penny, kept the title to the property, and put themselves under an obligation that would decrease with time. There was no chance that the replacement clause would be carried out so that land-clearers' acquired rights turned into negotiable assets that passed from hand to hand. With time, the value of these claims declined as the value of one arpent of arable land fell from 150 to 100 livres and then quickly to only 40 livres.[9] The economic situation favoured landowners, and it was to their advantage to retain such tenants as long as possible. The latter, for their part, were considered "habitants," a status which gave them the right to take part in the fur trade.[10] In order to increase the number of these tenants, concession declined and practically drew to a halt in 1663 and 1664. The colonial Council must have received complaints from people constrained to accept claims instead of outright title, for in 1664 the seigneurs were enjoined to give land to those who asked for it.[11] Concession increased. But the system had lasted long enough to produce a complicated web of claims on overlapping properties instead of the orderly and systematic division of the soil one might have expected to find.[12] The owners of such occupied properties appealed to the officials and law courts to recover the use of their land without incurring any costs, and the Council finally gave in to their demands in 1676.[13] The old landclearers' claims were annulled, and proprietors recovered their plots.

Other factors contributed to the initial confusion: the censives had not been surveyed, and some settlers, tired of waiting for a concession deed, squatted in various places. By 1666 the Sulpicians attempted to bring order to this chaos by preparing a *papier terrier*, by filling empty lots in settled areas, and by systematically opening up new areas to satisfy demand.[14] All *baux à cens* were witnessed by a notary after 1680.[15] As elsewhere in the colony, the seigneurs also granted "concession tickets," those claims to specific tracts of land that preceded the actual title deed. In theory a trial period separated the receipt of the ticket from the signing of the *bail à cens*. The colonist would have to start clearing the land to demonstrate that he intended to settle. Having no legal title to the property, according to the ordinances he could not sell it before it had been cleared. Yet the real situation was quite different. Some habitants sold their claims; what is more, most of the land sold in the year that followed the concession had not been improved. We might well wonder, therefore, whether the tickets stopped being issued, since they served no purpose.[16]

The new seigneurs' efficient management gradually sorted out the situation. There are two surviving assessments of the distribution of the censives: the first is a registry of occupiers dating from 1697, and the second a fuller description from 1731, when the seminary obtained Chancellery seals to force the habitants to declare their landholdings.[17] This last document, which was regularly updated, often contains the words "apparently owes," pointing to the uncertain status prevalent in the pre-Sulpician years. By 1731 three-quarters of the island had been conceded, meaning 1,047 arable plots and 487 lots in the town proper. The remainder would be handed over before the end of the French regime. The Sulpicians held on to three domains, covering a total of 2,800 arpents or less than 3 per cent of the seigneury. They could easily have doubled or quintupled their domain had they not been obligated to improve their holdings.[18] But the economic conditions prevalent in North America – an extremely favourable ratio of man to land – and the added difficulties of a colony away from the Atlantic sea routes put an effective brake on land ownership and discouraged speculation.

The significant point about the seigneurial regime in Montreal is that uncleared censives had absolutely no monetary value, as is shown in property appraisals. In 1660 thirty arpents were valued as follows: ten arpents under plough were worth 1,500 livres; five arpents tilled by hand, 500 livres; four arpents of pasture, 400 livres; four arpents of felled trees, 40 livres, while seven arpents covered with trees were deemed "worthless."[19] Only land that had been worked possessed any value, and this would not change for the next fifty years.[20] On such an economic vacuum was imposed a system of property that remained confined for centuries to narrow, limited, and much-coveted stretches of arable. We must therefore turn our attention to the evolution of this seigneurial system in its North American context.

2 THE EVOLUTION OF SEIGNEURIAL DUES[21]

Annual dues on land

The only fixed dues levied on the first plots consisted of a cens of 3 deniers per arpent – a mere trifle.[22] The Société de Notre-Dame made a short-lived attempt to incorporate real mortmain into their cessions, and this curious initiative should not be forgotten.[23] The following clause figures in five contracts: the taker had to reside on the Island of Montreal "or else, and should he be absent more than two years, he would forfeit his right to the granted property." He was also forbidden to sell any part of his land without the consent of the seigneur. Although the property bore this servitude, it spilled over to the taker, and these unusual contracts were swiftly denounced. The Colonial Council intervened, forbidding the use of such constraints, and freed the five colonists who had been taken in.[24] The Société's other concession deeds merely required the payment of the symbolic cens carrying subjection to a number of other charges. Yet around 1666 a new payment, which was not necessarily seigneurial, was superimposed on the cens. While the cens increased slightly, the newly established rente was paid in kind, first in capons, then in wheat.[25] To avoid any future arguments on the validity of this rente the seigneurs decided to tie it to the cens, rendering it indefeasible.[26]

By the early eighteenth century, contracts would state that the cens and rentes were indivisible, so that in the event of a lot's being subdivided, the various owners would be responsible together for payment of the entire amount.[27]

These dues slowly increased between 1666 and the first quarter of the eighteenth century.[28] (See Table 28.) The Saint Sulpice procurator advised that "there was nothing stopping the Seminary from charging as high a rate as the parties would accept."[29] But finally, "local custom," built up gradually by the population, placed a ceiling on seigneurial ambitions.[30] These foundered before the deep, passive resistance of the community. The habitants were reluctant to pay, and the seigneurs collected ten livres of cens and rentes with the greatest of difficulty. "I fully comprehend the distress that the multiplicity of debts and debtors is causing you, as well as the difficulty you have collecting them," the Saint Sulpice procurator wrote, "but it is common to all property-owners, and one can safely say both in France and in Canada that land equals war; you must be patient and get as much as you can out of these bad payers."[31] It proved impossible to raise the payments above a certain point, but they should not be dismissed as utterly insignificant, for they could prove relatively heavy on unimproved properties or for landclearers riddled with debts.

The seigneurs also granted common pastures. Since the Canadian seigneury originated from abroad and antedated the community, these were subject to annual dues, as well as all other ordinary seigneurial rights, including that of expropriation. There was a difference between the "commons" granted to residents of the côtes individually and not as a body (and which carried an additional small cens specified in the deeds), and the pasture ceded to the Communauté des Habitants de Ville Marie. That body did have the power to oversee and regulate the customary rights of various categories of residents, or to hire the cowherds, and so on.[32] But it could not alienate this holding, so this precarious ownership can be treated as mere usufruct.[33]

Occasional dues

The tax on the transfer of tenures was equivalent to the one charged in most regions of France, amounting to one-twelfth of the sale price. It was diligently collected and made up a significant portion of seigneurial revenues, perhaps as much as 25 per cent.[34] Buyers who paid the lods, in cash, within twenty days of the transaction, received a 25 per cent rebate. Proceedings were instituted against

Table 28
Evolution of seigneurial dues in three Montreal *côtes*, 1654–1731

Ward	Saint-Joseph	Saint-Martin	Saint-Michel
Date of concession	1654–1662	1665–1670	around 1700
Number of farms in 1731	16	11	51
Average size of farms	76 arpents	85 arpents	83 arpents
Average cens and rentes per farm	3l. 4s. 6d	7l. 6s. 7d.	8l 9s. 9d.
Average cens and rentes per arpent	10d.	1s. 8d.	2s.

late payers after the forty-day deadline.[35] From 1704 on, a new fine was laid on the exchange of all other kinds of property. Such exchanges were quite common in Canada and might have been used to disguise land sales and thus avoid paying the *lods*. After obtaining from the king the privilege of collecting these *droits d'échange*, the Sulpicians were in control of and benefited from all forms of property transfer.[36]

Montreal's seigneurs also collected the tithes, since parishes on the island within their seigneuries belonged to the Seminary. In 1663 the bishop had fixed colonial tithes at one-thirteenth of the crop – a hefty percentage for new settlements – but four years later royal officials decreed half that amount uniformly on all grains.[37] The first five crops on cleared soil were exempted, however. Unlike the French tribute, Canadian tithes were not lifted directly from the fields. Since few rural benefices were fixed in the seventeenth century, in order to curtail expenses habitants were required to declare their gross product, stow away the appropriate part, and take it to the tithe-collector once it had been threshed and winnowed. This was an open invitation to fraud and gave rise to countless lawsuits. The overall contribution of 3.8 per cent in tithes may appear modest, but it surpassed the tithes on new lands prevalent in France.[38]

Between 1658 and 1680 the Société de Notre-Dame and the Sulpicians conceded some fourteen arrière-fiefs on the Island of Montreal. Their vassals were either religious communities or military officers. Such fiefs were rather small, rarely more than double the average censive, and often strategically located to protect the island from invasion. Military and predominantly feudal concerns of this sort faded quite quickly, however, especially once the colony received and maintained royal troops. The seigneurs strove to get rid of these non-productive enclaves, and the merchants who bought them were only too happy to see them demoted to the rank of *rotures*, thus avoiding the payment of the *droit de quint* – a fine of one-fifth on the mutation of fiefs. Only the convents held on to their arrière-fiefs. In 1731 there were only six lay vassals left, and only two by 1781.

Personal rights – monopolies

The seigneurs of Montreal exercised high justice not merely on their seigneury but on the entire government of Montreal (one of three units of government, along with Trois-Rivières and Québec), since the privilege did not merely devolve from land ownership. Harried by the Crown, they relinquished those extensive powers in 1693.[39] They retained the administration of lower justice, which rested primarily on the cognizance of the censive, and was thus an essential tool in ensuring proper returns and obedience to the regulations. They made every effort to avoid prescription. The usual procedure was to bring a suit by summons, where the debtor was served with his notice to pay at his residence, or else, using subtler means, to request a distraint upon seizure by a third party.[40] The seigneurs showed patience and acumen, avoided lawsuits, and only seized property as a last resort. They kept their debtors in suspense, brought accounts regularly up to date, and made the debtors sign obligations to guarantee their arrears.[41] As long as they continued to control the courts, the interests of the seigneurs were fully protected.[42]

Banalité or gristmill monopoly – under which tenants' grain had to be ground in the seigneur's mill – was rigidly enforced in the colony. A hastily penned royal decision of 1686 transformed this personal prerogative into a *droit réel*, or at least this is how Canadian councillors, seigneurs every one, interpreted it.[43] Milling fees, set at one-fourteenth of the grain ground, were higher than the ones current in France, but this could be justified by the higher initial investment and the meagre yields in what were still scarcely populated seigneuries.[44] By the end of the seventeenth century the five banal mills on the Island of Montreal could not meet demand. This was partially due to technical problems: watermills only functioned in the spring and the fall, while windmills proved just as unreliable. These mills were leased, usually by a profit-sharing agreement, and commanded only a low rent. The millers, who were responsible for minor repairs and had to grind the seigneurs' grains for free, had a hard time meeting their commitments. In the early eighteenth century the seigneurs unloaded their responsibility for the building and upkeep of mills erected in newly settled areas (which were the least profitable) by ceding their rights in long-term leases. The number of mills rose, as did the bankruptcy of the leaseholders.

There were fifteen mills on the island in 1731, but the number soon dropped. More rational management and technical improvements would ensure a substantial increase in rent. Censitaires resented being subject to *banalité*. There were endless complaints about the unequal location of the mills, the slow service aggravated by preferential treatment, the squabbling, and the artificially high milling fees. The millers had a hard time ensuring that the habitants did not grind their grains outside the seigneury in mills accessible by water.[45] Illegally ground grain was confiscated.[46]

Not surprisingly, no one bothered to enforce hunting privileges.[47] By contrast, the seigneurs were quite keen on their fishing rights, which extended not merely to the seigneurial brooks, naturally enough, but to all navigable waters bordering on the seigneury. They had been granted this particular privilege in 1640 and as of 1678 began to demand that the fishermen pay them a fee. They tried to establish a custom by leasing these rights, hoping that this string of leases would strengthen their claims in the long run.[48] The habitants no doubt continued to poach for domestic consumption, but net-fishing, for commercial purposes, was confined to seigneurial fermiers.

Conventional rights – servitude

Besides these customary rights, the seigneurs further limited property rights by the clauses they managed to insert into concession deeds. The *retrait seigneurial*, or right to expropriate land that changed hands after its sale simply by reimbursing the buyer the full price and appropriate costs within forty days of the transaction, only appeared in Montreal at the end of the seventeenth century but would figure in all subsequent leases.[49] This prerogative was not covered by the Coutume de Paris. It was widely practised in Canada, however, and intendants who decried it at first eventually came round to ratifying it.[50] The seigneurs were thus able to speculate on the bad faith of censitaires who cheated on the *lods* and buy back the land for a fraction of its value. The Sulpicians also resorted to such measures to prevent the land falling into mortmain.[51]

Seigneurs had only one recourse against so-called colonists who took up properties and left them immediately to take part in the fur trade or for other reasons, and that was to take over the vacant lots.[52] They repossessed uncleared or minimally cleared properties where seigneurial dues were outstanding. They allowed the cases to pile up and then from time to time handed the intendant a list of twenty to thirty names, with affidavits from the curé and neighbours certifying the owners' absence. The procedure called for three public announcements and the owner had three months to come forth, settle his arrears, and begin improving the land. Seigneurs had no discretionary powers in this matter, and those of Montreal tried to be fair. Litigation proved unavoidable, however, when heirs with valid claims eventually came forth to contest the new censitaire's title deeds when the land had been granted anew.[53] The seigneurs looked for new tenants who agreed to pay all the arrears in cents and rentes that had accrued under the previous censitaires and the value of the labour and edifices, should it prove necessary.[54]

At first, habitants who had to yield part of their land for public roads were compensated; that soon ended. A further clause, tacked on around 1675, granted seigneurs the right to cut down one arpent of wood out of every twenty of the censive for their private ends, and allowed them to pick whatever building wood they might require, anywhere on the property, for the erection of churches, presbyteries, manor houses, mills, outbuildings, or fences for their farms, and for various public works. The censitaires received no compensation.[55] Later on a clause was added enabling the seigneur to repossess up to six arpents on a censive wherever a flour mill or sawmill could be built, with an indemnity covering only the value of the land expropriated. This is another example of seigneurial foresight.[56]

There can be no doubt, therefore, about the evolution of the seigneurial system. Seigneurs had no choice initially but to adapt to circumstances and demand little from those who had nothing to give. But as population grew and the land fell under the plough, they began to take advantage of all customary prerogatives, while introducing some novelties. Nothing was left to chance: one-page contracts lengthened to two or three by the eighteenth century. The seigneury became rigid and intrusive and could well vie with its French counterpart. Just as in the metropolis, the movement in annual dues did not fully express a hardening stance involving the stricter application of customary privileges and conventional rights, which provided so many brakes to the full enjoyment of property rights.[57] Montreal was no different from the rest of the colony, and its inhabitants would not escape such constraints for long by fleeing to other areas. They might at best gain a few years' respite by abandoning the more prosperous inhabited regions for lands whose absentee seigneurs hardly bothered to collect feeble rents or attend to their privileges. But this would entail a loss of security and of the comforts and services nurtured within a broader settlement. It would not be long, moreover, before all the obligations agreed to on paper would find concrete expression in those distant parts as well.

The seigneurial revenues were farmed out. It was usual for the same farmer to take on the tithes, the seigneurial cens and rentes, and the ground rent in a specific area for a period varying between three and nine years.[58] Depending on the period, the island had as many as four or five collectors. These individuals of modest extraction, more or less honest and solvent, often neglected to pay for the price of the farm but rarely showed leniency towards the debtors. The Sulpicians, however, could intervene to moderate their zeal. It was their rule to move gently because "a new colony is not governed like a full-grown country," and to connect possession with title deeds by "proceeding cautiously to avoid giving the habitants any cause for alarm, thereby securing the seigneurs' possession slowly but surely."[59] Less than a century after its establishment, this wise policy had propelled the seigneurial system beyond what some historians view as a simple means of land distribution or a debased institution serving the colonists to a truly restrictive property system that was resented as much in Canada as in the French countryside. The best weapon was passive resistance: to put off, forget, trust to circumstances, and let debts pile up. When times were hard, the colonists would "conspire" against the seigneurs, who read "sedition" into easily placated fits of anger. It was they who reported some of these "murmurings": the censitaires accused the Seminary of getting rich at their expense and saw the fire that destroyed the Sulpician's mill as divine retribution. "Although such practices were current in France," people argued, "they had no place in a land they had conquered by putting their lives on the line."[60]

CHAPTER EIGHT

The Pattern of Settlement

1 THE RURAL LANDSCAPE

The basic unit of the rural landscape was the individual farm on one unbroken lot. This the notaries called a concession or a habitation. Since land in the colony was not taxed, the need for greater precision never arose. A habitation was a property granted in one piece or composed of adjoining parcels, irrespective of the time and manner in which it had been acquired. The term applied to any type of farm regardless of its use and size.[1]

These farms were grouped in *côtes*. *Côtes* were areas with similar physical characteristics, delineated on either side, and often in all directions, by more or less obvious differences in terrain. The Island of Montreal contained more than thirty by 1731, and most had clear-cut features. Parallel elongated lots were common to all of them. Depending on location, however, these might be aligned in single file or else in two rows facing each other. This latter configuration, in herringbone pattern on both sides of a common pasture, could be found in several place in the interior of the island. Elsewhere they simply fronted the river, a barren declivity, or an artificial line drawn being another *côte*. The *côte* found its lateral border in a ravine, a change of gradient, or the indentations of the shoreline or jutting headland, which forced seigneurs to redeploy concessions. The varying topography meant that *côtes* included as few as ten or as many as fifty farms.

The term "habitation" derived from the word "habiter" (to reside). A habitant was therefore a free man who proved his permanent residence in the colony by taking on a farm (habitation). The origin of the term *"côte"* is harder to trace. It was apparently used in the colony before the founding of Montreal. Since the *côtes* usually bordered on rivers, this might refer to their "coastal" nature. Yet in Montreal the first *côtes* were located in the interior, on the hillsides, so that the reference might be to its meaning of "slope." Although the term "quartier" was used at the very beginning, *côte* soon replaced it. Each was given a name, a saint's name, prior to settlement, and this official nomenclature prevailed. Nevertheless, people insisted on keeping a number of local place-names (*lieux-dits*) such as Lachine, Pointe-Claire, Les Sources, La Grande Anse, l'Anse Fondue, le Bois brûlé, le Lac au Renard, or le Lac aux Loutres. Awkward circumlocutions were used for some geographically significant places, such as "the eastern tip of the island."

Parishes and villages were later superimposed on the *côtes* for purposes other than tillage. These divisions did not mesh as harmoniously with the landscape and lacked the unity nurtured by a common history. It should be added that the seigneury was not laid out in successive and similarly oriented "ranges" following the "geometric obsession" that geographers have viewed as typical of French Canada.[2] The lay of the land did not invite symmetry. The landscape was rather uneven and resembled the arable land of a French village much more than the townships that would be fashioned behind old seigneuries in the nineteenth century and elsewhere in North America.[3]

We can follow the formation of the Montreal landscape. The first farmsteads nestled on the terraces behind the town. This wooded, well-drained land was soon fully cultivated. The colonists then turned northeast, to the lowlands bordering the river, where the escarpment was sufficiently marked to prevent flooding. The censives, perpendicular to the shore, reached the end of the island and, before the end of the seventeenth century, had rounded back along the Rivière des Prairies. Agricultural imperatives accounted for the gradual settlement of this part of the seigneury, while the southwest developed by leaps and bound primarily in response to commercial and strategic considerations. The terrain was not as good, for one thing. Low-lying properties in Pointe Saint-Charles were basically used as pastures and remained, in the main, uninhabited. Southwestern concessions bypassed them by swerving towards the interior along two parallel *côtes* cut off by an elongated marsh known as "lake" Saint-Pierre. A road continued on to Lachine, the port of embarkation inland. Four forts along the river protected the most vulnerable approaches to the town.[4] Merchants had pioneered these projects to safeguard their warehouses. Colonists erected dwellings within the enclosures and claimed land in the surroundings. But cultivation lagged, since settlers in these parts were mostly interested in trading with the Indians, who had to unload at the top of rapids before making their way to the town. The forts were also used to house the troupes de la Marine. The seigneurs granted properties beyond Lachine that functioned as commercial and occasionally as military outposts, as did the arrière-fiefs of Boisbriant and Senneville at the very end of the island. Purely agricultural settlements eventually filled the area between these outposts, but until 1720 or thereabouts, the three riverside *côtes* of Lachine, Pointe-Claire, and Sainte-Anne-du-Bout-de-l'Ile remained sparsely populated.[5]

Requests for land rose in the early eighteenth century as demobilized soldiers and a generation of Canadians old enough to settle down created new demand. The seigneurs carved out new sections in the middle and subsequently on the northwestern side of the island. The *côte* of Rivière des Prairies and the inner western sections, however, would only be fully conceded by the middle of the century. The frontage of the new rectangular *côtes* extended six to nine kilometers; they stretched back two or three kilometers, were oriented differently, and were separated one from the next by declivities unsuited to farming. They had been surveyed, then conceded at one stroke, and the seigneurs waited until the oldest were fully settled before opening up new ones.

In 1731 eleven *côtes*, nestled close together, lay within three kilometers of the town and were part of the urban parish of Notre-Dame. These were the Montreal suburbs. The remainder of the seigneury was divided into seven rural parishes, four in the northwest, consisting of ten or so rather well-populated *côtes*, and the other three in the southwest, with five or six sparsely settled *côtes*. There were no villages other than the forts, where, until 1698, the rural population would huddle for safety for months on end in times of danger. Once peace was restored, the places were abandoned and the huts left to rot. A number of aged peasants who had handed down their properties to their sons spent their last years within these enclosures, where they found a church, or at least a chapel and cemetery. Two or three farmers whose land lay nearby found it more convenient to build houses inside the fort. On a slight elevation close by stood the windmill that doubled as a redoubt. In 1731 the island's biggest village, that of Pointe-aux-Trembles, had only twenty families and had barely begun to offer basic services to the surrounding population: a school, a forge, a store, and a notarial office.[6]

Habitants were not grouped in villages because it would take them too long to get to their farms, look after their plots, make hay, cut down wood, and tend their animals mornings and evenings. The village as an agglomeration of farmers is linked to small fragmented properties and collective rights; the village as a market centre between the farms and the distant town would only emerge once the countryside reached a certain population density. The lack of rural industry also pre-empted the rise of agglomerations. The forty to fifty households scattered on either side of a church could not provide sufficient livelihood for edge-tool makers, carpenters, masons, and the like. This explains the absence of villages and not, as one intendant suggested, the supposed odd temperament of the settlers, or their wish to escape from clerical and civil authorities.[7] There were no villages because the pre-conditions did not exist.[8] "Villages grow as parishes get older," Pierre Deffontaines observed correctly around 1940, about Quebec villages that had retained their original function as sanctuaries for retired farmers.[9] Is it any surprise that there were no villages in an era when parishes were new and people died young?

2 FARM SIZE

Montreal's first censives were small – no more than 15 to 30 arpents, and some smaller yet measured only 6 to 8 arpents. They had the same elongated shape, and the length was usually ten times the width. It soon became apparent, however, that the size was inadequate for the type of individual farm that had emerged spontaneously in the colony. Within ten to twenty years the habitant had turned his 10 hectares into arable land and vegetable gardens and had to look elsewhere for pastures, fodder, and especially wood. Dividing the commons among the settlers would not resolve the problem of finding feed to keep cattle in barns for seven months or wood for fireplaces and buildings. Canadian winters dictated the size of the farms.

This had already become evident when the Sulpicians took over the seigneury. Their policy was to grant concessions covering a minimum of 40 arpents, more commonly 60 arpents. With few exceptions, the soil was apportioned equally.[10] Their earliest concessions measured 20 by 300 perches, or 30 by 200, depending on the nature of the ground. Where the soil shared the same characteristics over the whole depth of the lot, parcels tended to be narrower in order to knit the farms closer together. The ideal distance was thought to be 20 perches or 117 meters, allowing for about nine farms per kilometer. This layout was no local innovation. Its origins can be traced to medieval Europe before subdivision blurred the sharpness of the outline and hedges hid the contours in many a region.[11] The layout was tied to a collective regulation of the arable land, but it responded also to other imperatives that agrarian individualism, spontaneously adopted in America, could not on its own render obsolete. Such an arrangement of long narrow farms brought the peasants closer together, reduced their isolation, and facilitated the building and common upkeep of the road linking their frontages. The wider the farms were, the greater the work of building up the road and digging ditches to drain the waters from the adjoining fields.[12]

This elongated pattern of settlement lining the St Lawrence also afforded colonists another means of communicating with the outside world. Although highly significant in other parts of the colony, this last factor proved less important in Montreal, where waterways were hard to navigate and the first settlements were removed from the river; the shortest and safest way to the town was across the fields, no matter where one lived. But there were other factors. In Canada, just as in Europe, these long fields made for easier ploughing by cutting the times the team had to be turned round. The pattern also led to a more equitable sharing of the terrain. Lots aligned in this way exhibited about the same characteristics, whereas cross-sectioning would have given one farmer soggy pastures, another fertile land, and a third rocky ground. Subsequent subdivisions would obey the same principle, creating strips within concessions, mirroring the original pattern. Again, this was no innovation but harked back to age-old habits, still perfectly suited to the life and work of these peasants.[13] The pattern was more or less untouched in years to come, and was even enhanced, creating the unique landscape of Quebec.

Seigneurs willingly extended concessions, wherever physical conditions allowed, by adding an extra 10 to 40 arpents, called an *augmentation*, behind the original farmstead. This was not automatic but rather a favour granted hard-working colonists with large families, and it served often to compensate widows and orphans. It was easy to lengthen farms fronting the river that ended back in the middle of nowhere. It proved more of a problem, however, in the interior. Take Côte des Neiges, for example, flanked against the mountain on one side and touching on the *côtes* Sainte-Catherine and Saint-Laurent, conceded in the same period, on two others, while bordered to the southwest by marshes. It was impossible to add to these 40-arpent censives distributed on either side of the common pasture. The same problem affected the earliest concessions granted by Maisonneuve on the narrow hillsides, or properties abutting on land of little value.

Yet the habitants came to realize that they needed more land. Up to one arpent of wood a year went to heating the household, especially if the trees were coniferous and burned up quickly.[14] It would take some thirty years' growth to replace them, so each farm needed at least 30 uncleared arpents. Montreal's seigneurs had no wish to encourage forestry and preferred land grants that increased settlement and wheat production, thereby enriching their mills and presbyteries and adding worshippers to their churches.[15] They were, however, concerned about their own future supplies and created wooded reserves that were carefully managed for their own use. The population's needs could not be met by gathering branches on the demesne. Besides, a forest guard patrolled them after 1682 (if not sooner).[16] On the mainland, beyond the twenty-kilometer radius of settlement, it was probably easy to forage without the seigneurs' knowing, but the wood still had to be lugged home, a hard if not impossible proposition given the prevailing conditions. In sum, the habitant's 60 arpents were hardly sufficient. The moment he became the least bit interested in his property or concerned about handing it down, he would naturally seek to enlarge it.

Efforts to enlarge original concessions began in the early days of settlement but cannot be inferred through the agricultural surveys, which provide no data on the size of the properties and their use. The large number of uncleared and unoccupied censives makes any averaging senseless. The phenomenon needs to be examined more closely.

Between 1698 and 1731 the overall size of the Côte des Neiges remained practically unchanged, except for one arpent added to the back of each lot after a survey. (See Table 29.) Eleven initial grantees sold their censives to their neighbours and the land was thus redistributed to suit eleven habitants who built up farms measuring 84 to 168 arpents. None of the original censives was subdivided. The 1731 figures show that the consolidation of property was not an ephemeral phenomenon, and it continued up to the end of the century.

The same could be demonstrated just as easily of any côte on the island. The movement was more noticeable in places where original concessions had been smaller and it proved impossible to enlarge censives. The habitant who could not obtain a free augmentation to extend his holding lengthwise paid whatever his neighbour asked in order to expand sideways.

Property distribution was more complex in the older côtes. Graph 18 illustrates the consolidation of parcels by residents of the Côte Sainte-Joseph. The first censives were granted in 1654. The seigneurs were able to concede a few later that they had repossessed through various transactions.[17] Here, as on the Côteau Saint-Louis, the size of

Table 29
Evolution of property in the Côte Notre-Dame-des-Neiges from the 1698 land grant
until 1781

Year	1698	1731	1781
Total area of the *côte*	1,940 arp.	2,078 arp.	2,078 arp.
Total number of farms	40	29	28
Number of farms by categories (size in perches)			
20 x 200	29	9	2
30 x 200	11	9	14
40 x 200	–	3	9
50 x 200	–	2	1
60 x 200	–	3	–
70 x 200	–	1	–
80 x 200	0	1	1
Irregular shape	–	1	1

Source: *Baux à cens*, Not. Rec., A. Adhémar and Raimbault, 1698–99, passim; seigneurial map of
1702 with list of landholders, NA, map Hi 340; *Aveu et dénombrement* of the seigneury of 1731 and
1781, RAPQ (1941–42): 3–176 and ASSM; Claude Perrault, *Montréal en 1781* (Montreal 1969).

the original concessions made it imperative to buy up adjoining
parcels, or land in another section.[18] Such dispersal of parcels
typified the suburbs. Elsewhere, the habitations formed an unbroken
lot, apart from a few meadows. In Pointe-aux-Trembles parish,
farms that had originally covered 60 arpents had increased to an
average of 112 arpents sixty years later by a combination of purchase and the generous extension of censives.

Let us conclude with the case of Julien Blois, a former indentured
servant who came to Montreal in 1659.[19] At the end of his contract
he married and spent 70 livres on a 30-arpent property on the Côte
Saint-François, conceded the previous year but barely cleared. Three
years later he purchased an adjoining property and nine years after
that a third border piece, which brought his holding up to 70
arpents. In 1686 he received his first concession, a large piece of
land at the end of his property, as wide as his own. He left behind a
210-arpent farm.[20] He was not an exceptional case. Many colonists
preferred to buy land in the *côte* of their choice rather than take a
concession in an imposed location, and like Blois, they waited
patiently for the chance to round out their property.

This ongoing process of property consolidation contradicts the
stereotype of prodigal seigneurs and carefree colonists with little
interest in agriculture, content with whatever land they were given,
letting it go to ruin, and abandoning it as soon as they could make

for the woods. This is not to deny that some did indeed fit the description, but on the whole many more worked hard to make the country habitable, build up a family holding, and recreate a familiar lifestyle, hoping that their labour and the practice of a tried routine would bring them security.

The assembling of parcels meant that settlement was spaced thinner than the seigneurs would have liked. There were 11.1 inhabitants per square kilometer in the countryside in 1731, though this average is skewed by the inclusion of about ten recently conceded *côtes* that were neither cleared nor inhabited. Older sections, such as Pointe-aux-Trembles, had a density of 19 inhabitants. This is the exact number recorded by Raoul Blanchard for the Montreal plain in 1953. From a European standpoint he found this figure disconcerting: "How can it be that the richest soil in the province supported no more than twenty persons per square kilometer, that excess population had been forcefully and systematically driven out over the last seventy years in order to maintain such a low ratio of residents?"[21] Yet from a North American standpoint, he added, this was rather a good showing, superior to that of Ontario, Vermont, or New Hampshire. What is there to add except that the process of expulsion was in fact three centuries old and had begun with the first concession? Unlike the English settler who was immediately handed some 50 to 70 hectares, if not more, the Montreal censitaire began with a 6- to 20-hectare property and had to struggle to enlarge it on a continent that made new demands.[22]

CHAPTER NINE

Occupying the Land

1 LAND-CLEARING

Few immigrants had come prepared for the long and difficult task of clearing the soil. Imagine a settler who was in a position to devote all his time to developing the wooded concession he had just been granted, thanks to the savings he had amassed during his years of service or to his soldier's pay.[1] It was April 1670, and the last of the snow was melting. His property was located in Côte Sainte-Anne with its two or three families and few clearings. The town, where he resided, lay twelve kilometers away, and the road barely covered half that distance. His first task was to fell trees for a small log cabin, measuring fifteen by twenty feet. He chose small trees, sharpening one end which he then stuck into the ground to fashion a crude dwelling with no floor or fireplace, yet sufficiently waterproof to allow him to withstand at least one winter. Thatch and bark would do for the roof and would fill the gaps. After three or four week's work, this cabin was ready to house his chest and supplies, even if it would need additional tinkering before the winter.[2] He now had to pick and cut down bigger and better-quality trees, more or less the same size, for the house he intended to build. His task would be simpler if this second site was close by and even in the original clearing. Everything hinged on the kind of trees growing there. His first choice was oak and then pine, the trunks of which he then cut into eighteen- and twenty-two foot pieces, which he set aside. This second stage took several weeks, for he worked with an axe and had no team to pull the tree trunks. Come June he went over the deforested section, one or one and a half arpents at a time, pulling up those tree stumps measuring less than one foot in diameter. The larger "unaxable" ones were girdled.[3] It would take four to five years for them to die and for the stumps to rot. Dead wood was bundled outside the cabin and kept as firewood or sold in town. The ground, still covered with brush, was then burnt. The arpent was "clean" and ready for breaking the soil. And so in the fall, the ashen topsoil between the heavy trunks was turned over to prepare it for a first sowing either late in the season or in the spring. Then it was time to ready the cabin for winter, and not a moment too soon to finish the timber that had been put aside. Squaring by means of an axe would provide sufficient protection. The colonist then spent the winter clearing a new site, chopping the trees off three or four feet above the ground, at snow level. This newly cleared ground was not suitable for spring wheat, but some settlers, following Indian custom, sowed corn, beans, and pumpkins, even if it meant deferring final clearing to the next fall.[4]

After a year's work the colonist had dug up one arpent and felled another two.[5] He increased his arable land by an additional two arpents a year, while erecting a permanent pièce sur pièce house with beam flooring, board roof, and cob fireplace.[6] He bought a heifer, a sow, a few chickens and turned the cabin into a barn as soon as he moved into the new house. Five years after he had started developing his property, he had no trouble pulling up the rotten stumps with the help of one or two oxen, and he found himself gradually in a position to plough his land. Tasks associated with land clearance receded as strictly agricultural ones took over. At this pace, he would have to wait a decade or more to have ten arpents under the plough, which was the minimum for the rotation of crops and fallow and for feeding his family. Should he take any longer, ground that had only been turned over lightly and sown every year would become exhausted. When he died, thirty years after taking over his property, he left behind thirty arpents of arable land, a pasture, a barn and a stable, a somewhat larger home, a road at the front of his lot, neighbours, and a pew in church. His whole life had been spent clearing and building.

Although the techniques always resembled those described above, not all colonists were so diligent. Few had saved enough to allow them to survive the eighteen months before the first harvest, pay notarial fees and surveying costs, or cover cost of the necessary tools, utensils, nails, and seeds.[7] And since these former soldiers and indentured labourers usually took a wife before or soon after settling on the land, they needed double rations, since the dowry, should there be one, was not enough to answer for the young bride over such an extended period. The immigrant who married a local girl, however, got a roof over his head and found seasonal employment on his father-in-law's farm in return for help, cartage, and loan of his plough. All land-clearers had to hire themselves out to avoid being crushed by their initial debt, and this meant putting off work on their own farms for weeks if not months.[8] The luckier ones rented a farm, which provided both temporary cover and income as well as some free time to begin developing their own land. Whatever the arrangement, it inevitably slowed them down.

There were also those who tried to combine occupations: more or less experienced masons, joiners, or shoemakers, who roomed in town, also worked at times on some distant rural lots. These remained uncultivated the longest, and arrangements had to be made with neighbours to have them cleared to avoid seigneurial expropriation. These lands provided no income, and often these part-time artisans moved to the *côtes* after years of eking out a precarious living in town, but little came of such belated endeavours and changes in orientation dictated by poverty. A number of settlers also gave up, lacking the stamina, health, or instinct to hang on to these sixty arpents of forest; and then there were those who had never wanted to be peasants and merely took a concession as a precaution, only to abandon it for the fur trade.

At the other hand of the scale we find the job-givers: the seigneurs, religious communities, merchants, judicial and administrative officers, some early settlers, craftsmen who made a good living, and voyageurs in the up-country – in short, anyone who did not rely on agricultural produce to survive. They either had servants clear the land or, up to 1664, used agreements with land-clearers, which cost them nothing (as described in chapter 7). Properties employing several hands were rapidly improved. But when immigrants began to get land on demand, clearers had to be paid. It is difficult, however, to establish the precise cost of this labour, for the clearer often received indirect, non-quantifiable benefits such as housing and tools.[9]

Land-clearing agreements were becoming adjuncts to straightforward leasehold. The owner leased out that part of his property that was already developed, including the buildings and stock, for the going price. He asked that the lessor clear and till a number of arpents for which he charged no rent as long as they were not under plough, after which the yields were shared on the same basis as the remainder of the leased property. The produce of the first three or four years served as the clearer's wages.[10] Clauses were strict: the tenant could clear only one arpent at a time in a specified location and never deforest more than he could till during the length of his contract.[11]

It follows, therefore, that any assessment of the overall rate of land-clearance should take the variety of these experiences into account and that quick progress on some plots balanced off delays and departures in other parts. The independent, isolated colonist is clearly a theoretical construct, a convenient average, and the economic conditions that obtained in the colony determined the pace of development far more than the more or less hard-working disposition of the population.

Let us take a closer look at a group of eighty-one farmsteads granted before 1666, at which date the censitaires had to present their title deeds and describe the state of their labours. (See Table 30.) At first, they would clear one arpent per year, and since the process was cumulative, they were soon able to add about two and a half arpents annually until they had ten to twelve arpents cleared. At this point they slowed down and reached their maximum when thirty to forty arpents had been put under the plough.

This sample includes the small lots that the seigneurs granted initially. After fifteen years these habitants had only four arpents of wood left, which would soon be used up. The 1666 document showed the new seigneurs that they had to double the size of the censives. A similar picture emerges (although the overall process was somewhat slower) when we look at the work done on ninety-three habitations between 1667 and 1681.[12] Those without any cleared land in 1667 had an average of 20 arable arpents fourteen years later. In 1667 the ninety-three habitants held 13 arpents of cleared land each, and 40 arpents by 1681. But the average was in fact lower, for a few important farms belonging to merchants and other notables who hired many labourers compensated for the slower pace of the ordinary settler.

Graph 22 shows the state of the censives in 1667, 1681, and 1731. About half of the censives in the first two censuses were new concessions, granted no more than four or five years earlier. In 1731, when the number of older farms becomes sufficient, a clearer picture emerges. The upper limit of the cleared area hovers around 40 arpents, and it had taken a long while to achieve this. Only a minority had cleared over 50 arpents, and only 1 per cent of landowners cultivated very large properties. Whereas only one-fifth of a Poitou *métairie*, which, for argument's sake, also covered 40 hectares, was uncultivated, in Canada three-fifths of the holding was left untouched.[13] For most farmers, who held smaller lots of about 20 hectares, these 13 hectares of meadow and arable land represented a threshold that could not be crossed without endangering the equilibrium of the enterprise.

Table 30
Progress of land improvement on the Island of Montreal between 1648 and 1666

Number of years farmed	1	2–4	5–10	11–18
Number of censitaires	13	18	20	30
Total arpents granted (100%)	390	320	582	910
Arable land (arpent)	12	48	230	639
	(3%)	(15%)	(40%)	(70%)
Meadows (arpents)	0	2	24	34
	(0%)	(0.6%)	(5%)	(4%)
Felled and pasture (arpents)	23	82	171	112
	(6%)	(25%)	(30%)	(13%)
Wooded (arpents)	355	188	147	125
	(91%)	(59%)	(25%)	(13%)

Source: *Aveu et dénombrement* of the seigneury, 1666, NA, MJH, 23, vol. 1.

The rate of land-clearance remained remarkably even for over a century. The arable land increased at the same rate as the population and the movement in concessions.[14] Land-clearance was far from a profitable investment responding to fluctuating external demand. It meant back-breaking, onerous work spurred by necessity, and the peasants persevered until they achieved some security and then stopped. The trend towards a similar amount of improved land, clearly noticeable in 1731, shows us that the countryside was shaped during a long recessionary phase.

2 DISTRIBUTION OF RURAL
PROPERTY AND TYPES OF
OCCUPATION

It was a regime of individual, middle-sized, rather undifferentiated property. At the end of the seventeenth century, four-fifths of the proprietors were peasants.[15] (See Table 31.)

If the distribution could be assessed in terms of acreage of arable land, including the Sulpicians' domains, the peasants' share would drop somewhat, for seigneurial and other religious holdings were extensive.[16] Officers and merchants, by contrast, rarely possessed more land than the peasants, whether in the form of arrière-fiefs or censives, so that all in all the peasants held at least three-quarters of the soil, until the middle of the eighteenth century. There were some large holdings, but they had not been created at the expense of any specific social group during this period. But the privileged few were allowed to accumulate uncleared plots, which would eventually

Table 31
Farm distribution on the Island of Montreal according to the owner's occupation, 1697

		Landholders	
Owners		Number	%
Peasants		262	80
Urban owners of farms:			
Religious communities	4		
Merchants	13		
Military and civil officers	13		
Artisans and fur traders	34		
Retired peasants and others	5		
Total		69	20
Total farm owners		331	100

Source: *Livre des tenanciers*, Dec. 1697, ASSM

brake the expansion of peasant properties inside the seigneury once all the land had been granted.

A sizable proportion of landowners actually lived in town and did not work the land. The commonly held view that the countryside was populated only by peasant owners is an oversimplification. Seigneurs, religious communities, merchants, and officers resorted to indentured labourers before 1660 to develop their land, but as time went on they relied more and more on leases.[17] In 1697 at least one-fifth of the rural holdings were permanently worked by fermiers or métayers, to which must be added a number of peasant holdings leased temporarily by aged habitants, or widows or guardians disposing of the land of their wards. One should also take into account a number of court-ordered rentals that followed crop seizures.[18] The 1721 inquiry on parish territories showed that 25 per cent of suburban habitations and between 10 and 15 per cent of those located further away were not farmed by their owners.[19] The island's average from the last quarter of the seventeenth century onwards was therefore something like 20 per cent.

Though there is nothing unusual about the presence of landlords, how could they find tenants in a country where property was so widely available? Who were the tenants, and why would they have preferred to work someone else's land instead of their own? Leaving aside happenstance and personal reasons, there are two permanent factors: the harsh nature of land-clearance and the poverty of the settlers. Except for the few cases of overseers and tenants of large properties who had definitely chosen this status, most of the tenants were potential owners.[20] They did not form a separate stratum, and one could find as many sons of habitants in their midst as immigrants. They had one thing in common: they could not afford to start their own farm. Rather than spend four or five years in a log cabin, clearing tirelessly while they watched their debts mount, they took on a properly cleared and well-equipped farm for as long as they needed. There were obvious attractions: income, a decent house, farming equipment, and the opportunity of raising a few head of cattle. They made few if any improvements on their own land in the first years, but in the long run a good farmer would manage to clear his property by hiring others – soldiers, for example – to do it for him.[21] Whenever possible he would try to make use of his landlord's plough and oxen. He built himself a house in his free time. At the end of five or ten years he was, therefore, in a position to settle on a productive farm and, what is more, in an inhabited côte, served by a road and integrated into a parish. Some tenants elected to buy a cleared farm rather than ask for land grants.[22] In either case, their financial status following these transactions was perhaps no better than that of their neighbours, but they had saved themselves several years of hardship and isolation.

The above suggests that tenants were usually young, restless, and poor at the outset, that they were little inclined to tend properties they would abandon sooner or later, and that they were very tempted to break the clauses in their leases that forbade them to use the landlord's equipment on their own land. This led to a fair number of lease cancellations and lawsuits.[23] Although the owners were in a delicate position, they were not at the mercy of their tenants. For despite the millions of uncultivated hectares surrounding the tiny agrarian settlement, the unfavourable ratio of men to the small arable area proved more significant in the short run. As long as there wee plenty of poor land-clearers, farmers could easily be replaced and the ablest and most honest would be preferred.

In the colony, the term "laboureur" gradually came to refer to tenant-farmers and sharecroppers, as opposed to the "habitants" who ran their own farms.[24] Temporary tenure was not considered a desperate measure in some way inferior to hereditary tenure.

It is possible to gauge the nature of the agrarian economy and the balance of power between farm capital and labour from the clauses in rural leases and the way they evolved.[25]

The titles of these contracts are somewhat confusing. Leases were made "à titre de ferme et moissons de grains" or "de ferme et loyer." Both cases involved a flat rate, payable in grains, for few rural leases in the colony were stipulated in cash.[26] Calculation shows that payments represented one-third of a farm's gross product. Another third was the tenant's net income, while the last covered production costs.[27] By the end of the seventeenth century "farming leases with half the grains" (*à titre de ferme et moitié de tous grains*) had begun to proliferate, and by 1720 such share-cropping agreements, as we now understand them, accounted for half the leases overseen by notaries.[28]

Irrespective of the type of contract, the owner always provided the farm's assets: the animals, the implements, as well as the lodgings and essential tools and utensils. The tenant arrived empty-handed, more like a labourer than a tenant. The landlord advanced him the seeds and was usually repaid from the produce of the first two or three years. Why, then, did it take so long for share-cropping agreements to take hold when they were so widespread in those poor regions of western France from which these colonists had come?[29] Landlords managed to collect fixed rents for forty years without sharing the risks. Similarly, the livestock leases that were always included in the contract put the tenant at a disadvantage for several decades. The animals were assessed by two experts at the start and the end of the contract, and the tenant had to repay the value no matter what happened in between. The burden of their depreciation was his alone, and losses were only shared when he could prove that the animals had died from natural causes and not through his negligence.[30] But the ordeals of wartime and the bad harvests after 1691 brought difficulties to a head.[31] The spread of share-cropping was a victory for the farmers who had suffered from the fixed rentals, as well as a manifestation of the owners' desire to oversee farming more closely and reduce carelessness.[32] With a greater amount of land under cultivation, rural livestock increased and peasant farms became better equipped, so that bourgeois or religious properties lost their attraction and an equitable sharing of losses and profits replaced the old system. This arrangement became the norm for livestock leases at the beginning of the eighteenth century. It was at this juncture that contracts came to include an option allowing either party to put an early end to the agreement – a wise precaution that would prevent flights far more effectively than would legal proceedings.

Leases remained niggling and rather strict, especially with regard to secondary obligations, various reservations and prohibitions. Besides his half-share of the harvest and of animals born during the year, the landlord collected a number of dues at a fixed rate.[33] Every cow he leased usually brought him ten pounds of butter a year; in return for oxen or horses, he demanded that fifteen to twenty *cordes* of firewood be carted to his home, which meant thirty or forty deliveries a year, not counting the ploughing he might request on another farm.[34] He also customarily took one fatted hog a year for every four he gave out, or one about to be fattened for every two. The rule was straightforward when it came to poultry: a dozen eggs and a dozen chickens for every one that had been supplied. Fruits of the orchard, should there be any, were evenly split. The owner usually held on to the vegetable patch, or took a number of cabbages. All this produce had to be delivered at specific times, at intervals that suited the landlord, and involved a considerable number of trips.[35]

Some landowners expected the delivery of several carts of hay, but the usual requirement was that the tenant leave behind what he had found when he arrived. He might occasionally be asked to feed an animal over the winter, most likely a horse, a duty not included in the lease.[36] The contracts included the ritual clauses: the tenant agreed to occupy the farm property and work it with care, to do minor building repairs, ditch cleaning, and so on. He was also responsible for all the utensils, agricultural tools, and implements entrusted to him. They were evaluated at both the beginning and the end of the lease, and the depreciation and necessary replacements were borne by him alone.

While the attitude towards the wooded part of the farm had been fairly lax at first, restrictions were soon placed on its use. The tenant could take what he needed for firewood or for repairs, but no more. Some leases specified the allotted quantity. Finally, he was strictly forbidden to use the equipment or animals for purposes other than those mentioned in the lease.[37]

These obligations, so common in France, seem out of place in North America. The landlords undoubtedly had some control over the rural labour force, since they found people willing to rent. The terms eased in the eighteenth century, although the process proved slow and irregular. The biggest landowners clung to their demands at least up to 1720. They could exercise this control because they invested more in the farms in order to produce a rent than did the average peasant. There was a ceiling on rents, however, since the share-cropper's net income could not fall below that of the ordinary habitants – but given the poverty of most of the peasants, this still left plenty of margin.[38]

Bourgeois and ecclesiastical property, however, did not expand. If anything, the relative importance of the first dropped between

1660 and 1720.[39] In 1697 only two-fifths of merchant outfitters and a slightly higher proportion of officers held any land in the seigneury.[40] These rural leases show that this was not due to any scarcity of labour but to the overall economic situation.

Beside the "laboureurs" that we have just described, and their strict leases, one finds a whole range of occasional tenants tied down by what notaries referred to as leases but which were actually only very vague agreements that suited both parties. The poor artisans who sought security in land ownership have already been mentioned. A concession gave small merchants and fur traders the status of habitants.[41] As long as their fur-trade activities were illegal, it was useful for them to have, at least on the surface, some other function, and to take cover behind a show of submissiveness and respectability, which eventually allowed even thee adventurers to secure their loans. One could easily get title to a censive, pay seigneurial dues, and nod towards the ordinances to avoid takeover by literally abandoning the land to the hands of an habitant for extended periods. A neighbour would most likely take over such property, and he brought his own farming equipment, in contrast with the arrangements we have met with previously. He cleared the land, thus giving his fields more daylight and saving his own wooded reserves. He dug the ground and sowed wherever he pleased, profiting from the high yields of this virgin soil. This form of leasing, which could be considered an extension of land-clearing contracts, was quite common and rarely became the object of notarized agreements. Improvements were slow and perfunctory, and the lessor got only a small fraction of the harvest without any additional returns either in kind or in services. But his outlay was nil, and he could potentially make some capital gains.[42] Other townsmen did not even go to such lengths and merely hired day-labourers to sow and harvest their fields. One can readily imagine the paltry results.[43]

3 APPARENT MOBILITY AND ACTUAL STABILITY

Not all the pseudo-setters were able to hold on to properties they did not till. In more isolated spots, where they were in the majority, as in the settlement along Lake Saint-Louis, there were no neighbours to take over the land. Intendants and seigneurs thundered to no avail, warning that the habitants had to reside or have someone else reside on the land (*tenir ou faire tenir feu et lieu*) and clear two arpents a year.[44] "One should consider," the supérieur of the Seminary declared, "that if all voyageurs who abandon their habitations and take them up again when they please are allowed to do so, the seigneurs will be unable to dispose of their land, and should peace be restored and the troops have leave to settle, we will be forced to grant land beyond the rapids, because the fur traders have claimed all the other lots."[45] The authorities were distressed by the abandonment of land, which jeopardized the proper running of the seigneury. The woods sheltered harmful fauna, cast shadows on the fields, and further inconvenienced the neighbours by breaking the continuity of the *côte*, forcing those on either side to build the road segments that ran along the abandoned properties.

The major culprits were the bachelors who joined the fur trade, but one should not forget those unlucky settlers who lacked the stamina and requisite skills to make it through the first years or were not cut out to be peasants. They gave up, and usually went back to France unless they were married, in which case they moved to town, where they continued to live in dire poverty.[46] One comes across a few small-time speculators who hoped to benefit from the location and development of adjacent holdings, and sell at a profit what they had got for free.[47]

These censitaires did their best to hold on to their lots, hoping to find either tenants or buyers. Otherwise their holdings reverted to the demesne, despite their opposition. The process of repossession cannot be quantified because it is not sufficiently well documented. It possibly involved as many as 150 censives between 1642 and 1731, or 15 per cent of the total. There were also a number of voluntary departures.[48]

While some abandoned their land and some lucky ones managed to rent worthless holdings, others sold theirs. From a hasty survey of the deed titles in the notarial records one might well conclude that there was an active real-estate market. Closer examination of the content of these land sales, in five sample periods, reveals the true state of affairs.[49] (See Table 32.)

Once transactions involving land-clearers claims (which do not imply cession of the lot) and lands located outside the seigneury are eliminated, the number of land sales in the Island of Montreal is relatively small.[50] The movement of land grants, more than the economic situation in each decade, commanded the volume of sales. On average, about 5 per cent of holdings changed hands every year. Basically, the condition of these differed little from that of abandoned holdings. They were practically uncleared, and if there was any building it was no better than a log cabin or a wretched *pièce sur pièce* house. They sold for between 30 and 50 livres, the amount

Table 32
Sale of farms on the Island of Montreal in the seventeenth century

	Periods				
	1649–63	*1667–70*	*1680–81*	*1690*	*1700*
Number of sale contracts	38	57	31	27	32
Sale of farms	24	52	27	11	29
Approximate number of farms	(50)	(150)	(250)	(350)	(500)
Sale within a year of the concession	3	34	1	3	19
Sale two to six years after the concession	19	14	1	1	1
Sale six to ten years after the concession	2	2	–	1	2
Sale more than ten years after the concession	–	2	8	6	7
Unknown	–	–	17	–	–
Sold by the first owner	10	28	7	5	17
Sold by later owners	14	23	13	4	12
Unknown	–	1	7	2	–

Source: Records of all the notaries working on the Island of Montreal in these periods.

representing the arrears in seigneurial dues, the cost of surveying and of the notarized land deed, and in some cases the value of clearings and building. Every lot sold less than six years after it had been granted basically answered to this description.[51] If it had been occupied longer than that, it was likely to be an unfinished, partly cleared property, with a few hand-tilled arpents that were neither ploughed nor stubbed, with crumbling edifices, which would be reckoned at 300 to 500 livres. Farms of such little value quickly changed hands as each buyer in turn proved unable to meet his payments and was forced to sell.

The buyers were mainly peasants who sought to increase the size of their holdings or even acquire some land in another *côte* on which to settle their children. Since they had no savings, they could not pay cash even when prices were low. Up to 1680 they needed only to provide a small down-payment, and the rest could be paid in equal instalments over several years, most often in wheat. Such agreements became more difficult to transact. The sellers and especially their creditors demanded to be paid on the spot either in cash or with card money. We should not be misled by the cash exchanged in the presence of the notaries, for the peasants borrowed the wherewithal, and the merchant who advanced it might witness the signing of the notarized deed and keep it as security for the loan. Those habitants who could borrow from the seigneurs in return for a *rente constituée* were in a better position. Land purchases were the main factor in peasant indebtedness. Some of the buyers were young men from the region who used their share of their inheritance or the wages they earned from their trips out west to acquire a somewhat productive farm, rather than staking wooded concessions.[52] The usual pattern was for immigrants to clear the land and open up the *côtes* while older settlers took over the partially cultivated lots of those who gave up.

These deeds of sale shows that peasant patrimony was not often sold on the market. A good farm with forty arpents of arable land, a meadow, and some buildings was worth at least 1,000 livres. There were no more than about twenty such sales in our sample, and half the sellers were either merchants who left the colony, couples without heirs, or religious communities. The buyers were a mixed lot: religious communities once again, merchants, two innkeepers, a miller, a locksmith, two habitants, and five voyageurs.[53]

Thus first impressions of high rural mobility, gleaned from administrative sources and notarial records must be tempered. Migratory patterns cannot be adequately measured because of the rarity and inadequacy of enumerations. It would be an overwhelming task to identify all of the owners on the island and locate their holdings. Without going to such lengths, it is nevertheless possible to see from the census that with three exceptions, the 111 families listed in 1666 still lived in the seigneury in 1667, while only 6 of the 27 bachelors remained. Over a longer period, 97 of the 123 families established on the island in 1667 still resided there in 1681. But all this remains somewhat vague since we have no proof that these families had been enumerated on the same habitations fourteen years later.

It is useful, therefore, to examine the process on a smaller scale, as in the two *côtes* of the parish of Pointe-aux-Trembles, Sainte-Anne and Saint-Jean, surrounding the fort, or village. (See Table 33.) This rectangular territory stretched two and a half *lieues*, while it varies in breadth from twenty to forty arpents, depending on the nature of the ground. The overall area covered two thousand arpents and could not be extended, as it bordered on the river and the interior *côtes*. The plots had been gradually conceded between 1669 and 1680, at a time when notarized deeds were not used systematically.

This particular example exhibits all the features encountered earlier. Mobility was high in the decade following the original con-

Table 33
Movement of property at Pointe-aux-Trembles between 1681 and 1781

Year	1681	1702	1731	1781
Enumerated landowners				
Grantees	20	–	–	–
Buyers	26	–	–	–
Total	46	–	–	–
Landowners on the following roll:				
Same family as on previous roll	–	41	41	–
New owners:				
Grantees	–	2	–	–
Buyers of recently conceded land	–	4	–	–
Buyers of older farms	–	5	9	–
Total owners	–	52	50	53

Source: AC, G1460; map of 1702, NA, Hi 340; Aveu et dénombrements, 1731 and 1781 in RAPQ (1941–42) and C. Perrault, Montréal en 1781.

cession. Over half the holdings changed owners before they were cultivated.[54] After the first decade, ownership proved less erratic. Four of the five habitants who sold their farms between 1681 and 1702 had died either prematurely or without any children. The seigneurs granted six new lots around 1692–97, bringing the total to fifty-two habitations on the two côtes, a figure that remained practically unchanged. Although the habitants had large families, holdings were not fragmented. Between 1702 and 1731 most of the land was purchased by sons of local habitants, and the same last names began to crop up time and again.[55] A glance at the situation in 1781 reveals the long-term trend. By that date the village, not included in the table, had grown to 38 houses, from 20 in 1731. A tighter network of kinship linked the habitants. Population density had not changed over the century, although properties increased in size and were more apt to be subdivided than those in the Côte des Neiges, examined earlier.[56]

4 INHERITANCE

How is this stability related to the system of inheritance? Based on their reading of customary law, historians have rarely failed to observe that until English practices were introduced in these parts, habitants could not leave their land to one heir but had to carve out equal shares, generation upon generation, ad infinitum. This would account in part, so the argument goes, for the backwardness of agriculture in the province.[57] The royal ordinance of 1745 would appear to lend weight to such an interpretation. It forbade habitants to build houses on properties with less than fifteen perches of frontage, in order, so it went, to end the excessive fragmentation of holdings that had brought on the harvest shortages of 1737–38 and 1742–44.[58] This curious regulation, hastily put together on the strength of some alarmist report, is invalidated by the seigneurial enumerations made circa 1730. The norm in the colony remained one house for every twenty or thirty perches.[59]

Those who speak of fragmentation fail to do one thing: examine the Quebec countryside today. One must search very hard, in places left untouched by urbanization, to find the slightest subdivision, and anyone who knows something about the size of the original concessions will easily observe how little the holdings have changed: they remain long and narrow, and small by American standards. Even the acute land hunger of the nineteenth century failed to alter this pattern.[60] An average farm on the island of Montreal covered eighty arpents in the early eighteenth century, as it did in 1851 in those parts still devoted to agriculture.[61] Can one not argue that the subdivision of holdings in France was related in part to the collective forms of farming? There, a peasant could survive on a small parcel of land because he had access to communal pastures and forest. Supplementary income from rural industry had the same effect. Without such complementary resources and given the agrarian individualism that prevailed in Canada, fragmentation was impossible. The habitant had to draw everything from his own land, and if it was too small, he sold it, became a day-labourer or emigrated. There was no middle ground.[62]

The relationship between the family and local inheritance customs is examined further in chapter 13. At this point, in order to explain the agrarian structure, it is important to state that despite the strong egalitarian tendencies of this society, land itself was not actually divided. When the marriage community was dissolved at the death of one of the parents, half the land was apportioned equally among heirs, and they similarly shared the other half upon the demise of the other parent. If there were five heirs to a sixty-arpent property, each would eventually receive two strips measuring two by three hundred perches. They drew lots, and the one who got the strip with the buildings had to return their value to the estate. Then four of the beneficiaries sold their "inheritance rights" to the fifth.[63] If the deceased left behind two properties of unequal value, each was divided by the number of heirs so that the shares could be evaluated more easily.[64] The division was always theoretical, and the cession of the shares restored the original holding.

When the father died first, which happened in a majority of cases, the heirs and their mother, if she did not remarry, would keep the estate intact until one heir requested its division. When that happened, whoever had claimed his share would sell it to one of the siblings, represented by a guardian if he was under age. One after another, sons leaving home and married daughters would negotiate their rights. Co-ownership most often involved minors who resided with their mother or with an older brother who had opted to keep the farm. Remarriage could hasten and complicate matters. When two or more heirs wanted the farm or disagreed about its worth, it was put up for auction, and the bidding determined the value of the shares. The creditors might sometimes demand an auction to establish the value of the mortgaged property. Outside bidding was then accepted, but, as merchants did not invest in land, one member of the family sometimes managed to recover the property.[65]

Some habitants left behind a number of farms or unusually large properties. This was true of the best farmers among the first generation, who received generous concessions and acquired many uncultivated lots. Although only the original concession tended to be properly cultivated, the rest did allow a genuine partible settlement. Therefore, it was unusual for the biggest habitations to remain intact. Land accumulation should be viewed as a strategy to provide for children rather than a trend towards large-scale agriculture. The successful habitant did not hoard his money. He naturally invested it in land for sons and sons-in-law. If large families automatically meant a greater subdivision of assets, it was also true that the presence of several older children stimulated and ordered the extension of the paternal property. René Cuillerier provides a good example. He accumulated several rural and urban holdings that he gave to his sons as advances on their inheritance.[66] One might also mention Toussaint Baudry, who left four properties behind – three lying one beside the other – which were split into eight shares so that each of his four sons, after compensating siblings, held 120 arpents.[67]

This pattern of extension and contraction of properties continued generation after generation, although generally on a smaller scale. An increase here balanced off a neighbour's loss there, and the rhythm paralleled the family's needs and ambitions, ordained by premature deaths and marriage strategies. It must be noted that this method of passing on property left peasants permanently in debt.

Whoever took on the farm assumed a heavy burden, for he often had to borrow in order to acquire his siblings' shares. It had taken the father thirty years to build up the holding; it now took ten to fifteen years for each generation to unencumber it. The *obligations* and *rentes constituées* strewn among the habitants' liabilities are usually related to such family transactions.[68] From a stable central core, the agricultural settlement gradually extended outward. The nucleus was bound to remain economically weak, for it bore the costs of colonizing the periphery.

CHAPTER TEN

Running the Farm

Few administrators or visitors who passed through the colony expressed any interest in Canadian agriculture before the end of the eighteenth century. Administrators might mention the bad harvests and the occasional very good ones, or complain about how slowly the land was being cleared and how often it was abandoned, but one is hard pressed to find in the official correspondence any details about the utilization of the soil or agricultural methods. The perfunctory agricultural surveys forwarded annually to Versailles bore no useful additional comments. Those who penned memoirs of New France dwelt on Indian customs, the local flora and fauna, cityscapes, military events, the fur trade, and some activities such as fishing, but seldom agriculture. These seventeenth- and eighteenth-century men were sensitive to the exotic and the picturesque, and more and more impressed by the austere beauty of the landscape. They were not interested in the settlers. As Pierre Goubert noted, they were "more sensitive to differences than to similarities they deemed self-evident, pertaining as they did to life in the country and to the peasants. What was evident to them may not necessarily be clear to us."[1] It remains that much less clear since it was not until the early nineteenth century that newspapers, memoirs, and travellers' accounts began to include descriptions of, and judgments concerning, French-Canadian agriculture.[2] It so happened that contemporaries with an interest in the question were Englishmen steeped in agronomic literature, who compared the habitant's methods to those that prevailed on the large estates of England, which were the models of progress of the time.

There is little doubt that Canadian methods left much to be desired both from their perspective and from ours, but it might be useful to place these in the context of the traditional agriculture familiar in both France and England in the seventeenth century.[3] What needs to be established is how colonial methods differed from those current in Europe at the same time.

Our information is based mainly on post-mortem inventories and rural leases, and applies to the average farm at its most developed.[4] Its various components look something like the schema put forward in Table 34, which we will now examine in detail.

1   THE FIELDS

Wheat was the dominant cereal, a northern variety chosen because it ripened quickly. It was well suited to Montreal's heavy, humid soil, more so than rye, which thrives on drier ground.[5] Little rye was harvested in Montreal, and hardly any barley. Oats ranked second in importance, followed at some distance by corn, originally known as *blé de Turquie* or coarse millet. Unlike their New England counterparts, the French colonists never substituted corn for wheat, even if they sowed small measures among their traditional crops.[6] If necessary they mixed corn or oaten flour into their wheat, made gruel out of it, and fed the surplus to their animals.[7] A whole range of legumes, encompassing a large number of indigenous varieties, were classified as pulse (*pois*) in the censuses. Leases contain an occasional reference to green peas, white peas, chick peas, beans, "faizoles" or *faveroles*, which were grown on the fields for the family soup or as food for the pigs. Depending on the year, wheat could represent as much as three-quarters or two-thirds of the total produce. However, since most of the newly cultivated plots were sown almost entirely with wheat, it is more than likely, given the sharecroppers' seed allocation, that on fully developed properties nearly half the harvest would consist of pulses and secondary cereals.

Fibre plants only made their appearance in the first quarter of the eighteenth century. Around 1668, Talon, the colony's first intendant, made some moves to encourage their cultivation.[8] The attempt was premature and reflected his lack of knowledge of the local situation, for if flax and hemp grew easily, they required heavy investments in time and labour.[9] The settlers, who had not cleared or sown a sufficient amount to ensure their families' subsistence and did not have grown-up children to help them, had other priorities. Flax would appear in good time, without special subsidies, on developed farmsteads with a large domestic labour-force. The cultivation of hemp, stimulated by demand from the shipyards in the early eighteenth century, would never be considerable. The habitants grew some white tobacco, which had to compete with an imported black variety.

Table 34
Division of a typical farm

Composition	60-arpent farm (%)	100-arpent farm (%)
Courtyard, vegetable patch, buildings	3	2
Arable land	58	35
Meadows	8	5
Wooded and untilled segments	31	58
Total	100	100

When a tenant-farmer leased a property, he agreed to plough, cultivate, and sow it with good grains in the appropriate seasons and to observe the usual crop rotation ("sans les dessoler ny dessaisonner"). Would the customary phrase have been used if crop rotation had not been practised in the colony? That is what every historian has claimed, based on the testimony of Pehr Kalm. He noted in 1749 that the soldier-landclearers who manned the Canadian frontier around Lake Champlain cultivated a plot until it was exhausted, let it lie fallow thereafter, and went on until they had used up all the land, then started all over again.[10] Fernand Ouellet and Jean Hamelin computed the colony's grain yields on the basis of this mistaken impression.[11] We know, however, that a large part of the holding was never tilled, and leases as well as inventories leave no doubt that the fields were divided into sections as soon as possible. Given a system of individual cultivation, there could be no fixed rule. One comes across specific references to triennial rotation: "The said taker will have to create three sections, one third sown with wheat, one third with minor crops, while another third lies fallow." Land was leased with the "middle piece lying fallow" or as "ten arpents four perches of arable land where one third is at present fallow."[12] The documents show that the autumn fallow, sown in wheat the following spring, which the outgoing tenant-farmer was supposed to have ploughed three times, often covered one-third of the arable land. The fact that over half the leases in the seventeenth century lasted three years and slowly replaced the older five-year leases strengthens the argument. This is not to say that the practice was universal – far from it. It looks as if the best land was usually divided into three sections while biennial rotation was common on a majority of farms. In that case, half of the surface lay fallow each year, while the other was sown with wheat, peas, and secondary grains, at a 3:1 ratio in favour of wheat.[13] There is no doubt that the habitants did not always follow a strict pattern and that the size of the sections could vary from year to year. They certainly worked the fallow (as its name of *guéret* clearly implies, for it refers to a field that has been ploughed but not sown), turning it over at least once or twice, but no more than three times.[14] With proper husbandry, the soil proved sufficiently rich to recuperate after only one year of fallow. Productivity could be maintained by moving the crop of peas regularly.[15] The *côtes* were dotted with "spoiled" fields, which had only been cleared half way, had not been ploughed over, and where the lightly raked soil no longer yielded anything. The habitant who took them over began by clearing the fresh growth and let the land rest for several years.[16] However, given the limited size of holdings and the need for an indefinite supply of firewood, temporary cultivation was out of the question for the great majority who aspired to be farmers and not perpetual landclearers.

Rotation was crucial because most of the land was not fertilized. Tenancy leases often specified that the lessors would have to cover the fields and meadows with stable manure, to "clean their stables once a year and cart the dung on to the fields except for fifty cartloads reserved for the garden and vegetable patch."[17] The hospital made money selling manure from its farm.[18] Everything seems to indicate, however, that only a minority of farmers, the seigneurs, and a few notables were concerned about fertilizing their fields. When Julien Blois, a retired farmer, prosecuted his tenant for not taking proper care of his plots, the latter admitted "that since he was going to throw the manure in the river like everyone else, he had given it instead to a neighbour who had spread it on his own land."[19] The basic problem was that the average farm did not produce sufficient manure to fertilize its fields adequately. It had few animals, and the custom of butchering before the winter to save on feed further reduced the possibilities. In short, the vicious cycle that plagued traditional agriculture operated here also.[20] There is ample evidence that vegetable gardens and meadows were properly fertilized.[21] If anything was left after this operation, few bothered to lug it on to the fields. No one attempted to collect the urban manure and cart it to the *côtes*, and whatever could not be used in the garden or vegetable patch was dumped in the river when the time came to clear out the courtyards. Besides, most of it was pig refuse, considered worthless. There was a widespread belief in the colony that fields located on good soil did not need any fertilizer "because the snow and very low temperatures kept the humidity in, and as it was locked in till spring, it manufactured a type of salt that ensured the speedy growth of the crops."[22] If administrators were prepared to believe this, should one be surprised by the habitants' negligence?

They were, in fact, much more concerned with draining their fields and especially their meadows, hard and costly work that was sometimes carried out on a co-operative basis. Seven habitants of the Côte Sainte-Marie signed a collective agreement to dig a nine-foot gulley along the front of their holdings. This would allow them to drain the waters that flowed from the perpendicular ditches located between their properties and direct them towards the river.[23] Habitant assemblies voted to finance the most urgent drainage. Leases commonly required that ditches be kept clean. Diligent farmers, bothered by their neighbours' inertia, had to call on the intendant time and again to make them "dig a channel for the waters that ran through their land," to avoid flooding.[24] Nevertheless, despite the evident good will of most of the peasants, it proved impossible to drain these low-lying fields adequately, given existing technology.

The habitant's stock of implements was representative for the period. The principal agricultural tool was the pick-axe, which often substituted for the plough. It was made of iron, as were spades, hoes, sickles, and scythes, while the two-pronged pitchforks and the shovels were made of wood. Hand tools also included hatchets, billhooks, a few carpentry tools, all-purpose chains, winnowing sieves, and compost hooks. Every peasant would own this assortment; what differentiated them was traction. The wheeled plough, with its ploughshare, coulters, two wheels, chains, iron bolts, axle bands, and what appear to be two handles and stationary mouldboard, was introduced in Canada in the early seventeenth century and does not appear to have changed subsequently.[25] It was a bulky, expensive implement that the Montreal peasants could not do without. But it did not dig deeply enough, and a century and a half later observers noted that only the surface of the soil was endlessly turned over.[26] It took a team of two if not four oxen to pull. The animals were harnessed two by two, yoked by the horns by means of leather straps.[27] This type of plough could be found on every middling farm. Poorer habitants' inventories sometimes mentioned a less valuable implement, which was never described.[28] The settler would spend a few years working his land with a pick-axe and, when it was ready for deeper ploughing, would use the services of a laboureur until he could purchase his own gear. Anyone in the Montreal area who had invested early in a good plough and team of oxen made a good profit.

An iron-wheeled cart with iron axles was worth about 1,000 livres, or twice the price of a plough, and was confined to the wealthier farmers. The average peasant fashioned himself a makeshift tumbril and put off most of his carting until wintertime. All that he needed then were good chains and the simple sleigh he had built. A poor-quality triangular wooden harrow would also be found on every farm.

The land was ploughed over completely in the fall. The sections about to be sown sometimes received a second dressing in the spring. Peas and wheat were sown as soon as the snow melted, from 15 April through the month of May, because the frost would not harm them.[29] Oats came soon after and then corn, once all danger of frost had receded.[30] The seeds were then covered by means of a harrow.[31] There are a few references to the cultivation of winter wheat, but the practice was not widespread and it is impossible to say whether the yields were any better. The fact that the seigneurs, who paid close attention to yields on their domains, planted in the spring would indicate the opposite. Some weeding would be done at the end of the spring, while the fallow would be turned over in summer.[32]

Wheat and pulses ripened in mid-August, and observers marvelled at the speed of the agricultural cycle.[33] Then came oats and finally corn at the end of September or early October. The habitant always needed extra help at the time of the harvest. Men were paid sometimes by the day and sometimes by the acreage.[34] It was cheaper to hire them by the month, for they could beat the pulses after the grain had been stored. Wheat was threshed as it was wanted, not before winter, however, for except in bad years the colony would not consume the new wheat before Christmas.[35] Threshing was another source of occasional earnings for settlers and labourers during the off-season. Straw went to feed the cattle, while the bales of "long straw" covered roofs, chairs, and other objects. The habitant would spend October and the first weeks of November plowing his fields and preparing for winter.

Until about 1675 tenant-farmers took over the farm in the fall, usually on the feast of St Michael but sometimes on All Saints Day or the feast of St Martin. Gradually thereafter they began to take possession in the spring, in March or early April, and this eventually became the norm. Twenty-three of the thirty-one leases examined between 1716 and 1721 started in the spring. The changeover is interesting because it reflects a quick adaptation to new conditions. The tenant who arrived in September took on the farm in mid-season, before the end of the agricultural cycle. Haycocks dotted the fields, the wheat lay bundled in sheafs, and the fields had not been ploughed. The new tenant would be left with the threshing and then be expected to divide the grains between the owner and the previous tenant, making do himself with the fodder left behind by the latter. Leases were short, tenants fickle, and the transition was anything but smooth. When the takeover was moved to the spring, once the granary was empty and the animals were ready for pasture, most of these problems disappeared. The lessee received everything from the lessor, which simplified the accounts. We can also assume that some people would have been tempted to take on a farm in the fall in order to spend the winter months in a decent house and enjoy five months of quasi-idleness, only to decamp in the spring. The new system offered better protection to the owner.

2 MEADOWS AND PASTURES

The average habitant usually owned a few arpents of natural meadow somewhere near his holding, which he supplemented with one or two hectares of cultivated grass. Meadows located on the river, on nearby islands, or in marshy areas in the interior had to be worked to yield minimally acceptable hay and were mostly used as pastures. When mown, they provided what was identified as "gros foin" or a mixture of coarse semi-aquatic grass, which did not fetch a higher price than straw, about ten livres per hundred bundles. Good farmers invested a lot of effort in planted meadows, and the fact that their monetary value rose over the seventeenth century while that of the wheat fields dropped or stagnated shows that good fodder was in demand. The chosen site was drained, ploughed, fertilized, and then sown. Pehr Kalm, the Swedish botanist who travelled up and down the colony in 1749, noted the presence of clover and other Eurasian grasses imported to America.[36] This "fine hay" was worth between 20 and 25 livres per hundred bundles. The habitants turned both new land and old sections of arable land into meadows. The lessors always insisted that tenant-farmers cultivate their meadows with care and protect them from wandering animals with fences. These enclosed meadows were exceptional in the otherwise open countryside.

July was haymaking season, and the grass was gathered in broad-based haycocks, rising eight to ten feet. When the peasants had no barns, or if these were too small, the haycocks would usually remain on the fields all winter long. The hay was valued by the bundle, whose average weight is unknown. Meadows were often leased in a separate contract, which sometimes stipulated an equal sharing of the produce but more commonly required a cash payment.[37]

Animals were put to pasture on communal grounds that had been conceded on an individual basis to those people who lived alongside. This was no real collective tenure, for each was responsible for the section beside his own property. Wherever low-lying fields had been considered good meadowland, they had been granted as common, but it did not follow that all farmers in the vicinity had automatic access.[38] Should the need arise, the seigneurs felt they were entitled to take back these pastures and use them for some other purpose.[39]

In the interior, a tract of forest in front of a *côte* was set apart for a common, and access was more equitable. However, as absent or negligent censitaires often forebore to fell and clear their portion, others preferred to renounce such ambiguous tenure and asked that the space be apportioned individually.[40]

No special place was set aside for pastures on the farm itself. The children led the animals on to the commons and, where there were none, on to the wasteland at the edge of the woods, on to the fallow, or along the roads. A few habitants let young animals roam freely in the St Lawrence archipelagoes. When the waters ebbed, the animals, branded beforehand, hopped from island to island.[41]

The fields were not enclosed. There were no hedges along the ditches. The habitant with rocky soil would try to bank it when he cleared his plots, but this did not provide sufficient protection. Only the gardens, meadows, and the front of concessions that abutted on the commons were fenced in with cedar stakes.[42] The properties themselves were almost never separated by fences.

Oddly enough, the habitants added a seasonal pattern of collective pasture to their system of individual farms, with foreseeable problems. Unlike access to the communal grazing grounds, which was basically an individual prerogative, *vaine pâture*, or the right of pasturing animals on the fallow, applied to everyone equally and was regulated by the courts. Horses and cattle were customarily allowed to roam freely from the end of the winter until the first of May. An ordinance reminded the habitants when the deadline had passed and that they now had to keep their animals in until all the grains had been harvested.[43] In the last week of September or first week of October at the latest, the *bailli* allowed "the animals to wander through the fields, but not on the meadows fenced in by hedges or stakes, to let them rebuild their strength before the long winter."[44] The habitants protested when animals were let loose in non-authorized periods, and such negligence was fined at three livres per head of cattle (ten livres as of 1674), above and beyond the damages collected by the owner of the field. A few peasants went to court over the issue, but most of the lawsuits involved damage done by pigs, who had to be kept in their pens at all times or else be ringed or collared.[45] These regulations could not have been well observed, for the law sanctioned the killing of any pig found on one's fields.[46] The habitants did just that, and in 1687 a new ordinance forbade them from killing more than one pig at a time.[47] Pigs outnumbered cattle, caused more harm, and often belonged to unscrupulous, ill-established settlers.

By prosecuting owners who let their animals wander off in the summertime, the administrators were slowly undermining the right of pasture on the fallow. They argued that the herds damaged the plowed ridges and endangered the winter wheat, that they interfered with the ploughing, broke doors and fences, and threatened individual safety.[48] There is no doubt that the *vaine pâture* contributed nothing to the biggest farmers, who had large areas in fallow and other good grazing areas on their land. The intendants insisted that the fields be enclosed. Any habitant could ask that a fence and a ditch be built at his and his neighbour's expense. If the latter refused, he was forced to repay his share at the rate of 30 sols per working day, materials included.[49] The expense was considerable because the farms were sometimes more than two kilometers deep. Enclosures advanced extremely slowly, and the court continued to regulate collective pasturing on the island long after the 1725 decree of the Sovereign Council abrogating such practices in the colony. The reiteration of the ordinances shows that this last vestige of communal practices still survived in some *côtes* at the end of the eighteenth century.[50]

3 LIVESTOCK

Cattle were brought to the colony very early and multiplied rapidly.[51] Table 35 summarizes the distribution on the Island of Montreal at the time of the first two censuses. Since the data include both urban and rural stock and do not specify the age and sex of the animals, they tell us very little. Those who owned four head of cattle usually had about twenty arpents "under the plough," while new settlers had none. Post-mortem inventories of peasants who had spent at least fifteen years on their farms and tilled between twenty and forty arpents give a much better idea of the size of the herds. (See Table 36.)[52]

The average habitant would be likely to own a team of oxen and make do with two or three cows. He kept very few young animals, barely enough to renew his stock. Raising livestock was secondary

Table 35
Cattle distribution on the Island of Montreal in 1667 and 1681

		Number of cattle				
Year	Number of owners	0	1–3	4–6	7–10	More than 10
1667	143	65	40	22	10	6
	(100%)	(45%)	(29%)	(15%)	(7%)	(4%)
1681	283	92	87	51	36	17
	(100%)	(33%)	(30%)	(18%)	(13%)	(6%)

Source: Census, AC, G1 460

Table 36
Average number of cattle per farm on
the Island of Montreal, 1673–1717

Type of cattle	Mean	Mode
Plough oxen	3.0	4.0
Cows	2.5	2.5
Young	1.5	1.5

Source: Notarial Records (65 peasants' post-
mortem inventories)

to grain production, and everything centred on the plough team. The biggest and best farmers, the religious communities, and the odd officer or merchant who tilled over sixty arpents owned three or four pairs of oxen and a proportionate number of cows. Suckling calves were sold to make room in the barn and so were animals more than ten years old who had become useless. The aggregate censuses list the volume of livestock almost annually until 1739, and they do not show any tendency to commercialize butter or meat production.[53] The small surplus sufficed to feed the town and provide new settlers with young animals, but no more. This was the weakest point in Montreal's agrarian economy. Heifers were not separated from bulls and were covered too young, before they were two, and at all seasons. Leases that fussed over every aspect of husbandry stated nothing about the care of the livestock. Since they were kept so long in stalls, the animals had to be fed properly, but all evidence indicates that the fodder was inadequate and the habitants mixed straw in with the hay.[54] The cows' milk dried up during the winter. Bulls were castrated when they were about two and a half. Their horns were bound as part of the breaking-in process, which lasted until they were four or five, at which point they really became valuable. Nothing is known about the origins of this stock, where red-haired animals seem to have been dominant.[55]

The renewal of the lease of the seigneurial domain of Saint-Gabriel illustrates the pattern of cattle reproduction. (See Table 37.) The six cows had produced thirteen calves in four years, an average of one birth every two years, assuming none were lost. In turn, the seven young cows would have been bred at a very young age to produce the calves listed in 1708. This ensured the renewal of the stock but did not go much beyond the balance that an average peasant had to maintain to keep up his plowing team.[56]

The habitants cooked with lard, but added butter, salted or not, by the end of the seventeenth century. Anyone who had two or three cows would own a churn. There was some local cheese – the Hôtel Dieu's account book vouches for that – but it is not clear whether its manufacture spread as quickly as that of butter. Candles were made out of tallow, and animal hides were used for bedding.

Livestock leases were quite common. This was how most land-clearers acquired their first animals. The lessee had to provide a certain amount of butter in return for the leased cow and was entitled to keep half its young. Other contracts at a set monetary rate were perhaps more widespread, and the fee was usually hefty relative to the animal's worth.[57] The peasant who needed money might sell his animals to a merchant who then leased them back in return for a half-share or set charge. The seizure of animals for debt had been officially forbidden in France in 1662 and again in 1667. The royal ordinance, registered by the Sovereign Council, theoretically had the force of law in the colony.[58] Creditors, however, were not impressed, as the reiteration of the decrees makes perfectly plain. They got around these by harassing the peasants until they sold their stock, and these private transactions were often followed by notarized livestock leases, which tell us the story.[59] In 1707 the Quebec merchants told the Council that they could not collect their debts "since animals were the habitants' greatest assets" and the various extensions of the prohibition had long since expired. It was then decided that cattle could be seized, excepting two cows per farm.[60]

There were hardly any horses on the Island of Montreal in the seventeenth century. Those that were brought to the colony around 1665–72 seem to have gone to the gentlefolk, who were in no hurry to breed them. The wealthier peasants began to acquire horses around 1695, and the animals gradually spread to most farms.[61] Prices that had once been prohibitive fell to the point where horses

Table 37
Cattle on the farm of Saint-Gabriel in 1704 and 1708
(valuation in livres)

6 December 1704		6 December 1708	
2 oxen at 55 l.	110 l.	————————	100 l.
2 young oxen at 40 l.	80	————————	80
6 cows at 30 l.	180	————————	180
Total	370	————————	360
		New breed	
		2 young oxen at 30 l.	60 l.
		2 bulls at 20 l.	40
		2 male calves at 10 l.	20
		7 young cows at 23 l.	161
		2 heifers at 16 l.	32
		5 female calves at 10.1	50
		Total	363

Source: Saint-Gabriel lease to Hilaire Sureau and wife, 6 Dec. 1704 and 1708, PAC, M-1654, sec. IV, no. 15 (Raimbault).

became easy to acquire. Around 1710–15 there was an average of one horse per farm. This was a major victory for the habitant, for oxen had proved extremely ill suited to a role in local transport, getting stuck in the snow or the mud. Horses would reduce the isolation of the rural families and allow grain and firewood to be carted more easily and with fewer delays. Horses did not replace oxen, which continued to plough. Their number increased at the same rate as that of the rural population. A new element had been introduced, intended for a different purpose.[62]

The sudden, spontaneous adoption of the horse shocked the authorities. Here were peasants riding about partaking in what had once been the officers' prerogative. They were losing the healthy habit of walking ten to twenty kilometers, with snowshoes if need be, from their farms to the town. They were becoming effeminate, and the intendant, who foresaw in this innovation the speedy decline of the colony, prohibited any habitant from keeping more than two horses and a foal.[63] The regulation was superfluous because before 1709 horses figured only rarely in inventories, and even thirty years later the official maximum had yet to be reached. Habitants gradually learned how to build carriages, beginning with sleighs, which glided over the snow, and in the middle of the eighteenth century, when the roads were in better condition, calèches. The horse had lessened the settlers' isolation and made life somewhat easier.

The peasants raised poultry as well as pigs. A sizeable farm might have two to four dozen chickens but few ducks or geese. Turkeys were raised in some places. The average peasant would own no more than a dozen chickens and a rooster. Only the raising of pigs exceeded the family's needs. The habitant might have four or five, including a sow which, given proper feeding, produced three farrows of twelve piglets annually. The habitant saved on feed by letting his pigs loose in the woods. There was a demand for suckling pigs. Also, each year the habitant fattened some of the young animals with peas and corn before slaughtering them at the beginning of the winter and preserving them frozen or salted.

Except for the two or three flocks of fifty to two hundred animals owned by the seigneurs and other big landowners, habitants kept no sheep before the eighteenth century, when some might possess four or five, solely for the family's needs. The development of sheep-raising, accompanied by the appearance in the inventories of spinning wheels, carding combs, hackels, and so on, and by the cultivation of flax, signals a certain degree of security: the food supply had been assured, and the sheep could be fed in the winter without endangering either the cattle or arable. Diversification of this sort did not mean that agriculture was expanding towards the market but rather that it was achieving an ideal level of self-subsistence.

4 GARDENS AND FARM BUILDINGS

We know very little about the vegetable gardens that peasants tended next to their houses, for the produce was mainly intended for their own kitchens. Cabbage topped the list because it kept so well over the winter.[64] It had a wider market than other vegetables and would be delivered by the hundred. Root vegetables came next, mainly carrots and turnips. At the end of the seventeenth century the Hôtel-Dieu planted onions, shallots, garlic, cucumber, and chervil. This last herb was found in the wild in the colony before it was transferred into the vegetable gardens. Although people preserved local berries, such as blueberries or cranberries, they did not grow them. The colonists had, however, soon learned from the Indians how to sow pumpkins and melons – ordinary melons and watermelons – and various types of squash. Montreal melons were renowned throughout the colony.[65] Canadian flora aroused much curiosity, and once the complete works of the botanists Michel

Sarrazin, Jean-François Gauthier, and Pehr Kalm have been published we should know more about various attempts at market gardening in the early days of the colony. Sarrazin, a retired army surgeon
who spent a number of years in Montreal between 1685 and 1712,
corresponded regularly with his teacher Tournefort, and summaries
of his observations periodically appeared in the *Mémoires de Trévoux*
and the *Journal des Sçavans.*[66]

It seems that the settlers lost no time in taking advantage of local
plants and incorporating those that could be grown into their
gardens. They gathered anything that could prove useful: medicinal
plants like maidenhair, dyes like tamarack or celandine, *cotonnier*
and later maple for their sugar and nettles for their fibre, *vinaigrier,*
and finally the cattail, which made much better mattress stuffing
than straw.[67] Certain plants were added to the settlers' diet but none
as substitutes for what remained a basically European regimen,
heavily centred on bread. Leek, celery, beet, and other vegetable
seeds would be imported from France somewhat later in the eighteenth century, and would complement market gardening.[68]

The island held ninety arpents of orchards in 1731, scattered in
various parts of the town and on the slope of the mountain. They
belonged to the Sulpicians and to a few notables. The owners
produced their own cider and sold apples outside the seigneury.[69]
Habitants planted a few apple trees in their gardens for their own
table, for this was the only fruit tree that grew easily in this climate.

Until the early eighteenth century, the homes in the *côtes* were
small, wooden, one-room, shaky structures.[70] They had been assembled very simply with pieces smoothed at the corners and cob
joints, and rested on four joists that raised the floor. They could be
taken apart easily, and when the habitant sold his land he could,
therefore, "lug" his house away, even if he had to rebuild the cob
fireplace.[71] As late as 1731, 93 per cent of houses in rural parishes
still fit this description. In the vicinity of the town, however, a
quarter of the houses were built out of stone, and a solid Canadian
architectural style would make its appearance.[72] At first, outbuildings were erected haphazardly. The stable and the barn might lie
cheek by jowl as well as apart, stand separately or lean against the
house. More often than not, the settler turned his old log cabin into
a stable. The presence of a barn already signalled more than average
wealth. This was a large edifice, stretching over fifty feet, which
housed the threshing floor and the winter fodder. The switch from
straw roofs (most commonly used on such buildings) to wooden
ones, and the presence of other outbuildings such as a dairy, pigsty,
or chicken coop spread very slowly and only figures on a minority

of farmsteads in the period under consideration. Ice-houses, which impressed visitors so, would not be found in the countryside before the middle of the eighteenth century.[73]

On the whole we must conclude that there was a close resemblance between French agricultural methods and those that prevailed in the colony. To deny this and speak of an original colonial agriculture implies an image of the French peasantry, based on literary rather than historical sources, that disregards all the recent work that has shed light on regional as well as local diversities. Since most of the colonists came from the western *bocages* and especially from the Poitou countryside, since the agrarian economy in both places encouraged improvisation while both areas had to contend with problems of distance and uncertain profits, one must compare New France with those regions.[74] Canadian agriculture in the seventeenth century was neither better nor worse than that of most of the French provinces. Although initially fairly open to innovation, it soon fell back upon the constraints of customary practices, and the slow rhythms of a tradition that it had never renounced.

CHAPTER ELEVEN

The Agrarian Economy

1 YIELDS

Wheat production on Canadian seigneuries never moved beyond the limits of traditional agriculture. Between 1820 and 1850, before the introduction of new techniques, it retreated drastically in favour of potatoes, barley, oats, hay, and eventually dairy farming. In the second half of the century the rural population, spreading beyond the confines of the valley on to practically sterile plateaux, combined a poorer sort of agriculture with employment in the forest industry.[1] The sudden transformation of the traditional husbandry practised in the old farming area, especially in the Montreal region, deprives us of a solid base on which to build a retroactive assessment of grain yields. Contemporaries and historians agree about the stagnation if not the gradual deterioration of agriculture over the preceding two centuries.[2] The habitant was indeed routine bound, but, given the lack of information regarding techniques and productivity under the French regime, we should be wary of pushing comparisons into the past. Besides, soil conditions varied widely from one corner of the St Lawrence valley to the next, and in the long term there could be significant differences in yields between the quickly eroded, thin soils on the north shore and the more fertile Montreal plain. Eighteenth-century observers did not take this into account. In fact, the productivity of the wheat fields was not properly assessed before 1760. Authors of memoirs, administrators with no grasp of the problem, or travellers in a hurry threw up a few figures which have been used to shore up the thesis of a deterioration in yields. These witnesses tended to overestimate the fertility of new land. One Sulpician reported that grain could initially be harvested at a ratio of 60 to 1.[3] "It is no exaggeration to say that [in 1659] one would reap as much wheat from a single *minot* as one now does from twenty-eight or thirty," the Hôtel-Dieu's chronicler wrote around 1700.[4]

The relatively abundant information for newly cleared plots reveals a fairly uniform picture: an arpent produced 6 minots in rent, which means a yield of 18 minots per arpent (20.5 hectolitres per hectare).[5] This is rather high but nowhere near the outlandish results one might have expected from seed-to-yield ratio, for as long as the land continued to produce at these rates, the settler sowed only lightly, all the more so since his partially cleared plot was still strewn with stumps and stones. He used a minot or a minot and a half of seed per arpent, and his yield hovered between 12 to 1 and 18 to 1. Such maximums were short lived. The results mentioned here approximate the balanced assessment of the Sulpician de Belmont and are slightly below those advanced by Pehr Kalm and those late eighteenth-century investigators who estimated yields on newly cleared plots as between 15 and 20 to 1.[6]

It is far harder to estimate the average yield on older lots that had lost their initial fertility and whose productivity depended on the quality of the soil and labour input. Using the census totals of arable land of wheat crops, historians have calculated average yields for the colony and for specific seigneuries. There are, however, good reasons to reject the method and question the accuracy of the results. We know that, depending on the time and the place, between half and a quarter of newly cleared land was not yet integrated into a system of rotation. Some of these plots, sown exclusively in wheat, yielded well above the average, while others were abandoned and hardly produced anything as they gradually reverted to a wild state. We also know that rotation was not uniform on older holdings, and that there were variations in the proportions of land planted in wheat and that sown with legumes and secondary cereals. It is pointless, therefore, to undertake any calculations that have to assume a uniform system of cultivation, with a given amount of seed per arpent, a three-to-one ratio in favour of wheat, and a fixed percentage of land sown annually. The method is flawed, as is shown by the inexplicable differences in yields from one seigneury to the next or from one year to the next on the same seigneury.[7]

For lack of other sources, it is best to examine thirty or so specific cases drawn from farm leases, post-mortem inventories, valuations of ploughed fallow or of crops, supplemented with other partial examples. Through the linkage of various bits of evidence, it is possible to establish the relation between seed, crop, and area sown in wheat on a few specific farms. The amount sown ranged between 1.5 and 2.5 minots per arpent, but in most of the examples at hand the peasant used 2 minots. Any farm that was reasonably well taken care of, meaning drained and rotated on either a biennial or a triennial basis even it if it was inadequately fertilized, produced between 12 and 15 minots per arpent (13.6 and 17 hectolitres per hectare), representing a seed-to-yield ratio of 7.5 to 1. This was true of the seigneurial domains and the property of some merchants, officers, and better farmers.[8] Most of the land would, therefore, have yielded less: between 7 and 11 minots per arpent (8 and 12 hecto-litres per hectare), or a seed ration between 4.5 and 6.5 to 1.

When one compares these figures with those that have been sug-gested for various parts of France in the seventeenth and eighteenth centuries, the argument that his colonial agriculture was an unprece-dented case of primitive husbandry, neglect, and systematic soil depredation is no longer convincing.[9] In fact the methods were fairly orthodox, as were the results. Using the data presented by Michel Morineau as a base of comparison, we see that the yields of a num-ber of farms – representing about 16 per cent of the island's arable land at the beginning of the eighteenth century – were more than adequate, on a par with those in northern France, the Paris basin, and other fertile regions. By contrast, productivity was mediocre on the majority of farms, as it was on three-quarters of French territory before the middle of the nineteenth century.[10] In fact, if Canadian yields excited so little curiosity or comment among administrators fresh from La Rochelle, Angoulême, or Bordeaux, could it not be precisely because these were exactly what they expected?

There should be some explanation for the disparities of yields in a region basically suited to wheat production. Except in a very few places the quality of the soil was not a factor. The means at the peasant's disposal could be much more significant. There is no doubt that religious communities and merchants capable of heavier investments seldom hesitated to undertake costly drainage, or to winter sizeable herds, or to plough the fallow several times over. It was not so much that they expected high profits, but only thus could they hope for a return on their property. Hard-working pea-sants who may not have had the wherewithal at the outset also managed to make the most out of their holdings. But the majority had no inclination to work their fingers to the bone just to make up for their initial lack of capital. Once they had attained the subsis-tence level, they did not undertake further improvements, dig more ditches, manure and plough the fallow, or increase their livestock and the size of their meadows. They stuck to a routine, and the rotation of their crops insured them fairly stable, if mediocre yields. In bad years, plots that had reached a ceiling of 4.5 to 1 barely

produced the amount of seed expended on them.[11] Should such conduct be blamed on the lack of farming experience of many of the
immigrants?[12] It does not seem likely. The job could be learned, and
there were many shining examples in the *côtes*. Rather than look for
cultural or psychological explanations, it would be more useful to
examine the overall context of this agriculture. The comparison
between the average mediocre yields on the Island of Montreal
between 1680 and 1715 and the higher ones mentioned by late
eighteenth-century investigators point to the importance of external
factors. Two people testified before the Assembly of Lower Canada
that the old properties produced an average of 10 to 12 minots per
arpent and that the seed-to-yield ratio lay between 8 and 10 to 1.[13]
Lower Canada was exporting wheat in this period, and prices were
very high. The lure of such profits proved a stimulus, and the
habitant showed renewed diligence in applying traditional agricultural techniques. The thesis that there was a gradual deterioration
both in methods and yields between the seventeenth and the early
nineteenth centuries has no apparent basis. At all times there were
both bad and good farmers, and, if anything, the latter became more
numerous once the market situation improved.

2 THE LIMITS OF THE MARKET

Given the lack of proper serial sources, Montreal wheat prices, on
which the following discussion is based, were collected from post-
mortem inventories and other notarized contracts, supplemented by
the well-kept account books of the Hôtel-Dieu and their monthly
price listings for the years 1698–1723.[14] The information for the
preceding period is highly uneven, and annual averages had to be
computed on the basis of six or seven monthly quotations, in some
cases only two. It was deemed necessary to use every scrap of
evidence on prices in order to delineate one of the fundamental
factors governing peasant behaviour: the depression of the rural
economy.

Such an unorthodox series called for a simplified presentation. It
is based on the harvest-year beginning 1 September, and calculated
in sols tournois and tenths of a sol, thus partly eliminating the fluctuations of the colonial currency but not those of the French one.
Conversion of the nominal prices in silver weight should use as a
base Colbert's livre, which remained stable between 1666 and 1684,
but this, like other statistical manipulation, such as index numbers
or moving averages, requires better, more complete data. It is hoped
that future researchers will correct these figures if need be. Yet,

despite all the reservations, this price series appears on the whole to be roughly accurate. Once the lag due to geographic location is taken into account, the prices fit those quoted by Jean Hamelin for the period 1674–1750, based on the Quebec Seminary's account books.[15] Some errors involving a few sols have probably crept in for those years with too few quotations, but they would not affect the overall trend.

Even if the series did not allow for the calculation of seasonal fluctuations, there are indications that these were not very marked, and practically non-existent in years with either low or average prices.[16] The Hôtel-Dieu's account books provide an example of pronounced monthly variations in 1699–1700. Since the previous harvest had been very good, stocks lasted until October, after which prices rose from 52 sols to 75 sols, climbing to 90 sols in March and 120 during the pre-harvest period, for the 1700 crop promised to be poor. In other years prices dropped even in summer, in anticipation of a plentiful harvest. From 1703 to 1707 the monthly price stayed at 30 sols, without the slightest rise at the end of the harvest year.

There is very little information on how the colony obtained foodstuffs before 1663. It took years for local produce to meet demand, and Montreal was in a more precarious position than Quebec. The trading post could more or less feed itself by 1659, but until 1668 the balance between population and food supplied was repeatedly threatened by the yearly influx of immigrants and the needs of the fur trade.[17] At some earlier date, the Quebec Council had fixed the price of wheat at 75 sols tournois to prevent speculation, and there is no better proof of a chronic shortage than the fact that grains continued to circulate at that rate in Montreal for some time.[18] But from 1659, prices achieved some autonomy, even if the regulation remained in effect until May 1665.

Short-term price movements were irregular and, on the whole, not very pronounced. Until 1688 the peak years measured against the preceding trough swelled to 29 per cent higher (1660–62), 12 per cent (1665–66), 66 per cent (1672–74), 25 per cent (1680–81), and all along the mean level drifted downwards. For the settler who came in 1660 twenty-eight years went by without a sudden shortage to remind him of the difficult years preceding his migration. The century's most severe crisis began in 1689. Military reverses compounded the agricultural setback. The island was invaded; the peasants abandoned their fields and sought shelter in the forts. Rain and mist destroyed the 1690 harvest. In 1692 caterpillars attacked a promising crop. This time the price swing was violent, with a fourfold increase from the 1685 trough. It would take until the Seven

Years' War to see a recurrence of such disastrous conditions. Recovery was slow, for the island was besieged and the fields lay abandoned. The town was full of refugees from other seigneuries, and this explains the high cost of wheat in 1696 (although the rise was no more than 87 per cent). Even with peace restored, the consequences of wartime population shifts, heavy damage to buildings, and the decrease in livestock accentuated the 1698–1701 cycle and prices doubled. Wheat production then entered a period of moderate fluctuations, marked by the 1703–06 slump and the continuation of the downward movement until the second quarter of the eighteenth century. Although prices expressed in card money between 1713 and 1719 were deflated according to the official rates, the perturbations due to colonial as well as metropolitan monetary upheavals, which were not completely eliminated, still blur the picture.[19] There would be a minor rise in 1713, followed by a drop (we know that harvests were good between 1714 and 1716) and a slightly higher increase in 1717–18.[20] The Montreal series ends in 1725, but thanks to the work of Jean Hamelin the trend can be represented up to 1750. Calculated by the calendar year and for the Quebec region, this series does not match the first exactly, but the general profile should be fairly consistent throughout the colony.[21] The bad harvests of 1736–37 and 1743–44 drove up prices on the order of 80 per cent. Other cyclical fluctuations proved as mild as those that had preceded the late seventeenth-century crisis.

The long-term trend is as plain as can be: a deep and protracted depression lasting three-quarters of a century. Prices only reached the pre-1670 level around 1745. Such is the trend revealed by nominal prices, but if the progressive devaluation of the livre tournois were taken into account (a 45 per cent decrease in value between 1660 and 1726), the decline would be spectacular, more marked, it would seem, than the one witnessed in various French provinces.[22] A rough comparison of the average price of a *setier* of wheat in Montreal and Paris, for example, with the Paris *setier* representing a base price of 100, shows that Montreal ratios moved from 97 for the years 1661–74 to 40.7 for the period 1705–17.[23] The depreciation of agricultural produce, the lack of accord between the cyclical peaks in the colony and the years of widespread shortages in France, demonstrate the colony's isolation.[24]

Prices of other cereals and livestock more or less followed the fluctuations in wheat prices, but the scarcity of quotations, the lack of precise units for volume and weight, and great differences in quality make it difficult to analyse their evolution.[25] In the early days of settlement a minot of corn was worth as much as a minot of wheat, after which the picture grows fuzzy. There was apparently a distinction between animal feed and corn intended for human consumption, whose value hovered near that of wheat. The variations for pulses could reach 30 to 40 per cent, depending on the vegetable. The prices of these products closely followed those of wheat in periods of high prices, falling behind in years of plenty. The movement in oats roughly agreed with that of wheat, though with more pronounced cyclical swings. Oats were not grown for human consumption but could replace wheat in times of shortage. Fodder production, it seems, was not sufficiently developed before 1725 to display an independent trend.[26] In any case, the long-term fluctuation in cattle prices mirrored the decline of wheat prices, but more strongly. (See Table 38.) Scarcity kept values high for about thirty years, but prices took a tumble between 1670 and 1688. When, from 1689 on, bands of Iroquois began to ransack the côtes and to slaughter cattle, there was renewed scarcity compounded by a shortage of fodder linked to the poor grain harvests. Prices climbed, but hard times had lowered demand. After the war, animal stocks were quickly replenished, and prices fell to such an extent that at the beginning of the eighteenth century habitants were loath to auction off animals as was customary upon the division of estates.[27] After the erratic fluctuations that characterized the period of monetary inflation, prices stabilized at a very low level. There is little data on swine and sheep prices but some indication of a long-term decline here also. Horse prices followed a different course. Few peasants could afford them before 1690. Once they were bred in the colony, however, their value fell very quickly. Around 1720 an ordinary draught horse cost less than plough oxen.

The Hôtel-Dieu account books list the monthly prices of some foodstuffs, but the span (1697–1723) is too short to permit any conclusions.[28] Moreover, can one really speak of a market price for poultry, eggs, milk, or butter? They were produced mainly for domestic consumption. Merchants might accept them for their own use in repayment of some debt, or as a favour to a customer, but townsmen who could afford such products usually had tenant farmers who provided them, and the traffic seems too limited to warrant close analysis of the prices. The market for beef and pork was somewhat livelier. Between 1696 and 1723 beef prices dropped 25 per cent, and through this whole period the value of a hundred pounds hovered around 40 per cent of the sum quoted for Beauvais.[29] Prices for pork, lean or fat, sold either by the pound or by the barrel, as well as those for pure lard, are too scattered.

The overall picture is fairly clear. The value of agricultural production declined, and the movement is underlined by the steady

Table 38
Average livestock prices on the Island of Montreal, 1650–1730*

	Average value at various periods (in livres tournois)						
Animals	1650–1670	1670–1680	1680–1689	1689–1700	1700–1708	1709–1720	1720–1730
Plough oxen (5 to 9 years old)	112–90	90–67	60–45	90–75	40–25	75–45	50
Milk cows	75	65–45	26–22	45–37	22–15	37–26	22
Mares	225	225	–	112–75	75–30	37–30	30
Lambs	–	–	–	11	4.5	4.5	4.5
Sows	18	18	6	–	10	–	8–10

*The quality of the animal affected its price. By looking at numerous quotations, it becomes possible to delineate the range in average prices of standard full-grown animals.

drop in farm prices. An arpent under the plough fell from 112 livres tournois before 1663 to 30 livres in 1668, and although it becomes impossible to find assessments per arpent after that point, its worth probably sank to about 20 livres in the early eighteenth century.[30] As long as cultivated land remained scarce and wheat sold for 75 sols a minot, rentes came to about 12 per cent. Once the habitants began to clear land in earnest, they foundered, and at the end of the century a landowner leasing his property was lucky to get a return of 2 to 2.5 per cent.[31]

The Sulpicians tried to get rid of their Sainte-Marie and la Présentation domains around 1683. The Parisian superior advised them that, "if indeed your other estates cost more to run than they produce, you would be well advised to sell them."[32] But they found no buyers, and two years later the issue came up once again. "People who understand the Canadian situation agree with you that the best course would be for the Seminary to get rid of as much land as possible."[33] "Land is worth nothing," the governor wrote in response to a suggested property tax. And he stressed that "with the depressed state of the colony and the daily drop in property values" it was impossible to tax anything except furs and imported goods.[34] In 1705 the seigneurs were still thinking of selling a fine piece of property: four hundred arpents of meadows and arable land.[35] Lastly, as we have already established, good farms hardly ever went on the market. Sellers were few because the price they could get did not compensate for the labour they had put in. The buyers were mostly peasants who were looking for means of subsistence rather than for a source of profit.

3 PRODUCTION AND SUBSISTENCE

"Non-value and abundance do not spell wealth; high prices and scarcity spell misery; abundance and high prices spell affluence," wrote François Quesnay.[36] Between 1642 and 1750 Montreal experienced some hard times. A collage of administrative testimony extending down through the period could easily suggest a darker reality than one which was in truth characterized by abundance and non-value.[37]

There were no outlets for local grain in the seventeenth century. Some people, eager to meet the initial demand and expecting that price controls would remain in effect, paid dearly for land and disbursed more to put it quickly under the plough, only to find themselves in straitened circumstances once immigration slowed down. The authorities concluded as early as 1669 that exports were the only solution.[38] But the sizable and reliable returns from the fur trade monopolized the attention of Canadian and Rochelais merchants. One could hardly find two ships a year to convey a bit of the surplus to the West Indies, where Canadian flour was not appreciated and could not compete with equally cheap metropolitan flour, which cost less to transport. And what would the ships carry back?[39] War as well as the uncertainties of oceanic travel delayed the commercialization of grain until the eighteenth century. Intercolonial trading revolved then around Louisbourg and was fuelled by the lag between Canadian prices and those of other exporting regions.

The town was too small to act as an important internal market. The habitants came to sell their eggs, chickens, vegetables, and other goods, but it was not a regional redistribution centre for grain. Unregulated deals between producers, bakers, and merchants were struck in the countryside.[40] In 1721 the town major arbitrarily decided to move the market stalls because they interfered with manoeuvres. The peasants who were thus driven away protested that they would never set foot in the town again, and as a result of this squabble, markets were only held on Fridays.[41] Both the initiative and the reaction show how inconsequential the institution was.

Montreal's nascent agrarian economy might have found a useful outlet in government contracts to supply troops during military campaigns. But this solution ran counter to Colbert's express policy of limiting currency exports outside France, and conflicted with the interests of French suppliers.[42] So, despite the glut of unsold wheat in the colony, flour and lard were regularly imported to feed the troops during the seventeenth century. Local officials argued year after year that it would cost the king less to buy food in the colony;

that profits from such sales merely accrued to metropolitan merchants; and that it was impossible to speed up land-clearance under the circumstances.[43] The royal imports were sometimes re-exported, and the intendants occasionally bought up some local produce.[44] "Wheat costs more to produce than it sells for," the Montreal seigneurs complained.[45] The intendant reported that, because there was no market, parish priests were unwilling to collect the tithe themselves and could not find tithe-farmers.[46] Officials went so far as to rejoice over the heavy rainfall that had fortuitously reduced the 1672 harvest, for otherwise wheat would have fallen below thirty sols and the disheartened habitants would have sown less.[47] One intendant spelled out the situation:

The habitants do not grow hemp because they get nothing for it. Wool is plentiful, but there is no market. They have enough to ensure their subsistence, but since they are all in the same position, they cannot make any money, and this prevents them from meeting other needs and keeps them so poor in winter that we have been told that there are men and women who wander about practically naked.[48]

The poor harvests of 1690–92 took the colony by surprise. The intendant, oblivious of previous circumstances, denounced the improvidence of the peasants "who were no longer producing beyond their own needs."[49] The crisis, barely relieved by shipments of French flour, was very severe. Bakers stopped baking bread in the spring of 1691.[50] Parish priests distributed peas to the poor.[51] Although times were hard, this cannot really be ranked as a "subsistence crisis." It does not look as if any local group, merchants or others, profited from the scarcity. The Seminary was the only major producer on the Island of Montreal that gathered the produce of its domains, from the tithes and from the seigneurial dues collected in kind. But it did not speculate on the high costs of grain. On the contrary, the seigneurs made grain available cheaply to the authorities as a way of getting into their good graces. This policy paid off in the long run and helped the inhabitants during shortages, but when it was continued in years of plenty, it helped to push down local prices.[52] Until the end of Louis XIV's reign intendants kept a watchful eye over wheat prices, controlling export levels and still importing flour.[53] The spectre of the famines that were taking their toll on France made the intendants intensify their precautions, and even a spell of overproduction such as occurred between 1702 and 1710 left them unmoved. According to seventeenth-century ideology, protection of consumers prevailed over the producers' interests.

The sluggishness of the agricultural sector nevertheless continued to hinge on the colony's isolation and was merely compounded by official bungling.[54]

The overall trend can be summarized as follows. Until the end of the War of the League of Augsburg, the output in wheat and pulses increased 7.5 per cent annually, while population rose by no more than an average of 3.4 per cent. In the period following the crises of the late seventeenth century, despite faster and more regular land-clearance, crop production sags and aligns itself to that of the population, as if the settlers had given up producing beyond their needs and those of the towns. If we assess consumption norms on the basis of a soldier's ration in Canada at the end of the seventeenth century, then it took 580 grams of wheat to produce a daily ration of 522 grams of bread, with what was lost in the milling.[55] (See Table 39.) This represented 211.7 kilos, or 7.1 minots of wheat a year.

In the period 1668–90 the island produced much more than what was required to ensure this ration of bread to everyone. After 1700 the farms continued to produce 30 to 40 per cent more wheat than necessary for their own consumption and seed supply,[56] but this surplus was insufficient to provide the townspeople with the same ration. There was no real decline in production, as the amounts harvested annually in Longue-Pointe and Pointe-aux-Trembles amply prove. This land had been cultivated since the early days of the colony, and each farm still produced between 145 and 165 minots of wheat in the first quarter of the eighteenth century – enough, in other words, to feed three families once the seed had been subtracted.[57] But the town had begun to grow faster than the countryside. Non-producers represented one-third of the seigneury's total population between 1665 and 1710 and 45 per cent by 1731. Yet this expansion in local demand did not stimulate higher wheat production. If we replace the maximum ration by a more balanced diet suited to all ages and incorporate peas into our calculations, there is no doubt that the island was still able to feed itself. But Montreal merchants had to buy from other seigneuries the grain they exported or turned into biscuit for the trips west and the outposts.

This accords with the evaluation of the arable land on these farms: an initial impetus soon reaching a plateau. As it attained self-sufficiency, the agriculture seemed to turn inward. It might be useful to recall that the price of imported goods had been rising since 1690, while grain prices hardly rose before 1740. How unusual was the peasant's response? Need one really invoke a genetic incapacity linked to the immigrants' social origins, laziness, frivolity,

Table 39
Soldier's daily ration

	Grams	Calories*
1.5 pounds of bread	522	1,764
4 ounces of peas	112.24	374
4 ounces of lard	112.24	820
Total		2,958

Source: "Mémoire concernant la paie et le décompte des troupes en Canada," 10 Nov. 1695, AC, C11A, 13, 367–8. These figures are based on Michel Morineau "Marines du Nord" in J.-J. Hémardinguer, ed., Pour une histoire de l'alimentation (Paris, 1970), 100–125.

or some other traits nurtured on the fur-trade frontier to explain this behaviour?[58] As long as his minot of wheat was worth 30 to 40 sols, the habitant made no attempt to break into a market where he usually lost out. This was the crux of the matter. Crises deserve less attention, for they were not deadly and had no long-term impact on production. Given the narrow surplus margin, poor harvests automatically meant a shortage of bread. Yet people still found something to eat, however doubtful the quality, and they survived.[59] Abrupt swings in prices could not rekindle the peasants' interest in the market. A protracted rise was necessary to convince them that this was no freak occurrence, and incited them to restructure their farms to suit the new conditions.[60] But it was common knowledge that in Canada "shortage was a natural consequence of a too great abundance" and that the cycle would merely repeat itself.[61]

The normal Canadian diet, based on starches and pork, was rich in calories and proteins but poor in vitamins.[62] Butter, eggs, cabbage, onions, turnips, and salted eel supplemented the basics, as did fruit when it was available. Most farms managed to fatten two hogs a year and could count on fifty kilos of meat per person for a six-member household.[63] Peasants only drank water at mealtimes. Wine and beer were consumed at the tavern along with brandy, which was also a tonic on journeys and was doled out to building workers and sometimes to harvesters. The pattern of drinking seldom but hard may have been due to the secular absence of a cheap local brew with low alcohol content.[64] Though there was malnutrition, the population was not undernourished.[65]

Habitants had to produce beyond their immediate needs. Self-sufficiency was desirable, but no farm could be complety autarkic. First, there were debts to be met, debts that harked back to the initial land-clearance, purchase of the farm, or payment of inheritance shares. A certain amount had to be set aside to cover the tithes, seigneurial dues, taxes for public works, the establishment and upkeep of the parish, harvesters' and threshers' wages (if the domestic labour force proved insufficient), not to mention the services of the blacksmith and so on. This accounts for the regular surpluses. Habitants had to be thrifty if they wanted to meet their current debts, the unexpected expense of an illness, or the calamity of a death that caught them off-guard and caused the ruin of more than one family. The countryside was not prosperous.

There is no point in assessing the relationship between wages and cost of living since there were no full-time farm labourers. Habitants and their sons may have done a day's work here and there, but no one relied solely on such income. It merely supplemented the farm production. Soldiers competed with the urban poor for seasonal work on the farms, and this easily available pool of additional hands also militated against the emergence of a specific group of farm labourers, thus reinforcing the domestic character of the rural economy.[66]

4 CONCLUSION

These last chapters have traced the development, in the absence of external stimuli, of a tight interplay between family needs and the options open to the peasants. In the last analysis this interplay determined the level of productivity. The fur trade, often invoked to explain some of the failings of the agrarian sector, had only a marginal influence – not necessarily negative – and no long-term effect on the peasant family economy. Moreover, the basic features encountered in the Montreal region, such as methods, yields, or the checks on farm expansion, were probably similar in the rest of the colony, including those areas outside the fur-trade network. It is also irrelevant to look for explanations in the so-called overly generous policies of the state in matters of taxation and land distribution.[67] They also were dictated by necessity. A levy on surplus production only made sense if it was marketable. In the face of an unchanging external and demographic situation, taxation could do little except further deflate the internal market, impoverishing some without enriching others.

After the initial confusion following migration, a traditional society emerged spontaneously. Commercial capitalism was not aggressive, while the monarchy was only too happy to allow the growth of a peasantry that provided a base for future consolidation.

PART FOUR

The Society

Social relations in the colony evolved from the economies of production and exchange detailed in previous sections. yet the link was not straightforward. Original attitudes changed slowly, while the institutional apparatus transplanted overseas recreated the social divisions of the old world, which had emerged in a different place and a different era. The social structure was still in a state of flux in the period covered by this study. Understanding its evolution requires analysis of the administrative framework, the characteristics of the different social groups, and the two institutions closest to the people: the family and parish.

CHAPTER TWELVE

The Setting

For the first seventy years of its history Montreal was involved in wars broken only by brief spells of armed truce. Strife was so constant that it must rank as one of the dominant elements of everyday life.

1 WAR

Montreal, the strategic nerve centre of the French colony, experienced the many faces of war: fear, devastation, conscription, and occupation. The authorities must be credited for their ability to contain the excesses of locally billeted troops. Although these were disciplined soldiers and not marauding bands, their relations with the residents cannot be assessed solely through official reports, for it was certainly not in the staff officers' interest to detail disturbances for which they were responsible.[1] Indeed, if we set aside all cases involving soldiers or officers, the crime rate drops drastically and, given the period, Montrealers appear a rather peaceful lot. While the military were the more likely victims of brawls, duels, or murder, the civilian population did not escape altogether, for even had this violence been exclusive to the troops, it still would have had local repercussions.[2] Soldiers also committed the most thefts in both town and country. They monopolized counterfeiting and generally violated police regulations at least as often as did the settlers. Had the soldiers departed, half the taverns would have been empty. As for the officers, they had nothing but contempt for civil justice.[3] Unfortunately, none of this can be quantified because judicial records are incomplete and most of the evidence from court martials has vanished.[4] Nevertheless, it seems quite likely that soldiers rather than Indians were the more unruly elements in the seigneury.

The officers' failure to discipline their men sanctioned disruptive behaviour. In theory, soldiers were required to take part in musket and grenade drills three times a week; sergeants were given twenty-four hours to report deserters; and captains were forbidden to employ their own men in their personal service. Yet these injunctions were rarely obeyed and had to be reiterated by the ordinance of 30 May 1695, which stressed quartering procedures.[5] Private billeting was enforced in the colony. It affected all but nobles, judicial and administrative officers, and the ecclesiastical property occupied and farmed directly by the Church.[6] Fief owners were exempted until 1673, but it is not clear whether they managed to hold on to this privilege.[7] Some of the hundreds of soldiers stationed in the island lived in forts, while the rest lodged with families compelled to offer them utensils, a mattress, and room at the hearth.[8]

The allotment of billets had originally been decided by the settlers' representative, the syndic, but later it presumably devolved to the intendant's deputy, the subdélégué, in concert with a few bourgeois. The subdélégué also chose local men to assign billets in the countryside. This arrangement usually worked where the people involved shared similar social backgrounds or wherever cohabitation was combined with some form of labour.[9] When conflicts arose, the householders appealed to the officer in charge, but these complaints have not survived, perhaps because they went unrecorded. Some captains openly flouted local authorities. The Sieur Du Vivier declared that "he would bind hand and foot and forceably remove any settler who refused to billet soldiers." As for the unfortunate who had denounced him, he sat in jail for his presumption.[10]

In 1673 the town assembly decided to raise an annual tax to provide lodgings for the garrison. Accommodations would be leased until permanent barracks were erected.[11] Although the intention was to replace private billeting, additional troops were still placed in individual homes, as was the case with officers who disdained barracks life. The bourgeois in particular resented this added burden. Milot, an edge-tool maker, paid 100 livres' rent a year to be rid of the Sieur Caron, "whom it was his duty to lodge, for he hoped to put an end to their daily quarrels."[12] It seems that any who could preferred to pay to safeguard their privacy.[13] The intendant or subdélégué intervened when officers' demands exceeded the bounds of common sense, as in the case of Captain Subercase, who expected twenty cords of wood and twenty pounds of candles besides his lodging, costing his host 160 livres over four months.[14] In short, the presence of the military created problems and weighed heavily on a population already burdened with frequent calls for labour and cartage.

Whereas in France in this period war usually signified a rise in taxation, in Canada exactions mainly took the form of personal service. Montreal's first militia was established in 1663 under the command of the local major. All able-bodied men were divided into twenty squads, each electing its own corporal.[15] This primarily defensive, communally based force was revamped several years later when the government reorganized colonial institutions. All men except the handicapped and certain office-holders became liable for duty. Regrouped according to seigneury, district, or town, the militiamen had to purchase a rifle, drill and march off to war when "so ordered," with no other reward than their daily rations.[16] Relatively little information has emerged on how the system actually operated. On some campaigns the intendant ordered massive levies that drained town and country. In 1687 a third of all those over fifteen followed the governor on a distant expedition.[17] At other times only some of those liable for service were recruited, perhaps by lot, as in France. Two substitution contracts from 1684 hint at this for 30 livres purchased replacements for two heads of household aged forty-three and forty-four.[18] Such agreements were rarely overseen by notaries. Besides the militia, a small elite corps of volunteers was recruited among young coureurs be bois, whose enlistment gained them a pardon and who were sent on dangerous missions in enemy territory.[19] We should keep in mind that all the settlers and craftsmen were liable for service. There were no exemptions either for family responsibilities or for urgent agricultural work. The intendant assured those concerned about the fate of their harvest that the men who stayed behind, including vagrants, would replace them on the farms.[20]

Military levies were under civil jurisdiction, just as in France. In town, the responsibility fell to the syndic and, after 1667, the intendant's *subdélégué* assisted by the captains of the urban militia. These were notables, nobles, and merchants. The first took part in campaigns but the second did not.[21] By the eighteenth century membership in this corps, with its six or seven captains and one major, had become essentially bourgeois and primarily honorary.[22] Since the king maintained a garrison at Montreal, the militia did not ordinarily mount guard, and the urban population served on the frontiers.

In rural areas the intendant named a representative, a literate habitant of some standing, to draw up the muster, summon the men to drills, and serve as an intermediary between the administration and the rural populace. He assigned billets, organized the labour for public works, and gradually assumed numerous responsibilities.[23] In fact he took the place of non-existent village councils.[24] We know that he had trouble imposing his will, that he was not paid for his work, and that his duties took up much time, but it is not clear whether the honour of being chosen or the attendant privilege of following the churchwardens in procession was enough to compensate for all the inconvenience – as the intendant clearly expected.[25] These *capitaines de côte* or "militia captains" as they were sometimes called were usually middle-aged, and their services were deemed so valuable to the community that they rarely saw active duty. When they did, however, it was always in the ranks. They should not be confused with officers commanding the militia, and their position cannot be viewed as a means of social advancement.[26]

Members of the local nobility with military training led the forces, followed by their sons, who gained their experience from such service. The nine squadrons that set off from Montreal in 1673 for Iroquois country were staffed either by veteran officers of the Carignan regiment or well-born men who had come to Canada without commissions. Captains and lieutenants of the militia involved in the campaigns of the last two decades of the seventeenth century all came from such families, including the Lemoyne who benefited from recent enoblement.[27] The convergence between social status and access to commissions is obvious. By demonstrating their ability to command the militia, well-born Canadians eventually obtained commissions in the Free Companies of the Marine. The experienced soldier who had served the colony ten or twenty years without pay began to realize his dreams when he was named an ensign or lieutenant.[28] In the eighteenth century, these young men would be incorporated directly into the regular force. In the previous period, however, the officers were recruited in France, and the only way Canadians could accede to the military hierarchy and financial security was by distinguishing themselves as leaders of the militia.

These inducements must have stimulated the spirit and initiative shown under fire. Officers anticipated the governor's wishes, led war parties of Indians and Canadians to the far corners of colonial territory, and returned decimated but triumphant, frequently laden with spoils.[29] Meanwhile, the regular troops, who saw no reason to run risks, guarded the rear, harvested when needed, and kept up their strength. The settlers who took part in these forays clearly fought well. "Their feet are bloody," Frontenac reported, "but they keep up their spirit."[30] Yet rumblings grew frequent in Montreal in this period and some complaints even trickled into official correspondence. There was indignation that married men were called up while coureurs de bois continued to roam in the wilds; the populace was "most displeased" at being ordered out but had not "refused to march yet."[31] Guerrilla warfare caused numerous casualties, and failure to register them fostered the myth of a privileged population paying no taxes and playing at soldiering.[32]

The forays of the Indians and the British expeditionary forces into the Montreal area are well documented. The enemy never reached the town palisades but regularly laid waste isolated farmsteads, rekindling the ever-present fears of rural settlers, who paradoxically were poorly protected. It was easy to play on these fears and "harangue the masses" until they believed that continuing the fight elsewhere was their only hope of preserving peace at home.[33]

2 VIEW OF THE TOWN

In 1715 half of the 4,200 inhabitants of the seigneury resided in the town. Despite the small population, the rural and urban components cannot be studied together as one would do for a village society. Very rapidly they came to form two distinct societies, but before analysing them we must look inside the closed area of 37.6 hectares that was Montreal.

This small North American frontier town exhibited features common to the oldest urban centres as well as specifically seventeenth-century notions of spatial organization. Above all it was a stronghold, or so it claimed to be. The stockade, fashioned from posts struck into the ground and pegged together, had five gates, guarded and locked each evening at set times by the royal garrison supervised by the town major.[34] These measures aimed to protect the residents and regulate the movement of Indians and soldiers, shipments of trade goods, and new consignments of furs. Yet nothing was easier than to cross the palisade through gaps breached by the inhabitants. Lodged behind these paltry defences, Montreal became a place of refuge in the last decade of the seventeenth century. Victims of enemy raids and the terror-stricken poured in from the countryside and built temporary shelters within the walls, where room was still plentiful.

The inhabitants were responsible for the building and upkeep of the stockade.[35] In 1714 the government decided to erect stone fortifications, sixteen feet high, sporting bastions and other embellishments. The project was only completed in 1741, at a cost of 500,000 livres. The residents, who had contributed 4,000 livres annually, still owed the crown 164,808 livres, the remainder having been graciously remitted at the end of a bitter struggle marked by a number of violent incidents. It had been necessary to force the peasants to share in these expenditures on the pretext that they too would benefit from such an impregnable fortress. They had not been easy to convince.[37] The bourgeois, however, supported a plan they felt would embellish as well as increase the stature of their town and which, in the meantime, provided work and contributed to the town's development.

The more primitive aspects of this fur-trading post began to disappear between 1710 and 1730 as a result of faster demographic growth. The number of houses rose from two to four hundred.[38] As in the countryside, most were simple wooden cottages, or half-timbered, two-storey houses with an extra room or two, pressed one against the other. In the aftermath of the great fire of 1721, the use of stone became quite common, and according to the 1731 *aveu et dénombrement*, 44 per cent of dwellings were made from that material. Some even had three floors. The town boasted a rather impressive parish church and four convents as well as the Hôtel-Dieu and the Hôpital général near the city gates. These religious communities all undertook construction and renovation projects at the turn of the century. Public as well as private buildings of a commercial or industrial nature numbered no more than a school, a jail, a slip for making canoes and small craft, six or seven royal and seigneurial granaries and warehouses, and a guardhouse. Two tanneries, four grist mills, and a couple of sawmills dotted the nearby suburbs. The urban layout was spacious and regular. Two major arteries, theoretically twenty-four feet wide, stretched parallel to the river, intersected by ten or so narrower streets. The homes and shops of the leading families bordered on the marketplace, the town's nerve centre, where people gathered once or twice a week. Market times were strictly regulated, in the French manner.[39] Religious property and other private enclaves created open spaces without encroaching on residential blocks, which were still studded with large yards and gardens. A few animals, pigs mainly, were sheltered in sheds or barns at the back, and often ran loose despite police regulations.

Streets were muddy, dirty, and congested. No one paid any heed to ordinances that forbade butchers and builders to empty their stalls or dump materials on public thoroughfares, ordered inhabitants to keep latrines and remove all refuse, compelled statutory labour for the drainage, levelling, and stone-lining of the carriageway, or to any other for that matter.[40] Poorly aligned houses and shops that spilled on to the road constantly undermined the neat checkerboard pattern depicted on maps. Only after the fire of 1721 could the "highly uneven" St Paul Street finally be straightened.[41] Streets were not fit for traffic, and the bourgeois kept neither horse nor carriage for personal outings. Wagons could barely pass, and nuns reported how each spring carters pulled up their fences in order to negotiate the gulleys.[42] Repeated taxation, statutory labour, threats and indictments gradually improved matters, but the town did without basic utilities, street cleaning, fresh water, sewers, and street lighting until the end of the eighteenth century.

The residential pattern was also chaotic. Except for the small central core inhabited by the leading merchants, rich and poor rubbed shoulders, artisans and officers lived cheek by jowl, and wooden habitations destroyed the effect that the new residences strove to achieve. Property was clearly not concentrated in 1715, since this was still the case fifteen years later.[43] At least three-quarters of the residents owned their own homes, while a minority possessed one or two houses that they let at a profit.[44] Rents apparently doubled between 1670 and 1715, partially through inflation, but it is difficult to analyse this trend as significant results emerge only from longer periods. Our analysis of merchants' inventories has already shown that real estate made up a minor part of assets. People built their own dwellings and leased their old lodgings and whatever housing they might have inherited, seized, or otherwise acquired. Landlords frequently shared premises with their tenants, and some surprising instances of overcrowding could be seen within a town where space was not a problem. These reveal both the lack of means and the sluggishness of building activity.

3 A SEIGNEURIAL TOWN

The seigneurial regime did not stop at the city gates. The urban community evolved within the seigneurial system, and this peculiarity weighed heavily on its development and quickly provoked friction and unease.

The Société de Notre-Dame had only collected a nominal cens on plots. In 1665 the Sulpicians raised it to six deniers a *toise*, which represented a return of 5 per cent on 450 livres, the market value of an arpent within the town limits in that period.[45] The new seigneurs endeavoured to regain some of the urban space that their predecessors had too generously granted to religious institutions and private individuals. Around 1677, for example, they cunningly managed to recover the communal pastures that the Communauté des Habitants had received in 1651.[46] This narrow strip of land, separating the town form the river, accommodated the annual fur market, and thereafter merchants paid dearly for the right to keep stalls.[47] In exchange the Communauté received another pasture on the west side whose only value lay in its grazing properties. The seigneurs also profitably dismembered part of their close beside the marketplace. The plots that they granted, or re-granted, bore the same rate of cens, with an added ground rent based on the value of the property, a novelty that elicited protests. "In order to avoid these complaints," the seigneurs' attorney suggested, "it might be better to demand higher cash payments and lower the dues."[48] Indeed, this became the norm in the eighteenth century, when plots carried low annual dues and varying entry fees, especially in outlying and suburban areas, which only developed after 1725.

All landowners behaved in this way, but the rights of *lods et ventes*, levied on urban real estate – which changed hands more often than did rural property – were clearly feudal in character, and the inhabitants resisted their application. Unwilling to fuel the hostility of the leading citizens, Saint-Sulpice remained attentive to its interests in this regard but bided its time and advised its collectors not to prosecute offenders. Disdaining shows of force, the seigneurs chose to wait until buyers died or property changed hands to re-establish their prerogatives.[49]

Seigneurial authority affected nearly every aspect of public life until 1693. Nothing of a civil or criminal nature exceeded the competence of its court, the *bailliage*, whose decisions were appealed directly to the Sovereign Council. The seigneurs further decreed police regulations, named all administrators, and more profitably all notaries, by a privilege called *droit de tabellionnage*, which had fallen into disuse in France.[50] The staff of the seigneury included, in order of importance, a judge, seigneurial attorney, registry clerk, up to five notaries dispersed about the seigneury, several sergeants and bailiffs, a jailer, a road inspector, and a forest guard. Rights of escheat and confiscation, summons and legal fees, court costs, fines, and registration fees contributed to the income generated by the *bailliage*. Though sparsely populated, Montreal was a commercial centre, and its judges had to be of a higher calibre than those usually found on small seigneuries. Montreal was also a rough town, and the officers of the court had a hard time enforcing regulations, especially those pertaining to the fur trade and the sale of liquor to the Indians. Early on the notables challenged the competence of the court and openly exposed its venality.[51] Yet the real opposition lay elsewhere. The Crown regularly confronted a seigneury to which it had ill-advisedly granted too many powers. In short, this was an anachronistic episode in the long drawn-out battle between feudal institutions and centralizing forces. The state gave Saint-Sulpice's opponents free rein and used the Sovereign Council to undermine a court that stood in its way.[52] Worn-out, the Sulpicians gave in at the end of the century and their *bailliage* was replaced by a royal court.[53]

Royal or seigneurial, colonial justice was expensive even when honestly administered – which was not always the case.[54] Whatever the proceedings, the legal fees, which stood more or less on a par with those of the Paris vicomté, quickly spiralled. A foreclosure involving a verdict, summons, placarding, and public auction cost approximately 110 livres tournois; surveying cost between 7 and 20 livres; guardianships coupled with inventories and divisions of estates came to a minimum of 37 livres and more likely 150 in the case of a sizeable inheritance.[55] Criminal proceedings could prove calamitous for the accused, who was responsible for fines but also had to pay jail and court costs before being released.[56] Plaintiffs had to be sure that they were in the right before they embarked on a suit whose costs they could well end up paying themselves. An appeal to the Sovereign Council in Quebec, with its attendant travel expenses, lay beyond the reach of most people. Lawyers had been barred from the colony, supposedly to simplify proceedings, so notaries, bailiffs, surgeons, and other practitioners represented the opposing parties to the best of their abilities, and were handsomely rewarded for their service. The intendant and subdélégué mediated some disputes, but if a record was wanted or the situation grew more ticklish, the inhabitants would still have recourse to the judiciary. The myth that justice in New France was free must be abandoned once and for all.[57]

Townsmen were helpless before the seigneury's other intrusions. Merchants were resigned to taking second place when seized goods were allocated among creditors.[58] They also faced competition from seigneurial grains, which defeated almost all attempts at speculation, and had to contend with the millers whenever they shipped wheat out of the seigneury or brought in flour from elsewhere. Prodded by their Parisian attorney, the seigneurs gave up taxing these last activities at the beginning of the eighteenth century. Unyielding towards peasants, they closed their eyes to merchants' infractions, "lest by over-extending their prerogatives they occasioned their restriction, banalité in and of itself being heinous and opposed to the commonweal."[59]

4 A TOWN GOVERNED FROM ABOVE

Shortly after their arrival the Ville Marie colonists incorporated themselves and began meeting regularly to discuss communal affairs and to elect a syndic each year by majority vote, spontaneously transplanting a familiar rural organization that served their collective interests.[60] Communal bonds took shape around the fur trade and the initial area of settlement, confined within a narrow cultivated and inhabited zone, bounded by the river and the forests. This tiny stretch, both home and workplace, had to be guarded against enemy raids and the monopoly of the Quebec trading company; it had as well to be developed at common expense. The syndic and other elected representatives ordered periodic levies, supervised the raising of militiamen, and allocated military billets.[61] The only local authority at the time was that of Monsieur de Maisonneuve, who embodied all seigneurial, judicial and governmental powers. He was compelled to rely on the Communauté, which therefore played an essential role. It included all those who held property, barring non-residents and servants. Most syndics were common people, which does not mean that the society was homogeneous but rather that its small elite – which lacked the support it would later muster from the Crown – had to contend with the assembly's democratic nature.[62] Besides, it was easier to commit local affairs to the care of the willing and focus needed energies on trade. The inhabitants elected their first vestry in 1657, but the two bodies remained autonomous.[63]

In 1677, following seditious activities on the part of the inhabitants and syndic, the governor of the colony published an ordinance prohibiting "all assemblies, covenants, and joint signatures."[64] The "Communauté des habitants" had ceased to exist. That such an arbitrary measure could be carried out without triggering a full-scale rebellion indicates that the institution had already lost any real substance.

Settlers and traders no longer shared a common habitat. The first had migrated to the countryside, and Montreal had become a strictly commercial enclave. The communal bonds, rooted in rural traditions, could hardly survive such a transformation. Collective interests, which had rested on participation in the fur trade (an unequal, but nevertheless real participation), had also fallen apart. "The chief or leading elements residing on the island" included a growing number of merchants and other worthies who had little in common with the twenty-odd inhabitants – representing approximately one-tenth of householders, tailors, carpenters, or farmers – who attended the last town meetings.[65] The Sulpicians had transformed the seigneury into a powerful institution, and royal authority had also made headway in Montreal. Through these establishments the elite gained control of public affairs. Possessing no property or collective rights except a pasture transferred at the will of the seigneurs, unable to raise monies – for in France a locally based tax system strengthened local ties – the Communauté could not survive.[66] Everything conspired to promote the domination of a small group of merchants and officers in the town, leaving only a single outlet for rural collective organization: the parish.

Notables were always party to decisions affecting public life. The *bailli* regularly called together "the local merchants and bourgeois" or "oldest bourgeois families" to consider sundry administrative matters, bread and meat assizes, public works, wages, statute labour, and so on.[67] From their midst were either selected or elected (the procedure varied but never allowed genuine representation) the prudhommes who drew up the tax rolls, the captains of the urban militia, the churchwardens, and the assessors who seconded the judge at some criminal trials.[68] Representatives of the trades were only summoned once in a while. Only merchants were allowed to convene to conduct their own affairs and, when necessary to dispatch delegates to Quebec or Versailles.[69] A document from 1729 styles them "town spokesmen," but in fact they represented themselves.[70]

The notables did not try to set up a municipal body because its powers would have been far too restricted. They were satisfied to make their voices heard throughout the seigneurial, administrative, judicial, and military framework. In a period when communal institutions were on the decline, when French towns retained but shreds of their former privileges, it is not surprising that this tiny new settlement exhibited only spasmodic forms of public participation, bereft of a popular base.

Canada received the institutional apparatus of a French province, with one major exception: offices were not for sale.[71] Colbert made a noteworthy effort to simplify and improve the governmental framework he was transplanting to the colony, but he could not manage to eliminate the overlapping powers that were a basic feature of French absolutism. Colonial officials wasted a great deal of energy trying to delineate their particular sphere of influence, and the vitality of the military sector only made matters worse. In Montreal, for instance, ordinary by-laws issued from six different authorities: the local judge, the Sovereign Council in Quebec, the intendant or his *subdélégué*, the local governor, the town major, and the governor of New France. Each kept a jealous eye on his domain and spared no effort to impress Versailles with his zeal – for these precarious positions were dispensed and maintained according to the Court's whims. Six ordinances were no better than one, and frequently each cancelled the next. Coercive force proved weak and ineffective.[72] This legislative mania would have been more oppressive if meagre salaries had not been augmented by private business.[73] So Montreal's civil and military cadres devoted much of their time to the pursuit of their own interests, thereby granting the citizens some respite.

It did not take many people to govern Montreal. Some twenty individuals only staffed the court in 1700: a judge, a crown prosecutor, a deputy-prosecutor, a registry clerk, four or five notaries, some sergeants and bailiffs, a jailer and an interpreter, as well as some petty seigneurial officers. They were all recruited in the colony, and posts were often handed from father to son.[74] Even the administration employed no more than twenty officials in the town: a local governor who took precedence over all others, a Marine commissioner who doubled as *subdélégué*, an agent of the colonial treasurer, a representative of the tax farmers, a keeper of the royal stores, a road inspector, a constable and a small company of archers, along with six staff officers attached to the garrison. Except for minor appointments, all these posts were filled from France. Montreal's elite may have hankered after offices as eagerly as others did elsewhere, but precious little was available. They used both craft and energy to secure the creation of new positions, such as that of official surveyor. Yet there was little likelihood that many of them would be able to crown a life of hard work with a respectable sinecure, and merchants generally spent their declining years behind their counters.[75] If the local elite exerted constant pressure to enter the military hierarchy, it was because other avenues for advancement were rare.

Officers of the Crown and their employees enjoyed exemptions from public wardships, billeting of troops, and other burdens, as well as sundry privileges, including the free transport of goods on royal vessels or the possibility of appealing to Versailles for favours. They served and participated in the system, each according to his rank, and thereby they helped to maintain, with a certain economy of means, the social fabric of the Ancien Régime in the colony.

CHAPTER THIRTEEN

Social Groups

1 OVERVIEW

In 1715 4,700 people lived on the Island of Montreal. The active population numbered some twelve hundred individuals, who can be grouped by occupation as follows. Two-fifths were peasants who drew their income mainly from the land. Some also performed other functions and worked as carters, lime-burners, or blacksmiths, since villages were not yet capable of supporting full-fledged artisans. There were also five or six millers in the countryside, along with two notaries, five curés, a group of nuns in the Lachine and Pointe-aux-Trembles convents, and about ten small merchants, sometimes acting as voyageurs, as well as one hundred to one hundred and fifty people whose primary activity was fur trading – at least for a while.[1] There were few married men in this last group. Most came from peasant families and went home to the farm between trips. Agricultural labourers did not form a distinct category, as we have already remarked.

The 650 individuals who made up the town's active population can be divided into four categories. The first comprises the 40 per cent who performed services of some sort, and includes 24 clergy-men – Sulpicians, Jesuits, and Récollets – and about 75 nuns; the resident military officers and their families (35); judicial and admin-istrative office-holders (14); minor officials (12); surgeons (4); and maybe a hundred or so servants, children and adults.

Trade accounted for 20 per cent of occupations, including mer-chant-outfitters (25); professional voyageurs and small merchants (60); innkeepers and tavern-keepers (30); bakers and butchers (5); and a few carters.

The secondary sector consisted of those in the building trades (40); blacksmiths and cartwrights, locksmiths, edge-tool makers, and gunsmiths (20); 4 tanners and a dozen cobblers; tailors and especially seamstresses (40); and a number of other craftsmen, such as a brewer, cooper, gardener, weaver, clog-maker, wig-maker, goldsmith, hat-maker, and so on. Together these independent artisans gave work to perhaps 50 apprentices at most, for they rarely employed more than one or two at a time. This sector involved no more than a quarter of the town's active population.

Last came a mixed bag of day-labourers who worked wherever they could, sometimes in construction, sometimes as *engagés* for the fur trade, and sometimes as harvesters. This loose contingent made up 15 per cent of the labour force.

Urban development in this period was neither important enough nor sufficiently sustained to support a greater reservoir of labour. Access to trade was limited, and the small body of artisans already met both local demand and that of the fur trade adequately. Although construction was increasing, large-scale projects were rare.

The town did attract voyageurs, who had previously lived in the country. As their occupation became more professionalized, they grew closer to the merchants, their partners and outfitters. But apart from a few suburban farmers who settled in town when they reached retirement age, the voyageurs were practically the only rural population that was tapped by the town. The inherent limitations of the colonial economy meant that the winds of change would not blow over this occupational pattern in the eighteenth century.

The few tax rolls that have survived are poor substitutes for the fiscal documents used elsewhere to reconstruct income levels. Although tax levies were frequent, each was too slight to provide an adequate gauge of the taxpayers' means. The categories defined by the assembly that drew up the list for a public works tax in 1681 teach us more than the actual range of assessments. (See Table 40.) Only the garrison staff was exempted. The names of those in the lowest category were left out of the tax roll, but I was able to identify them by referring to the nominal census taken that year. They were recent settlers.

For the sake of comparison it is useful to analyse a more important assessment levied in 1714–15 for the building of the fortifications.[2] This particular tax was assessed by head rather than household and, given its defensive purpose, allowed almost no exemptions. Unlike earlier levies, which were expressed in terms of money, this one imposed so many days of statute labour, valued at 2 livres per man-day and 5 livres per "draught-day." Although the

Table 40
Distribution of the public-works tax raised in 1681 on the Island of Montreal

Description of the categories	Taxpayers	Assessment (in livres)
Important merchants	6	20
Lesser merchants	13	12
Comfortable	58	8
Less comfortable	67	6
Poor	161	3

Source: NA, M-1584: 38.

analysis is based on these equivalents, the reader should be aware that they do not reflect current wages. A day-labourer generally earned 30 sols, while a day's carting was usually worth over 100 sols, depending on the nature and quality of the team. The discrepancy favoured the merchants, who drew up the rolls and put themselves down for draught-days, which most of them remitted in cash. But it added to the burden of those in the lower categories, who, for one reason or another, would have had to pay their share in coin. It obviously tended to lessen the spread between assessments.

Contributions ranged between 2 and 75 livres, and the mean was 11 livres.[3] Using the method devised by J. Dupâquier, based on a geometric progression distributed on either side of the mean, I charted a histogram that, despite the imprecision of the source, reflects, up to a point, the overall income distribution in this society.[4] There are only seven tax brackets – six actually, for only two persons figure in the seventh – and there is a marked concentration in category a, where payments lay between 5 1/2 and 11 livres. The very small spread around an homogeneous mass of moderate revenues fits what we know about this economy: it arose from the split between trade and agriculture, and the long-term recession accentuated the trend towards equality.[5]

This concentration is even more obvious when we turn to the countryside, where we find a mixture of wealthier farmers, voyageurs, and a sprinkling of notables in the top 17 per cent, and a much larger category of habitants who had done well for themselves without producing sizeable surpluses. The other two-fifths were recent settlers, in more or less straitened circumstances, although for most this would only be temporary. The town had its contingent of untaxed paupers, who do not figure on the rolls, but the portion was insignificant. Montreal offered so little occasion for scraping together a living that those who did not have a steady income moved away.

The roll yields little information concerning the professions. Although I was able to reconstitute three small categories, only the merchants emerge with a clear profile. They did not over-assess themselves, and from what is known of their business at least three should figure in category D. If we suppose that the group's mean revenue hovered around 1,200 to 2,000 livres, or ten times that of craftsmen, this would give a fair idea of the extent of inequalities. The artisans identified belonged to the upper strata of the trades, but even they were hardly well off. The broader spread of assessments among military officers points to diverse material conditions.

The purpose of this overview is to establish a backdrop for the analysis of socio-economic groups based on a more or less trustworthy source: the post-mortem inventory. Two hundred and fifty of these were used, supplemented by other notarial documents such as curator's accounts, divisions of estates, sales, adjudications, marriage contracts, and wills.[6] Inventories alone do not provide an accurate picture of the distribution of wealth because they give pride of place to the more affluent. Notaries never charged less than 7 livres tournois (and usually an average of 20, with the authenticated copy) for making inventories of the peasants' movables and effects, and this did not include the property valuations. Another 7 livres would go to the two livestock appraisers should they refuse to be paid from the brood, as custom dictated. What with costs for electing a guardianship or dividing the estate, the total fees could easily mount to 5 per cent of an ordinary inheritance, and common people would do all they could to avoid such an outlay.[7]

A careful curator would request an inventory in order to protect the interests of the minors when the surviving parent remarried, while unclaimed successions were inventoried on order of the court, so that we do, after all, get a glimpse of the poor. The reliability of the declarations, however, raises another problem.

The notary who returned to complete the inventory of the late Pierre Gadois tells us of the widow's welcome, "screaming that he had no right to do it, that he only did it to despoil them and ruin her children, calling down a thousand curses, that the devil should take him, that he should die of shame for trying to include in the inventory some eight cords of wood belonging to her as well as many chickens that she and her late husband had owned together, and that, since he was so interested in how many there were, he should count them himself ..."[8]

Not everyone was as hostile, but people had no qualms about concealing as much as they could. Yet relatives of the deceased kept their eyes open, and besides, most had little to hide. Even if the notary did not reckon every one of the widow Gadois' chickens, enough information was recorded to show that this family was better off than the average and to reveal its material environment, which is what we are after.

Grain and cattle were appraised at their market value. Merchants stocks were valued according to the invoice price, with or without the mark-up, but this being always specified, it is easy to standardize these estimates. Only movables were assessed at less than their sale price, and this *cru* came to about 25 per cent, if not more.[9] Since this procedure was common to all inventories, and movables represented only a minor portion of the total assets, the figures are tabulated as given. One cannot compare overall levels of wealth at different periods to measure overall impoverishment or enrichment, since the various categories of estate would not be equally represented in the samples. However, a close look at the changes in the nature and distribution of the assets can indicate the trends. Price fluctuations create a problem. Thus, all the inventories taken between 1715 and 1719, valued in card money, had to be eliminated, and those taken prior to 1670, when prices were very high, were analysed separately. What remains is more or less comparable.

The inventories rarely assign a value to real property, but they describe the buildings and the state of the land. I dealt with this problem by assigning a standard value of 50 livres to every arpent under the plough (the market price around 1675, halfway through the period) and by adopting the appropriate price range for the buildings. The method is obviously crude since land value could vary from one farm to another and also over time (decreasing gradually from 1650 to 1720), but the data are too scattered to permit any refinements.

Stocks, securities, and cash were entered separately. Other items were divided into four categories: durable and perishable consumer goods and durable and perishable producer goods, each with twenty to thirty subheadings.[10] Perishable goods were left out of the overall calculations because the contents of the barn or the cellar differed from season to season, while pantries were not consistently inventoried. This classification allows us to isolate expenditures related to the running of the enterprise from those meant to make life more pleasant.

2 THE SEIGNEURS

The fiefs that the trade companies and the French monarchy granted to gentilshommes and to religious bodies did not generate revenues until enough people settled on them and their owners put up mills and invested on their domains. Since most lay seigneurs had not undertaken such improvements by the beginning of the eighteenth century, relying instead on the slow and spontaneous influx of settlers to populate their land, there were no seigneurial revenues (with a few exceptions), and we cannot speak yet of a seigneurial class.[11] But the institutional framework was there to promote the rise of such a group, and a few proprietors did not wait to take advantage of their privilege.

Thus, although fourteen small arrière-fiefs had been granted on the island between 1658 and 1690 and a number of the town's officers and merchants owned large, nearly empty seigneuries off the island, these landowners are classified according to their occupations and the origins of their revenues, which were not seigneurial.[12]

The seminary of Saint-Sulpice stands alone as truly seigneurial, but the Sulpicians left no balance sheet of their administration. A 1704 lease indicates that the revenues from all seigneurial dues, mill rights, and rentes foncières came to about 6,500 livres. The lease of two domains brought in 2,500 livres. In the same period, net income from the tithes appropriated by the Seminary can be estimated at 3,250 livres. Rental from houses, forge, warehouses, and other properties, and income from rentes constituées held both in Canada and in France amounted to at least another 3,000 livres. Sulpician revenues were therefore in the order of 15,000 to 20,000 livres tournois, and since three-quarters were feudal in origin, there were safe from economic fluctuations.[13] Expenses long exceeded revenues, for the seigneurs worked tirelessly to exploit their privileges as well as their demesne. Small acquisitions of rentes show that by the early eighteenth century their income had risen to cover their outlay. "And since we do not deem it wise at present to make any further purchases in Canada, because they are not safe," the Superior wrote, "we must send this sum as well as other payments and reimbursements which come our way to Paris, where they can be properly invested."[14] These sure investments turned out to be rentes on the Hôtel de Ville, whose fluctuations the Seminary watched, with some consternation, over the next twenty years. The portion of the censitaires' savings drained off in this fashion was still small, but it would soon increase. By the middle of the eighteenth century rumour had it that the seigneurs had an annual revenue of 70,000 livres and that a large proportion ended up in France.[15]

As for the men who personified the seigneury, they were educated French clerics of good birth, from families of the robe and the sword, who looked on this society of commoners and adventurers with a mixture of severity and condescension.[16]

3 THE NOBLES

Their titles were recent: four or five generations, at best, fewer in many cases, and the eleven Canadian families ennobled in the seventeenth century formed part of this group.[17] However recent, they had a recognized status that included a number of privileges. "Monseigneur," the governor wrote, "I beg leave to tell you that Canadian nobles are no better than beggars and that increasing their number would only inflate the number of idlers."[18] No one, not even the common criminals sent over in the eighteenth century would cause so much anxiety for the authorities as these arrogant, ignorant nobles, who could not take care of themselves. The intendants would variously explain that such people were accustomed to "what is known in France as the life of country gentlemen, which is all they had ever known or seen." "They spend most of their time hunting and fishing, having no other skills, not being born to till the land, and having no means that would allow them to take part in business."[19] This is hardly surprising, but the royal authorities behaved in an irresponsible manner by doing all they could to attract this class to the colony, only to reprove them for living on government handouts as they waited for the emergence of seigneurial revenues. The occasional liberality of the authorities was not enough to solve the problem; that took the elaboration of a system of economic promotion that gave this petty nobility access first to the army, where it belonged by right, and then to trade and even to the civil establishment if it showed the least aptitude.[20] But until then the disturbances created by this "armed idleness' grew more frequent, for these families proved highly prolific.[21] The young Le Gardeur and d'Ailleboust "ran about the streets of Montreal and the surrounding countryside in the middle of the night disguised as Indians, carrying guns and knives and stealing money from the purses of those they encountered ... while threatening to kill and burn anyone who denounced them."[22] This is just one example of disorderly conduct where the suit was dismissed or the penalty remitted.

When the authorities deplored the flightiness, pride, and laziness of "our" youth, they meant the group they represented and knew intimately.[23] Its rowdy habits were an integral part of the nobiliar lifestyle of seventeenth-century Montreal.

Loss of rank was not something that worried colonial nobles, so the 1685 decree allowing them to take part in trade proved irrelevant.[24] Although they felt no compunction about running illegal taverns, they turned up their noses at manual labour. The governor, arguing on behalf of Monsieur de Saint-Ours, assured the minister that he "had seen the two eldest sons cutting hay and leading the plough."[25] A touching scene, but hardly the norm. A few may have sunk so low in the early days, but the Saint-Ours boys would soon be off trading furs, and like many others this family would spend more time in Montreal than on its seigneurie.[26]

Some recipients of arrière-fiefs on the Island of Montreal proved to be talented traders. Berthé de Chailly, the son of a poor Amboise nobleman, absconded via New York with the 40,000 livres he had amassed on his Bellevue property, where he detained Indians headed for Montreal with their furs.[27] Picoté, Carion, and La Fresnaye did the same and were equally successful.[28] These petty nobles tried to compete with the merchants, but few succeeded in creating going concerns based primarily on circulating capital.

As a captain in the troupes de la Marine a noble would earn 1,080 livres, while staff officers made two to three times as much. Such salaries helped to make ends meet but did not leave surpluses. Seventeen post-mortem inventories describe gross fortunes among this group of 3,000 to 8,000 livres, the same as those of good artisans.[29] These inventories are incomplete and poorly drawn up, as if the notaries were reluctant to intrude into the privacy of households. Marriage arrangements and various legal subtleties helped somewhat to keep creditors at bay, while royal bounty "in lieu of patrimony" could come in handy in safeguarding belongings.[30] The inventories also list heavy liabilities, which reveal the odd trading activity. These nobles owed money to merchants, to the treasurer, to the intendant, to their soldiers, to the convent where they placed their daughters, to tradesmen, and to their servants.[31] One fief, with its six thousand hectares of wood and eight censitaires, its ten or so cultivated arpents adjoining the house and barn, and a small crumbling mill, would be worth no more than an ordinary censive.[32] It was hard to keep up appearances in a three- to four-room country house or, as often was the case, in the smaller quarters that officers owned or rented in town.[33] But these nobles tried. Their inventories leave an overwhelming sense of overcrowding: countless children, one or two servants, and much more furniture than a merchant would have. It cost officers nothing to ship their belongings on royal vessels, and this explains the presence of expensive pieces: an ebony cabinet, a morocco-covered chest, armchairs with silk-woven patterns, West Indian rugs, and those high-warp tapestries valued at four hundred livres that hung about a room. There was an abundance of chairs with pillows, tables covered with rugs, feather beds even for children, sheets, utensils, gold-framed mirrors, knickknacks, china, and silverware. All owned silverware, dinnerware, candelabra, and so on, which could be pawned on occasion. Five of these families possessed a few books, and six boasted a religious painting or a portrait or two. Duplessy Faber, who fought on every European front and spent the last twenty-five years of his life in Canada longing for the Saint-Louis Cross, kept a portrait of Vauban, his protector, and a picture of "a Dutchman, reading while another looked on," which he probably brought back from some campaign on the New York frontier.[34]

And when dire poverty struck, when the last armchair, ivory crucifix, and last silver spoon had gone, one might still find on the wall a "worthless, worn-out" strip of Bergamot tapestry.

4 JUDICIAL AND ADMINISTRATIVE PERSONNEL

When the Sulpicians looked to replace their *bailli* d'Ailleboust, a career officer who had no legal training and was the nephew of a former governor of the colony, they were lucky enough to find a law graduate on the spot, said to have been a lawyer at the Parlement of Paris before he came to Canada as a clerk of the Compagnie des Indes occidentales.[35] Migeon held the post between 1677 and 1693, all the while working as a merchant, and left behind one of the finest farms on the island as well as urban properties. He paid his daughter's 4,000-livre dowry in cash, which was quite unusual. Although he left no inventory, he appears to have been worth altogether at least 50,000 livres and to have owned what was no doubt the best library in the seigneury after that of the Sulpicians. Since his sons opted for military careers, he was succeeded by his son-in-law, who is better known for his adventures in Mississippi than for his career as a judge.[36]

There was no social status attached to the other judicial functions. These were left to individuals of all stripes who performed them with varying degrees of competence. Bénigne Basset would have been a decent notary and clerk if "tobacco and debauchery" had not "so affected his wits that he could no longer think properly or remember anything."[37] He had to be relieved of his duties. His wife and children found consolation in the bosom of the Church. The notary Adhémar, son of a Languedoc bourgeois who had come to Canada as a soldier, earned the merchants' trust, and most of the fur-trade *obligations* passed through his office.[38] He loaned money, oversaw successions, and left behind about 5,000 to 6,000 livres, once the mortgage on his house is deducted. His son succeeded him.[39]

Jean Gervaise, one of Montreal's first settlers, acted as attorney to the *bailliage* in respectable obscurity and died on his farm at Coteau

Saint-Louis. His heirs were peasants, as their father had been before them.[40] For lack of a better candidate, the seigneurs took on a merchant's clerk as their court clerk and later attorney, but he was troublesome and went back to La Rochelle at the end of five years.[41] The other local notaries were not up to performing such duties. Modest careers could be forged when an ex-soldier turned school-master, then sergeant of the *bailliage*, bailiff, sometimes jailer, and even notary, without any hope of further upward mobility.[42] Claude Maugue's possessions were worth only 600 livres at his death, and his widow married a cobbler.[43] Yet with proper training and initiative one could go much further. Did a Sulpician suggest that the carpenter Raimbault send his ten-year-old son to France? Whatever the reason, the boy was away fifteen years, studied, and eventually became a notary, *subdélégué* of the intendant, *bailli* for the seigneurial lower court, and, from 1727 to 1740, judge of the royal court.[44] In his early days he occasionally took on the lease of tithes and seigneurial dues. Pierre Raimbault owned some fifty books: Greek and Roman classics, law books, edifying works, and a horticultural treatise.[45] In this tiny society where everything devolved from trade or warfare, this is the sole example of education's becoming a means of preferment.

5 THE MERCHANTS

Trade was the most common means of social promotion open to the dynamic elements of the lower classes. Success was commensurate with the milieu and with the potential offered by this activity. Although the wealth of the outfitters whose post-mortem assets are summarized in Table 41 bears no comparison either quantitatively or qualitatively with that of the French urban bourgeoisie, they dominated the fur trade and played a primary role in the small colonial town. (See Table 41.)

Those at the bottom are underrepresented in this sample. Dozens of persons became outfitters at some point in their lives, working with a capital of 8,000 to 10,000 livres until they sank into oblivion. Those who endured had every reason to believe that they would leave behind some 20,000 to 35,000 livres, which was about average. Besides the five wealthiest merchants included in the table, two other individuals, whose inventories were not available, held assets of more than 150,000 livres at the beginning of the eighteenth century.[46]

These men's assets differed significantly from those of their metropolitan counterparts. Seven of the inventories did not include

Table 41
Distribution of the assets of merchant-outfitters based on post-mortem inventories, 1680–1718

Categories	Net value of the estate in livres tournois							
	5000–10,000	10,000–15,000	15,000–25,000	25,000–35,000	35,000–55,000	100,000–200,000	260,000	Total
Merchants under 45	4	4	3	1	1			13
Older merchants	1	2	6	3	1	2	1	16

even one plot of land, while the single farm that figures in the other inventories amounted to no more than 20 per cent of the estate. Urban properties represented 30 per cent, movables 5 per cent. Stocks and commercial claims accounted for 40 per cent, while rentes rarely rose above 5 per cent, if there were any at all.

There was also a marked contrast in lifestyles. The merchants' stone houses, lining the marketplace, each contained perhaps six large rooms and a number of smaller ones (*cabinets*), with the shop at street level and the storeroom one story above. Wheat and furs were kept in the attic. These were fine residences by Montreal standards, although in reality they were no more than upgraded peasant cottages. The furnishings depended upon the degree of wealth. At the outset of their careers merchants lived as sparely as the lower classes. Whenever business took a turn for the worse, the furniture was the first to go. Wealthier merchants would own cupboards full of linen, kitchen utensils, an abundance of pewter, beds and covers, and silverware weighing seven to twelve marks. All had an iron stove, worth about 150 livres, set in the main room, a symbol of comfort not yet within the reach of the common people. They relied on locally produced pine and cherrywood furniture; a mirror, one or two upholstered armchairs, a tapestry, and the occasional painting complemented this spare assortment, which we find, for example, in the houses of J.-B. Charly and Pierre Perthuis, men worth at least 40,000 and 50,000 livres respectively once their debts have been subtracted.[47] Jacques Leber, the richest of them all, and Charles de Couagne did not live on a grander scale.[48] The latter's two inventories, taken 25 years apart, reveal that while his assets quadrupled, his furnishings remained practically the same except for a clock, a pedestal table, and two armchairs.[49] Wardrobes, valued at 200 to 300 livres, were not extravagant.

The merchants were not a cultivated lot. If their inventories can be trusted, two-thirds never opened a book. The others possessed 10 to 40 volumes, mostly of a religious nature. Couagne, who enjoyed historical accounts and covered his walls with plain paper maps of the world, of France, and of Paris, seems to have been something of an eccentric.[50] Jean Quenet owned seven family portraits, including those of five brothers living in France, but it was above all religious subjects that adorned one-third of these bourgeois households.

Theirs was not a nobiliar lifestyle: idleness was reproved, and no one retired prematurely. The women learned how to keep accounts and how to manage the business while their husbands were away. Boys were sent to school until they turned fourteen, when they began their apprenticeship with Canadian or French merchants. For these men, growing richer, becoming respectable, and becoming respected were serious concerns. They did not participate in the scandalous and boisterous pleasures of the officers. Fines for contravening fur-trade ordinances may have been an unavoidable occupational hazard, but they were otherwise orderly citizens. They took part in public life, became churchwardens, and donated generously to charitable works.

6 TRADERS AND ARTISANS

The forty-five-year-old voyageur who found himself too old to pursue an occupation that had become too strenuous came home to his family with no more than 4,000 to 5,000 livres in savings. These had been invested in some suburban property or urban building and provided a small income in his declining years.[51] He kept an eye on his son's affairs, a son he had trained himself and who, as conditions improved in the eighteenth century, would make a better living from his trips to the west than his father had. But Jean Lorain was already able to leave his children twice as much as he had received from his own father, a peasant, and this explains both his choice of career and the attraction it exerted on the next generations.[52] For if modest success was less common than failure and poverty, it was more likely to impress the youth of this region.

The innkeeper Isaac Nafréchoux had begun his career as a miller. The money he left behind allowed his son to outfit fur traders and his daughters to marry, the one an army officer and the other a sergeant in the constabulary. The daughter of another innkeeper, Abraham Bouat, married Pacaud, one of the major merchants of the colony, while his son went to France to study law and, having made a good match, received a commission in the troops and eventually became judge of the *bailliage*. This is enough to give the impression of an unstructured society. We should nevertheless remember that these were exceptional cases and that the 50 or so individuals who ran taverns or inns at one time or another in Montreal had a different fate. This was an attractive occupation that brought easy returns, especially when one had no scruples about cheating the Indians, or intoxicating servants and soldiers, or staying open on Sundays to attract country residents who came in to hear mass, an activity they were all guilty of, without exception. Whatever dire penalties the ordinances may have prescribed, the Court showed little zeal, and the mitigated fines had no effect.[53] Theoretically, only twenty or so individuals were entitled to sell drinks, but there were at least ten transgressors a year, besides other illicit establishments the authorities failed to track down. Tavern-keepers were a mixed lot: former voyageurs, a notary, a bailiff, many artisans who left the running of the business to their wives, and a large number of widows.[54] They were grasping and unscrupulous. The accusations of the Court attorneys are convincing: all of the inns were bawdy houses, and many taverns were dens of iniquity. The proprietors did not make a fortune. Vincent Dugast, who left 4,500 livres after 20 years of keeping judge and curé on the alert, probably did better than any others.[55]

There were no guilds in Canada. This was a deliberate ministerial decision, and masters who occasionally sought letters patent or exclusive rights met with repeated refusals.[56]

At first people worked as they pleased, and this could give rise to incongruous associations, such as that of the butcher and the clog-maker who decided to join forces to sell liquor on the side.[57] But from 1680 onwards crafts became more organized.

Butchers and bakers were regulated by the judge, assisted by a few chosen citizens who determined their number, the quality of their products, and their prices.[58] The response of the assemblies to market fluctuations proved so slow that the butchers and bakers were forever at odds with the *bailli*, or with the merchants who interfered with their monopoly, or with peasants who sold meat at the market.[59] Given the economic priorities of l'Ancien Régime, the decisions usually came down in favour of the consumers, all the more so in this town, where merchants were the biggest customers. They were the ones who fixed the assize and denounced the slightest contraventions. Sentences were not only frequent; they were also quite heavy.[60] Most of the assets left behind by two butchers, between 3,000 and 5,000 livres each, went to repay their debts. The only inventory left by a baker shows that he was penniless.[61] Most probably did better, but in this period these were not profitable trades.

Tanning was one of Montreal's few viable industries. The two firms that competed for business in the early eighteenth century had a turnover of about 10,000 livres and employed no more than five or six workmen and three shoemakers each, if they obeyed the intendant's ordinance.[62] He meant to put a stop to the beginnings of an association between butchers and tanners that threatened to absorb the shoemakers as well. The inventories of the town's first tanners have not survived, but since we know that the families ran the concerns for several generations, these were obviously worth maintaining.[63] The shoemakers remained independent, multiplied, and functioned on a very small scale.

In 1663, eleven years after he arrived in the colony, the former *engagé* Jean Milot *dit* le Bourguignon, a good edge-tool maker who could not sign his name, owned 10,000 livres in assets, while at his death in 1699 he left behind some 35,000 livres, consisting of urban and rural properties.[64] He was exceptionally successful, although the iron trades were generally sound, armory in particular. Fezeret and Turpin owned houses on the marketplace and stood out from the crowd with their savings of 7,000 to 10,000 livres.[65] Two blacksmiths, dead by the age of thirty, had already amassed net assets of 4,000 to 5,000 livres, something most peasants would only achieve in a lifetime.[66] There was an unflagging demand for guns and tools in the colony and also in the west, where these artisans were called by the administration to set up forges under highly favourable terms.[67] The seigneurs and a number of merchants owned forges, which they rented completely equipped, while the lessees in return provided whatever wares they ordered.[68] Although access to these trades was open, they demanded skills and a basic investment beyond the reach of adventurers.

The situation in the building trades was quite different. The mass of semi-rural part-time carpenters and masons who obtained contracts in the seventeenth century did not live well. In order to be awarded the projects they underestimated the costs, and this inevitably landed them in trouble. The *bailliage* registers are full of lawsuits involving carpenters who were demanding their money and town dwellers who were clamouring for them to finish the work.[69] They left construction sites as soon as anything became available in the royal outposts, and exchanged their high wages for trade goods. The shrewdest were eventually able to give up an occupation they had never really been good at and that paid so little. At the end of the seventeenth century there were no competent major contractors in Montreal, but this is hardly surprising since no important projects had yet demanded their permanent presence. Quebec workmen were used on the major building sites, such as churches, convents, mills, fortifications, and boatyards for small craft, and eventually they settled in Montreal and trained the local labour force.[70]

The first surgeons combined medicine and farming. André Rapin left his family a prosperous farm near Lachine as well as a house in town, and his sons were apprenticed to a shoemaker and an edge-tool maker.[71] Later on, a few of the better-educated surgeons, especially those who acted as public and private curators, would rank among the minor notables. Whatever they earned from such tasks, combined with their salaries at the Hôtel-Dieu and the emoluments received from their patients, ensured them a decent lifestyle, even if they left behind little more than 4,000 to 5,000 livres.[72]

Craftsmen were a close-knit group. Their families were bound by wedlock – often within the same trade – and through apprenticeship. Most apprentices were the sons of artisans and often related to the master, or they were the sons of surgeons or merchants. Since the trades were expanding in this period, they offered a few openings to boys from the country. A well-off habitant with more than one son to succeed him on the farm could settle one of them this way. The cost was not very high, and all that some masters required was that the parents provide their children's clothing.[73] The apprenticeship usually lasted three years and began when the child was anywhere between twelve and nineteen years old. Conditions were stringent and sometimes harsh, especially in the more profitable trades like iron and leather, where tradition was strictly observed. Fathers were keen to pass on their skills to their sons, and one coppersmith had his apprentice promise that after his death he would teach the craft to one of his late master's children, under the same conditions he had been trained himself, "if the said child was so inclined."[74]

The lowest rungs of the urban society were occupied by the small contingent of unskilled labourers who had either given up land-clearing or never tried it at all. They earned 30 sols a day, with a meal added, it seems, when they worked for masons or carpenters. Although these were high wages by any yardstick, this proved irrelevant. "It may be true that the workers are well paid," the intendant wrote, "but one must keep in mind that they can only work five months of the year because of the cold winters and that they must therefore earn enough to see them through the other seven months."[75] In fact, work was interrupted for about six months, but the 30 sols a day did not apply to those employed for long periods, who generally earned only 12 to 15 livres a month.[76] If we allow 4 sols a day for the equivalent of a soldier's ration, a labourer would need a minimum of 50 livres to keep alive during the period of inactivity. Include the rent for a heated room, between 50 and 70 livres a year, and his entire income is spent. When the price of bread rose, the labourer could not feed himself. His lot was that much more uncertain in those periods when there was little construction, as in the last decade of the seventeenth century. If he built himself some cabin in the suburbs, he might save on rent, but should he have a family to feed, he would have to go begging. Some of these men were hired by the fur traders, but the labour supply was greater than the demand, and not everyone was strong enough to paddle to Lake Huron carrying hundred-pound packs. The rest were better off staking some land where they might keep body and soul together by combining some agriculture with part-time employment. Yet the town still sheltered a number of paupers who do not figure in notarial records and who more or less lived off charity.[77]

7 THE HABITANTS

The inventories of the habitants present a three-tiered picture. At the bottom, and severely under-represented in the sample, is the contingent of poor peasants, whose goods were never valued at more than 100 livres, a value that falls close to zero once their debts are taken into account. (See Table 42.)

Hugues Messaguier dit La Plaine came to Canada as a soldier. He lost his wife after eight years of marriage and was left with two children. When he contemplated remarrying in October 1695, he had his possessions inventoried. He then owned forty arpents in Lachine, six of them hand-ploughed, a few more barely cleared, a twelve-foot post-in-ground cabin with timber flooring and thatched roof, a shed, a "nearly fatted" pig, and two chickens. His harvest had brought in 35 minots of wheat and 17 minots of oats, barley, and pulses, a bare subsistence given the amount that had to be set

Table 42
Distribution of wealth of the peasantry, based on post-mortem inventories

Value of the assets (in livres tournois)

Periods	Less than 500	500 to 1,000	1,000 to 2,000	2,000 to 3,000	3,000 to 4,000	4,000 to 5,000	5,000 to 6,000	6,000 to 7,000	7,000 to 8,000	8,000 to 13,000	Total
1650–1669	2	4	3	–	2	–	–	–	–	–	11
1670–1689	1	5	9	3	2	1	1	–	–	–	22
1690–1715	3	5	12	12	2	3	2	–	1	1	41
1720–1729	–	–	1	3	3	1	–	–	–	–	8
Total	6	14	25	18	9	5	3	–	1	1	82

aside for the tithes, rentes, and seed. The inventory also mentions a chest, a bread bin, an old wooden canoe, a few tools and utensils, three worn-out blankets, and his family's clothing. He had also gathered white tobacco, which could possibly bring in 36 livres. His debts, which came to 212 livres, amounted to half his assets: he owed money to a merchant, to the surgeon who had taken care of his wife, and the vestry had to be paid for the funeral. There were also arrears on seigneurial dues and an obligation to the curé who had loaned him wheat for seed and for the family subsistence.[78] After eight years of work most colonists had got over the initial stage of destitution, but bad luck, inadequacy, and often unsuccessful experiences in the fur trade could account for such failures.

Half the rural dwellers left behind 1,000 to 3,000 livres, and, as Table 42 shows, the distribution remained unchanged. The peasants' primary asset was land. (See Table 43.) Their 30 to 40 arpents of arable land and meadows amounted to 50 per cent of the value of inventories. Next came a small, still rudimentary dwelling, no larger than eighteen by twenty feet but resting on foundations and roofed with planks. It included partitions, an attic, and a fireplace adequate to keep it warm in winter. Jacques Beauchamp of Pointe-aux-Trembles owned such a house. He died at the age of fifty-eight, leaving behind a widow, five married daughters, two boys aged fifteen and seventeen, and a net worth of 3,000 livres.[79] As in this case, the barn and cowshed together, with their thatched roofs, were often worth as much as the house: as we have seen, when profits were available, they were first expended on the farm's productive assets. The year was 1693, the time April, but although prices were high, there was

Table 43
Composition of peasant assets, 1670–1715

Average assets	2,200 livres	(100%)
Real estate		66%
Durable producer goods		23%
Durable consumer goods		6%
Claims and cash		5%
Liabilities		15%

enough wheat in the attic to suffice for the critical period before the next harvest.

Such tiny dwellings hardly contained any furniture: two chests, a bread bin, a folding table, three or four chairs. The kitchen utensils and tableware were always worth more than the furniture. The parents slept in an alcove, called the "cabane," which was often nailed to the wall and appraised along with the house. A "furnished bed," including curtains, a bolster, feather mattress and pillows, blankets and quilt, worth as much as 150 livres, would only be found in the better-off peasant households. Children apparently slept on the floor, on mattresses filled with straw or cattail grass and rolled up in dog-hair blankets, or in bear, elk, or ox skins. There were few woollen blankets, and half the inventories reported no linen. A chest filled with sheets, tablecloths, and napkins signalled a higher standard of living than the one attained by the Beauchamps. The habitants had a supply of flour, peas, lard, and sometimes butter, but never of imported goods such as pepper, wine, or brandy. The inventories do not mention salt.

It has become commonplace in Canadian historiography to claim that habitants were vain, that cowgirls went to the fields decked out like duchesses, and such conspicuous consumption is continually invoked to account for agricultural backwardness.[80] Could habitants who otherwise spent so little on their creature comforts have lost all restraint when it came to clothing? It does not seem so from the inventories.[81] Beauchamps' wardrobe consisted of the basics: a coat, a jerkin, and because nothing was ever thrown out, a second worn-out and worthless jerkin, a pair of hide hose, woollen breeches, a hat, a pair of shoes, stockings, four used shirts, and, two nightcaps, worth altogether no more than 40 to 50 livres. Even by doubling this amount to account for any omissions, we do not exceed reasonable bounds. A bride could well be endowed with a trousseau worth up to 150 livres, but it was made to last a lifetime.

A number of factors allowed about 10 per cent of habitants to rise above the mass. Success might depend on unstinting labour and the help of a number of sons, or a secondary occupation compatible with agriculture, such as carting or lime-burning, while a few were exceptionally lucky individuals who had been granted a large urban lot in the early days of the colony and had held on to it long enough to sell it at a profit.[82] It is notable that the better-off these peasants became, the more land they acquired, and if they patched up their buildings, they did not alter their lifestyle. The house was enlarged now that they could afford two stone fireplaces. They added chairs here and there, a panelled armoire, symbol of their success, blankets and sheets, more pewter, and sometimes a small mirror. Here as well there was no hint of ostentation.

One-quarter of inventories list only those debts brought on by the illness and demise of the individual in question. Half the successions recorded between 150 and 400 livres, representing mainly family debts such as unpaid succession claims or money owed to children for loans or services they had performed for their parents, along with arrears in seigneurial dues and outstanding accounts with merchants and artisans. If the liabilities proved any heavier, as in one-quarter of the sample, the movables had to be sold. The land was not affected because the merchants would not take it and usually did not extend loans beyond the value of livestock, tools, and other moveables. But without these, the farms could not be cultivated.

There is no sign of hoarding among these peasants. Two or three among the richest may have kept some gold or silver coins, but we find in the inventories neither card money nor beaver. The sums owed to the community included returns from grain, cattle, or land sales as well as anticipated inheritance shares. The peasantry took part in exchanges, as shown by these inventories, but they were never sufficiently important to disrupt or to strengthen their position.

8 THE SOCIAL DIMENSION

How much of the social system of Ancien Régime France survived in this small shoot transplanted to the American continent? Although occupational boundaries may sometimes have been hazy – which was not atypical per se – there was a fairly well-defined professional hierarchy. Still, the brakes on the colonial economy and easy access to land tended to reduce material differences and to bring the members of the various social groups to the same level.

This apparent equality masks the cleavages that remained under the surface. We must be able to recognize them and to follow any possible realignments in order to discover both the nature and the direction of social mobility.

Those who deny the existence of a coherent hierarchical structure invoke the fluidity of titles and of the vocabulary of appellation.[83] Yet the evolution of the terminology would seem, on the contrary, to indicate a very precise awareness of concrete realities and of the underlying subordinations. Take the word "habitant," which has been used throughout this work as a synonym for peasants, although this meaning only evolved very slowly. The term was first used to refer to free property owners, who were therefore differentiated from those who were not: servants, soldiers, and non-propertied volunteers.[84] This status entailed some privileges. Notarized deeds and enumerations mention "carpenter habitants" and "merchant habitants" or simply "habitants," meaning those who had no other occupation than clearing and tilling the soil.[85] Around 1675 notaries began to distinguish between merchants and masons "residing on the Island of Montreal" and the "habitants on this island"; and at the end of the century we read: "Pierre Désautels habitant resident of this island."[86] In the intervening period, ordinances defining the status of habitant ceased to have any effect. People without resident status and who did not own land in Montreal came to work in the town. Servants and soldiers alike took part in the fur trade. Shedding the restrictive distinctions that it had first acquired in the colony, the term came to denote no more than the age-old notion of a holder and tiller of a censive.[87] The *bailli* makes this plain: "*Manant*, habitant, tiller of the soil," he once shouted at a churchwarden who vied with him for the best place in church.[88] When Bacqueville de La Potherie wrote around 1700 of "the habitants of the countryside who would be called peasants in any other country," he was slightly mistaken, for the notion of land ownership remained tied to the term habitant, which is why tenant-farmers were referred to as "laboureurs."[89] Should one both own and rent, one became a "laboureur and habitant." No other distinctions were evident in the countryside, and the uniformity of the vocabulary expresses the absence of hierarchy that we have already noted.

As the meaning of the word "habitant" narrowed, the term "bourgeois" made its appearance. At first there were only "bourgeois merchants," but the appellation gradually spread. Yet it was not enough to reside in the town to earn this form of respect; one had also to hold a certain rank. Notaries, bailiffs, surgeons, and innkeepers, artisans and fur traders employing other men, even re-

tired habitants living in town in homes of their own either adopted
the title or were sometimes accorded it. The term basically referred
to people who did not perform lowly tasks. The distinction was
bolstered by the widespread use of the word "bourgeois" to mean
"master." Voyageurs, apprentices, and servants worked for "their
bourgeois." All this denotes a clear perception of the evolution of
the society.

What of the question of the particles and titles that have repeatedly led historians astray? Canadian usage did not really differ from
that current in France. Men who called themselves "écuyers" in
Montreal were either noblemen or reputed to be noble, and managed to retain that status. Surnames may have been more prevalent
in Canada than elsewhere. Immigrants came with them, but most
originated in the fur trade. The traders, influenced perhaps by the
particularism prevalent among the military, institutionalized the
adoption of surnames, which eventually eclipsed family names.[90] A
number of Trottiers went out west at the beginning of the century,
yet they appear in the merchants' account books under the names of
Desauniers, Desruisseaux, and Des Rivières, along with La Feilliade,
La Fortune, La Déroute and so on. When these adventurers became
more established, they dubbed themselves "Sieur des Rivières," and
the particle might well stand separately. Because this practice was so
widespread among the lower classes, it leaves no room for misinter-
pretation, while a reverse snobbery may well have impelled some
people to use only their names or surnames as their signatures.[91]
Whatever the case, a change of patronym never propelled anyone
upwards. The bulk of the habitants, small artisans, and workers
continued to be known by their first and last names or surnames
and were often tagged "le nommé" (known as). The "Sieur" and
parallel "dame" and "demoiselle" tended to be confined to those
who called themselves bourgeois. This may have included quite a
variety of humble folk in the case of notarized deeds or parish
records, which they dictated themselves, but in the tax rolls, or in
the list of creditors recorded in post-mortem inventories, such usage
was restricted to the upper echelons of the bourgeoisie. It could also
depend on the writer. The Sulpicians were grudging with titles and
in their enumerations would accord the petty nobility only the right
to a "Sieur," like the rest of the notables. They kept "monsieur" for
the governor, the lieutenant du roi, and the crown's top representatives. Notaries were more liberal. Officers were invariably dubbed
"monsieur," and merchants often were as well. A property trained
notary knew how to respect traditional gradations, something the
merchants were also aware of. When Raimbault made a few slips in

an inventory list of over two hundred pages, the son of the deceased corrected the erroneous titles and had the notary add those he had omitted.[92] These Sieurs altered to monsieur or vice versa, these carefully crossed-out prefixes of "ma" or "la," show the survival of a "chain of contempt," and the squabbles over precedence reveal the tensions that accompanied it.

This society was obviously not fixed. To see it clearly, it is useful to make a distinction between the mobility of entire groups, involving changes in their composition and in the gaps that separated them, and the social mobility of individuals.[93] Promotion was most noticeable at the bottom of the social scale. A loose group of destitute and unemployed individuals turned into small landowners and within one generation attained a certain level of security and respectability. This is the fundamental phenomenon.[94] Another slower ascension, which affected fewer people, was the transformation of coureurs de bois into voyageurs. An entire group pulled itself up from the lowest and most discredited of social positions and succeeded in carving itself a niche within the mercantile hierarchy. The casualties were heavy, and once the group had been safely installed, it pulled away the ladder. Yet this remains a clear example of the transformation of the socio-professional structure. The group achieved a level of social recognition that it had been denied at the outset.

Other categories were not affected: the nobility remained at the top, followed by the most successful merchants. The entry of individuals from the lower ranks into the upper may look impressive because the latter group was so tiny, but viewed from the standpoint of the number of persons who rose from the masses, upward mobility appears rather insignificant. In the first fifteen to twenty years there was enough room at the top to create some social stir. Of the 270 immigrants enumerated in 1667, 5 per cent had risen in the social scale or were about to.[95] But the higher echelons soon closed ranks, and thereafter only a handful would be allowed in. Altogether, between 1642 and 1715 there were barely ten people who had initially performed some manual work in the colony and then managed to have others forget this. The gunsmith Fezeret may have had his finger in many pies, but at the end of his days his contemporaries still referred to him as the "bonhomme Fezeret" who paid in labour for his pew in church.[96] His daughter would marry a lieutenant, scion of a metropolitan family of the robe, but the match would do nothing to improve the craftsman's status.[97]

Actually there was a great deal of downward social mobility. The volume of external trade did not keep pace with the population;

capital did not multiply as fast as the offspring of merchants. Thus the proportional difference between the members of the upper crust and the rest declined steadily, which meant that the excessive numbers produced by the first generation of merchants were relegated to the lower ranks. The Perthuis family is a good example. Pierre Perthuis was the son of a small Amboise merchant and came to Canada around 1667. He was twenty-three and could rely on the support of a number of relatives living in the colony.[98] In 1681 he already figured in the second stratum of merchant-outfitters. He was a man of good reputation who traded cautiously and led a modest life. His net assets at his death were of the order of 50,000 livres.[99] His two surviving sons and six sons-in-law were unable to maintain his socio-economic station. Two branches played some role in the trade, but as simple voyageurs.[100] The other descendants were habitants. There is no doubt that the sharing of the inheritance into eight equal parts brought on this fall. A single heir would probably have been able to hold on to his position within the merchant community, but any others would inevitably have been driven back. The ascent of a merchant could be speedily reversed.

More money and fewer children might halt this downward pressure, as would close ties with the class that was safeguarded from the vagaries of trade, whose reproduction was therefore not constrained by economic fluctuations. There was only one sure way to keep one's social status for more than one generation, and that was by joining the colonial nobility. Of some 120 merchants whose concerns were thriving at one time or another between 1650 and 1724, three were accorded this ultimate sanction in their lifetimes, while the descendants of another four would eventually achieve it.

There were few avenues of ascension. The Crown had begun by conferring nobility in order to encourage colonization: seven Canadian merchants were granted such letters gratis before 1669, as were four others later in the century, before the practice was abandoned.[101] Charles Lemoyne, ennobled in 1668 as a tribute to the handsome fortune he was amassing and for services rendered, was the only Montrealer in this group. Jacques Leber purchased one of the blank letters of nobility sold by Louis XIV during the War of the League of Augsburg. His ships were sailing the high seas, and he had a capital of about 250,000 livres. He could well afford to spend the requisite 6,000 livres.[102] There were fewer handouts of this sort in the eighteenth century, and no Canadian was either able or bold enough to request them.[103] Ennobling offices, so common in France, did not exist in the colony. Possession of a fief, of course, did not convey nobility, and it did not necessarily signify upward mobility.

By confusing the issues of seigneury, nobility, and prestige some Canadian historians have constructed a completely muddled picture of this society. "It is not fitting for an ordinary habitant to hold fiefs," but there was nothing to stop commoners from buying those that the Crown had granted to noblemen.[104] There were a number of seigneurial properties on the market, and these were purchased mainly by merchants, sometimes by artisans or peasants. Why else, we might wonder, if not for prestige? If that was what the landclearer Laurent Bory had in mind in 1672, when he settled on his fief of La Guillaudière, two thousand arpents of forest, then he was in for a terrible disappointment. He would never be known as Bory, Sieur de Grandmaison. He remained a peasant, and when his son wed the daughter of a carpenter, he did not marry beneath him.[105] Pierre Lamoureux bought the arrière-fief that the brothers Berthé owned on the west end of the Island of Montreal, but this did not improve his social standing, and despite the excellent location, neither father nor sons made a go as outfitters.[106] The edge-tool maker Milot bought the fief of Cavelier de La Salle in 1669 and continued to work at his craft, leaving some money behind. In 1700 Montrealers continued to refer to him as "le bourguignon," as they always had done.[107] His children had decent dowries but made ordinary marriages, and even the descendants of the eldest son, who inherited the fief, remained people of low status. Other such examples could be found. There was more prestige attached to the title of "merchant bourgeois of Montreal" than to that of "seigneur" of such and such a place, a title that was in fact used rarely, those with land merely mentioning if need be that they were the "owners" of a particular fief.

Merchants sometimes bought fiefs because they came for nothing and in many cases were cheaper than a good censive on the outskirts of Montreal. The grantees were badly in need of money and let thousands of uncultivated arpents go for 2,000 to 3,000 livres. A merchant could well afford to invest such a small sum, and even if he did not improve this distant property, he could look forward to some capital gains once settlement spread.[108] Charles Lemoyne acquired Ile Perrot for 825 livres in 1684, and his son resold it twenty years later, unimproved, for 2,625 livres, which represented a decent profit.[109] Those who made a bigger outlay expected immediate returns. Couagne, for example, began by taking an option on La Chesnaye. He farmed out the domain and granted a few censives, yet six months later allowed the deal to drop. A little later he acquired an uninhabited fief on the Richelieu for a song.[110] For such merchants, who showed little interest in developing these properties, did not live on them, and sold at the first opportunity, these were mere speculations without any social significance.[111]

Jacques Testart, a merchant's son who distinguished himself in the militia, managed to enter the officer corps and was awarded the Saint-Louis Cross, becoming ipso facto integrated into the colonial nobility.[112] But this was a rare occurrence. Officer families produced a surfeit of candidates for the military, and commissions could not be purchased, leaving little room for merchant ambitions in that direction. Exceptional valour might earn one a place, but it was difficult to outdo those who had natural claims.[113]

The right marriage might further a family's social advancement. "I will insist," the governor wrote the minister, "that in the future officers make marriages that are both suitable and profitable."[114] The authorities showed great interest in these matters. One way to help poor noblemen was to encourage them to make good matches. One widow brought 10,000 livres to an officer discharged from the Carignan regiment who had survived on government bounty, and this pleased the intendant no end.[115] The union of the ensign Leber, who was already well off, with the daughter of a merchant worth 50,000 écus, was of course sufficiently noteworthy to be mentioned to the minister.[116] A *mésalliance* was only noticed when a young man of good birth took it into his head to marry a commoner who brought him nothing. Yet on the whole the nobility tended to close ranks. The exogamy rate for a sample of fifty officer families with a total of ninety-two first- and second-generation marriages stands at 33 per cent.[117] Since the group represented no more than 2 per cent of the population, it was relatively homogeneous, especially since most of the exogamous unions adhered to the classic schema, meaning that it was only women of the lower classes who were raised up. The inverse was exceptional.[118] In most cases these unions had no effect on the status of the bride's relatives, although in a few instances where the commoner family had some means, it did trigger upward mobility. Couagne's children were able to pursue military careers because his widow remarried a young officer. The same advantage accrued to the sons of J.-B. Charly, whose wife was a d'Ailleboust. However, the business relations sealed by such unions have more importance, for we should never forget that this petty military nobility was involved in the fur trade. In Canada it was not the bourgeoisie that set itself to conquer the nobility's economic bastions but the officers who invaded the world of commerce. The Crown did all it could to help them: they were handed trade permits and the leases of the western outposts, and they did not lose their noble status. The merchants had no choice but to stick with them, to finance and support them, in order to profit from privileges that they as commoners would never be given directly and without which, ironically enough, the merchants might eventually have lost their hold on trade. This was a very odd situation, filled with the potential for conflict, to say the least, but one that the merchants accepted passively until the end of the regime. There were no "bourgeois-gentilshommes" in New France, in spite of the title of a well-known study.[119] There were gentilshommes and there were bourgeois, the latter too insecure, too few, not rich and experienced enough to be fully conscious of their position. Unconcerned with the nature of the regime, they accepted the alliance they were offered, and they worked tirelessly to cement it until they lost their partners, a century later, and found themselves alone, facing a group of foreign officers who could well dispense with their services.

CHAPTER FOURTEEN

The Family

There are no diaries, no family record books, not even any worthwhile travellers' accounts that might help us better understand this society and its mental universe. We must therefore turn once again to the notarial records. Those which deal with family matters seem the most likely to bring us into contact with the world of the average settler and allow us to examine the values that prevailed there. This is an approach which goes against the historiographic tide of recent years: Quebec historians have been more inclined to search the past for anything that foreshadows present-day restlessness and have therefore highlighted disorder and deviance in their portrayals of New France.[1] On the surface, my views appear closer to those of an earlier generation of historians who saw the fate of the community as determined by its domestic virtues and the zeal of its priests. Ideological considerations apart, it should be possible to demonstrate the truth of what other scholars grasped by intuition, namely that the family became particularly important because of the initial isolation of the settlement and, eventually, to the weakness of public institutions. When Léon Gérin, the eminent Canadian sociologist, delved into these questions at the end of the nineteenth century, he discovered in the Quebec countryside the stem-family so dear to his teachers in France, Le Play, Tourville, and Demolins.[2] The following generation of sociologists took exception to some of Gérin's generalizations, but the issue was left hanging for lack of historical evidence.[3] Whatever new information is offered in the following pages may perhaps serve to reopen a debate that has not lost any of its relevance.

1   TYPES OF HOUSEHOLD

The last nominal census taken in New France dates from 1681. Despite its proximity to the last wave of immigration, which maintained the imbalance between the sexes and an abnormal age structure, this document still yields some worthwhile information about households.[4]

Trips out west and late marriage meant that this society would always have a certain number of independent bachelors. But the sizable proportion noted in Table 44 was short-lived and can be traced to a lack of females and the recent release of indentured servants and soldiers. Besides, not all of these fifty-seven bachelors actually lived alone. Other documents show that some immigrants boarded with families. Peasants' sons usually continued to live with their parents until they married, even when they were granted a censive (a grant of land). In short, the compilers of the census listed property owners separately, without paying heed to the residence of these single individuals. Still, the grouping of households is easy to understand.

In the early days non-relatives often shared living quarters. For instance, two men turned to a notary to put in common all their earthly belongings, including the lot that they held together from the seigneurs. They promised to help each other in sickness, and to leave everything to the survivor.[5] There is no better illustration of the anxiety of these unattached males. The marriage of one of the partners without a prior dissolution gave rise to a tripartite community of assets. Henri Perrin went on living in the Jarry household. He was godfather to the first child and, after Jarry's death, fathered the fourth, whereupon the bishop granted the necessary dispensation to put an end to this legal and moral imbroglio.[6] Later on such male households would not be defined in this formal way. The arrangements would be more ephemeral – as for those young men who leased a farm together – and the authorities would not find them as suspect as they were in New England.[7]

As we might expect, the Western European family structure predominated. There were, on average, 3.4 children per family, which is relatively high. The modal structure was four children, or six people per household. Rough calculations, based on later aggregate censuses, indicate that the number of children per family remained more or less stable until the beginning of the eighteenth century. The slowdown in immigration and consequent effects on the marriage rate subsequently brought it down and kept it around three.[8] Even poorer parents kept their children at home for a long

Table 44
Structure of households on the Island of Montreal in 1681

Types	Percentage of households	Number of households
1. Single people (presumed)	21	2 widows 57 bachelors (or civil status unknown)
2. Household with no family structure	0	1 co-residence of two unrelated men
3. Single family households	76	28 married couples 164 married couples with children 7 widowers with children 9 widows with children
4. Extended family households	2	2 extended upwards 1 extended downwards 2 extended laterally
5. Multiple family households	1	3 descending joint family
Total	100	276

Total population: 1,390
Average household size: 4.6
Modal household size: 6.0
Extreme sizes 1–13
Average number of children per family (households type 3, 4, and 5): 3.4
Average number of servants per family: 0.2
Source: AC, G1, 460.

time. Only a minority went into service or became apprenticed at an early age. Household size had little to do with the number of servants, who represented only 7 per cent of the overall population.

More complex households were not common: two old people living with their married offspring, four young couples residing with their parents, brothers and sisters who had emigrated together and continued to share quarters after one of them married. There was a tiny range of possible combinations, which would swell only when the population had fully developed and as successive generations made new demands.

Demographic patterns, however, imposed limits on this growth in the number of secondary family units in the existing household. Take a simple example. A man and a woman married at the ages of twenty-eight and twenty-one respectively, had a child every two years, and produced ten children, five or six of whom survived.

When the father began to decline physically in his fifties, he still had a brood of young children, his eldest no more than seventeen. At sixty he was still the master of his farm, with one or two sons under twenty-five still living at home. Running the farm required no added labour, and the presence of married children would merely reduce the living space. This was how things stood when he died. Later on the children would have to come to some arrangement with their mother, who was more likely to live to see them all settled.[9] Large families, high mortality rates, the spread between births, and especially the fact that men married late combined to reduce the number of complex households. Nevertheless, if later nominal censuses were available, they would chart the rise of such households, for even if the system of inheritance did not require it, familial solidarity encouraged the incorporation of various relatives into the nuclear family.

2 MARRIAGE COMMUNITY AND INHERITANCE

The marriage community

Signing marriage contracts before a notary was a common practice in Montreal, as it was, apparently, throughout the colony. It must initially have been one of the many ways of celebrating what was a rare and welcome event. Thus we see the local notables clustering around newlyweds from the lower classes. The first contracts represented no more than a promise of marriage stipulating that the couple would form, for legal and property purposes, a corporate entity, the "marriage community," as set down in the Coutume de Paris.[10]

Even after the first decades the ratio of contracts to marriages remained very high. The proportion seems to have been the same at the end of the seventeenth century as the 96 per cent calculated for the period 1750–70.[11] Whereas in France only the comparatively well off procured a notarized marriage contract, Canadian settlers of all classes went through the signing ritual as a matter of course. Why? Is this an indication of some sort of social pretention or of a weakness for formalities? I think not. It was rather the exceptional circumstances of colonial life that made these legal conventions a necessity.

The family law sections of the Coutume de Paris, with its protective provisions ensuring the maintenance of widows and the preservation of the estate against alienation or the claims of creditors, were based on several important concepts and distinctions.[12] Property was divided into "biens de communauté" which were owned by the marital community and "propres" which were attached to an individual. Virtually all moveable wealth fell into the first category, as did land that was purchased after the couple's marriage. Immoveable property (essentially land) inherited by the husband or wife remained his or her personal "propre" and, as such, was treated differently in the inheritance settlement that followed the owner's death. But in Canada the first colonists had no *propres*. Land granted them before or during the marriage was treated as an acquiest and automatically included in the marriage community.[13] Subsequent generations sometimes mentioned *propres*, but since estates were never large, given the effects of equal division among heirs, the concept was largely inoperative. In many cases the lot was almost worthless at the time of marriage and would only acquire some value after years of combined labour. In order to avoid arguments about initial and added values, land was often simply incorporated into the marriage community. "The future couple's lot located in the Côte Saint Leonard ... will be part of the marriage community since it is unimproved."[14] In the case of a developed farm, only the heir who took control by buying all his siblings' shares truly had a *propre*. Even if his brothers and sisters claims legally fell into the category of immoveable property, they were nevertheless treated as moveable wealth and merged in the coheirs' marriage communities. Moreover, a number of marriage contracts specifically transformed inherited land or a share in the same into movable assets.[15] This meant that the surviving spouse came into possession of property that normally should have reverted to the deceased's family, where it originated. In the event of remarriage, this property, or half of it if there was progeny, became part of the new marriage community. Rarely did estates revert to parents; instead, the universality and centrality of the marital community ensured that property passed into the hands of the surviving spouse.

Although provided for in a general way by the Coutume de Paris, the marital community afforded little protection from lawsuits unless its individual features were specified in a marriage contract. According to the law, a widow was automatically entitled to half the revenue derived from her deceased husband's personal property during her lifetime (*douaire coutumier*). In the absence of any *propres*, this revenue was replaced by a lump-sum payment specified in the marriage contract, to be taken from the marriage community (*douaire préfix*). "The groom endows the bride-to-be with the *douaire coutu-*

mier or, if she prefers, the sum of 300 livres as *douaire préfix*, which she can take from the ready and available liquid assets of the community.''[16] The amount, based in principle on the couple's potential earnings, would be about 300 livres for the peasants. Officers might go as high as 4,000 to 6,000 livres, such sums reflecting the groom's social pretensions and the bride's parents' anxieties rather than actual or anticipated assets.[17] Merchants provided smaller *douaires* of 1,000 to 2,000 livres. Notaries obviously advised their clients to take such basic precautions, but since all the settlers, even the poorest, availed themselves of their services, they must have deemed them necessary.

People of rank always added another safeguard called the *préciput*, giving the surviving spouse, whether male or female, the right to retrieve a certain amount prior to the division of the estate. This gradually trickled downward in society, but more slowly than the *douaire préfix*.[18] In short, widows of all classes held preferential claims against the marriage community, and if the latter was encumbered with debts, it was to the widow's advantage to renounce this community and stick to these conventions.

An attempt to study social stratification through the dowries and other personal assets listed in marriage contracts would not be very revealing. Over half the hundred or so contracts analysed for the period 1650 to 1701 did not mention any dowry at all. This is hardly surprising in the case of brides recruited in France to populate the colony.[19] But in the case of local girls there appears to be no obvious correlation between the parents' means and the presence or absence of a dowry.[20] Yet most young couples were helped by their parents, and the sums were scrupulously entered in private accounts or figured in post-mortem inventories in the form of various obligations. It hardly mattered whether the value or nature of such endowments was mentioned or not in the marriage contract, for they were not permanent but simply advances on the inheritance (*avance d'hoirie*).[21] These liberalities, or rather their value, would eventually be restored to the parents' estate, subject to equal division by inheritance.

When they were specified, these endowments turn out to consist of such things as livestock, ploughing or cartage, wheat seed, household goods and garments (beds with bed linen or wedding clothes), room and board in the parents' home, or sometimes a piece of land.[22] Should a sum of money be mentioned without further details, chances are that the young couple received a milch-cow and fatted pig rather than cash.[23] These advances, whether recorded or not, were obviously limited by the parents' available assets. When they had none, inheritance records indicate that the 200- or 300-livre endowment specified in the marriage contract would never be paid.[24]

Lack of information was also frequent among the upper classes. The groom's personal assets were rarely recorded in the contracts, although other sources may reveal their existence. These were passed over in silence and incorporated into the community.[25] The new couple brought to the marriage community movable and landed property, inherited or to be inherited; the failure of the marriage contract to mention this does not mean that they were poor, any more than the promises of 10,000-livre dowries constitutes proof of wealth.[26] It became necessary to state the amount and nature of the advance only when the parents or the couple wished to transform these endowments into personal property (propres). This was common practice among the officers, and sometimes among the merchants. These same families also resorted to the notion of "côté, estoc et ligne," to make sure that such propres would remain in the endowed offspring's lineage, but these concerns were foreign to popular mentality.[27]

Marriage contracts also included the mutual gift of all movables and real estate to the surviving member provided there were no children living at the death of one spouse. This was important to the first colonists, who had no kin in the colony. If they were to die intestate, the deceased's half of the marriage community would not fall into escheat and be appropriated by the seigneurs. The clause became more and more common in the following generations: in most cases it took the form of clear-cut donations, which allowed the recipient to enjoy and dispose of the assets "as if they were his own" and "he had acquired them himself"; this sometimes even extended to propres.[28] The colonists were obviously averse to ascending or collateral forms of devolution. One should be aware that the Coutume de Paris forbade such donations. The notaries were well aware of this, since such contracts had to be registered.[29]

To summarize, a very powerful centripetal force affected the marital unit. The marriage agreements do not point to confrontations between two families involved in a business deal. Rather, they testify to the good will of the parents, who collaborated in the formation of a new marriage community and tried to protect it as best they could. The marriage community was also the norm, though less absolutely, among the local upper class.[30] If indeed French jurisprudence tended more and more to maintain each spouse's patrimony by limiting the principle of acquests, the contrary held true in Canada. This trend distanced the society from aristocratic values and brought it back to an older, simpler, and more generous tradition.

Inheritance

The same simplicity and generosity guided the sharing of estates, and in this case there were no initial equivocations. The settlers opted straight away for equality, thereby embodying the levelling tendencies that had already been evident among the common people of central France since the fourteenth century. It is quite likely that the availability of land on the new continent, the freedom from crippling fiscal pressures, and the small number of true nobles strengthened and even accelerated this trend.[31] We might be tempted to link the provincial origins of the Montreal colonists, who came primarily from western France, with this preference for complete equality and the restoration of endowments to the estate, a preference so systematic that it appears mandatory. This was, after all, typical of Normandy and western France. But archaic traits such as the notion of lineage underpinning these customs, the dominance of *propres* and the absence or weakness of the marriage community, were not transplanted overseas.[32] Canadian procedures were in fact rooted in the Coutume de Paris, but there was a wide gap between this sophisticated legal corpus and the inheritance practices of the habitants.

As André Morel argues, legal writers have placed too great an emphasis on the testatory restrictions imposed by the Coutume, and the same criticism can be levelled against Canadian historians imbued with the superiority of the English tradition.[33] Take the case of an average peasant at the end of the seventeenth century who left four children and a farm worth 2,000 livres, with its livestock and other movables worth another 1,200. There was nothing to stop him from giving the land to only one of his children. The movables divided equally among the other three would have covered their *légitime*, in this case 400 livres, which was all they were legally entitled to.[34] Even so, the concept of the *légitime* was never applied in Canada, at least in the period and region under review.[35]

A father had three ways of favouring one of his heirs: through a dowry, a bequest in his will, or a donation *inter vivos*. We have already seen that children did not receive permanent dowries but only an advance on an inheritance. Some families granted equal endowments; others did not. There was no hard and fast rule. The advance was not necessarily given as part of a marriage settlement. This lack of rigidity and uniformity, as well as the puniness of the advances, shows that the parents had no intention of using them either to exclude children from an inheritance or to set them up once and for all. Endowment and inheritance were never considered alternative choices. Dowries were only granted to daughters entering into religious orders, who were legally excluded from the inheritance.[37]

If we add the notarized wills that have been found to the wills made under private seal mentioned in inventories, we find that about one-quarter of the inhabitants expressed their last wishes in this fashion. A man who died in his prime and who had direct heirs did not bother to make a will. The aged were more likely to think of it, widows especially. The testators worried about their souls and the people they left behind, but rarely about material things. We find the traditional clauses: choice of burial place, masses and funeral, repayment of debts, settling of grievances, bequests to the poor, to the parish or some convent, practical concerns accompanied often by fair words and advice to the living. The testator might sometimes express his gratitude towards a member of his family who had treated him particularly well by leaving that person a small legacy. "He bequeaths a seven-month-old chestnut foal to his son, Louis Chauvin, in lieu of the wages he would have earned had he not stayed with him to help him with his work, without his needing to restore its value to his brothers and sisters when the estate is divided."[38] There were similar token gifts to godchildren or grandchildren.

Merchants had fewer scruples about imposing their wishes. The seventy-five-year-old Jacques Leber left some 200,000 livres to his grandson "to keep the property in the family, given the poor husbandry and bad conduct of his son Jacques Leber and the way he has squandered his own property." The latter obtained only the usufruct of the fortune. Leber left nothing to the children of an eldest son who had died in France, where he had taken his family, nor to another who had renounced worldly goods to found a hospice, nor to a devout daughter who lived as a recluse in a convent.[39] All the children had been amply provided for at the death of their mother, and the father had shown himself generous during his lifetime. Yet this did not give him the legal right to disinherit any of them.[40] Not all merchants adopted the principles that guided this will – protection of the patrimony and perpetuation of the lineage in the country that had witnessed its rise.[41] Snobbery did contribute to the spread of these values, yet not without an equal measure of resistance: some years earlier the eldest Leber had renounced the privilege of primogeniture in favour of an equal division of a fief acquired by his father. The Lemoynes, another wealthy family, made no distinction between fiefs and common land when they divided their estate equally among the heirs, and in the following century a baker asked the seigneurs to change his fief into a censive "to ensure equality among his children."[42]

Merchants adhered to the notion of partible inheritance and, to a man, used their wills as a means of inventorying their worldly goods and establishing the value of advances on the inheritance and other gifts in order to prevent squabbling among their heirs. They used them as well for small bequests, but not to favour one heir over the rest.[43] Yet it may have been more natural (and this is where the Leber example comes in) for a man of means to dispose of his fortune as he pleased than for a poor father to deprive his children of the few livres they might expect to receive.

Parents who decided to favour one of their heirs relied on the third option provided by the coutume: that of donations *inter vivos*. Such contracts were characterized by two conditions: they were drawn up by elderly parents who depended on the goodwill of their children for their livelihood and security, and they were made in the presence and with the assent of all the heirs. They were therefore family agreements born out of necessity rather than unilateral decisions of the donors. Since there were few old people in the first decades, such arrangements were not legion. In 1680 Mathurin Lorion, attended by his wife, informed his three sons-in-law that "old age and infirmities made it impossible for him to support himself by his own labour, that his twenty-one-year-old son Jean, who had been a great help to him, wanted to leave him and go into service in order to put something away for his own future, and should this happen, he would be in dire straits." Mathurin begged the heirs to take this into consideration and to accept his decision to turn over all his goods (and he pointed out their meagreness) to Jean, who would become responsible for his debts and for keeping him and his wife, paying for their funerals, and having masses said for the repose of their souls. The son "favoured" in this way fulfilled his filial duty for eighteen years until his mother died, whereupon he married at the age of thirty-seven.[44]

These gifts could sometimes appear as sales. Jean Lacombe and his wife, "totally incapable of running their property" and wanting to express their gratitude towards their son Jean-Baptiste, who had stayed with them and helped them, sold him one-third of their farm, with the consent of the co-heirs. Presumably this was a fictitious sale. When his parents died, the son was still entitled to his share of the remaining two-thirds and of the movables.[45] Such pre-

cautions are surprising, since these arrangements in no way deprived the other heirs of their *légitime*, and the parents were legally free
to dispose of this portion of their property as they pleased. Yet they
did not feel that they were morally empowered to do so.[46] Parents
had other ways of providing for their old age besides such gifts.
They might give up the usufruct of their property in return for a
fixed pension, without sacrificing the equal division of the land.
This presupposed, however, that the farm yielded enough to tempt
one of the heirs.

Remarriages offer another measure of the strength of the conjugal
unit and of the egalitarian values underpinning this society. Take
the case of a widow with small children, the most common occurrence. While she held to her half of the marriage community, the
orphans had a claim on the other half. However, her remarriage
called for a dissolution of this community, preceded by an inventory, in order to establish what she and the children were entitled
to. The widow's share, with the added provisions of the *douaire* and
préciput, was incorporated into the new marriage community. As
long as the orphans remained under the family roof, they had no
right to the usufruct, or their inheritance, and their stepfather
managed the whole estate. They could demand their share when
they came of age.[47] Normally the girls lived at home until their
weddings and the boys until the age of fifteen to twenty, but rarely
until the age of majority, legally set at twenty-five. Relatives kept an
eye on these marriage contracts, all the more so when the parent
who married again was old and rich.[48]

These were the proper procedures, but the lower classes were
inclined to jettison such agreements in favour of a second marriage
as simple and economically coherent as the first. They managed this
by adopting any children from the first marriage. "The groom
promises to adopt the child she is carrying in her belly and which
may be born to her as if it were the issue of their own legitimate
marriage."[49] "The groom adopts as his own and legitimate children
Catherine and Martin Coureau, who will receive an equal share in
the future estate along with whatever legitimate children might be
born to the future couple."[50] The children's mother took everything
she could claim from the estate of her first husband into the new
marriage community, leaving so little that there was no point in
reserving anything for the orphans, who would eventually have to
share the consolidated inheritance deriving from both marriages. In
all cases, the first household had broken up early on and the
children to be born to the second marriage were the only ones likely
to suffer from the arrangement. We find instances of mutual adop-

tion, as in the following example involving two families of voyageurs. Pierre Lamoureux, with his three children, and Barbe Lecel, with her little girl, agreed to pool all the assets derived from their previous marriages and to adopt each other's children, "who would share equally the inheritance with those who might follow later."[51]

It then became a simple matter to divide the estate. Each child declared what he or she had received during the parents' lifetime. The value of these endowments was added to the stock of movable property and credits due to the estate, while outstanding debts, pious bequests, and other expenses were deducted. The remainder was split into as many shares as there were heirs. Each was entitled to the difference between this amount and whatever he or she had already received, and those who had received more were bound to turn the excess over to the others.[52] Real estate was then shared in the manner already described.[53] The dilemma of legacy versus inheritance never became an issue.[54]

As long as the surviving spouse did not remarry, the estate usually remained undivided and this normally lasted until the youngest child came of age. After the dissolution of the community, and even anticipating it, the co-heirs effected various transactions among themselves, which resulted in the concentration of land and movables into the hands of one, two at the most.[55] The fact that inheritance claims were often treated as a negotiable asset before the division of the estate and that strangers accepted this form of payment even before the parents died shows the extent to which this society took equal division for granted. The buyer could make a rough estimate of the value of the succession and rest assured that the claims he had acquired would not be deflated.

Indebtedness remained a problem, however. Families faced with this external threat suddenly realized the value of customary provisions. Young widows who retrieved their *douaire* and *préciput* salvaged a sizable portion of their marriage community, but it was unusual for the heirs to refuse the estate of a more established peasant family. Bourgeois and especially officer families offer better examples of the subtleties of the Coutume, the intricacies governing *propres*, the recourse to *douaire* bestowed on children, and other tortuous contrivances that exasperated creditors.[56]

The common people adhered to a tradition that had been profoundly altered by the release of medieval constraints. The settlers brought this tradition with them from central, northern, or western France; the place is immaterial, for the essence was the same. And where would it flourish better, unhampered, than in this empty land?[57]

The economic repercussions of the system of partible inheritance may be obvious,[58] but its causes are less clear, for the Coutume de Paris did not impose such strict equality.[59] A look at future developments might round off this discussion. Families were able to multiply and spread across the colony as long as land remained available and there were no market stimuli. They could ignore the legal mechanisms designed to halt the fragmentation of rural capital, and continue to give each offspring an equal chance. Little of this changed before the nineteenth century, and the testamentary freedom introduced in 1774 was not taken up in the countryside.[60] Traditional practices would only die out once land became scarce and a large part of the agrarian sector became regularly involved in the market economy. At that critical point, rigidly egalitarian inheritance laws could have set off a Malthusian reaction.[61] But the English legal system provided less drastic options. The stem-family that the sociologist Gérin observed at the end of the nineteenth century may not have been widespread, but it became common practice to exclude from the succession children who had been endowed at marriage. They heeded the call of near and far-off industries. Yet there were places, the towns, for example, where these constraints did not apply and egalitarian intestate successions still remained the norm.

The practices described in this section tell us not only about material conditions in the early days of the colony but also about the prevailing values of this society. The absence of a distinction between *propres* and *conquets* property implies that family land was not the cornerstone of the family, and that the latter's unity was not tied to its preservation. The lack of differentiation between endowed and non-endowed children shows that people did not think of the family as a unit of production where members' rights would be strictly defined according to their contribution. The roots of family solidarity lay elsewhere.

3 FAMILY RELATIONS

Philippe Ariès has described the seventeenth century as a time when centrifugal social forces and centripetal familial forces entered a period of equilibrium. The modern family emerged at the end of the Middle Ages and began to supersede other types of human relations, less favourable to the development of domestic intimacy.[62] For a long time, according to Ariès, these changes affected only nobles, the bourgeoisie, and wealthier artisans and peasants. The poor, by contrast, were slow to develop a sense of the family, partly because of the custom of apprenticeships, which separated young children from their parents, and partly because their overcrowded, uncomfortable lodgings forced them to spend much of their time out of doors.[63]

The Canadian family of the seventeenth century fits into this broad trend, although the special conditions of colonial life hastened its modernization. Traditional forms of sociability such as guild or religious associations, village feasts, and neighbourhood and kinship ties did not exist at first and were never fully reconstituted. There was nothing to threaten the isolation of the first households, and, when new poles of attraction developed outside the family, they did not conflict with the sense of privacy nurtured early on. Furthermore, since the colonial economy required few artisans and consequently there were never large numbers of children leaving home to become apprentices; consequently the feeling of belonging to a closed family unit did not take as long to develop as in France.[64]

There is ample evidence that the family was a strong institution, especially among the lower classes, but some qualifications are needed. Traditional traits, hostile to intimacy and paternal authority, indifferent to the need for education, had not completely disappeared. A casual, tolerant attitude continued here as elsewhere to regulate family relations. Colonial authorities viewed it as an unhealthy adoption of Indian mores, although its roots in fact lay in the European past. "The local residents imitate the Indians and manifest an immoderate affection for their children, which prevents them from chastising them and developing their sense of honour."[65] This contemptuous view is expressed even more forcefully by those historians who believe that any display of individualism, as distinct from present-day middle-class family values, must be a sign of savagery and constituted a break with ancient European peasant traditions.[66] In fact there is evidence of the influence of both the French past and the need to adapt to a new continent.

Husbands and wives

In the early days of the colony people were quick to tie the knot, especially when the bride had been shipped over at government expense for that very purpose. But this involved no more than 10 per cent of the couples who married on the Island of Montreal before 1715. Normally, young people got to know each other better, particularly because so many men were tied down by indentureship contracts or military service, which they had to complete before marrying. The maturity of couples at marriage and the concentration of weddings in a few months of the year also show that they had plenty of time to think things over. According to the standard formula, the ceremony followed "an engagement and publication of three banns." It is impossible to say whether engagements were formally blessed or not in the seventeenth century. Because priests were so scarce and the parishioners so scattered, such practices were probably reduced to a minimum. In 1698 the synod made them illegal because the betrothed supposedly took too many liberties, and this may indicate that the custom was already dying.[67] The marriage bed was blessed, at least in theory, right after the ceremony and before the wedding meal.[68]

In 1717 the bishop issued a pastoral letter threatening to excommunicate any couples who stood up during mass and announced they were married without the proper sacrament, but such nuptials "à la gaulmine" were infrequent.[69] Antoine Boyer *dit* Lafrance, a native of the Ile de Ré who had been stationed in Montreal for four years, confessed that he had resorted to it because the governor would not give him permission to marry.[70] The *bailliage* registers record only one other case, with a similar excuse.

To what extent did parents influence the choice of a spouse? They certainly had a say in upper-class families. Philippe Carion bequeathed his entire fortune to his eleven-year-old daughter and the husband he had chosen for her. In the meantime she was left in the care of her future father-in-law. No provision was made for the possibility that she might eventually reject these paternal wishes.[71] The little information that survives, allied with evidence of the strong endogamy of these social groups, attests that marriages were not merely affairs of the heart.[72]

Parental interference was far more rare among the lower classes. Though young people were free to make their own choices, there is every reason to believe that girls were under pressure to marry young. Large families and precarious economic conditions made this imperative, for girls contributed little to the household. There was hardly any domestic industry, and they had practically no opportunity of bringing in wages from the outside. Unless the mother died or was ill, girls who stayed at home became a burden, and if they never married, they remained a problem for their parents and for their brothers and sisters.[73] Parents who had no sons and whose future depended on their daughter's union would do all they could to get her settled. Rather than wait for her to marry a local boy with better prospects, they would encourage her to marry a soldier or other recent immigrant. As long as his background seemed decent and there was no hint of impropriety, no one objected to these leaps into the unknown. After all, the parents had married in exactly the same way.

Unmarried sons, however, could prove an asset. A boy helped his father and ran the farm when he grew weak or died; he took care of his aged parents and younger siblings. All this was easier to arrange if he was single. A son might become a voyageur and contribute to the household finances, by settling outstanding debts, for instance. The liabilities listed in post-mortem inventories demonstrate that such contributions were quite frequent.[74]

There was little about courtship or married life that was out of the ordinary. According to Henripin's calculation of the rate of pre-marital conceptions in the colony in the eighteenth century, some 10 per cent of brides came to the altar pregnant.[75] There were few paternity suits, and they seldom took long enough to set tongues wagging. One could use the cases of debauchery before the courts to paint a picture of an amoral society, but it would simply not be true. Montreal had its share of prostitutes and procuresses. We know their names because they repeatedly appear in the court records.[76] Yet sexual mores were remarkably tame for a garrison town and an area with a sustained and marked imbalance between the sexes. This is not to deny that behaviour was coarse, that seventeenth-century morality differed from that of the nineteenth, and that peasants continued to display a surprising degree of freedom and immodesty in their personal relations. A young bride complained to her parents that her husband was impotent. She harangued her unfortunate spouse in front of witnesses, calling him a "gelding," while her mother charged that "he had nothing stiff under his shirt" and "only tripe in his breeches," and defied him then and there to prove her wrong.[77] The importance accorded virility comes to light in a number of disputes. A marriage that was not consummated would be annulled after public proceedings that no one found embarrassing.[78]

That prosecution for adultery was always directed against women, and that their accessories tended to be soldiers rather than married men, tells us more about what was expected of women than about the virtue of local men.[79] Yet husbands who had been deceived nearly always kept their wives and even found excuses for them. Claude Jodoin denounced the officer who had got his wife to go to bed with him "by promising to give her presents ... and taking unfair advantage of their poverty," and he added that after four months' "separation from his wife, he felt so desperate that he was ready to go off to the enemy ... he took her back and now lives peacefully with her, for he understands that all this happened because of La Freynière's powerful solicitations."[80] Although the court had ruled that the surgeon Bouchard could have his wife locked up or sent back to her parents, he made repeated attempts to straighten her out, if only out of "duty to God."[81] Claude Leblond made similar efforts to get his wife back, despite her unforgivable public misdemeanours.[82] Recourse to the judiciary appears to have been a way of bolstering an obviously shaky marital authority. A more irritable man, the tenant-farmer Julien Talua, fired point-blank on the man he discovered in his marriage bed.[83]

Despite these atypical excesses, the absence of charges of wife beating is striking. Were the women simply resigned to being beaten? Their aggressiveness towards neighbours and outsiders and their quick tempers would argue against a natural submissiveness. Could this outward violence have been a way of compensating for strains inside the household that husband and wife struggled to repress? We have no way of answering this question. Women in the colony were neither better nor worse off than anywhere else. They took part in family decisions and accompanied their husbands to the notary's to sell property, sign leases, or put children out to learn a trade. As widows they often showed themselves efficient managers, which indicates that they already had a hand in the family concern, whether rural property or urban commerce. There was nothing unusual about that, for it was common practice, especially among the lower classes in France under the Ancien Régime, and there is no reason to give credence to hasty assertions that colonial conditions altered relations between the sexes.[84] In Canada as well, men remained their wives' legal "lords," and the wives' participation in daily activities posed no threat to male dominance.[85]

We know even less about the feelings of these couples than about their behaviour. The phrases that appear in wills were most often inspired by notaries, and offer no real insight. The husband thanks the wife for her good services and for the way she raised the children, and he reminds the latter to treat her with "tenderness, respect and warmth ... help her, honour her, and obey her."[86] Spouses requested that joint masses and prayers be said for them and their long-departed wife or husband. Amid his credits and debits, one merchant recorded in his account books the passing of his wife: "1721, October fifth, on Sunday at about six in the evening died Marie-Louise Zemballe, the Sieur Monière's English wife, and was buried on October the sixth, a Monday, between ten and eleven, in the parish church."[87]

Marital life was usually short, and as soon as it was interrupted survivors would look for a replacement, without which both their livelihood and their children's survival would be severely threatened, for they had nothing else, no neighbours and no large kinship network to lessen their isolation. At the turn of the eighteenth century widowers remarried on average after twenty-five months and widows after thirty-eight.[88] The nature of the feelings between spouses, however, cannot be determined from either the frequency or the very existence of second nuptials, which in the previous century probably took place even sooner after the death of the first spouse.

Parents and children

There were many children in this society, but they appear to have counted for little. Parish records monotonously register their burials, and yet the authorities, so concerned about peopling the colony, paid no notice to the fact that children died. Parents accepted it.

Documents like post-mortem inventories tell us nothing about children's home life.[89] As soon as they were seven they were assigned various duties, like keeping the cows; they were taught the catechism on Sundays, and if they lived in town, could go to school.[90] The girls followed in their mothers' footsteps. Often a boy's father would be dead by the time he reached the age of apprenticeship. If there was no stepfather, an elder brother or brother-in-law would act in loco parentis. A fourteen-year-old boy had to have a gun and know how to use it, but he would not go off to war or take part in the fur trade until he turned eighteen. If he went into service, he left the house very young, but if he was sent off to learn a trade, he would only do so at the age of sixteen or seventeen.[91] But few did either in the seventeenth century, and even a century later, when domestic servants and apprentices represented 18 per cent of the urban population, there were few children in their midst.[92] Chronic underemployment among the adult urban work-force did not encourage the drafting of country residents. Large households remained the most common arrangement, and children continued to live at home until they married. In the meantime, about one-quarter of the local youths divided their time between the family home and the western outposts.[92]

These young people – between the ages of eighteen and twenty-eight – who had managed to pull through a mean and hazardous childhood, had special privileges. Their lack of discipline, their vagabondage, their contempt for regulations worried the authorities: it was said that the youths of this country will not obey; children do not respect their fathers; parents give them too much freedom; as soon as they can carry a gun, fathers lose all control over them and "are afraid to contradict them."[94]

This insubordination must be placed in its context. There is no doubt, first of all, that parents made no attempt to stop sons who wanted to go out west and that, if anything, they prodded them to leave. The widow of a merchant baker explained how she had wanted her son Henri to get some education and how the curé had kindly taken him in and sent him to Brother Gentot, who kept the local school. But Gentot taught him nothing, and the young man fell into bad habits. Seeing this, his mother "had taken him back home, and in order to keep him busy and free him from his bad habits, particularly gambling, she had outfitted him for the trade in the Upper Country."[95] This attitude towards the fur trade was typical: farming was not considered morally superior to trade and the settlers understood very well that a young man would be better off gathering some savings while he had the strength than spending his youth clearing land with little return and no profit for his family. When his father died in the fall of 1684, Nicolas Desroches, aged thirty-two, was off trading in the Ottawa country. He was one of the first coureurs de bois so decried by the intendants. Back home there were still three sons, aged six, eleven, and twenty-one, two young girls, and his mother and grandmother, as well as a brother and sister, both married, who lived on their own farms. Nicolas would trek west another two years and continue to support his mother. He settled all his late father's debts, amounting to 625 livres. In 1686 Jean, who had run the farm up to that point, married and left home. As his mother would explain in her will, she was then getting on and found herself alone with the grandmother and young children. She therefore called on "her child" Nicolas to take care of the family holding and in return gave him her half of the property, with the consent of all the heirs. He bought back the remaining shares from his brothers and sisters, gave up fur trading, and supported the entire household as well as his own bride and growing brood. Nineteen years would go by before he had married off all his siblings and buried his mother and grandmother.[96]

This case, which was hardly exceptional, should demonstrate that these youthful voyages were not a source of conflict and that one set of values did not replace another, but rather that a new occupation became integrated into a traditional lifestyle.

The control exercised by the family was not based on material considerations. Parents had too little to offer their children to be able to impose their will in this fashion, and as we have seen, they did not even consider themselves in a position to buy their collaboration. Paternal authority was not brought into play either. Living conditions and especially the proximity encouraged by the climate, which forced family members, sometimes of several generations, to live in close quarters for months on end, were coercive enough. Discipline owed little to the intervention of parents. And when they were gone, family solidarity continued to prevail.

Everything took the form of reciprocal services. Thus parents would help newlyweds by offering them board for a year or more. "The future bride's parents promise in favour of the marriage up to 500 livres as an advance on the inheritance, 300 of which will go towards a year's board, beginning the day of the wedding."[97] One out of every eight marriage contracts over the period 1670 to 1700 included similar clauses.[98] The parents did not require any work from the young couple, who could devote their energies to improving their nearby lot and building their house. These boarding arrangements could involve either a son or a daughter, who brought a spouse to live in a household that still included unmarried siblings. Co-residence of this sort would rarely last beyond the weaning of the first child. Purchases of land for young children testify to the same concern.[99] Pierre Jousset and his wife paid a rente of 50 livres for the sixty arpents they had bought "for Lamothe, soldier in the La Chassaigne company, and Marie Jousset, their daughter, if he marries her. If he does not, it will go to their daughter and whomever she marries, as long as they pay the rente and release the above-mentioned Jousset for this debt."[100]

One of the children's primary and unavoidable duties was caring for their aging parents. When the father was no longer able to care for himself, usually at between sixty to seventy years of age, he turned his property over to his children. In the majority of such cases all of the children accepted the gift, and they were jointly responsible for an annuity paid either in cash or in kind.[101] Circumstances and individual bonds determined whether the old man would spend his declining years with one or another of his children or, if he preferred and if his allowance was large enough, move to the village or the town or else live in a separate house on his old farm.[102] Couples usually tried to find separate lodgings. Widows followed the same procedure, without waiting for old age. They helped the family that took them in, and the allowance was adjusted accordingly.[103] When only one child was responsible for the allowance, the others compensated him accordingly from their own shares in the inheritance. These arrangements were not profitable.[104]

This form of assistance was not affected by the remarriage of one of the parents if the children were still young at the time. But children felt they owed nothing to a stepmother who came into the family at a later stage, when all the children had grown up.[105]

Arrangements concerning the care of orphans and of their inheritance underline the importance of fraternal ties. Custom dictated that fathers, mothers, or stepfathers if they remarried, take on such responsibilities, assisted by a surrogate guardian chosen from among the deceased's family. In the early days of the colony it proved difficult to fulfil this last obligation. It was easy to find next-of-kin on the mother's side, but most fathers had no families in Canada. Brothers and brothers-in-law took the place of the missing or dead uncles and grandparents. If one son had come of age, he would be named surrogate guardian and full guardian if the other parent died. Since daughters married earlier and took older husbands, these brothers-in-law would usually be elected surrogate guardians. The tendency to restrict these responsibilities to the narrow family circle outlasted the first generation.[106]

The next of kin called to decide on such matters recognized that brothers and brothers-in-law effectively raised the children. Uncles intervened only when all the orphans were very young. The creation of a number of "sibling communities," a temporary version of the frérèches, insured that the family would not be scattered once the parents died.[107] Take the case of twenty-one-year-old Louis Beaudry, who in return for wages paid by the estate took charge of the farm as well as the six minors "since the revenues were too small to board them elsewhere." A brother-in-law who worked as a blacksmith in the town was elected guardian. The estate and the children were parcelled out after three years. Louis kept two of the minors; the eldest, Toussaint, returned from the Ottawa country and settled on one of the lots with a younger brother; two young girls went to live with a recently married sister.[108] When the household had to be broken up, the married offspring took in the younger ones, with the usual requirements that they "raise them in the fear of God" and see to all their needs in return for whatever services they could render. The eldest brother unquestioningly assumed the paternal role, protecting the younger or handicapped ones and defending his sisters' honour.[109] A brother-in-law who also played an important role in these families was called a "brother," but it is impossible to say whether this was peculiar to the colony. Permanent co-residence of married brothers was a rare occurrence. Only two such cases were found: the Dumets and the Décarri brothers, who ran large farms together. Temporary fraternal partnerships, however, were often formed for the purpose of participating in the fur trade or for farming.

Brotherly solidarity also shines through the wills of voyageurs who, in some cases, left all their worldly goods to the brothers or sisters who had taken them in and cared for them.[110] Jean Magan, a thirty-eight-year-old bachelor, bequeathed 1,500 livres, his clothing, feather bed, and six beaver pelts to his sister Louise, married to Giguère, who had nursed him during his last illness. He left 375 livres to his mother and the same to another married sister, and 500 livres to each of his three illegitimate children, a sum his brother Antoine would hand over when they turned twenty-one. The rest went to charity. Surviving receipts show that his family carried out his wishes in the same way it had apparently accepted his way of life.[111]

The insistence with which the testators asked their children to "maintain among them a perfect unity ... and settle disputes in a peaceful manner, without noise, lawsuits, or squabbling," suggests that quarrelling was frequent.[112] The fact that marriage endowments were scrupulously recorded and notaries were called on to legalize agreements shows a desire to forestall any difficulties. If we hear so little about disputes, it is because they were usually settled out of court. The family chose conciliators among the propertied folk in the area and accepted their decisions.[113] The intendant and his *sub-délégué* were sometimes called upon to resolve these sorts of problems. They were rarely taken before a judge because the value of the estates did not justify the legal expenditure and material uncertainties did not encourage long-standing feuds.

These examples all come from the countryside. The small body of craftsmen and day labourers was not yet very visible in the notarial records, and when they did not own property, their negligible estates were settled without much ado. Merchants and officers did not assign responsibilities quite so simply. They appointed executors and guardians who were not young men but other officers or merchants, relatives, or friends of the deceased. Assistance was not necessarily reciprocal. Parents in these social groups tended to do more for their children, and children in turn did less for the family, which could rely on other resources besides the charity of its members. Ensigns in the Marine companies did not return from Newfoundland or Louisiana to raise their brothers and sisters or take care of their old mothers. The Crown and the Church took on those responsibilities.

The kinship network

Kinship ties developed rapidly. Michel Dumets married Isabelle Jetté in 1685. A year later André Dumets married another Jetté. The next ten years would witness another three unions between the two families who lived in the same *côte*. The sheer size of these two families and the intensity of their relations make them exceptional, but double unions between two lines in the second and subsequent generations were frequent enough. One might end up as someone's aunt as well as sister-in-law, or be both husband and cousin. Every combination was possible.[114] Social relations were limited to a very small group, and a marriage stimulated friendly relations between the spouses' families, which then gave rise to new unions. Extensive genealogical research would no doubt show that this behaviour was typical of most traditional rural communities, yet it seems particularly frequent here. Isolation cannot explain this phenomenon entirely. In the seventeenth century the families on the Island of Montreal came into contact with a large number of immigrants and took the comings and goings of strangers for granted. These were more noticeable in the town, especially among merchants. Yet the endogamous tendencies exhibited by all urban classes were as strong if not stronger than those prevalent in the countryside.

This population had its beginnings in the experience of an often traumatic emigration, of insecurity and loneliness. These anxieties would be appeased within the family, which became, during the colony's chaotic first half-century, the only effective and truly compelling instrument of social control. The division of labour and the allocation of responsibilities were ordered first by these elementary units, and disorder declined gradually as individuals were integrated into and socialized by them.

Religion is a second arena of social participation, one that involves wider networks of solidarity. Yet we find in this case none of the spontaneity and harmonious development that marked the elaboration of the family. The evidence that survives is scarce and difficult to interpret. This explains why the following section will be mainly descriptive, although it will attempt to trace the origins of the tensions and contradictions that accompanied the creation of a religious framework.

CHAPTER FIFTEEN

Religious Life

Of all the religious projects that marked the beginnings of New France, that of the Société de Notre-Dame was the most ambitious. It meant to do more than open convents or missions with the help of the Crown and trading companies. Its avowed purpose was to create an alternate, autonomous settlement, fundamentally religious in nature, that would serve as the model, orderly, and prosperous base for its evangelical work among the natives.[1] This project sprang from the piety and reforming zeal that marked the reign of Louis XIII. It was abundantly funded and supported by devout personages – and it failed. The Montreal that survived the founders' apostolic visions drew nothing from them. The town was no different from other commercial outposts, but those first years, excruciatingly difficult, often exalted, would forever be remembered by the religious elite. Tales were spun about what might have happened, about what could have been.

They lived like saints ... Every working settler would come to early Mass before dawn in wintertime and at four o'clock in the morning in the summer, while all the women attended a later service at eight ... Things were never locked up in those days, neither houses nor chests; everything was left open, and nothing ever went missing. Those who had some means helped those who had less, without waiting to be asked, happy to offer them this expression of their love and esteem; people who had grown excited and spoken roughly to their neighbours, or anyone else, would not go to sleep before begging forgiveness on their knees. There was no hint of vice and impurity, which was abhorred even by those who seemed the least devout. In short, Montreal in its beginnings embodied all the principles of the early church.[2]

Our only direct witnesses for this period, the notarial and judicial records, do not echo this beautiful picture. It may well be that the first settlers, terrified of the Indians, found some solace in the religious fervour that prevailed at the fort and tried to conform to the wishes of the pious leaders with whom they were trapped. Once the gates were opened, normalcy reasserted itself. Then as later one senses the gap between the traditional and comfortable religion of the people and the demanding, enlightened, and anxious beliefs of the founders and priests who were there to guide them.

1 THE PRIESTS

The Seminary of Saint-Sulpice, which had not been directly involved in the founding of Ville-Marie, began to send out priests in 1657. They took over the organization of religious life from the laymen who, assisted by itinerant Jesuits, had seen to it up to that point. Despite their importance in the rest of the colony, the Company of Jesus played only a minor role in Montreal itself.

The Congregation of Saint-Sulpice was established in Paris in 1645 to instil ecclesiastical dogma and morality in the clergy. At this period it attracted mostly men of the upper class. Many of the members, including those who came to Canada, such as de Queylus, Fénelon, d'Urfé, Dollier, Pérot, Vachon de Belmont, and Rémy, had large private fortunes. The priests, who had taken no vows, deferred to the decisions of the supérieur général in Paris, who oversaw the various provincial seminaries and a few parishes and missions, assisted by a dozen councillors. The convent in Montreal was known as a seminary, although it would not provide any regular teaching before the middle of the eighteenth century. It had a supérieur and a procurator and housed all the clerics who were not responsible for rural parishes or missions. The community grew from its original three or four members to some fifteen in 1730, in the Montreal area. The Seminary controlled all the seigneury's parishes, and the priests could be removed at the supérieur's pleasure.[3] Although these parishes fell under the authority of the bishop of Quebec, spiritual and temporal decisions were actually made in Paris by the Sieurs Bretonvilliers and their successors, de Tronson and Leschassier. They were wise men and clever politicians who never lost sight of Canadian interests. Saint-Sulpice did all it could to stay on good terms with the bishop without allowing him to dictate its conduct.

Montreal Island, with its excellent priests, was privileged in comparison with other places in the colony. "Three-quarters of the

Canadian settlers barely attend four masses a year and often die without the sacraments. They know as much about our religion as the Indians do," wrote de Meulles.[4] This intendant loved to exaggerate, but the situation was far from ideal. In 1730 only twenty of the one hundred parishes had their own permanent curés. The others relied on the services of itinerant priests, and the quality of all clergy was uneven.

The Sulpicians who came to Canada in the seventeenth century harboured missionary hopes, but few had the chance to realize this dream. The Jesuits, abetted by the Séminaire des Missions étrangères, had a monopoly over native territories. The Sulpicians had to resign themselves to caring for the people on their seigneuries. They had to accept that they would not carry the Lord's message to foreign parts, and renounce not only the excitement of converting the heathen but also the ever-present chance of martyrdom, in order to undertake the bland task of ministering to the settlers, who expected concrete services rather than evangelical messages.[5] The disappointment was all the greater and adaptation the more difficult since most had no previous experience of the French countryside. They judged their parishioners harshly; their spiritual guides had to remind them that French peasants were no different, and entreat the priests to be patient, modest, and tolerant. There was no need to prod them to be generous. The curés were unstinting with personal and material help. They wore themselves out and despaired of succouring all the poor, lightening their burdens, and triumphing over vice and indifference. Their supérieur begged them to be more reasonable, to become good managers, to control the ardour with which they denounced injustices and risked upsetting the local community, and to take better care of their health. Some became "unhinged" and had to be called back. Others grew sick of Canada, tired of their thankless task, and asked to go home, creating vacancies that were hard to fill. "French missions" elicited few vocations in the metropolis.[6] We can follow the moving correspondence between the Parisian supérieur and these priests, who turned to him when their spiritual loneliness became unbearable, when they wondered about their vocations and how well they served where God had sent them. A number persevered, eventually achieved serenity, and probably became more effective.

The Montreal clergy was animated by Gallican and Jansenist sentiments. Their Gallicanism expressed itself primarily in their suspicion, if not antagonism, towards religious orders, specifically the mendicant orders and the Jesuits. The Seminary was forced to yield to the combined pressure of the population, the bishop, and the intendant and allow these orders to open convents in its seigneury. Dollier complained that "it was an evil thing to have allowed the Jesuits come to Montreal, for it will sow division and ruin the parish."[7] It took all the diplomatic skills of the supérieur général to prevent open conflict over the right to preach and hear confession.[8] Although Paris had no use for the Jesuits, Montrealers were repeatedly exhorted to hold their tongues in order to avoid aggravating matters. Rome is never mentioned in the voluminous correspondence. Solutions to local problems were sought at Versailles or the Sorbonne. The Seminary took note of the civil authorities' infringements on its territory, but without alarm. The colonial Church would also make its peace with Crown interference in its affairs, something the Sulpicians had accepted at least half a century earlier.[10]

The term Jansenist is used in its broadest sense, meaning a spiritual outlook rather than a theological or political platform. It was a demanding brand of Christianity that did without compassion or concessions.[11] The Sulpicians were rigid. They "rattled men's consciences," "tyrannized souls." Their rigour can hardly be discerned in rural parishes, where the priests made allowances for poverty and ignorance. But in urban parishes their intransigence against overdressed women, captains who mistreated their soldiers, or merchants who got the Indians drunk landed them in trouble.[12] Beginning with Fénelon, who dared in an Easter sermon to remind the governor of his duty towards the people – for which he went to jail and was sent home to France – and continuing on through the denunciations from the pulpit, the refusals to grant absolutions, and the accusations of laxity levelled against the Jesuits, especially in the matter of conversion, the Sulpicians' attitudes could only offend the colonial elite.[13] They also showed an exaggerated respect for the sacraments, followed rules to the letter in matters of morality and ritual, and were wary of spontaneous piety. "A native woman died at the Sault in the odour of sanctity. All of Lachine makes its novenas and confesses there, even the biggest sinners, which saddens the curé and undermines the parish."[14]

The Seminary was vigilant. When Monsieur Bailly began to take cases of witchcraft seriously, he was promptly shipped home.[15] Spirits ran high during the calamities of the end of the century. Priests, unable to stem the tide of violence and adversity, grew restless and cried out for vengeance from above. A visionary nun claimed to know the true state of communicants and maintained that there were hardly sixty people in the colony in a state of grace, which her confessor willingly believed. "Idle fancies of empty brains," wrote Tronson. "Dismiss anything out of the ordinary or in any way odd that will divert you from the path of our Fathers."[16]

These were the clerics who took it upon themselves to organize religious life on the Island of Montreal. They were educated, demanding, their behaviour beyond reproach. Their individual characters tempered what had been a rigid and cold training. The social and intellectual gap that separated them from the faithful did not lessen – quite the contrary. The Seminary did not accept any Canadian priests before the end of the eighteenth century, and thus the new curés who arrived from Paris or Clermont seemed, more and more, like strangers.

2 THE PARISHES

Notre-Dame

For thirty-five years the island had a single parish. Holy offices were celebrated in the fort, then in the chapel of the Hôtel-Dieu until the consecration of the church in 1678. While it still ministered to a large number of rural residents, Notre-Dame parish soon took on an urban flavour. As Pierre Goubert puts it, the vestry was the religious corollary of the village council, and indeed the minutes of its meetings and annual accounts outline the evolution of the urban community.[17] It was organized as in France, with an assembly of residents, yearly elections, and annual accounts tendered by the outgoing churchwarden that had to be made public and approved by the bishop. The curé took part in the meetings, as did all the previous elected wardens and, in the early days, a number of honorary members. Between 1657 and 1685 five merchants, three officers, one innkeeper, two surgeons, one baker, and fourteen peasants and craftsmen served as churchwardens. Only bourgeois, merchants in particular, would fill the post in the following period.[18] Accounts began to be better kept, and the common people ceased to have any say in the running of the parish once the commercial structure became well established. The position of churchwarden, which was not scorned even in more exalted circles, became a form of consecration for those who had not yet made their fortunes.

Creating a religious organization from scratch proved a costly operation. In 1654 Montrealers were asked to contribute towards the building of the Hôtel-Dieu chapel and the establishment of burial grounds. The receiver of the alms managed to raise some 2,000 livres in cash, kind, or statute labour from this tiny community.[19] In the early days a large part of vestry revenues consisted of the fines that the *bailli* turned over to the parish, legacies from fur traders who had no relatives in the colony, and properties that fell into escheat and that the court then awarded to the parish and the Hôtel-Dieu. Payments were made in kind, mostly in the form of trade goods. This explains the existence of a "parish store," where the churchwarden housed his stock at the beginning of the financial year and which he ran like any private business.[20] The building of the church in the upper town, somewhat removed from the first urban nucleus, would commence in 1672. It was a large stone structure, befitting a *bailliage* seat and locus of government. It was officially opened in 1678, before the work had been completed. Contracts for the bell tower, side-chapels, embellishments of the portal, and the lateral windows would wait until 1710–20.[21] It is impossible to estimate the total costs. Saint-Sulpice contributed large sums. Curés put their names down on the subscription lists, and the king contributed some monies.[22] But the inhabitants bore a heavy share of the expense. No one was forced to contribute, but when the churchwarden went door to door to draw up lists of "donations and promises" for the following year's work, the social pressure was sufficient to open the purses. Artisans and peasants promised up to 12 livres, equivalent to a labourer's monthly wage. Everything was assessed in money terms, but contributions included timber, grain, stones, lime, or so many days of labour or cartage as well as cash.[23] The churchwardens instituted proceedings against those who did not honour their pledges.[24]

These frequent special levies came in addition to the tithes and fees for religious services (*droits casuels*), and certainly cut into the Sunday collection and other offerings. If we divide these last two by the number of inhabitants, we get an annual average of 15 sols per family. At the end of the century parishioners contributed no more than 20 to 30 sols to the Sunday plate.

Funerals came in four categories: 3 livres 7 sols for children and Indians; 6 to 10 livres for adults, or twice as much for additional pomp; and 60 livres for burials in the church.[25] When the vestry began selling pews around 1690, they were auctioned off for 37 livres. The price rose to 90 livres by the beginning of the eighteenth century. The buyers paid an additional annuity of 7 livres 6 sols. In 1707 the pews were owned by 16 military and civil officers, 17 merchants, and 2 notaries; 12 belonged to a number of bakers, butchers, tanners, and blacksmiths, and another 2 to a surgeon and an innkeeper – a total of 47 families in a parish that numbered 355. That same year the churchwarden collected 262 livres from the plate and donations, 334 livres for funerals, and 372 livres for pews.[26] This took care of the consecrated bread, wax, oil, charcoal, cloth, washing of the linen, the beadle's wages, the officiants' and choir boys' remuneration, the upkeep of the church, and sundry expenses. In this period the religious communities and the poor received most of the legacies that had earlier been earmarked for the vestry. Annuities never amounted to much, and small foundations grew at a very slow pace. The *casuel* fees from baptisms and marriages, exemptions from fasting and dispensation from banns, were not listed among the churchwarden's receipts.[27]

The urban parish was more or less in place by the early eighteenth century. The tithes it drew from the oldest and best-cultivated sections were the largest on the island. In 1705 the auction started at 650 minots of various grains and rose to 950 minots. The average would have hovered around a minimum of 600 minots a year, or some 1,125 livres, which Saint-Sulpice used to bolster the revenues of new parishes because that sum was more than enough to support a curé and a vicar.[28] In 1721 the 150 or so habitants and tenant-farmers scattered in the rural suburbs declared that they were happy to be part of the Notre-Dame parish.[29] The dignified locale, the spectacle provided by properly conducted ceremonies graced by an elegant company, and often enhanced by the presence of the governor, intendant, and other distinguished visitors, must have assuaged the sense of anonymity that the peasants shared with the small artisans and labourers.

Rural parishes

As early as 1665–68 the Sulpicians had to minister to more distant parts of the seigneury. For three years a priest trekked out each Sunday to say Mass in François Bot's house in Pointe-aux-Trembles. In 1674 the residents elected two churchwardens, who collected the subscriptions and signed and supervised arrangements for the building of their church.[30] The Lachine parish was organized at about the same time. After a hiatus in wartime, new parishes were created to keep step with settlement: Rivière-des-Prairies, Pointe-Claire, Sainte-Anne, Longue-Pointe, and Saint-Laurent. As habitation spread, places of worship multiplied. As long as the island was not completely settled, boundaries were continually redrawn and old sections merged into new ones to establish parishes of fifty to one hundred farms, with a church right in the middle. Few habitants agreed to travel more than a league and a half (six kilometers) to hear mass "because it was too cold in wintertime, in summer too hot, and there were too many mosquitoes."[31] It was up to the priests to visit isolated households, and settlers complained if the mission proved irregular. The moment thirty families had settled in one area, they started to clamour for a church and a curé.

There was nothing more heartwarming than the enthusiasm mustered at these first meetings. All the settlers were present. The need for donations did not frighten them. They promised money and the best trees on their land; they offered to cart stones and provide food for the workmen; they bound themselves to furnish whatever additional statute labour the foreman might require. The work was begun and then abandoned for lack of funds, materials, and labour. The receiver called assemblies to which no one came. He crisscrossed the côte in vain to remind settlers of their promises. The Sulpicians and the bishop intervened, to no avail. The intendant had to be called in, and it was only when settlers were threatened with a lawsuit, with a doubling of their contributions and the fining of offenders, that the frame began to go up.[32] A few well-publicized penalties did the trick.[33] Five years went by before the settlers rallied in Longue-Pointe, "although they had all seemed very eager before the first stone had been laid down."[34] It took even longer in Rivière-des-Prairies, while in Lachine the curé, tired of waiting, paid a large part of the expenses and also guaranteed the loan raised by the churchwarden to cover the remainder, for the habitants "had left the parish in debt by failing to provide the necessary contributions, labour, and other things they had promised, and no longer wished to give, used as they were to promising a lot and not keeping their word."[35]

The first churches were usually built out of wood. They were no more than plain, poorly insulated chapels that soon crumbled and had to be replaced with longer-lasting stone edifices. More established habitants manifested as little enthusiasm for building them as did newly arrived settlers, for these were costly propositions. When, one way or another, the church was finally up and the curé demanded a house for himself, he met with passive resistance, and he was lucky if he could find a churchwarden to undertake the collection. Priests on the Island of Montreal often had enough private means to advance the necessary funds and eventually remitted the parish's debt in their wills.[36]

It took a long time for the habitants to get over the trauma of the impositions made on them to establish the churches. Vestry revenues did not cover the expenses of worship. Churchwardens prosecuted people who did not pay for funerals, and the bailli had to order settlers to take turns providing the consecrated bread and other necessities or else face penalties.[37] There were similar problems with the tithes. Saint-Sulpice was in favour of traditional levies on the fields "to prevent fraud and sin," but it could not drum up enough support in the colony to make the Sovereign Council alter the regulations.[38] The lawsuits instituted by tithe farmers, which we can follow in the *bailliage* registers, kept pace with the rate of settlement and economic conditions. Tithe collection was a process of trial and error. Saint-Sulpice had no desire to request dues directly "because demanding them and taking people to court over them would make them hate the clergy," but it had a hard time finding solid lessors.[39] Bankruptcies and a lack of continuity emboldened the habitants, who accumulated arrears. The inevitable, if sometimes delayed penalties were harsh, terminating often in the seizure of crops.[40] Proceedings were generally meant to recover both seigneurial dues and tithes, the latter accounting for the bulk of the debt.[41]

The Seminary's procurator administered the income from the tithes and supplied the curés with whatever they required for their sustenance, taking into account their personal revenues. The king subsidized new colonial parishes, and Saint-Sulpice obtained some of this bounty.[42] These supplements were not really crucial because, despite the difficulties of collection, wheat found its way into the seigneurial granaries as returns from older parishes compensated for the paltry revenues from new ones. Curés reported that the set allowance provided by the Seminary did not permit them to ease their parishioners' poverty.[43] The latter were quite aware that the product of their tithes was allocated not only to other parishes but also to unrelated expenditures incurred by the Seminary itself, including the improvement of its farms and the upkeep of its missions. The widespread belief that the Church, and the Sulpicians in particular, had untold riches excited some animosity. The settlers' initial poverty, however, accounts for most of the difficulties. No sooner had they cleared a few acres of land than they were asked to contribute, and the mobility of the first settlers reduced the base of the assessment even further.[44] Some of the better-established colonists felt that they were being penalized for their hard work by being made to pay for the absent or down-and-out, and added this to their list of grievances. Finally, since there were no wealthy residents in the countryside, individual generosity, donations, legacies, or foundations could not compensate for the paucity of contributions, as they did in Notre-Dame parish.

Despite these conflicts, the habitants were intent on running the parish, and this became another source of friction between the clergy and the faithful.[45] Yet the inhabitants grew deeply attached to the curé who lived among them some years running, and complained if he spent too much time ministering to other areas or if the Seminary tried to transfer him.[46] Nor did they gracefully accept the remapping of parishes that wrested them from a home church, from the cemetery where their parents lay buried. In 1714 the Seminary decided that Côte Saint-Léonard would henceforth belong to the new Rivière-des-Prairies parish. The residents of Saint-Léonard resisted, and petitioned the bishop. When they heard that he had upheld the decision, they became indignant and seized the bread that a more docile member was taking to the new church. The bailiff sent to deliver summonses to the rebels reported that the women had waited for him "armed with rocks and sticks with which to do me in" and that they ran after him "screaming: Stop, thief, we are going to kill you and dump you in the marsh."[47]

It would be a mistake to equate the resistance to taxation with indifference to religion. The way in which rural communities threw themselves heart and soul into these costly projects, which no one asked them to undertake, is more telling than their refusals. The parish was a symbol that spelled the end of their isolated struggle to domesticate this foreign land, and a revival of normal social intercourse. The church and the curé defined their religious identity. To dismiss these outward signs of commitment would be to deny too easily the depth of the settlers' Christian faith, for it rested on collective practices and a conformity that itinerant religious services could not create. The priests, who nurtured a greater inner piety, seem to have been unaware of these dangers and to have thought that all they had to do to keep religion alive was to visit the families and bring them the sacraments once in a while. They readily ascribed the lackadaisical attitude in the "French missions," which were long bereft of tokens and devotion, to the deplorable character of the habitants and the pernicious influence of the fur trade.[48] The habitants, however, sensed the importance of the parish, as their premature commitment to building projects witnesses, despite their subsequent ambivalence.

3 SCHOOLS

Since primary education was a parish matter, these duties were first discharged by the priests, and then, in the French tradition, by schoolmasters under their supervision.[49] The town's primary school opened in 1664. The boys learned to read and write French and to do arithmetic. In 1680 the supérieur congratulated the curé on the progress of his pupils' writing skills but advised him to apply himself to teaching them the catechism and to begin training choir boys.[50] Later on, laymen or young clerics hand-picked by the Sulpicians would take over these functions.[51] M. de La Faye "was no great genius, but he was good-natured and had a pleasant disposition."[52] He would soon be replaced. In the early eighteenth century the schoolmaster tried to keep the children quiet, "as in Monsieur de La Salle's schools," but since he taught two classes in a single room, with the older children to one side and the younger ones to the other, his task was anything but easy.[53] In 1719 the correspondence discloses another arrangement, with one group gathering between six and eleven and the other from noon to five o'clock.[54] Schooling was apparently free.

In 1642 a devout native of Champagne, Marguerite Bourgeois, came to Montreal, where she founded a teaching order to instruct Indian and French girls. The nuns had a school in town, a second in the La Montagne mission, and gradually opened boarding schools in Lachine, Pointe-aux-Trembles, and other parts of the colony.[55] We know nothing about their urban day-school. Fees were probably assessed according to each family's means. Girls most likely were taught to read and write while they were trained in the catechism and needlework, as in the boarding schools. The latter cost 90 livres a year and therefore appealed to well-off families, although we find the odd orphan peasant girl among their pupils. The nuns took in lower-class girls free of charge in a house known as La Providence or in their other convents, and trained them in domestic duties. "And since experience shows that all these young girls are somewhat backward, they should not be accepted before the age of twelve so that they might get the best from their education ... and be in a position to contribute to their upkeep ... Given their poverty, there is no need to teach them how to write, for it would just be a waste of energy that might be more usefully directed elsewhere. If any prove capable of taking the veil, they should then be sent to school to learn how to write."[56]

The school system appears to have fulfilled its function in Notre-Dame parish. Judging by the signatures of spouses in the parish registers between 1657 and 1715, 45.5 per cent of the men and 43 per cent of the women born in the colony could sign their names.[57] We might recall that in the same parish the figures for French-born spouses, 38.4 per cent for the men and 31.7 per cent for the women, were already relatively high.[58] The second generation did even better, while the gap between educated males and females lessened.[59] The sample in question is, of course, largely urban. The rural parishioners lived close to the town and profited more than other peasants from the occasional visits of itinerant teachers.

It proved very difficult to set up schools in other parishes. The curés of Lachine and Pointe-aux-Trembles promptly hired teachers, but they lacked qualifications and were often unstable, and the dispersion of settlement, combined with the calamities at the end of the century and the poverty of vestries, prevented any progress.[60] Children from isolated areas were merely taught the catechism.[61] Soldiers sometimes gave lessons wherever they set up winter quarters, and the priests supported these initiatives.[62] It was not unusual for some children in a family to know how to write when others did not. Education was a matter of circumstances and individual motivation. The schoolhouse, or whatever was used in its stead, was far away; the roads were not always safe, and education was basically not terribly useful to these peasants. Yet a young man who hoped to become a voyageur had to have some notion of arithmetic and writing, without which he would always remain a porter. The abécédaires that the merchants sold in the countryside were probably also destined for those youths who realized the drawbacks of ignorance somewhat late in life.[63] The level of education of rural women remained far below that of the men. Rural parish registers were not well enough kept before 1715 for us to hazard any percentages, but the literacy rate in the second generation seems to have been much lower than that of the immigrants. Some progress would be possible in the eighteenth century, once parishes became properly established. The delays can be traced to material circumstances rather than to the priests, who always held religious and secular education to be closely linked and waged war on ignorance to conquer sin.[64]

Attempts to educate the masses stopped at the elementary level. The Sulpicians and other regulators tutored some of the well-born privately, but only the Jesuits in Quebec taught Latin in the early grades and offered secondary and college education.[65] The nearby Petit Séminaire provided accommodation for boarders for the duration of their studies.[66] Few Montreal families could afford the requisite fees, however, and the college did not recruit among the lower classes, at least in Montreal. In 1727 the notables, "seriously concerned about their children's ignorance and idleness," petitioned the governor to ask the Jesuits to open a college in Montreal, but to no avail.[67] People with means, and relatives or connections in France, had their children educated overseas. Saint-Sulpice accepted a number in its metropolitan seminaries.[68] In the European tradition, the urban parish school alone provided a rudimentary education to children of various social backgrounds, and this remained the norm in this distant outpost.

4 RELIGIOUS PRACTICES

Worship in an urban parish

The well-run parish of Notre-Dame, organized early on, gives us an inkling of religious practices in the seventeenth century.[69] There were about thirty-seven mandatory religious holidays a year, and Easter dominated the liturgical calendar.[70] It began with Confession and Communion, and the insistence on these rituals would seem to indicate that they were not frequently observed. Alms-giving, perhaps as penitence, accompanied these services.[71] From Maundy Thursday to High Mass on Sunday, the parish collected over half its annual revenues. By contrast, Christmas did not loosen the purse strings, while the Circumcision and Epiphany were not treated differently from ordinary Sundays. The churchwardens faithfully recorded the forty-hour devotions in February and the feast of St Joseph on 19 March. The feasts of the Holy Family, St John the Baptist, the apostles St Peter and St Paul, and Corpus Christi limited the number of working days in June. There were a number of processions around the church, but that of Corpus Christi surpassed all others. The residents cleaned the streets and "decorated their houses in the customary fashion," while the soldiers fired their arquebuses to punctuate the shows of piety.[72]

People had been unwilling to adopt the name of Ville-Marie, chosen by the founders. Yet the Marian cult on which the priests placed so much emphasis eventually marked many of the island's place-names, and the feasts of the Assumption and the Nativity of the Virgin became important celebrations. This worship did not supplant the more spontaneous cult of the dead, however, which revolved around the observation of All Souls' Day and countless Masses for the souls in Purgatory. The fall saw an additional array of feast days, with Michaelmas, Ste Catherine's Day and St Nicholas' Day, while St Crispin and St Crispinian's Day on 25 October, although it was not a day of obligation, was celebrated twice: on the day itself and on the following Sunday. They were officially the patron saints of shoemakers, but perhaps also of most everyone in a town where hides and leather played such an important role.[73]

Individual piety

It is a delicate matter indeed to decide which of the numerous ceremonies – frequent benedictions of the Holy Sacrament, Masses and processions down to the Bon-Secours chapel, public prayers, jubilees, and so on – awakened the fervour of the parishioners and answered their expectations, and which merely devolved from the clergy's desire to emulate French practices, leaving the spectators cold. The petition that the inhabitants addressed to the authorities to attract a mendicant order, despite the opposition of the parish clergy, shows at least that the latter had not succeeded in slaking the people's spiritual thirst.[74] The Récollets, who arrived at the same time as the Jesuits, after a period of intense bargaining, found a small and none too prosperous town. As the Sulpicians had predicted, their presence undermined the authority of the Seminary and cut into the parish revenues.[75] Most of the alms were already earmarked for the Hôtel-Dieu, which administered charitable donations. After 1692 it was the Récollets who benefited from the most generous gifts, inscribed in every will. Such legacies allowed these two regular orders to establish themselves quite comfortably. The tiers Ordre, introduced by the Récollets, and the Jesuit Congré-gation des Hommes exercised a strong attraction for the inhabitants, who had previously known only one religious association, that of the Holy-Family, established in 1651.[76]

Social cleavages were more apparent in the Jesuit chapel than in the parish. Merchants and officers who spent their lives jeopardizing their eternal salvation relished the Fathers' soothing words. Charity could make amends for anything, and Montrealers who had the means gave generously, both in their lifetimes and on their death-beds, either directly to the parish poor or else to the four convents, which redeployed a part of these alms in various forms of assis-tance, without neglecting their own material interests. As far as we know the town had only four craft confraternities. Those of the surgeons, armourers, and shoemakers obviously had limited mem-berships, which clubbed together to pay for a Mass for their patron saint and a repast to commemorate the festive day.[77] Only the merchants were sufficiently well represented and powerful enough to be able to found a full-scale organization. With the onset of Anglo-Iroquois attacks, which threatened their livelihood, they began to feel a need for it:

We, the undersigned merchants of Ville-Marie, in the face of the calamities that assail us from all sides, and in order to quell God's ire, have hereby resolved, after asking the help of the Holy Virgin, to take and choose the holy souls in Purgatory as our intercessors before God. And to express our trust in their help we promise not to sell any goods to the residents of this parish, either on feast days or on Sundays, except for perishables that can be consumed that very day, like candles, oil, pepper, or vinegar, etc. As for the non-residents from the nearby *côtes*, we will sell them nothing without the written permission of our curé or some other priest from the Seminary so that they [the Holy Souls] might grant us what we ask. We have resolved to build a side-chapel next to the St Joseph chapel across from the sacristy where these souls can be properly served and which will be used for the meetings of the gentlemen of the association of the Holy Virgin, and until the said chapel is completed we will conduct services for the dead in the St Joseph chapel, done at Ville-Marie ...[78]

After mature reflection, four of the thirty-nine signatories specified that they would only respect their vow on Sundays and not on feast days. The others soon came round to this wise decision. There were penalties for offenders. The following year the members reached an agreement about their "everlasting monument," settled on minimum donations of one hundred livres, and determined how best to conduct the services.

The ordeals of this period incited unusual fervour. During the wars and epidemics the people prayed to St Roch and consecrated a chapel to him in the parish church.[79] They gave credence to any miraculous and providential event, such as the cures effected in the Notre-Dame-de-Bon-Secours chapel, which housed a number of imported relics, or the favours granted on the tomb of the young Iroquois woman Kateri Tekakwitha.[80] Ste Anne, near Quebec, was the colony's oldest sanctuary, and its renown had spread even to Montreal. Unfortunate settlers, captured by the Indians, begged Madame Ste Anne for a miracle that might transport them back to their homeland.[81] The *bailli* shared these beliefs, for he dismissed a surgeon's suit for payment for drugs and treatment, accepting the defendant's argument that his wife's leg had not been healed by the surgeon but by a pilgrimage to Ste Anne's.[82]

Most of the inhabitants never faced the question of heresy. Supposedly, only Catholics were permitted to settle in New France. Yet a number of Protestants, merchants and soldiers mostly, did live in the colony, although they were forbidden to assemble for religious purposes. There were ninety-nine of them in 1686, according to the intendant – one-twelfth of the troops, in other words – but they were too scattered to voice any opposition to the regulations.[83] Those who intended to go home once they were through could turn a deaf ear to the exhortations of the clergy. But those who meant to settle had no choice but to give in if they wanted to marry and live in harmony with the rest of the community. The priests also proselytized among the people of the neighbouring colonies, whether they were prisoners, or Englishmen and Flemings who decided to transfer their business to Montreal, or the few Huguenots who came to Canada via New York or Boston.[84] They also brought back into the fold Canadians who had returned after several years' stay in the British colonies, sometimes with children baptized by Protestant ministers.[85] There is something pedestrian about these recantations, as if adherence to a particular religion was a matter of time and place. The prodigals abjured with neither pomp nor circumstance.[86] Orthodoxy easily reigned supreme, and since nothing occurred to excite strong sentiments, the people experienced no religious conflicts and remained basically tolerant.[87]

Extent of religiosity

When religious consensus prevails, indicators of spiritual sensibility are few. Take away the public ceremonials and the generosity inspired by fear of retribution or social pressure, and what have we got? How can we measure individual acceptance of Christian ideals? It was rarely expressed in a domestic setting. One-third, but no more, of the forty-six post-mortem inventories of merchants and officers reveal outward displays of piety: four crucifixes, three fonts, and a number of religious paintings.[88] Personal libraries contained more pious works than any other writings, but since there were few readers, more often than not we do not even come across a catechism.[89] Sparely furnished artisan and habitant dwellings did not include devotional objects, but from the early eighteenth century onwards, merchants began to offer customers religious pictures, rosaries, small crosses, and books of hours and hymns. It was perhaps in this same period that the roadside crosses mentioned by travellers at the end of the regime made their appearance. They replaced the church steeple hidden from the view of settlers scattered farther and farther across the countryside.

Can overall piety in this period be measured by the number of vocations undertaken? It is a commonplace that Canadians expressed a "natural distaste" for religious life. The Sulpicians saw no point in investing time and money appealing to local youths, "since they had so few chances of success."[90] This was no passing phase due to the settlers' numerical weakness and initial material constraints, but a situation that would prevail as late as the nineteenth century and would compel the Church to import most of its priests.[91] Without completely dismissing the possibility that there was among the colonists a certain spiritual lukewarmness, we must consider two other hypotheses.

The first centres on the prestige of the secular personalities of the colonial Church, especially in Montreal. Ville-Marie owed its existence to inspired laymen who rejected traditional approaches and clerical moderation, and dreamed of a regenerated Church. While such ardour was being stilled in France, it lived on in the colony. There were highly devout men and women, but they spurned ordinary ways. In 1691 Charon and Leclerc, both merchants' sons, dedicated themselves and their worldly goods to the founding of a new religious community – a questionable enterprise that was cut short. Enthusiasts both male and female donated their wealth to the Church and buried themselves in convents without yielding to the routine of a regular vocation. Oddly enough, none of these elite Christians, whose lives would be celebrated for their virtue, ever considered serving a parish. This penchant among the privileged for inordinate piety deprived the country of the sort of dedication that could have proved fruitful in the more modest framework of clerical organization.

It was, however, the colonial Church, which had always banked on upper-class recruitment, that was primarily responsible for the lack of priests. There was no system whereby a country boy might graduate from catechism lessons to the urban schoolroom, from there on to college and finally to the grand Séminaire in Quebec. This was a costly itinerary, foreign to rural thinking, since the priests seldom spoke of it. Yet in 1743, when the consequences of this attitude were already plain, the French minister and the Quebec bishop were still discussing ways of "getting young men of good birth to consider an ecclesiastical career."[92] But those on whom they placed such hopes, who had access to secondary schooling, soon succumbed to the attractions of trade or military careers. The intermediate urban groups – the innkeepers, bakers, notaries, surgeons, and so on – proved more steadfast, for they valued education even if they could rarely afford it. It took endless petitions to obtain a bursary, reported the widow of an innkeeper who managed to get her son into the grand Séminaire.[93] At least another century would go by before the Canadian Church began to consider using peasants to staff its rural parishes.

The two female orders, by contrast, had no difficulty finding recruits throughout the seventeenth century. If anything their numbers continued to swell until about 1715, when they totalled a hundred or so members in a town with a population of fifteen hundred. A more rigid enforcement of the dowry system slowed down further recruitment. The settlement theoretically amounted to 3,000 livres for a choir-nun at the Hôtel-Dieu and between 600 and 1,000 for a servant-nun, above and beyond their trousseaux and maintenance during their noviciate.[94] These sums had rarely been demanded in the seventeenth century, and the Congrégation de Notre-Dame proved even more accommodating. This led to chronic deficits, appeals to royal largesse, frequent collections, and finally to government intervention in 1722 to force these communities to put their affairs in order and lighten the state burden.[95]

What was the attraction of these convents? There was a higher percentage of vocations among the upper classes, who made a greater show of piety and whose young women were often condemned to years of idle waiting, given the extended celibacy of the young men and the even more prolonged absence of those who pursued military careers. Lower-class women did not wait for men of their own generation and married soldiers, but the officers were harder to catch. If the four d'Ailleboust des Muceaux sisters, who turned twenty between 1690 and 1700, took the veil, it is perhaps because they could not find a suitable match.[96]

The differences in income perpetuated social barriers inside the convents. With a few exceptions, peasant girls were recruited as servant-nuns and admitted with a wheat allowance, a straw mattress, a bowl, a few utensils, a few ells of cloth for their noviciate, and their inheritance claims in lieu of a dowry.[97] Their parents did not encourage such vocations, which put a strain on family revenues and deprived them of help in their old age.[98] Nevertheless, the trend continued.

This overview is obviously incomplete: no mere summary of established ritual, orthodox belief, and a few instances of tangible, if never exaggerated, devotion can do justice to this society's religious attitudes. What sort of popular beliefs were transplanted overseas, for example, along with official religion? The sources are silent, but this may reflect more than mere inadequacy of data. Since here it did not have to combat a common, deeply rooted tradition, the Church found it easy to purge error and to mould a greater orthodoxy. Superstitions were doomed by their variety to be replaced by official doctrines. Popular religion would experience a temporary setback until the communities were sufficiently well organized and homogeneous to allow age-old traditions to surface in ordinary life, taking on here and there some local colour. This is no more than a hypothesis, but an attractive one.

The initial impoverishment of popular religion may have contributed to feelings of estrangement among settlers scattered in distant côtes. Physical and cultural isolation generated disorderly behaviour. These remained, however, individual responses, and the settlement's lasting features cannot be read in the judicial records. The communities as a whole conformed to the rules, but this does not mean that they were submissive. We have seen how parishes were established by mutual consent to fulfil communal needs as much as religious ones. The fact that the priests provided both material and spiritual support does not invalidate this claim. The tensions that devolved from this collaboration, along with an inherent anti-clericalism that surfaced continually, fuelled by Saint-Sulpice's dual role of seigneur and pastor, cannot be read as signs of disaffection.

"Canada's spiritual state is appalling. The inhabitants misinterpret everything they are told," wrote the priests. "One has to be very virtuous to agree to serve parishioners who display as much ill will as the French in these parts do." To reinforce this vision, we could cite an endless string of ordinances against those who assembled and amused themselves on Sundays, who were noisy during services, who brought their dogs to church, wandered off for a breath of fresh air during the sermon, worked on holidays, swore, sold wine during mass, and so on.[99] But what curé of the Ancien Régime did not despair of his parishioners?[100] What people did not display similar signs of insubordination and disrespect? Halfway between the belief that this society was in a complete moral shambles and the alternative and no less fictional view, that this was an intensely Christian community (the view long advanced by a clerically inspired historiography), there is an ordinary reality no different from that of any society where religion permeates everyday life but does not stimulate in popular consciousness an unusual intellectual or moral drive.

CHAPTER SIXTEEN

Conclusion

We have covered over a half a century, or two generations, with these few thousand colonists, and the time has come to pull together the various threads of this discussion and draw some conclusions.

The evidence mustered in the course of this research, fitted into a broader comparative context, has corroborated my initial impression that the Island of Montreal would provide a good vantage point from which to map the development of the colony's socio-economic framework. If there are differences between this region and others (Quebec was somewhat more in touch with the world beyond it while the rural areas were more isolated), there is also a common experience that allows me to advance a number of generalizations.

In order to provide a complete picture of this society, I adopted a now widely accepted structural approach, with an emphasis on economic activities. Quantitative data take up little room in this study. I sometimes regretted my inability to round out arguments with good time series. But these lacunae, which others will no doubt fill in one day, do not affect the main argument, which does not rest on conjunctural fluctuations, since these had limited repercussions on the commercial structure and even slighter ones on the pattern of settlement. Any overall explanation that means to do full justice to the colonial experience cannot be based solely on cyclical and intercyclical variations, or even on long-term trends. This country, created in the midst of a recession, kept its characteristic features for two centuries, while upward and downward economic phases alternated. The development of an export sector engendered a growing vulnerability. Whatever the conjunctural strains, they gave rise to minor adjustments only.

This study had to begin with what was produced and what was exchanged. Yet at first I feared that this might lead me nowhere. No one had ever attempted to study the evolution of the colony except through the official policies it embodied. Since the settlement was so new and so scantily populated, would anything coherent be left once the economic activities were separated from the framework of metropolitan projects and directives? Would such empirical research on a small region, removed from decision-making, merely reveal haphazard initiatives and contradictory or anarchic behaviour patterns? Was the rationale of this early period to be found only in the ideology of the agents of colonization?

These fears proved groundless. The economy had an autonomous existence. It evolved according to its own rhythms, and the manner in which it interacted with the rest of the system was neither preordained nor pointedly dictated by the authorities. This rereading of the nature of French colonization in America encourages us to reconsider what effect government has on development and the effectiveness or pertinence of regulation. An analysis of the public sector would demonstrate the financial links between government and private sector and highlight the nature of social relations on which this study has touched only briefly. It would not, however, change the main trends delineated in this study.

Canada was created by merchant capital as an offshoot of metropolitan interests to which it remained subservient. This reality governed the development of all colonial societies. A polarity was established between the centre and the periphery on the one hand, and the latter and its own hinterland on the other.[1] Yet I would argue that Canada in the seventeenth and eighteenth centuries provides a poor illustration of the links that are usually forged at the upper level. The metropolis invested heavily in the colony, and its merchants received only paltry returns. The drain of the economic surplus, which was far from considerable, cannot in and of itself explain why the undertaking proved so shaky. The fur trade garnered its profits from the surplus created by native peoples. Once the system was in place, it could do without further European immigration: the offspring of the first generation of colonists more than sufficed to manage the cargoes and keep the trading posts supplied.[2] The internal market developed more slowly than the productive capacity of the countryside. Its geographic location prevented the colony from competing with France or the American colonies in the West Indies. Merchants made timid attempts to sell wheat, meat, and wood in the eighteenth century, but the returns were too unpredictable to redirect merchant capital away from its initial focus, which generated sound profits with fewer risks. Even when its metropolis changed, when one group of merchants took over from another, Canada could not avoid these basic contradictions.

Economists have described this schema on more than one occasion.[3] Historians have never challenged it directly, choosing rather to ignore it. No one has attempted to demonstrate the inevitable repercussions of such a system on the internal economy, institutional development, and social structures of the colony, or on the colonists' outlook. Yet such linkages emerge very clearly as soon as we leave events behind and try to isolate permanent features. The analysis of the movement of men, credit, and price differentials between town, distant outposts, and countryside, and the study of land ownership, have consistently shown the effects of a gap between two sectors: the export sector and colonial production.

The trading posts' links with the countryside, which had initially ensured their survival, loosened as settlement spread. The significant phenomenon of the period under study is the depreciation of the rural output. A system of appropriation cannot rest on occasional scarcity. There were no long-term inducements to entice merchant capital to the land or tempt it to bank on rentes. This meant that peasants were not threatened with dispossession but also that sources of credit were rare and incentive to produce beyond their own needs were almost absent. The situation engendered a certain degree of independence, a transient sense of security, and brakes on both production and social development. This is the background that cannot be obscured by the limited market activity of Montreal and environs. The deeper one delves into the evidence from the countryside, the more one feels the effects of this dislocation. Even in Montreal's suburbs, the rise of some enterprising and ambitious farmers was associated with favourable family circumstances. Their relative number did not increase, and since household circumstances and personal motivations varied from generation to generation, so did the composition of the group. Stimulated from within and not from without, large properties did not have to be handed down fully from father to son. It took time and effort to develop a farm, and this led to obvious inequalities, although these were short-lived. Time levelled out differences in this rural society.

The lack of integration of agricultural production within the market economy accounts for the type of "frontier" found in New France, for the regular expansion of settlement on both banks of the St Lawrence. Settlers were periodically driven by demographic pressures to seek out new land, a movement abetted both materially and morally by the family nexus. Colonists who moved to the fringes of the cleared land reproduced the features of the *côtes* they had just left, which lay just a few hours away. Nothing changed on the frontier. The conquest of virgin soil does not, by itself, generate social and cultural change. Capitalism, advancing with rapid strides on Virginian plantations or other settlements in the Appalachian valleys, as it would later accompany American and Canadian settlers in the west, was the prime factor of transformation. These outlying regions would immediately be integrated into a dynamic network of exchange that would overhaul ancient values and create a new breed of men. The Turner thesis, which mistakes the locale for the cause, still has its champions, who either disregard this early Canadian example, which will not fit the pattern of geographical determinism, or else assign the anomaly to cultural differences.[4] In both cases they dodge any analysis of the relations of production between the frontier and both local and distant metropolitan centres.

However burdensome for the peasantry, the levy of tithes and seigneurial dues did not govern the production or marketing processes and did not give rise to the apposite social formations. No rural elite, and no body of tenant-farmers, money-lenders, merchants, and large landowners lived among the habitants on the fruits of their labour, acting as economic and political intermediaries between town and country. The settlers were very much on their own, and their geographic dispersal compounded the difficulties when the simplest infrastructures, such as parishes, were set up.

Cushioned against economic pressures, people formed strong, harmonious ties with the land promoting close family bonds, neighbourliness, and, in the aftermath of a turbulent immigration, the elaboration of those traditional practices with which we are familiar since they disappeared only recently.

If the French peasantry of the Ancien Régime can be defined by its relation to the rentier class, the Canadian experience was different: the regime required of the small landowners tribute in a number of forms, such as statute labour and militia service, but they were granted a kind of respite at the material end. Once they began to run out of the empty stretches of potentially arable land that ensured their autonomy, the *côtes* nurtured armies of proletarians, and colonial capital proved just as hopeless at utilizing them.[5]

Many of the rural inhabitants of the Island of Montreal and surrounding areas were drawn to the fur trade, either temporarily or for their entire lives. This study has shown that we must be careful to differentiate among young men who regarded the trade as a source of savings for their future farms, those who tried to ally farming and trading, those who became professional voyageurs, and those for whom such expeditions proved a pathway to permanent emigration, notably to Louisiana. For the first group, trading was merely a temporary activity. By this route a tiny fraction of mercantile profits were redirected towards the countryside, making life easier for some young couples.

The fur trade's demand for manpower was not sufficient to support a body of labourers in the côtes. The first settlers who travelled west while attempting to run a farm fell into dire straits, and soon such cases became rare. Trade investments imposed a limit on the number of professional traders. After 1700 it was highly unlikely that a habitant's son would be found in their ranks, for recruitment was essentially urban.

As for emigration, it has to be placed within the context of an economy where the only other outlet was farming. The west beckoned those who were either unsuited to or disliked agricultural work and who dreamed of greater riches than those afforded by this traditional sector. Without this constant appeal, most would probably have come to terms with their restlessness, as they did in those parts of the colony that remained completely outside the fur-trade network. As many as 1,000 men might have left the Montreal region over a hundred years. In the end, however, this phenomenon had few short-term repercussions. A larger population would not have made this country easier to defend, and a speedier proliferation of units of subsistence could not have altered the course of economic development. In short, the colonists' peregrinations and emigration were mostly the consequence of the general conditions prevailing in the colony.

No sooner was it settled than the counrtyside began to exhibit the familiar, unchanging features of Quebec rural society – and this despite the closeness of the warehouses – encapsulated in its uniform farms and lifestyle, stable land ownership, strong family ties, and entrenched routines. The fur trade not only did not disturb this pattern but, by systematically relieving the rural sector of its most enterprising and unruly elements, actually hastened the development of such particularism, such conformity.

In stark contrast, the merchants pursued their own interests with great logic and boundless energy and perseverance. Colonial and metropolitan on both sides of the Atlantic combined their labour and capital to promote this joint undertaking. They may have experienced temporary strains, but no real antagonism divided them. The entire debate around the bourgeoisie of New France is a non-issue.[6] The merchants were equal to the activity that sustained them. It did not engender untold profits, but it certainly justified their efforts. They had to set up the trading networks, and the organization that emerged testifies both to their foresight and to their flexibility.[7] Wary of government interference, yet always ready to take advantage of it, they cleverly managed to bypass obstructive monopolies, policies, and government agents. There were a few major winners in this game, and a number achieved both comfort and respectability.

There was no marked difference between the income and lifestyle of the merchants and that of traders and artisans and this seems to remain stable. Within the mercantile community distinct functions soon evolved that were likely to underscore financial inequalities. However, social cleavages grew far more pronounced than the spread between incomes would suggest. The town had its own hierarchical structure, and the barriers between one level and the next proved progressively harder to bridge. These traits were largely determined by the close ties that bound the colony to the mother country. Yet the interplay between colonial staple production, the local social structure, and the institutional framework was somewhat atypical.

The privileged class had only weak bonds with the land and was characterized primarily by its military role and by the preferential treatment it received within the fur-trading organization.[8] Craft production remained marginal and did not depend on merchant capital. The scattered workshops provided basic necessities and trained a sufficient number of artisans to ensure a continuity of services, while the excess urban population swelled the number of day-labourers, only partly absorbed by the fur trade.[9]

Merchants could never rest on their laurels. Their success depended on the uninterrupted reinvestment of profits in trade goods and furs. Here they did not have to contend with social pressures urging them to invest heavily in land purely for prestige, rather than in commercial undertakings. They let the Crown chance a few diversified ventures and assume the subsequent losses.[10] They were far more likely to maintain their positions by continuing to invest in the activities that had allowed them to rise.

If we look at the long-term development of this colony, then, there is no doubt that all categories of merchants who continued to take advantage of various regional disparities and bank everything on distant markets held pride of place whatever the changes in political regimes. The petty military nobility that underpinned their earliest endeavours would eventually disappear, and artisans would remain a relatively small group. That left only one other permanent category, whose importance lay primarily in their numbers: the habitants. They figured only marginally in mercantile enterprises. There is a timeless quality about the way they continued to reproduce, generation upon generation, static communities that more or less resembled those that emerged soon after their arrival. The polarization of these two societies, which was already apparent in the seventeenth century, would dominate this region's subsequent history.

Do such comments stray too far afield from the limited case study on which they are based? I do not think so. The history of New France, as it appeared to me at each stage of this study, is not a self-contained story, a quaint prologue to more telling accounts, but a first chapter that embodies the essential problematic of the nation's socio-economic development.

PART FIVE

Appendices

Weights and Measures

The colony's official weights and measures were those of Paris. The following were used in this book:

Area measures

1 arpent = 100 perches = 34.19 acres (approximately 5/6 of an acre).

Linear measures

1 toise (6 pieds) = 1.94 metres (or about 2 yards)
1 perche (18 pieds) = 5.84 metres (or about 6 yards)
1 lieue (league) = 4.91 kilometers (or about 3 miles)
1 aune (ell) = 1.188 metres (or about 1 yard)

Volume measure (for grain)

1 minot (0.25 setier) = 39 litres (or 8.75 imperial gallons)

For a number of decades Montreal settlers occasionally used measures from their provinces of origin. They might talk of a *journée* as an area measure of their arable land, or the *poinçon* or the *provision* when weighing their crops. I was unable to find exact equivalents for these measures. Other units used for liquids, wood (cords and *trainées*), or hay (*gerbe, mulon* and *barge*) were often very localized and since they did not enter into any quantitative analyses, I did not dwell on the problems of their measures. A uniform system of weights and measures was well established by the end of the seventeenth century.

Supplementary Tables

Table A
Structure of the population on the Island of Montreal, 1666–1739

| | Males | | | | | Females | | | | | |
| | Married or widowers | | Single | | | Married | Single | | | | |
Year	Fifty years and over	Under fifty	Fifteen and over	Under fifteen	Total	and widows	Fifteen and over	Under fifteen	Total	Total population	Population of Canada
1666	11	95	153	144	403	111	15	130	256	659	3,246
1681	54	155	149	321	778	214	78	316	610	1,388	9,742
1685	324		300	383	1,007	259	115	339	713	1,720	11,030
1688	254		247	278	779	252	133	249	634	1,413	10,038
1692	78	175	192	290	735	222	130	254	606	1,341	11,114
1695	135	247	274	458	1,114	383	224	440	1,047	2,161	12,786
1706	143	441	440	884	1,908	552	314	831	1,697	3,605	16,788
1707	132	445	404	926	1,907	541	303	875	1,719	3,626	17,615
1713	168	407	385	931	1,891	658	546	1,053	2,257	4,148	18,467
1714	180	418	402	854	1,854	603	592	957	2,153	4,007	18,741
1716	211	527	523	922	2,183	688	588	950	2,226	4,409	20,896
1718	770		1,581		2,351	824	1,582		2,406	4,757	23,125
1719	316	484	417	1,010	2,227	689	678	1,072	2,439	4,666	22,530
1720	338	493	536	890	2,257	791	727	1,086	2,604	4,861	24,544
1721	342	543	607	900	2,392	795	722	1,100	2,617	5,009	24,946
1722	342	555	631	750	2,278	799	726	1,130	2,655	4,933	25,106
1723	327	596	628	1,200	2,751	949	742	1,173	2,864	5,615	25,972
1726	319	720	684	1,246	2,969	957	822	1,198	2,977	5,946	29,836
1727	323	646	573	1,370	2,912	974	828	1,282	3,084	5,996	31,169

1730	370	739	751	1,424	3,274	1,126	861	1,366	3,353	6,627	34,188
1732	401	762	781	1,515	3,459	1,132	881	1,407	3,420	6,879	35,525
1736	458	854	725	1,368	3,405	1,251	773	1,572	3,596	7,001	39,220
1737	329	964	789	1,533	3,615	1,376	823	1,544	3,743	7,358	40,143
1739	381	994	863	1,443	3,681	1,420	918	1,717	4,055	7,736	43,264

Table B
Population on the Island of Montreal according to sex, marital status, and age categories (1666 census)

	Males				Females				Both sexes			
	Single	Married	Widowers	Total	Single	Married	Widows	Total	Single	Married	Widowed	Total
0–4	75			75	71			71	146			146
5–9	56			56	43			43	99			99
10–14	13			13	16			16	29			29
15–19	22			22	3	7		10	25	7		32
20–24	62	5		67	4	30	1	35	66	35	1	102
25–29	30	11		41	2	19	1	22	32	30	1	63
30–34	18	29		47	1	24		25	19	53		72
35–39	6	20	1	27	1	9	1	11	7	29	2	38
40–44	3	22		25		3		3	3	25		28
45–49	5	7		12	2	6		8	7	13		20
50–54	3	3		6		2	1	3	3	5	1	9
55–59	4	2	2	8	1	3	2	6	5	5	4	14
60–64		3		3	1			1	1	3		4
65–69						1		1		1		1
70–74		1		1						1		1
75–79							1	1			1	1
Total	297	103	3	403	145	104	7	256	442	207	10	659

Table C
Population on the Island of Montreal according to sex, marital status, and age categories (1681 census)

	Males				Females				Both sexes			
	Single	Married	Widowers	Total	Single	Married	Widows	Total	Single	Married	Widowed	Total
0–4	113			113	121			121	234			234
5–9	116			116	105			105	221			221
10–14	92			92	91			91	183			183
15–19	60	1		61	45	22		67	105	23		128
20–24	51	2		53	9	29		38	60	31		91
25–29	27	7		34	7	29	1	37	34	36	1	71
30–34	32	37		69	4	34	2	40	36	71	2	109
35–39	16	50		66	4	24		28	20	74		94
40–44	25	36	2	63	3	23	2	28	28	59	4	91
45–49	17	20		37	2	19	2	23	19	39	2	60
50–54	13	23	2	38		13	3	16	13	36	5	54
55–59	2	12	1	15		4		4	2	16	1	19
60–64	5	11		16	3	2	2	7	8	13	2	23
65–69		1		1						1		1
70–74	1		1	2	1			1	2		1	3
75–79		3		3						3		3
80–84							1	1			1	1
85–89						1		1		1		1
90–94				0				0				0
95–99							1	1			1	1
Totals	570	203	6	779	395	200	14	609	965	403	20	1,388

Table D
Average annual prices of wheat per minot, Island of Montreal, 1650–1725
(calculated for the harvest year in sols tournois)*

Years	Sols	Years	Sols	Years	Sols	Years	Sols
1650–8	75	1675	71.2	1692	117	1709	45
1659	67.5	1676	71.2	1693	60	1710	35.6
1660	63.7	1677	67.5	1694	37.5	1711	30
1661	82.5	1678	63.7	1695	60	1712	37.5
1662	82.5	1679	45	1696	75	1713	45
1663	71.2	1680	45	1697	52.5	1714	50
1664	67.5	1681	56.2	1698	43.8	1715	52.5
1665	60	1682	46.5	1699	90	1716	60
1666	67.5	1683	41.2	1700	92	1717	60.5
1667	60	1684	37.5	1701	45	1718	60
1668	60	1685	30	1702	37.5	17179	30
1669	45	1686	31.5	1703	30	1720	30
1670	52.5	1687	37.5	1704	30	1722	40
1671	45	1688	41.2	1705	30	1722	40
1672	60	1689	60	1706	30	1723	50
1673	60	1690	112	1707	45	1724	55.5
1674	75	1691	90	1708	37.5	1725	40

Source: Notarial records, principally after-death-inventories, and the account books of the Hôtel-Dieu of Montreal for the years 1698–1723.
*The harvest year 1659 runs from 1 September 1659 to 31 August 1660.
One Canadian sol = 0.75 sols tournois (1650–1712), 0.375 (1713–19), 1.00 (from 1720)

APPENDIX THREE

Graphs

Graph 1
Canadian population and population of the Island of Montreal according to census, 1650–1770, with an approximate distribution of Montreal's rural and urban populations.

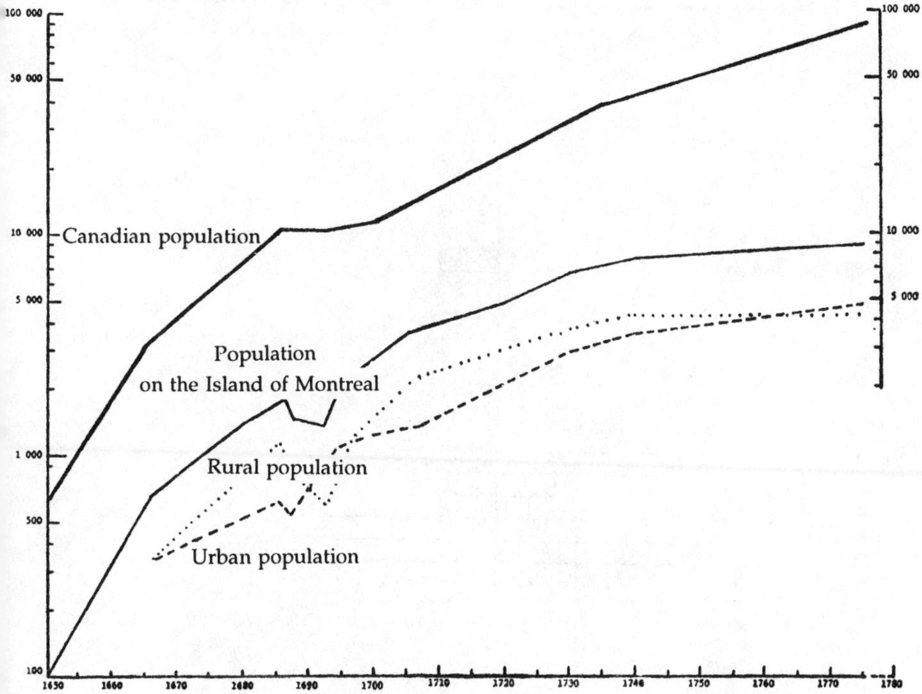

Graph 2
Age pyramid of the Montreal population, based on the 1666 and 1681 censuses,
according to marital status

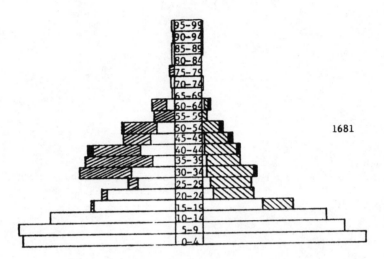

1681

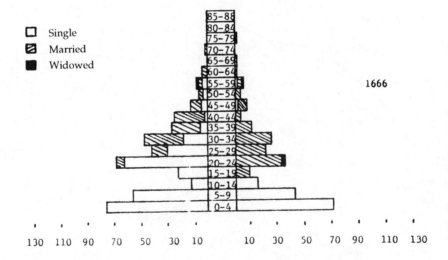

☐   Single
▨   Married
■   Widowed

1666

130   110   90   70   50   30   10   10   30   50   70   90   110   130

Graph 3
Age pyramid of the Montreal population, based on the 1666 and 1681 censuses,
according to the country of origin

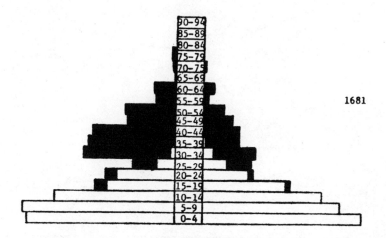

1681

☐ Born in Canada
■ Born in France

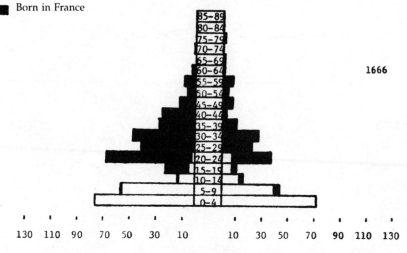

1666

130   110   90   70   50   30   10   10   30   50   70   **90   110   130**

Graph 4
Distribution of the Montreal population by sex,
age group, and marital status, 1666–1739

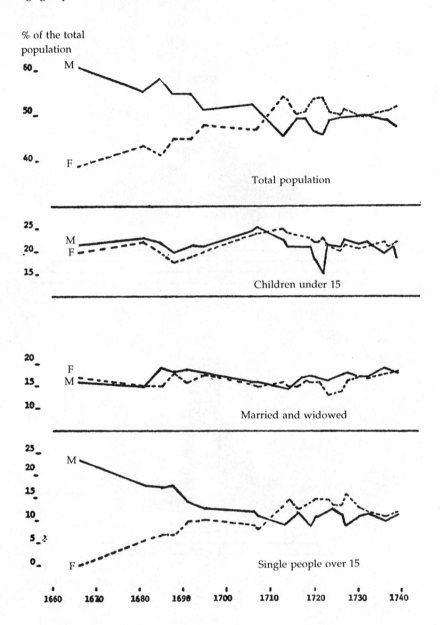

% of the total
population

Total population

Children under 15

Married and widowed

Single people over 15

Graph 5
Annual number of baptisms, burials, and marriages, Island of Montreal, 1643–1715.
(The dotted lines for the years 1712–15 were adjusted to fill the voids in the
registers of the rural parish of Lachine.)

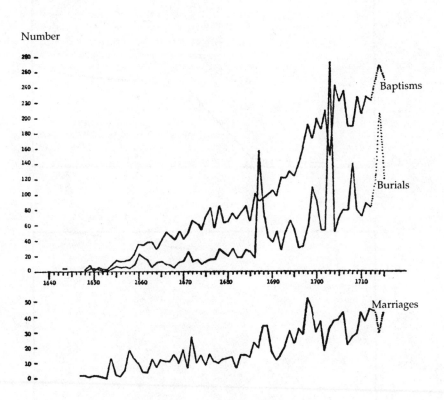

Graph 6
Marriage distribution in the Montreal parish of Notre-Dame, 1650–1715, according
to the spouses' country of origin

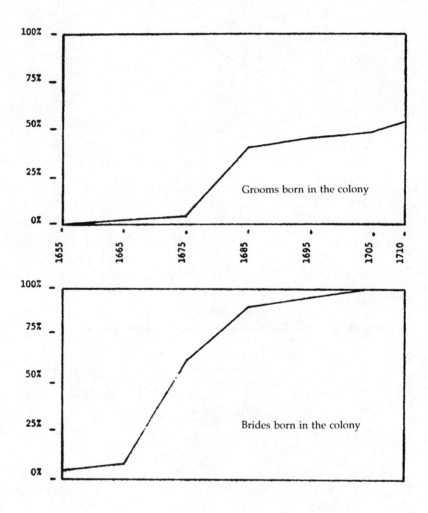

Graph 7
Monthly distribution of marriages (corrected index) on the Island of Montreal,
1646–1715

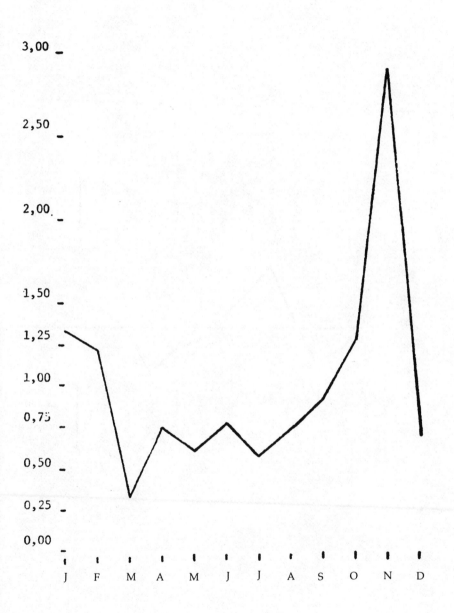

Graph 8
Monthly distribution of births and conceptions (corrected index) for the Island of
Montreal, 1646–1715

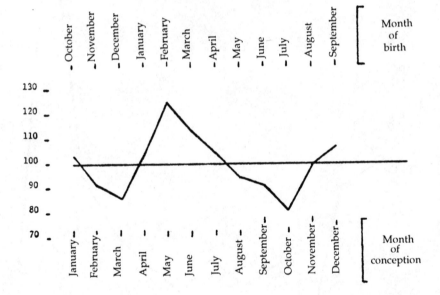

Graph 9
Quarterly distribution of deaths, conceptions, and marriages and price of wheat,
1686–94

Number

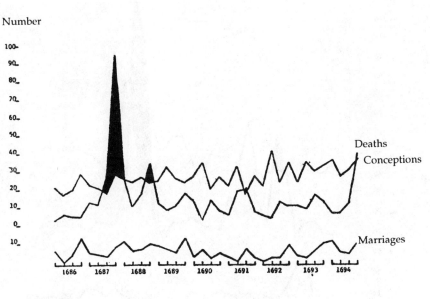

Deaths
Conceptions

Marriages

Sols tournois

Price of wheat

Graph 10
Quarterly distribution of deaths, conceptions, and marriages and price of wheat,
1698–1704

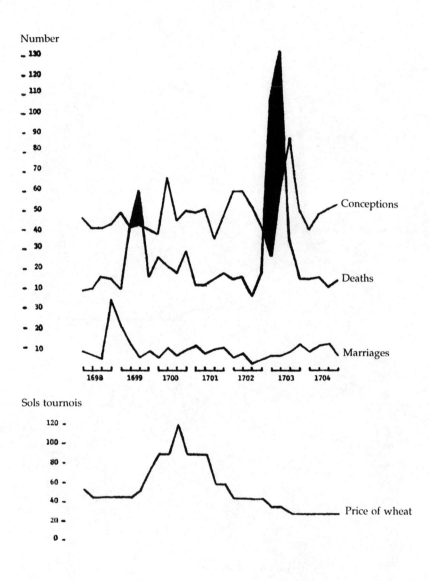

Graph 11
Distribution of the goods sold by Alexis Monière, 1715–25
a. Goods purchased by Indians 100% = 63,375 livres tournois

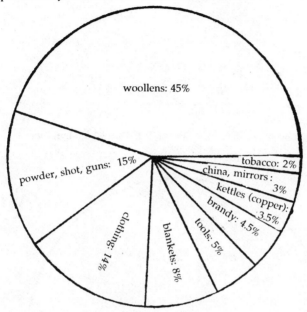

woollens: 45%

powder, shot, guns: 15%

tobacco: 2%

china, mirrors: 3%

kettles (copper): 3.5%

brandy: 4.5%

tools: 5%

blankets: 8%

clothing: 14%

b. Goods purchased by the colonists 100% = 25,846 livres tournois

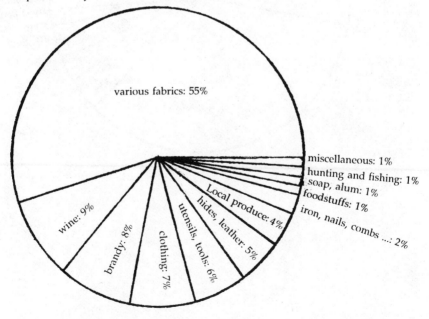

various fabrics: 55%

miscellaneous: 1%
hunting and fishing: 1%
soap, alum: 1%
foodstuffs: 1%
iron, nails, combs ...: 2%

wine: 9%

brandy: 8%

clothing: 7%

utensils, tools: 6%

hides, leather: 5%

Local produce: 4%

Source: Account books, NA, M-847, 848

Graph 12
Forms of payments according to Alexis Monière's account books, 1715–24

a. Payments by voyageurs and their *engagés* 100% = 52,440 livres tournois

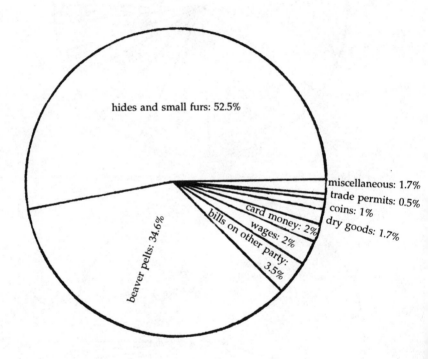

hides and small furs: 52.5%

beaver pelts: 34.6%

bills on other party: 3.5%

card money: 2%

wages: 2%

miscellaneous: 1.7%

trade permits: 0.5%

coins: 1%

dry goods: 1.7%

Source: NA, M-847, 848

b. Payments by other clients 100% = 26,820 livres tournois

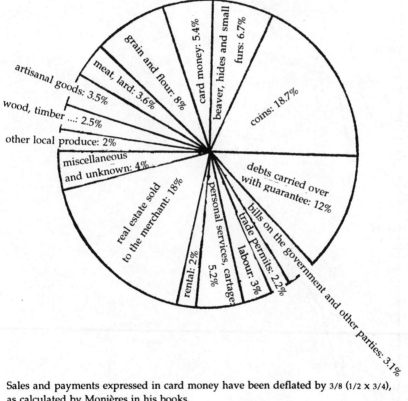

Sales and payments expressed in card money have been deflated by 3/8 (1/2 x 3/4), as calculated by Monières in his books.

Graph 13
Credit sales and cumulative payments in Alexis Monière's account books, 1715–24

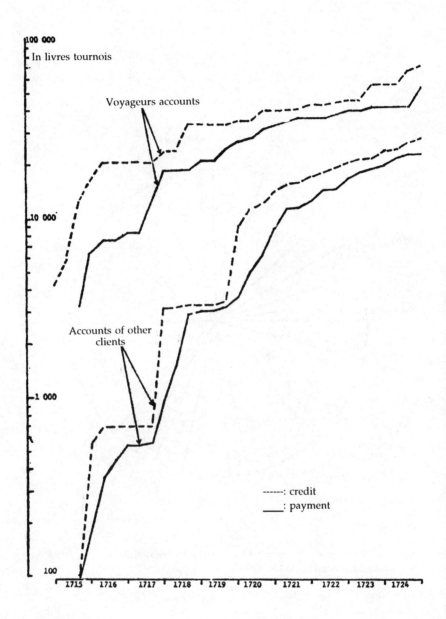

Graph 14
Quarterly movement in credit and payments in Alexis Monière's account books,
1715–24

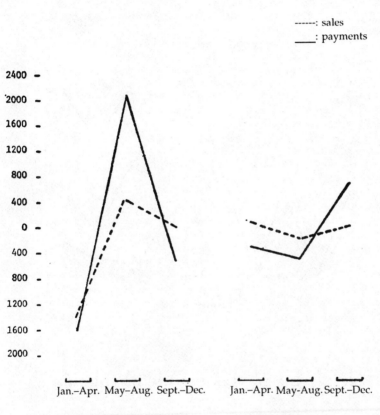

------: sales
_____: payments

2400

2000

1600

1200

800

400

0

400

800

1200

1600

2000

Jan.–Apr. May–Aug. Sept.–Dec.   Jan.–Apr. May-Aug. Sept.–Dec.

Voyageurs accounts   Other clients' accounts

Graph 15
Annual departures for the fur trade, 1708–17

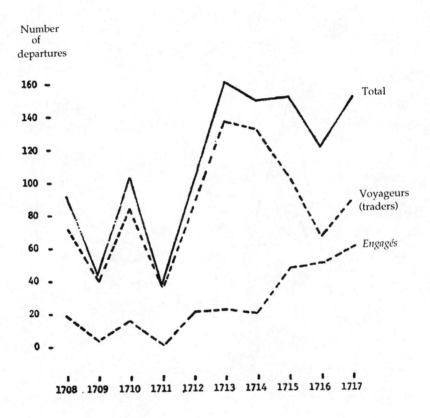

Number
of
departures

160 -

140 -

120 -

100 -

80 -

60 -

40 -

20 -

0 -

Total

Voyageurs
(traders)

Engagés

1708 1709 1710 1711 1712 1713 1714 1715 1716 1717

Source: obligations, partnerships, hiring, and other deeds related to the fur trade in
Notarial Records

Graph 16
Distribution of voyageurs and *engagés* 1708–17, according to their age at first voyage in this period

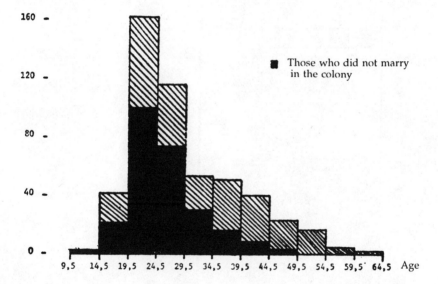

Graph 17
Regional distribution of the voyageurs and *engagés*, 1708–17

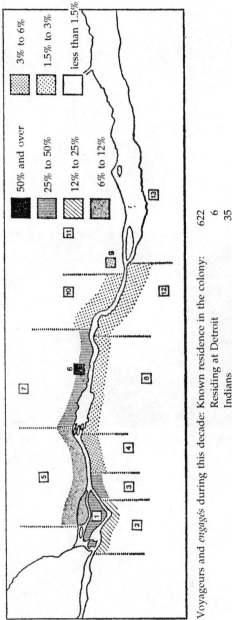

■ 50% and over	▨ 3% to 6%
▤ 25% to 50%	▧ 1.5% to 3%
▨ 12% to 25%	☐ less than 1.5%
▨ 6% to 12%	

Voyageurs and *engagés* during this decade: Known residence in the colony: 622
Residing at Detroit 6
Indians 35
Unknown residence 35
Total 668

Regions	Total population in 1716	Adult males (a)	Voyageurs and *engagés* Number	%(b)
Colony as a whole	20,530	5,520	657(c)	12.0
Montreal district				
1. Island of Montreal	4,276	1,230	337	27.4
2. *South Shore: west* (Châteauguay, Laprairie, Longueuil, St.-Lambert, Tremblay)	905	202	42	20.7
3. *South Shore: centre* (Cap St.-Michel, Boucherville, Varenne, Trinité	705	170	66	38.9
4. *South Shore: east* (Chambly, Verchères, Vitré, Contrecoeur, St-Ours, Sorel, Iles Bouchard and Ste-Thérèse	824	212	11	5.2
5. *North Shore* (Ile Jésus, Lachenaie, Repentigny, Dautré, St.-Sulpice, Berthier, Lavaltrie, Lanoraie, duPas)	1,138	272	17	6.2
Trois-Rivières district				
6. Town proper	279	54	29	53.7
7. Trois-Rivières, North Shore seigneuries	956	221	67	30.3
8. Trois-Rivières, South Shore seigneuries	430	106	2	1.8
Quebec district				
9. Town proper	2,440	578	29	5.0
10. North Shore: west	1,669	360	9	2.5
11. North Shore: east (including Ile d'Orléans)	3,793	855	9	1.0
12. South Shore: west (from Lauzon)	1,138	242	4	1.6
13. Lower St Lawrence	2,093	480	0	0

(a) 15 and over
(b) Of the adult male population
(c) Known and unknown residence

Graph 18
Size and structure of farms in the Côte Saint-Joseph, 1697

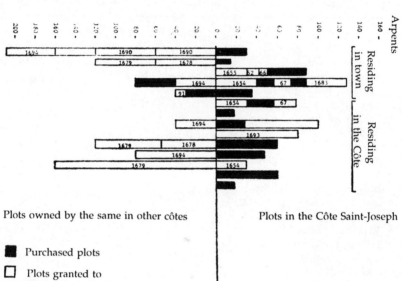

Plots owned by the same in other côtes   Plots in the Côte Saint-Joseph

■ Purchased plots

☐   Plots granted to
     the family (with date)

Source: "Livre des Tenanicers," 1697: Séminaire de Saint-Sulpice Archives, Montreal

Graph 19
Size and structure of farms in the Côte St-Louis, 1697

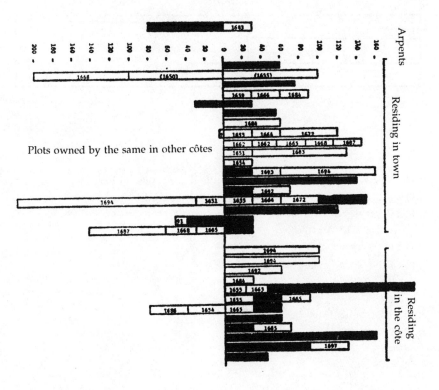

Plots owned by the same in other côtes

Graph 20
Example of consolidation of a holding: the farm of Julien Blois in the Côte Saint-François, 1704

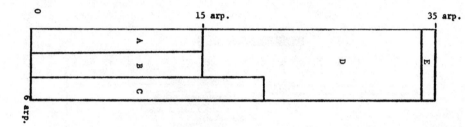

Plot A: granted in 1665. Blois purchased it from the grantee in 1666.

Plot B: granted in 1666. Blois purchased it from the third owner in 1669.

Plot C: granted in 1665. Blois purchased it from the second owner in 1678.

Total: 100 arpents

Plot D: 90 arpents granted to Blois in 1686.

Plot E: bit of land granted to Blois in 1690.

Graph 21
Changes in the arable land and meadows of 93 farms on the Island of Montreal
according to the 1667 and 1681 census returns

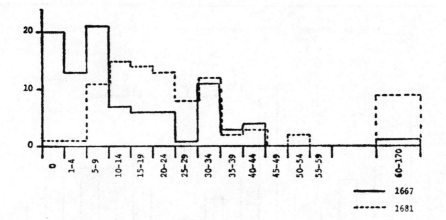

———— 1667

------- 1681

Graph 22
Size of arable land and meadows on all the censives on the Island of Montreal,
1667, 1681, 1731

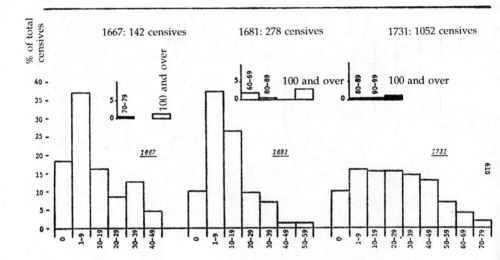

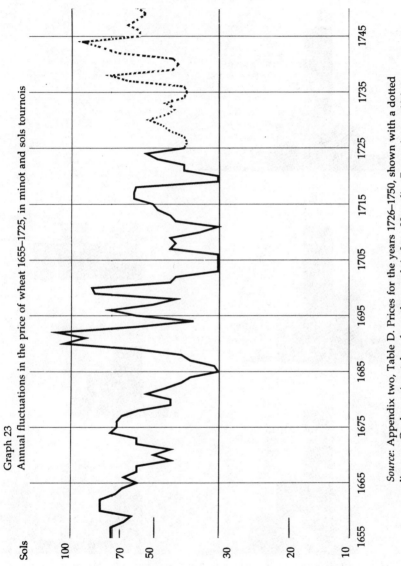

Graph 23
Annual fluctuations in the price of wheat 1655–1725, in minot and sols tournois

Source: Appendix two, Table D. Prices for the years 1726–1750, shown with a dotted line, are Quebec prices taken from the graph in Jean Hamelin, *Economie et société en Nouvelle-France* (Quebec 1960), 61.

Graph 24
Tax categories in the Island of Montreal according to the 1715 assessment

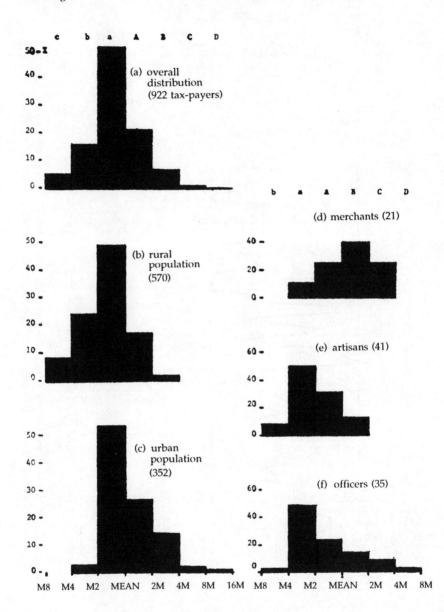

Notes

AC   Archives des colonies
AN   Archives nationales (France)
ANQ   Archives nationales du Québec (Québec)
APND   Archives de la paroisse Notre-Dame (Montreal)
ASSM   Archives of Saint-Sulpice in Montreal
ASSP   Archives of Saint-Sulpice in Paris
BN   Bibliothèque nationale (Paris)
BRH   Bulletin des recherches historiques
CHAR   Canadian Historical Association Report
CHR   Canadian Historical Review
CJEPS   Canadian Journal of Economic and Political
          Science
DCB   Dictionary of Canadian Biography
JDCS   Jugements et délibérations du Conseil souverain
NA   National Archives of Canada
Not. Rec. Notarial Records (ANQ, Montréal)
PCRS   Proceedings of the Canadian Royal Society
RAPQ   Rapport de l'archiviste de la province du
          Québec
RHAF   Revue d'histoire de l'Amérique française
SCHEC   Société canadienne d'histoire de l'Eglise
          catholique

CHAPTER ONE

1 D. Jenness, *Indians of Canada*, National Museum bulletin no. 65, 3rd ed. (Ottawa 1955); L.H. Morgan, *League of the Ho-de-No-Sau-Nee Iroquois* (New York 1904); A.C. Parker, "Origins of the Iroquois," *American Anthropologist* 18 (1916); Geroge T. Hunt, *The Wars of the Iroquois: A Study in Intertribal Relations* (University of Wisconsin Press 1960); W.N. Fenton, "Problems Arising from the Historic Northeastern Position of the Iroquois," *Essays in Historical Anthropology of North America*, Smithsonian Miscellaneous Collections no. 10 (Washington 1940); W.A. Ritchie, *Prehistoric Patterns in Northeastern North America*, Viking Fund Publications in Anthropology no. 23 (1956); B.G. Trigger, "Settlement as an Aspect of Iroquoian Adaptation at the Time of Contacts," *American Anthropologist*, no. 65 (Feb. 1963).

2 Hunt, *The Wars of the Iroquois*; Leo-Paul Desrosiers, *Iroquoisie*, vol. 1 (Montreal 1947); B.G. Trigger, "The French Presence in Huronia: The Structure of Franco-Huron Relations in the First Half of the Seventeenth Century," *CHR* (June 1968); 107–41, and "The Mohawk-Mohican War, 1624–1628: The Establishment of a Pattern," *CHR* (Sept. 1971): 276–86.

3 See the works of W.J. Eccles, in particular *Frontenac: the Courtier Governor* (Toronto 1959).

4 Hunt, *The Wars of the Iroquois*, 158.

5 This is based on D. Jenness, *Indians of Canada*. See also L.E. Hamelin, *Le Canada* (Paris 1969), 136–42; J.N. Biraben, "Le peuplement du Canada français," *Annales de démographie historique* (1966): 105–38. These are obviously tentative figures, advanced already long ago, but unlike current research on Latin American demography, more recent work has not tended to reinforce them.

6 In addition to the works already cited, see H.F. Driver, *Indians of North America* (Chicago 1969); C. Wissler, *Histoire des Indiens d'Amérique du Nord* (Paris 1969); B.G. Trigger, *The Huron: Farmers of the North*, Case Studies in Cultural Anthropology (New York 1969).

7 Benjamin Bissell, *The American Indian in English Literature of the Eighteenth Century* (New Haven 1925); Gilbert Chinard, *L'Exotisme américain dans la littérature française au xvie siècle* (Paris 1911), and *L'Amérique et le rêve exotique dans la littérature française au xviie et xviiie siècles* (Paris 1913); René Gonnard, *La Légende du bon sauvage* (Paris 1946); Paul Hazard, *La Crise de la conscience européenne, 1680–1715* (Paris 1935).

8 R.G. Thwaites, ed., *The Jesuit Relations and Allied Documents*, 73 vols. (Cleveland 1896–1901), in particular 5:107 (1633 relation) and 2:283 (1648 relation). Louis Armand de Lom d'Arce, baron de La Hontan, *Nouveaux voyages de M. le baron de La Hontan dans l'Amérique septen-*

trionnale, 2 vols. (The Hague 1704) and *Supplément aux voyages du baron de La Hontan où l'on trouve des dialogues curieux entre l'auteur et un sauvage de bon sens qui a voyagé* (The Hague 1703).

9 In his work on the Micmac at the time of contacts, Alfred G. Bailey slides rapidly over the impact that native culture had on the French. *The Conflict of European and Eastern Algonquin Cultures, 1504–1700* (St John, NB 1937), 117–22. See also H.A. Innis, *The Fur Trade in Canada* (Toronto 1962), 386–93.

10 W.J. Eccles, *The Canadian Frontier, 1534–1760* (Toronto 1969), 91–2; A.L. Burt, "The Frontier in the History of New France," CHAR (1940): 93–9; Bailey, *The Conflict*, 123; G.F.G. Stanley, "The Policy of 'Francisation' as Applied to the Indians during the Ancien Régime," RHAF 3 (Dec. 1949): 333–48; C.J. Jaenen, "The Frenchification and Evangilization of the Amerindians in Seventeenth-Century New France," SCHEC 35 (1968): 33–46.

11 Marcel Giraud, *Le Métis canadien: son rôle dans l'histoire de l'Ouest* (Paris 1945), 297ff, 312ff.

12 On this question consult Michael Bantom, *Race Relations* (London 1967), chap. 4; Z. Barbu, *Problems of Historical Psychology* (London 1960); W. Stark, *The Sociology of Knowledge: An Essay in Aid of a Deeper Understanding of the History of Ideas* (London 1960); G. Gurvitch, *Les Cadres sociaux de la connaissance* (Paris 1966).

13 Champlain sent his young *commis*, Etienne Brûlé, to winter with the Huron to learn their language and cement trading agreements.

14 See the various accounts of discovery and Marcel Giraud's work on the Métis.

15 Parish records of Notre-Dame de Montréal (APND), birth, marriage, and burial registers.

16 Olivier Maurault, "Les Vicissitudes d'une mission sauvage," *Revue trimestrielle canadienne* (June 1930): 121–49.

17 The La Montagne mission, founded in 1671, contained Huron and Algonkian and a minority of Iroquois. "Etat de ce qui a été dépensé pour l'entretien de la Montagne" (1697), NA, M.G.17, A7, 2, 1, vol. 1, 221–6; ASSP, doss. 109, doc. 1, item 16. The slavery practised by the Iroquois was, like adoption, a means of recouping the tribe's losses. A.G. Bailey, *The Conflict*, 91; D. Jenness, *Indians of Canada*, 51.

18 Maurault, "Les Vicissitudes"; Charles P. Beaubien, *Le Sault-au-Récollet: ses rapports avec les premiers temps de la colonie. Mission-paroisse*, (Montreal 1898), 226; G.F.G. Stanley, "First Indian Reserves in Canada," RHAF 4, no. 2 (Sept. 1950): 199–202. On exhausted soils at La Montagne, see ASSP, letter of M. Tronson, (ca. 1695), XIV:250.

19 ASSP, letters of M. Leschassier, 21 Mar. 1701, 15 May 1703, 18 Mar. 1706, 229, 294, 356.

20 The Sulpicians were hesitant to baptize girls since circumstances would probably force more than one to marry a pagan. "Mémoires sur les missions," ASSP, doss. 109, no. 1, item 15, letter of M. de Tronson, 25 Mar. 1686, XIII:473, 561.

21 "Native women are rather sterile, either because the hard work they must perform retards their childbearing or because they nurse their children too long; but such an impediment to the speedy peopling of the colony can be overcome by some police regulations that would be easy to introduce and carry out." "Mémoire sur l'état présent du Canada," BN mss, fr. N.A., fols. 73–7.

22 Bailey, The Conflict, 56–7.

23 Memoir by Denonville of 10 Aug. 1688, AC, C11A, 10, fols. 72–3. See Bailey, The Conflict, 104 and 114–15, on the various causes of depopulation among the Algonkians; Pierre Chaunu's synthesis, L'Amérique et les Amériques (Paris 1964), 104; and especially the studies by W. Borah and his group.

24 Namely the forays against Corlar and Dearfield in 1704 and Haverhill in 1708.

25 Some prisoners crop up in parish registers. On this question see E.L. Coleman, New England Captives Carried to Canada between 1677 and 1760 during French and Indian Wars, 2 vols. (Portland 1925), and Beaubien, Le Sault-au-Récollet, 164–213.

26 The Jesuits took advantage of the Iroquois Confederacy's neutrality to visit their settlements and to try to attract converts to Kahnawake. Trade relations between the mission and homeland remained close, and despite the split between non-Catholic Iroquois allied with the English, and the "praying Indians," the Iroquois always refused to bear arms against each other. One gets a good idea of these links in An Abridgment of the Indian Affairs Contained in Four Folio Volumes Transacted in the Colony of New York from the Year 1678 to the Year 1751 (New York 1968). In 1752 Louis Franquet found two hundred warriors at Sault-Saint-Louis and 228 and Lac-des-Deux-Montagnes, Voyages et mémoires sur le Canada, 119–21. The Jesuit Nau also mentions some figures in his letters of 29 Oct. 1734 and 2 Oct. 1735, RAPQ (1926–7): 272, 286.

27 The presence of Indians who had "retired" to the côtes and who were protected by the inhabitants is confirmed by the enquiries and various testimonies contained in the Montreal bailliage records. Copy Faillon, GG 213–17 and FF 68. A small group of Indians settled in the seigneury of Chateauguay; authorities who wanted all Indians confined to reservations disapproved of their presence. "There are many Indians wandering about the seigneury," wrote the governor on 13 Nov. 1685. AC, C11A, 7, fol. 9. The Sulpicians did likewise. Mémoires sur les missions, 1684, ASSP, doss. 109, doc. 1, item 23.

28 The inhabitants felt that it was less profitable to hire young Indians than colonial children. Letter from the intendant, 13 Nov. 1681, AC, C11A, 5, fol. 291v. Such adopted children took on new last names and are therefore difficult to trace. There is only one recorded case where the Indian remained with his adopted family till adulthood. André Kayanis Rapin did not figure among the seven heirs to the estate but received a heifer and a bull in the will "for the services he had rendered to the family he had joined at the age of five." He settled on the land and married a colonist's daughter. Not. Rec, 24 Oct. 1699, A. Adhémar.

29 Marcel Trudel, L'Esclavage au Canada français: histoire et conditions de l'esclavage (Quebec 1960).

30 Since 1627, according to the edict creating the Compagnie de la Nouvelle France. Edits, ordonnances royaux, I:7ff.

31 "To increase the population ... it seems to me that without waiting to capitalize on new colonists sent from France, nothing would be more useful than to attempt to civilize the Algonkian, Huron, and other Indians who have embraced Christianity." Colbert to Talon, 5 Apr. 1666, AC, C11A, 2, fol. 205.

32 Colbert's instructions to the Sieur Bouterou, 5 Apr. 1668, AC, B1, fol. 88v. Arrêt of the Sovereign Council of 10 Nov. 1668: "In order to execute his Majesty's wish that the Indians dwell among his Natural subjects in harmony and togetherness, so that the desired alliance between them be fostered and grow stronger each day by means of such renewed contact." JDCS, vol. I.

33 "They stated that they did this because they thought they might better preserve the tenets and holiness of our Religion by keeping the converted Indians' ordinary lifestyle than by bringing them among the French. Since it is only too obvious how such a course is harmful both to Religion and the State, one must act gently to get them to change their mind." Colbert to Talon, 5 Apr. 1666, AC, C11A, 2, fol. 205. Frontenac wondered at the fact that none of the Indians at the Notre-Dame de Foy mission spoke French, "although they have numerous contacts with us." Letter of 2 Nov. 1684, ASSP, doss. 109, doc. 1, item 1.

34 Ibid., item 2.

35 Ibid., item 3; letters of M. Tronson, 20 Mar. 1680, 13 Mar. 1683, ASSP, XII:160, 324.

36 Rather than adopt Indian names for objects they borrowed from these cultures, the colonists burdened their own language. They thus spoke of "French shoes" to distinguish them from "Indian shoes," of Indian cabins, and so on. A.G. Bailey mentions numerous borrowings, but he relies on a nineteenth-century Acadian Dictionary, The Conflict, 211. The documents that permit a glimpse into the Montreal vernacular, such as depositions before the bailliage, merchants' account books,

inventories, and so forth, lead me to suspect that common terms such as moccasin, wigwam, squaw, and so on, entered Canadian vocabulary only at a later date, through English. The thirteen colonies were much more receptive.

37 Giraud, *Le Métis canadien*, quoting Marie de l'Incarnation, *Lettres historiques*, 632–3.

38 One should note that the Jesuits would also fail to establish isolated enclaves in the west, and the history of their far-flung settlements consists in the futile struggle against the disturbances wrought by voyageurs and outlying garrisons. Even if they had, at the dawn of New France, conceived a grand plan in the manner of Paraguay, the destruction of Huronia brought such dreams to an end.

39 Eccles, *Frontenac*, 86; Sister Marie Morin, *Annales de l'Hôtel-Dieu de Montréal*, 24–5; report on the conduct of the Sieur Perrot, 1681, AN, F3, vol. II, fols. 76–7. Frontenac commented that eight hundred Indians had shown up at the 1674 fair. 14 Nov. 1674, AC, C11A, 4, fol. 69.

40 Letter of the intendant, who sought to revive the fair, ruined by the coureurs de bois. Ibid., 12 Nov. 1684, vol. 6, fol. 408.

41 Arrival of five hundred Indians on 18 Aug. 1690. Ibid., vol. 11, fol. 23v.; 1,200 Indians assembled in Montreal in 1701. Letter of M. Leaschassier, 3 Nov. 1702, ASSP, XIV:242. "Relation de ce qui s'est passé," by Monseignat, 22 Aug. 1690, AC, C11A, 11, fol. 23v. Letter from La Barre of 4 Nov. 1683, ibid., vol. 6, fols. 135–6, from Frontenac and Duchesneau, 1682, ibid., fols. 5–15.

42 Letter from the intendant, 10 Nov. 1679, AC, C11A, 5, fol. 45. See the description of the fair in *Nouveaux voyages de M. le baron de La Hontan*, I:64–5.

43 The intendant retold a quarrel between "a young Indian and the son of a Frenchman ... with drawn weapons ... for each had taken his nation's side." AC, C11A, 5, fol. 45.

44 Letter by the same, 13 Nov. 1680, ibid., fol. 173.

45 Letter by Father Nau, 2 Oct. 1735, RAPQ (1926–7): 283–4; Beaubien, *Le Sault-au-Récollet*, 282, 187; letter of M. Leschassier, 13 Mar. 1702, ASSM, XIV:247.

46 Letter of the intendant, 28 Sept. 1685, AC, C11A, 7, fol. 152v.; also by the same, 4 Nov. 1683, ibid., vol. 6, fol. 193; letter of M. Tronson, 8 Apr. 1684, ASSM, XIII:361.

47 Ordinance of M. de Lauson, 12 May 1656. This policy was clearly stated in the act ratifying the cession of the seigneury of Sillery in July 1651. See Léon Gérin, "La Seigneurie de Sillery et les Hurons de Lorette," TRSC, 2nd ser., 6 (May 1900): sec. 1, 80–5.

48 B.G. Trigger, "Settlement as an Aspect of Iroquoian Adaptation at the Time of Contact," *American Anthropologist*, 65 (1963): 90.

49 M. Baluze to M. Rémy, 23 Apr. 1697, ASSM, copy Faillon, H 351 and 357.

50 M. Magnien to M. de Belmont, 5 Apr. 1702, ASSP, XIV:411.

51 Letter by M. Tronson, 15 Apr. 1699, ibid., 192.

52 Letters by M. Leschassier, 1707 and 14 May 1708, ibid., 382 and 403.

53 Response of the Séminaire de Saint-Sulpice to a report on Canada, NA, M.G. 17, A7, 2, 1, vol. 2, 388–435.

54 The Hurons of Lorette who met a similar fate sent, on 22 July 1791, the first of a series of petitions to the governor-general demanding the return of the seigneury of Sillery, which had been granted to them. Léon Gérin, "La Seigneurie de Sillery."

55 Letter by M. Tronson, 1686, ASSP, XIII:438, and by the same, 19 June 1689, ibid., 561.

56 Letter by Denonville, 13 Nov. 1685, AC, C11A, 7, fol. 106. Letter of Father Nau, 2 Oct. 1735, RAPQ (1926–27): 284.

57 Report on the missions, ASSP, doss. 109, doc. 1, items 18 and 23. Bailey, The Conflict, 50–5. The Indians took longer to adopt European garb. In 1683 the intendant reported that the girls at La Montagne only wore a blanket, which left bare their legs and almost half their bodies. AC, C11A, 6, fol. 194. "If you could introduce skirts to Indian women and have their children wear pants, and win them over to present fashion, you will become famous," Tronson wrote to M. de Belmont, the La Montagne missionary. ASSP, XIII:416.

58 Breakdown of the Seminary's expenses for the running of the La Montagne mission, NA, M.G. 17, A7, 2, 1, vol. 1, 221–6.

59 Eighty men from La Montagne took part in every campaign between 1676 and 1697, according to the same report. See also ASSP, XIII:418; AC, C11A, 6, fols. 143 and 267; state of the troops in Fort Frontenac. These raids terrorized English villages. Cotton Mather describes them as "The French withe Indians being half one, half t'other, half indianized French and half Frenchified Indians." Cited by I.K. Steele, Guerrilas and Grenadiers (Toronto 1969), 2.

60 According to the intendant, it was impossible to enumerate the Indians, because they spent only the spring and summer in their villages. AC, C11A, 5, fol. 68. Letter by Father Nau, 2 Oct. 1735, RAPQ (1926–27): 284.

61 The advances were never huge: 100 to 200 livres at most. The debt was tallied in pelts and not in the money of account, and the composition of the goods remains unknown. Each Indian, identified by name, nickname, or ties with a better-known customer, was credited for so much beaver or otter, etc. These ledgers, which the merchants named "catalogues de sauvages," have not survived, but their contents are described in the estate inventories.

62 See the analysis of debts in chapter 5, sec. 2. The authorities castigated the tavern-keepers who enticed the Indians to spend their furs on drink, leaving in the lurch the merchants who had granted them credit. Ordinances of 3 Sept. 1700, *bailliage*, copy Faillon GG253; letter by M. de Longueuil, AC, F3, vol. 2, fols. 273–6.

63 Breakdown of expenditures ... at La Montagne, 1697, NA, M.G. 17, A7, 2, 1, 221–6.

64 Minutes of 7 Sept. 1713, *bailliage*, copy Faillon, FF116.

65 Raudot's ordinance authorizing nine beer-selling establishments for the Indians: three for those of the Jesuits, two for Sault-au-Récollet, two for the Algonkians at the end of the island, and two for the visitors, 23 July 1710, *Edits, ordonnances royaux*, III.

66 These regulations were legion, dictated by every administrative and judicial body in the colony. Their sole achievement was to raise monies for the Hôtel-Dieu and other charitable institutions and for the informer, who received half of the fine. These ranged from 50 to 100 livres for a first offence to 300 and 500 livres for subsequent offences, or else the lash for those who could not pay. Minutes, May 1703, *bailliage*, copy Faillon, GG184. Authorized publicans were careful because they could lose their permits. Private individuals offered drink in their sheds or poured the liquor into the small pails that the Indians then carried until they had filled them. Vachon de Belmont, *Histoire de l'eau de vie au Canada*, passim. Drunkenness is a complex question. Contemporaries saw this attraction to alcohol as a root cause of disintegration when it was really the result of a moral and cultural breakdown traceable to violent cultural shock. The Indian accused of a crime committed under the influence blamed it on his intoxicator, thereby demonstrating his dependence. See André Vachon, "L'Eau de vie dans la société indienne," CHAR (1960): 22–32; R.C. Dailey, "The Role of Alcohol among North American Indian Tribes as Reported in the Jesuit Relations," *Anthropologica* 10, no. 1 (1968): 45–57; Bailey, *The Conflict*, 95.

67 No complete series of *bailliage* records has survived, so it is impossible to carry out a quantitative analysis of criminality. Indians appear to have been disproportionately implicated in acts of violence. It also appears that they were not prosecuted for minor misdemeanors, assault, and the like, or for violence to their own group. What struck the population was less the number of murdered Frenchmen than the gratuitous nature of such crimes, as the victims quite often were children.

68 By an *arrêt* of the Conseil of 13 Mar. 1664, and another of 11 May 1676, Indians became liable to the same laws as the French. JDCS, I and II. The Indians stated explicitly that they would not allow one of their

kind to be subjected to demeaning punishments such as the yoke. Minutes of 21 Jan. 1686, ibid., III:7–8.

69 Such cases were often dismissed. The culprit was sent back to the mission "to appease the Indians, who were convinced that the guilty were in their right, that it had been an accidental and fortuitous meeting, and moreover they seemed intent on removing themselves from our midst, which would be detrimental to the colony." Minutes of 15 and 16 Aug. 1722, bailliage, copy Faillon, HH122. Or again: "Since there was no convincing proof of the said crimes, and since it was of the utmost importance for the king's rule and the interest of the colony not to keep the said Indian prisoner for too long, and the Christian chiefs of his nation and his relatives were asking each day for his release and were ready to leave the country and go off to our enemies, on account of this arrest ..." Sentence of the governor and intendant, 4 Aug. 1689, ibid., FF15. The king approved these reprieves and provided pardons to still any criticism. AC, C11A, 10, fol. 18. The victims' parents, however, cried out loudly for blood. Pierre Gagné and his wife took their dead child to the murderer's cabin, where all his friends and relatives joined in bewailing the tragedy. Minutes of 25 Feb. 1719, bailliage, copy Faillon, HH98; Vachon de Belmont, Histoire de l'eau de vie, passim.

70 On 4 Nov. 1683, the governor suggested abolishing the fund, "which had been a mistake since none of them married and this money had always been settled on Frenchwomen." AC, C11A, 6, fol. 140v.

71 Giraud, Le Métis canadien, 349–50.

72 This was done "to win over the Indians." Report of M. Tronson to Seignelay, 1682, NA, M.G. 17, A7, 2, 1, vol. 1, 140–3. His name was Alexandre Botté. See C. Tanguay, Dictionnaire généalogique des familles canadiennes françaises depuis la fondation de la colonie, 7 vols (Montreal 1871–90) 1: 141.

73 For instance, the case of Pierre Boucher, governor of Trois-Rivières.

74 Jenness, Indians of Canada, 154–6, 303; La Hontan, Nouveaux voyages, 118–23.

75 Testimony by three Indians from La Montagne with regard to the affair of a mission woman "who no longer lives with her husband because of her conduct and has had her head shaven." June 1701, bailliage, copy Faillon, HH34. The curé of Lachine baptized the child of a loose-living Indian woman, "famed for it throughout the region, who was in the habit of producing such children." 1780, Lachine registers.

76 Jenness, Indians of Canada, 306, about reserve Indians. The effect on the white population was greater where there were proportionally more Indians, as later in the further reaches of the province. The transformation gradually took place over three centuries.

77 Chaunu, *L'Amérique et les Amériques*, 25–6.
78 Each mission had its tribal council, but it is quite likely that the destruction of ancient tribal structures and their replacement with an assembly of converts from various clans reduced its prestige. Much power lay in the hands of the missionaries.

CHAPTER TWO

1 The society, founded in 1640 by Jean-Jacques Olier, was part of the network of the Société du Saint-Sacrement. Léon Gérin, *Aux sources de notre histoire* (Montreal 1946), 175–7; Marie-Claire Daveluy, *La Société de Notre-Dame de Montréal* (Montreal 1965).
2 E.-Z. Massicotte, "Les Colons de Montréal de 1642 à 1667," BRH 33, nos. 3–11 (1927): passim; and Marcel Trudel, "Les Débuts d'une société: Montréal 1642–1663: Etude de certains comportements sociaux," RHAF 23 (Sept. 1969): 185–207. The colony's first census was taken in 1666. See App. 2, Table B, and App. 3, Graph 2.
3 See App. 2, Table A, and App. 3, Graph 1.
4 Every effort was made to identify these individuals and to ascertain their means of entry into the colony. After 32 soldiers discharged from the Carignan regiment and 123 ex-indentured servants were isolated, this left 54 unidentified cases, which were then distributed equally among the two groups, since they could not possibly have belonged to any other.
5 A. Chatelain, "Les Migrations françaises vers le Nouveau Monde aux XIXe et XXe siècles," *Annales ESC* (1947): 53–70.
6 Prisoners were only deported systematically after the Treaty of Utrecht (1713).
7 There was no upsurge in recruitment during the crises of 1693 and 1709, as Robert Mandrou believed he noted in the movement of departures from La Rochelle, which were too few to establish a trend. R. Mandrou, "Les Français hors de France aux XVIe et XVIIIe siècles," *Annales ESC* (Oct. 1959): 671–2.
8 "So many lost to the Kingdom, already suffering from underpopulation," Maurepas remarked on 7 Jan. 1699, concerning Vauban's proposals to revive emigration to Canada. L. Dechêne, *La Correspondence de Vauban relative au Canada* (Quebec 1968), 27.
9 Including some that broke up prior to the census.
10 We estimate that about 500 people immigrated between 1642 and 1666, a figure that comes close to that cited by Marcel Trudel, who found about 400 at the end of 1662. Trudel, "Les Débuts d'une société," 185–207.

11 Audiot *dit* LaFlèche, recruited in 1651, and Auger *dit* Baron, recruited in 1753, went back to get their families in 1659. René Fezeret, who had arrived in Quebec in 1648, came to Montreal in 1659 with his wife and son. Picoté de Belestre, a soldier in 1659, went back to France to find himself a wife in 1662.

12 Minutes of 10 Oct. 1663, *JDCS*, I.

13 Saint-Père in 1643, Leduc in 1644, Beauvais in 1651, and Jarry and Prince in 1646. Contract of indentureship of 10 Jan. 1646, Archives départementales de l'Orne, Sorand, Bélème notary.

14 Louis Tuety, *Les Officiers sous l'Ancien Régime: Nobles et roturiers* (Paris 1908); André Corvisier, *L'Armée française de la fin du XVIIᵉ siècle au ministère de Choiseul: le soldat* (Paris 1964), 118–19.

15 These first arrivals included Closse, Dupuis, Picoté, Robutel, Philippe, and d'Ailleboust.,

16 "The man-of-war is already something of a bandit; the bandit is still something of a soldier," wrote Richelieu. Cited by G. d'Avenel, *La Noblesse française sous Richelieu* (Paris 1901), 80.

17 For further details see Gaston Zeller, "La Vie aventureuse des classes supérieures en France sous l'Ancien Régime: brigandage et piraterie," *Aspects de la politique française sous l'Ancien Régime* (Paris 1964), 375–85, as well as Fléchier, *Mémoires sur les Grands-Jours d'Auvergne*.

18 Minutes of 1 July 1664, *JDCS*, I.

19 Letter from Talon to Colbert of 2 Nov. 1671, AC, C11A, 3, fols. 178–9.

20 Gabriel Debien, "Engagés pour le Canada au XVIIᵉ siècle vus de La Rochelle," *RHAF* 6, no. 2 (1952): 196–7. The author takes Canada's present-day boundaries. Newfoundland and Acadia were not then part of Canada, and if we take away all the sailors recruited for these two destinations, the similarities between fishing contracts and ordinary indentureships no longer stand out.

21 A.E. Smith, *Colonists in Bondage* (Chapel Hill 1947), 8–16; Debien, "Engagés pour le Canada," 191, and "Propagande et recrutement pour les îles au XVIIᵉ siècle," *La Porte océane* (1956), 3–39.

22 The society's account books have not survived. It was munificently endowed, but its sponsors lacked perseverance and very quickly lost interest in the venture. This led to bankruptcy. See Gérin, *Aux Sources de notre histoire*, 170–91.

23 The society thus got rid of preferred debts and, by having the amount owed by the taker stated in the contract, avoided prosecution in the event that it would be unable to fulfil its commitments.

24 I found 26 servants freed in this way, in contracts dating from Jan. 1654 to Sept. 1655. NA, M.G. 17, A7, 2, 3, vol. 1. According to Faillon, they numbered 35. *Histoire de la colonie française au Canada*, II: 187–8.

One hundred and one *engagés* arrived in the fall of 1653. The Hôtel-Dieu and a few colonists bought back a number who were still in service.

25 Decisions of the Conseil, 18 July 1664, following a petition presented by R. Bondy, P. Godin, and Marin Janot, NA, M-1654, sec. III, no. 1.

26 See notarial records: transfer of claim by Bouchard, 8 Nov. 1658, Basset; exchange contract, 27 Dec. 1655, and sale of 25 Aug. 1657, Saint-Père.

27 1647 Regulation. See Paul-Emile Renaud, *Les Origines économiques du Canada: l'oeuvre de la France* (Paris 1928), 237; Debien, "Engagés pour le Canada," 190–3; hiring by Pierre Boucher, minutes of 17 Oct. 1663, *JDCS*, I.

28 Debien, "Engagés pour le Canada," 191; Smith, *Colonists in Bondage*, 12–13.

29 The society only transferred the Island of Montreal to the Saint-Sulpice Seminary in 1663, but the priests arrived four years earlier with their capital and undisputed authority.

30 Arrêt of 15 Oct. 1663, and report of 19 June 1664, *JDCS*, I. If they were granted land immediately, the councillors wrote Colbert, three-quarters would starve.

31 Debien, "Engagés pour le Canada," and M. Gaucher, M. Delafosse, and G. Debien, "Les Engagés pour le Canada au XVIIIe siècle," *RHAF* 14 (1960–61): 597.

32 Three *engagés* for a sixty-ton burden and six for a one-hundred ton burden. Ordinance of 1716, cited by Jean Hamelin, *Economie et société en Nouvelle-France* (Quebec 1960), 78.

33 Smith, *Colonists in Bondage*, 28–9.

34 Once the colony maintained the compagnies franches de la Marine (1683), the distinction between recruits for military or domestic service no longer obtained. The men sent by the navy were sorted out on arrival: the fittest were enlisted, while the less fit were passed on to the colonists. Denonville correspondence, 4 May 1685 and 20 Nov. 1686, AC, C11A, 7, fol. 21v., and vol. 8, fol. 140; letter by De Meulles, 28 Sept. 1685, ibid., fol. 150.

35 Like those who accepted three years' service in return for 300 pounds of sugar or 10 livres a year. Gaucher *et al.*, "Les Engagés ... XVIIIe siècle,' 595.

36 Pierre Harvey, "Stagnation économique en Nouvelle-France," *L'Actualité économique* 37, no. 3 (Oct.–Dec. 1961): 546. The Sulpicians continued to recruit part of their help in France. Letter by Tronson, May 1679, ASSP, XIV:145–58.

37 B. Porchnev, *Les Soulèvements populaires en France de 1632 à 1648* (Paris 1963), 534–5; J. Dupâquier, M. Lachiver, and J. Meuvret, *Mercuriales du*

pays de France et du Vexin français (1640–1792) (Paris 1968), 236 and graph 5.

38 R.J. Auger, *La Grande recrue de 1653*, and Marie-Claire Daveluy, "Le Drame de la recrue de 1653," RHAF 7, no. 2 (Sept. 1953): 157–70.

39 The average age of the indentured servants enumerated in 1666 was 25 and the mode 23. This also applies to the earliest recruits.

40 For example, two youths taken on for four years by the hospital "merely for their room and board." One was only sixteen and died two years after he arrived.

41 Such information is only rarely included in marriage records and cannot supply an overall picture.

42 One might try, however, for the canton of La Flèche what Hubert Charbonneau has begun in Tourouvre, *Tourouvre-au-Perche aux XVIIe et XVIIIe siècles: Etude de démographie historique* (Paris 1970).

43 Anonymous description of Canada, 1671, AC, C11A, 3, fol. 201.

44 Letter from de Meulles to the minister, 4 Nov. 1783, ibid., vol. 6, fol. 184.

45 As between the Clermont recruits: Jean Gasteau, who arrived in 1653, and his cousin Julien Blois, who came in 1659; close links existed as well between natives of Igé, Marans, and La Rochelle. Because this aspect has not been studied, numerous examples must escape us.

46 See the power of attorney granted by S. Audiot, P. Chauvin, Antoine Courtemanche, Thomas Monnier, Mathurin Langevin, No. Rec., 22 and 30 Sept. 1658, 3 Feb. 1669, 13 Apr. 1670, and 13 Oct. 1675, Basset.

47 Corvisier, *L'Armée française*, I:498.

48 The letter was deposited at the office of the notary Basset on 25 Mar. 1670. Averty had come to Montreal in 1653 as a landclearer and died in the colony well on in years.

49 There were eight girls among the Canadian servants and four others recruited in France, whereas previously all servants had been men.

50 These suits were judged directly by the Sovereign Council. See JDCS, vols. I and II passim.

51 "The indentured labourer lived with the family, often married one of the daughters, and settled down near his former master." Renaud, *Les Origines économiques du Canada*, 242.

52 M. Tronson congratulated Maître Jacques for the zeal and vigilance with which he kept order among the labourers. Apr. 1684, ASSP, XIV:90–100.

53 Report from Governor Frontenac to Seignelay, 1681, RAPQ (1926–27): 123.

54 His term began the day of his arrival. Minutes of 4 July 1678, JDCS, II.

55 Letter to the king, 19 June 1664, ibid., I.

56 Gabriel Debien, "La Société coloniale aux XVIIe et 'XVIIIe siècles: Les

engagés pour les Antilles, 1634–1715," *Revue d'histoire des colonies* 38 (1951): 64. The regulations of 1670 and 1672 were never put into effect. See the arrêt of the Conseil d'Etat of 28 Feb. 1670, AC, B2, fol. 54v.

57 Lawsuits by servants requesting unpaid wages or for other grievances were exceptional. See the minutes of 30 Oct. and 10 Nov. 1663, JDCS, I.

58 Letter by M. Tronson, 2 May 1686, ASSP, XIII: 461.

59 The Council allowed one master to get rid of a sick or disabled engagé as long as he found a new master. Minutes of 20 Feb. 1665, JDCS, I. The servant thus dismissed recognized a debt of 149 livres 10 sols, which he would reimburse upon request. Not. Rec., 11 May 1661, Basset.

60 Renaud, *Les Origines économiques du Canada*, 240.

61 Sale of a farm by the merchant Médéric Bourduceau to F. de Sailly. Not. Rec., 20 Sept. 1661, Basset; re-engagement of Claude Pugies to Jean Magnan, 25 July 1684, ibid.

62 Lease by Lambert Closse to Pierre Papin, 4 Oct. 1660, ibid., Basset.

63 Debt acknowledgment by Jean Armande to Vincent Philippe, 21 Apr. 1675; debt tally between J. Décarri and A. Chevasset, 15 Dec. 1658, ibid.

64 Transfer and retrocession of the journeyman Jean Senelay between Pierre Gadois and the Hurtebise family, 14 Mar. and 15 May 1672, ibid.

65 Debien, "Engagés pour le Canada," 216.

66 Minutes of 7 Oct. 1663, JDCS, I, and of 9 Sept. 1664.

67 Letter from Talon to Colbert, 21 May 1665, AC, C11A, 2, fol. 138.

68 Suit by Claude Chamberry against Louis d'Ailleboust, 10 June 1689, *bailliage*, 2nd ser., vol. I, 752. D'Ailleboust, who was unable to come up with the contract, had to free the wig-maker.

69 It seems unlikely that a Canadian seigneur ever refused land to freed men who requested it. For the land policies followed in Montreal before 1662, see below, chap. 7, sec. 1.

70 Letters by M. Tronson, 5 Apr. and 20 May 1677, and 15 May 1682, ASSP, XIII:50–60, 99–100, and 288.

71 Petition by the Jesuits' procureur against Jean Brusseau, hired in La Rochelle on 5 Apr. 1680, minutes of 27 July 1682, JDCS, II:803 and 806.

72 Arrêt of the Conseil du roi forbidding residents of New France from leaving the colony without the permission of the governor, 12 Mar. 1658, AC, C11A, 1.

73 Arrêt of 10 Dec. 1664, JDCS, I.

74 Reported in Apr. 1653 in the *Journal des Jésuites*, 183.

75 Sentence of 24 Mar. 1665, JDCS, I.

76 Arrêt of the Conseil of 2 June 1673, registered in Montreal on 10 Nov. 1675, E.-Z. Massicotte, *Répertoire des Arrêts*.

77 Sentence of 5 Dec. 1663, JDCS, I.

78 Sentence of 10 Dec. 1664, and other similar convictions between 1663 and 1665, ibid., I.

79 Lawsuit between Pierre Rivière and the bishop of Quebec, 4 July 1678, ibid., II.

80 Lawsuit between Charles Le Gardeur and Jean Denison *dit* le Gascon, 12 Aug. 1686, ibid. III.

81 Appeal to the Conseil of a sentence rendered by the Quebec *Prévôté*, by Chartier, 30 June 1692, ibid.

82 Sentencing of 5 Dec. 1663 and 10 Dec. 1664, ibid., I. Talon planned a regulation relative to the punishment of servants, but it was not adopted completely. 10 Jan. 1667. See P.-G. Roy, *Ordonnances, commissions, etc., des gouverneurs et des intendants de la Nouvelle-France, 1635–1706*, I:51.

83 Smith, *Colonists in Bondage*, chap. 12, "The Servant in the Plantations"; O. and M.F. Handlin, "Origins of the Southern Labor System," *William and Mary Quarterly* (Apr. 1950): 199–222.

84 Debt tally between J. Décarri and his servant. Not. Rec., 15 Dec. 1658, Basset. See also the contracts dated 14 Mar. 1672 and 21 Apr. 1675, and the inventory of 5 May 1661, in ibid.

85 Indentureship of Jean Senelay to M. Hurtubise, 14 Mar. 1672, ibid.

86 Minutes of 10 Nov. 1663 and of 30 Oct. 1663, *JDCS*, I.

87 See the inventories of Jacques Boisseau and Tècle Cornélius of 5 May 1661, of Jean Beaudoin, Michel Paroissien, and Charles Roqueville of 25 May 1660, and Pierre Couasné, 23 Dec. 1663, etc., in Not. Rec., Basset; Adrien Pouliot and S. Dumas, *L'Exploit du Long-Sault* (Quebec 1960), 13.

88 This was the case with Urbain Baudreau and Michel Bouvier, hired in 1653 and rehired in 1659; of René Fezeret, a Quebec locksmith who went into debt to return to Canada in 1659, and of Pierre Mousnier, who came back in 1663 under a new indentureship agreement. The curé of Notre-Dame attempted to have this second contract annulled, but his request was rejected by the Conseil on 16 Oct. 1663, *JDCS*, I.

89 Gaucher *et al.*, "Les Engagés ... XVIIIᵉ siècle," *RHAF*, 13:257ff, and 14:108.

90 Especially the *Dictionnaire généalogique des familles canadiennes françaises* by Mgr C. Tanguay, and the previously cited studies by R.J. Auger and A. Godbout.

91 Description of Canada ... 1671, AC, C11A, 3, fol. 201; Report from Patoulet to Colbert, 25 Jan. 1672, ibid., fol. 274.

92 Recruited by the merchants of La Rochelle, Rouen, and other places for their own ends or on behalf of the Compagnie des Indes occidentales. See Debien, "Engagés pour le Canada," 190–3.

93 Letter from Colbert to Talon, 3 July 1669, AC, B1, fol. 138v.

94 According to A.E. Smith, only 7 per cent of the 5,000 indentured labourers who came there between 1670 and 1680 took up any land. *Colonists in Bondage*, 298–9.

95 I counted 650 unions of male immigrants.

96 Gustave Lanctôt, *Filles de joie ou filles du roi* (Montreal 1952), 121–5. According to this writer, 360 girls from the *Hôpital général* came to the colony between 1669 and 1673. See also Renaud, *Les Origines économiques du Canada*, 258–63.

97 The dowry might consist of personal effects or a cow. After 1663 dowries were no longer provided due to lack of funds. Letters from Duchesneau, 10 Nov. 1679 and 13 Nov. 1680, AC, C11A, 5, fols. 54 and 249v. The governor asked that this gift be reintroduced, as "many complained that they had not received a thing for several years." 13 Nov. 1685, ibid., 7, fol. 106.

98 La Hontan, *Nouveaux voyages*, I:11–12. Letter of 2 May 1684. The 165 girls shipped in 1670 were married before the winter. Letter from Colbert to Talon, 1671, AC, B3, fol. 23.

99 See the intendant's letter of 12 Nov. 1684, which mentions six poverty-stricken servants found on La Rochelle streets "who would not fail to find husbands in this country." AC, C11A, 6, fol. 401.

100 Colbert to the archbishop of Rouen, 27 Feb. 1670, on the girls from La Pitié, AC, B2, fol. 15v.

101 Cited by Lanctôt, *Filles de joie*, 213.

102 Governor d'Argenson decried the insolence of a Rochelais merchant (Péron) who had shipped "some low-life, presently with child, as well he knew. I sentenced him to take her back to la Rochelle and to court costs ... and to an additional 150-livre fine." Letter of 14 Oct. 1658, copy Faillon, X, 136.

103 Colbert to Talon, 1671, AC, B3, fol. 23. If, on the whole, judicial archives provide some insight into the nature of this immigration, these women behaved better than Canadian women would twenty years later. There were no reports of prostitution in this period, but there were the expected occasional insults, and bodily harm, and one murder attributed to a girl recruited by the Hôtel-Dieu.

104 The accuser, Roberte Gadois, was sentenced to damages and to a 20-livre fine following the surgeon's negative report. *Bailliage*, minutes of Sept. 1676, copy Faillon, KK, 328.

105 Account of the bonuses, 26 Mar. 1669, AC, B1, fols. 110v.–112; Talon report of 10 Nov. 1670, C11A, 3, fol. 83v.

106 W.J. Eccles, "The Social, Economic, and Political Significance of the Military Establishment in New France," *CHR* 52, no. 1 (Mar. 1971): 1–22.

107 Ordinance of M. de Courcelles of 25 Oct. 1665, in Massicotte, *Répertoire des arrêts*. About 300 men had their winter quarters in Montreal, while 700 to 800 circulated on the island in other seasons.

108 G. Roy and G. Malchelosse, *Le Régiment de Carignan* (Montreal 1925), 24. It was important to keep this plan secret prior to sailing, but the minister's letters hint at the fact that the decision had already been reached. Copy of a letter from Louvois to M. de La Galissonnière. Service historique de l'armée, France, A1, vol. 191, fol. 228.

109 Letter from Louvois to M. de La Tour, 6 Jan. 1665, ibid., fol. 44.

110 Since the regiment was headed for Canada, His Majesty was lenient towards the recruiters, Louvois reported to La Galissonnière on 27 Jan. 1665, ibid., fol. 228.

111 See the letters of the minister to De Launay, *prévôt des maréchaux* of Saint-Jean-d'Angely, 26 Feb. 1665; to M. Du Chaunay, war commissioner, 28 Feb., 15 and 30 Mar. 1665; to the *syndics* of the same town on 17 Mar. 1665, ibid., fols. 445, 446, vol. 192, fols. 88, 93, and 96.

112 Louvois to Colbert de Terron, 15 Feb. 1666, ibid., vol. 199, fol. 467.

113 A better showing had been expected in the hope that the officers would set an example to their men. They could, if they insisted, return to France, but they would be penniless, thundered Colbert. Letter in Clement, III: 395, cited by Renaud, *Les Origines économiques du Canada*, 243.

114 Representing 333 soldiers and non-commissioned officers according to Eccles, "The Social, Economic, and Political Significance," 3. See the bonuses granted these new recruits, 11 Feb. 1671, AC, B3, fol. 19.

115 According to the list drawn up by Roy and Malchelosse, *Le Régiment de Carignan*, 85–111. No similar search was made for soldiers discharged in 1669 and 1670, there being no official rolls of discharged soldiers.

116 There were only a few natives of eastern France among the veterans, and they had joined the regiment before it reached Aunis.

117 According to Corvisier, sons of notables made up 6.9 per cent of the corps prior to 1716, after which their proportion decreased. Corvisier, *L'Armée française*, 484–5. They were relatively more numerous at the beginning of Louis XIV's reign.

118 Pierre Perthuis, François Noir, and François Pougnet, who opened shop as soon as they were discharged.

119 Eccles, "The Social, Economic, and Political Significance,' 3.

120 Ibid., 5; letter by de La Barre, 12 Nov. 1682, AC, C11A, 6, fols. 59–65.

121 Plan of M. de Callières, Jan. 1689, AC, C11A, 10, fol. 26. They began by calling for 35 companies of 50 men, then 32, and finally 28, after 1689, to ensure that all would be complete.

122 In 1689, up to 22 companies were scattered around the town. Letter to Champigny, 6 July 1689, ibid., vol. 10, fols. 233–5. See also vol. 12, fol. 87v., and fols. 99–100.

123 The number of officers remained the same, but the troops dwindled for lack of reinforcements during the War of the Spanish Succession. Letter of the governor and intendant, 15 Nov. 1713, ibid., vol. 35, fol. 4.

124 The intendant began by converting those unfit for duty into servants and replaced them with more vigorous indentured labourers who arrived that same year. After 1685, however, the force apparently made do with whomever it got. Letters from Denonville of 4 May 1685 and De Meulles of 28 Sept. 1685, ibid., vol. 7, fols. 21 and 150.

125 Corvisier, L'Armée française, 149–50.

126 Eccles, Frontenac, the Courtier Governor, 214–15.

127 "They are a pitiful lot," the governor commented on 6 Nov. 1688, AC, C11A, 10, fols. 9–11. Fatalities at sea seem quite high. In 1693, one-sixth of the recruits died aboard ship, but the authorities considered this normal. Ibid., vol. 12, fol. 211v. In 1685 perhaps a third were missing on arrival. The embarkation and arrival rosters have not survived, so it is impossible to examine this further.

128 Ibid., vol. 8, fol. 43v.

129 Response to letters from Canada, 8 Mar. 1686, ibid., vol. 10, fol. 17.

130 Very few were demobilized until 1669, but these soldiers did not get the promised bonus. Ibid., vol. 10, fols. 233–4. The intendant's letter of 13 Oct. 1697, asking the minister whether he could allow the soldiers to marry and settle down, indicates that discharges had long since been suspended.

131 Letter from Denonville and Champigny of 6 Nov. 1688, ibid., vol. 10, fols. 9–11.

132 Pastoral of the bishop of Saint-Vallier of 1721, cited by E. Salone, La Colonisation de la Nouvelle-France (Paris 1905), 345. Tried for scandalous behaviour, Antoine Boyer from the Ile de Ré, garrisoned in Montreal for four years, protested that he had not been allowed to marry as promised. Minutes of 30 Oct. 1715, bailliage, copy Faillon HH89.

133 See the letter by the curé of Lachine on behalf of Saint-Olive, soldier and apothecary, asking leave to marry, attached to the marriage contract. 1 Dec. 1701, P. Raimbault, notary.

134 Letters from Frontenac and Champigny, 10 Nov. 1695 and 13 Oct. 1697, AC, C11A, 13, fol. 302, and C11A, 15, fol. 83.

135 Corvisier, L'Armée française, 828–30.

136 Ordinance of De Meulles, 26 Apr. 1685, Roy, Ordonnances, commissions, etc., II:96–7.

137 Letter from Frontenac, 19 Oct. 1697, AC, C11A, 15, fol. 43.

138 Letter from Champigny, 5 Nov. 1687, ibid., vol. 9, fol. 202.
139 In which case, the whole exercise brought in about 4,000 livres.
140 Eccles, *Frontenac, the Courtier Governor*, 219–20.
141 About 3,000 soldiers came to the colony between 1683 and 1700.
   About a quarter might have died. A number of disabled men left each
   year, and many deserted. We know, moreover, that the population's
   real growth was only slightly superior to its natural increase.
142 The war had lasted thirteen years. Those who left the troops in 1697
   were about forty years old. In 1745 Peter Kalm described recent
   veterans as being in their forties. *Voyage de Kalm en Amérique* (Montreal
   1880), 3.
143 Letter from Champigny, 14 Oct. 1698, AC, C11A, 16, fol. 39; letter from
   Frontenac, 19 Oct. 1697, ibid., C11A, 15, fol. 43.
144 Guy Frégault, "La Nouvelle-France, territoire et population," *Le XVIII*
   siècle canadien: Etudes, 50–1.
145 Report by Ruette d'Auteuil of 25 Jan. 1719 in *RAPQ* (1922–23): 75;
   Salone, *La Colonisation de la Nouvelle-France*, 339–42.
146 Ordinances of 1714 and 1716, cited by Salone, 343.
147 Letter from Colbert to Talon, 1671, AC,. B3, fol. 23.
148 According to the list drawn by Roy and Malchelosse, checked in
   genealogical and biographical dictionaries.
149 Carion, Dugué, and Gabriel de Berthé. Most of the officers of the
   Carignan regiment received seigneuries in the Montreal region but
   chose to reside in the town.
150 Some twenty fiefs were created. R.C. Harris, *The Seigneurial System in*
   Early Canada (Quebec 1967), 39–40.
151 They received at first about 500 livres. Captain Pécaudy, who married,
   received 600 livres. La Mothe de Saint-Paul was awarded 1,500. See
   various accounts and bonuses for the years 1668–69, AC, C11A, 3, fols.
   35–6, and B1, fols. 110v., 112; B3, fol. 19.
152 Three hundred livres to help M. de Chambly build a sawmill. Letter
   of 26 Mar. 1669, AC, B1, fols. 110v., 112.
153 Letter from La Barre of 14 Nov. 1684, C11A, 6, fol. 363; letter from
   Captain Duplessis Faber to Marchal Vauban, 16 Sept. 1698, in *La*
   Correspondance de Vauban relative au Québec, 19.
154 P.-G. Roy, *Lettres de noblesse, généalogies, érections de comtés et baronies*
   insinuées par le Conseil souverain de la Nouvelle-France, 2 vols. (Beauceville 1920), passim. See the examples of Saint-Ours, Pécaudy, Da-
   mours, etc. Their titles were rarely older than the sixteenth century.
   Those threatened with invalidation dated from the seventeenth and
   consisted mainly of a petty, non-hereditary nobility of office.
155 Jean-Vincent Philippe, born in Normandy, had the letters granted his
   father in 1654 confirmed in 1671 under this proviso. See Roy, *Lettres de*

noblesse, and the intendant's letter on this question, 10 Nov. 1670, AC, C11A, 3, fol. 88.

156 List of vacant posts, 15 Oct. 1691, AC, C11A, 11, fols. 221–4.

157 In 1689 two died and two returned to France. Ibid., fols. 102–3.

158 Taking into account the still limited number of postings granted Canadians in the seventeenth century, which were deducted from this crude estimate.

159 The officers of the troupes de la Marine who settled in Montreal in the seventeenth century did not receive seigneuries, but some held censives.

160 Over half the officers of the troupes de la Marine who married in the colony before 1700 later left the country, according to data in Mgr Tanguay's *Dictionnaire généalogique.*

161 The way to hold on to a good officer was to get him on the general staff. This was done in the case of Captain de Monic, named major of the troops in 1691, who nevertheless returned to France, where he died after a brief command in Newfoundland. Letter from Frontenac, 14 Aug. 1691, AC,C11A, 11, fol. 108; *Dictionnaire biographique du Canada,* II: 503–4, entry by J.F. Thorpe.

162 List of censitaires of 1697, ASSM; tax roll of 1715, NA, M.G. 17, A7, 2, 1, vol. 2, 487ff. Officers rarely resided in the *côtes,* and the fifteen enumerated in the town represent in all likelihood the near-totality of French officers living in the area, with two or three exceptions.

163 Letter from De Meulles, 12 Nov. 1684, suggesting this cutback to the minister, AC, C11A, 6, fol. 402.

164 Ibid., vol. 7, fols. 94–5, vol. 9, fols. 192–3. See Eccles, "The Social, Economic, and Political Significance," 7–8.

165 The association between Médéric Bourduceau and Anne-Françoise Bourduceau, married (under separation of assets) to Louis Artus, Esq, 29 Mar. 1658, AN (France), minutier central, LXXXVIII, Richer et Monnet, notaries.

166 Tally of accounts between Artus de Sailly and M. Bourduceau, Not. Rec., 17 Jan. 1600, Basset.

167 If they married in the colony, their origins appeared in the contract. There is no reason to suppose that those who were already married when they arrived came from different backgrounds.

168 Departures of Raymond Amyault, A. Hattanville, the Bourduceaus, C. Tardiff, Hilaire Bourgine, the brothers Arnaud, Simon Despres, Antoine Galiber, etc. It made little difference if their stay had been long or short.

169 Louis Charbonnier, for example, the son of a bourgeois from Cognac, came with his family in 1675; Charles Alavoine arrived at the end of the century with his wife and children.

170 M. Delafosse, "Le Trafic franco-canadien (1695–1715): Navires et marchands de La Rochelle," paper presented at the first Colonial History conference, held in Ottawa, Nov. 1969, passim.

171 Bernard Bailyn underlines the significance of family ties in the credit structure supporting colonial trade. *The New England Merchants in the Seventeenth Century* (Cambridge 1955), 34–8; see also P. Léon, *Marchands dauphinois dans le monde antillais du XVIIIe siècle* (Paris 1963), 30–1.

172 For more on this question see below, chap. 5.

173 A. Godbout, *Origine des familles canadiennes-françaises: Extrait de l'état civil français* (Lille 1925); and "Nos ancêtres au XVIIe siècle," RAPQ (1951–60), passim; Renaud, *Les Origines économiques du Canada*, 274–84.

174 "Pour le Secours qu'il plust au Roy donner au Canada l'an 1664," from a "mémoire" in AC, C11A, 2, fols. 93–5.

175 Tronson correspondence of May 1679, 4 June 1680, and 15 May 1682, ASSP, XII:145, 158, 287.

176 Based on a 1716 roster, André Corvisier calculated that 63.4 per cent of the troops came from the countryside. *L'Armée française*, 389–90. Cole Harris, basing himself on a list of 286 immigrants who settled throughout Canada, found a slightly lower proportion, 60 per cent, with rural origins. R.C. Harris, "The French Background of Immigrants to Canada before 1700," *Cahiers de géographie du Québec* 16, No. 38 (Sept. 1972): 317.

177 *Dictionnaire géographique, historique, et politique des Gaules et de la France* (Paris 1762).

178 Pierre Goubert, "Les Cadres de la vie rurale," in F. Braudel and E. Labrousse, *Histoire économique et sociale de la France*, vol. II (Paris 1970), 104–11.

179 See Lionel Groulx, *Histoire du Canada français* (Montreal 1960), I:163–4, quoting La Potherie and Charlevoix.

180 Michel Fleury and Pierre Valmary, "Les Progrès de l'instruction élémentaire de Louis XIV à Napoléon III," *Population* 1 (1957): 71–92.

181 See G. Gini, "La Théorie des migrations adaptives," *Etudes européennes de population* (Paris 1954), 422–32.

CHAPTER THREE

1 See App. 2, Tables B and C, and App. 3, Graphs 2 and 3.

2 By 1715, immigrants made up 10 to 15 per cent of the population.

3 See App. 2, Table A, and App. 3, Graph 4.

4 Jacques Henripin, *La Population canadienne au début du XVIIIe siècle* (Paris 1954), 18–20.

5 In France one finds a greater number of widows. Pierre Goubert, *Beauvais et le Beauvaisis, de 1600 à 1730* (Paris 1960), 38.

6 Hubert Charbonneau, Yolande Lavoie, and Jacques Legaré, "Le Recensement nominatif du Canada en 1681," *Histoire sociale / Social History* 7 (Apr. 1971): 84. Besides, these coureurs de bois, peasant or peasants' sons, are well accounted for. They were enumerated along with their families, even during their absence.

7 A percentage of 30 to 35 between those under 15 and the whole population was usual in eighteenth-century France and in many parishes in the seventeenth. J. Bourgeois-Pichat, "Evolution de la population française depuis le XVIIIe siècle," *Population* 4 (1951): 661–6; J. Ganiage, *Trois villages de l'Ile de France* (Parius 1963), 35–7; R. Noel, "La Population de la paroisse de Laguile," *Annales de démographie historique* (1967): 197–226; Marcel Lachiver, *La Population de Meulan du XVIIe au XIXe siècle* (Paris 1969), 43; Pierre Valmary, *Familles paysannes au XVIIIe siècle en Bas-Quercy* (Paris 1965), 60–1.

8 The percentage of individuals 60 and over would have been no more than 5.5.

9 Jacques Henripin, *Tendances et facteurs de la fécondité au Canada* (Ottawa 1968), 5.

10 See App. 3, Graph 5.

11 Graph 6 in App. B illustrates the distribution of marriages between Canadians and immigrants, by decade, in Notre-Dame parish.

12 Compare the mobility in Montreal and that observed in Meulan in the same period, where 40 per cent of the grooms and 60 per cent of the brides had been born in the town. Lachiver, *La Population de Meulan*, 94–5; Hubert Charbonneau, *Tourouvre-au-Perche aux XVIIe et XVIIIe siècles: Etude de démographie historique*, and Marcel Couturier, *Recherches sur les structures sociales à Châteaudun* (Paris 1969), 130–1.

13 Based on 390 grooms and 381 brides. Ages were only systematically recorded after 1696, and I am only using the Notre-Dame parish records, which are more complete than those of rural parishes.

14 Pierre Goubert, "Le Régime démographique français au temps de Louis XIV," in F. Braudel and E. Labrousse, *Histoire économique et sociale de la France*, 29. In Dedham, Massachusetts, the average age for first marriage was 22.5 for women and 25.5 for men. K.A. Lockridge, "The Population of Dedham, Massachusetts, 1636–1736," *Economic History Review*, 2nd ser., 19 (1966): 329.

15 With an intergenesic interval of only 23 months. See J. Henripin, *La Population canadienne*, 66, Table 18b.

16 This aspect cannot be quantified, for the age of the spouses was not yet recorded. Only family reconstitution would show how common child marriages were.

17 This happened with Marguerite Sédillot, who was eleven when she married Jean Aubuchon for the first time. She gave birth to her first child five years later. Tanguay, *Dictionnaire généalogique*, I.

18 Letter from the bishop to the curé of Notre-Dame de Montréal, 12 Jan. 1684, recorded in the parish register, about the union of Jacques Lemoyne and Jeanne Carion.

19 The girl was twelve when the marriage was celebrated in 1657. It must have been annulled, since both he and she found new spouses in 1663. Tanguay, *Dictionnaire généalogique*, I:150, 239; JDCS, I, 3 Nov. 1663.

20 In 1683, Marguerite would seek to have this 1661 contract nullified: JDCS, II: 863.

21 Transaction between Mathurin Thibaudeau and Francois Brunet, Not. Rec., 9 Dec. 1669, Basset. The marriage did not take place, and in 1673, Brunet married another girl, hardly any older.

22 Should this happen, they received 20 livres. Arrêt of 3 Apr. 1669, AC, B1, fol. 113. Not a single case of this turned up in the Montreal records.

23 This would indicate that the last recruits, least accustomed to military life, asked to be demobilized.

24 Jacques Henripin proposes 27 per cent as the average rates for the eighteenth century. *La Population canadienne*, 95. The short span of unions has been highlighted by M. Baulant in her study of the Meaux region, where the ratio was 30 per cent. "La Famille en miettes: Sur un aspect démographique du XVIIe siècle," *Annales ESC* (July–Oct. 1972): 959–68.

25 In the eighteenth century men remarried in 18.5 per cent of cases and women in 14.1. Henripin, *La Population canadienne*, 95–101.

26 Henripin found also a mean age of 34 for widows in this category, but only 28.6 for their husbands. Ibid.

27 In this age category Henripin found an average of 50.3 for men and 43.9 for women. Ibid., 96.

28 See also App. 3, Graph 7.

29 Henripin, *La Population canadienne*, 92–5.

30 Henripin, *Tendances et facteurs*, 7. This supposes that the censuses were correct. The author recently proposed a new means of evaluating population size. Based on higher denominators, rates are lower and more regular over a longer period. But uncertainty remains. J. Henripin and Yves Peron, "La Transition démographique de la Province du Québec," in H. Charbonneau *et al.*, *La Population du Québec: Etudes rétrospectives* (Montreal 1973), 23–44.

31 The curés almost never stated the residence of the parents of the baptized child.

32 Based on 6,599 legitimate births divided by 1,312 marriages.

33 A GRR of 4.4. Henripin, *La Population canadienne*, 74. See also G. Sabagh, "The Fertility of the French-Canadian Women during the Seventeenth Century," *American Journal of Sociology* 47 (1942): 680–90.

34 Report by De Meulles (1684), AC, F3, vol. 2, fol. 204v.

35 Royal arrêt to grant a pension to large families, 3 Apr. 1669, AC, B1, fol. 113. In 1671 the Crown spent 4,000 livres under this heading, for a dozen or so cases. Accounts of 11 Feb. 1671, ibid., vol. 3, fol. 18v.

36 According to the 217 families enumerated in 1681, supplemented by information found in Tanguay, who lists the children born to these families.

37 They were those of Gilles Lauson, Etienne Campeau, and Charles Lemoyne. The d'Aillebousts would also have been eligible were it not for four daughters in convents.

38 See also App. 3, Graph 8.

39 Henripin, La Population canadienne, 42–4.

40 "This gives us a way," wrote Pierre Goubert, "of following the arrival of spring, south, north, east, and west." Quoted in Braudel and Labrousse, Histoire économique et sociale de la France, 34.

41 This would require citing the numerous instances recorded in bailliage minutes regarding live or dead foundlings. The bailli repeatedly ordered the public reading in church of Henri II's 1556 edict on pregnancy and infanticide. See E.-Z. Massicotte, Repertoire des arrêts, passim.

42 Bishop's pastoral of 5 Feb. 1672, to be read in every parish church every six months. Copy in the Notre-Dame parish registers, Mar. 1677.

43 Cited by Henripin, La Population canadienne, 104.

44 Letter from De Meulles, 4 Nov. 1683, AC, C11A, 6, fol. 182, and letter from La Barre, ibid., fol. 144.

45 ASSP, mss, Bretonvilliers, box 3.

46 Henripin, La Population canadienne, 106.

47 Ibid., 15, 103, as well as Tendances et facteurs, 7.

48 Hubert Charbonneau, Yolande Lavoie, and Jacques Legaré, "Recensements et registres paroissiaux du Canada durant la periode 1665–1668," Population 1 (1970): 97–124.

49 See App. 3.

50 App. 3, Graphs 9 and 10.

51 (Vachon de Belmont), Histoire de l'eau-de-vie en Canada, 16–17.

52 Soeur Morin, Annales de l'Hôtel-Dieu de Montréal rédigées par la soeur Morin, 187. Letter from Champigny, 6 Nov. 1786, AC, C11A, 9, fols. 4–18.

53 Goubert, Beauvais et le Beauvaisis, 46–7.

54 Letter from MM. de Callières and Beauharnois, 27 Apr. 1703, AC, C11A, 21, fols. 41–3.

55 Letters of M. Leschassier, 22 Mar. 1701 and 20 May 1706, ASSP, XIV:229, 36–8.

56 They were generally identified as vague "pestilences." Against true plague administrators took the most serious measures. A 1721 ordi-

nance required all vessels coming from the Mediterranean to anchor 50 kilometers downstream from Quebec. AC, C11A, 124. In 1734 the Hôtel-Dieu sealed the joints of coffins that were carried through the streets in order to prevent a malignant fever from spreading through the town. M. Mondoux, *L'Hôtel-Dieu*, 285.

57 R.G. Thwaites, ed., *The Jesuit Relations*, vol. 19, cited by A.G. Bailey, *The Conflict of European and Eastern Algonguin Cultures, 1504–1700*, 94–5.

58 Given the large numbers of unrecorded burials, these trends are too uncertain to warrant any comments.

59 Letter of Denonville, 8 May 1686, AC, C11A, 8, Feb. 16–17.

60 Among 240 soldiers and labourers at Cataracoui and Niagara the intendant counted 180 dead in two years. Letter of Champigny, 8 Aug. 1688, ibid., vol. 10, fols. 121v.–122.

61 Memoir of De Meulles, 1684, AC, F3, vol. 2, fol. 204.

62 See n 61.

63 See App. 3, Graph 1.

64 Elsewhere I have described the basis for these calculations, namely the seigneurial enumerations, that allow us to correct a current misconception – that is, of strong urban growth in New France. See L. Dechêne, "La Croissance de Montréal au XVIIIᵉ siècle," *RHAF* 27, no. 2 (Sept. 1973): 163–79.

CHAPTER FOUR

1 "Grande rivière" was the name commonly given to the St Lawrence.

2 The Prairies, where the French began to travel in the early eighteenth century, were known as the "mer de l'Ouest," or Western Sea.

3 Marcel Trudel, *Histoire de la Nouvelle-France: I. Le Comptoir* (Montreal 1963), 375–6. M. Delafosse also estimated that the voyage between La Rochelle and Quebec lasted two to two and a half months and less than one month on the way back. M. Delafosse, "Le Trafic franco-canadien (1697–1715): Navires et marchands à La Rochelle," presented at the first Colonial History Conference, Ottawa, Nov. 1969.

4 Raoul Blanchard, *Montréal: esquisse de géographie urbaine* (Grenoble 1947), 39–48.

5 Pehr Kalm, *Voyage de Kalm en Amérique*, 59, 183; E.R. Adair, "The Evolution of Montreal during the French Regime," *CHAR* 23 (Mar. 1942): 31.

6 The boat used by the Sulpicians was 35 feet long and, with a slight break for the cabin, could carry approximately a 40-ton burden. Transaction of 17 Aug. 1670, Not. Rec., Basset. The merchant J. Leber had to get rid of a larger boat, meant for inshore navigation, because he did not have enough cargo. Letter from the Intendant de Meulles, 24 Sept.

1685, AC, C11A, 7, fol. 138v. The *La Marie*, owned by two Montreal merchants, that plied the route between Quebec and Montreal in 1715, had only a 30-ton burden. Not. Rec., 4 Sept. 1715, Le Pailleur.

7 Pierre Rousseau, "Notes historiques sur le canal et le moulin de Lachine," unpublished study, NA, M-1654.

8 G.P. de T. Glazebrook, *A History of Transportation in Canada* (Toronto 1964), I:27; H.A. Innis, *The Fur Trade in Canada*, 59.

9 Letter from Denonville, 20 Nov. 1686, AC, C11A, 8, fol. 142; C. de Rochemonteix, *Relations par lettres de l'Amérique septentrionale, années 1709 et 1710*, 11.

10 It took seven days to transport a prisoner to Quebec and return to Montreal by four-paddle canoe (1706). JDCS, V: 308.

11 Minutes of Mar. 1683, *bailliage*, 1st ser., reg. 2 (copy Faillon FF 52).

12 For more on horses, see below, chap. 10.

13 "Due to the dangers of the voyage," one Jesuit wrote in 1636, cited by E. Salone, *La Colonisation de la Nouvelle-France*, 127. The practice, therefore, had clearly begun before 1661. It probably originated during the first years of the Compagnie des Cent Associés' administration.

14 See below, sec. 6.

15 Report of 1663, cited by Adam Shortt, *Documents relatifs à la monnaie, au change et aux finances du Canada sous le régime français*, 2 vols. (Ottawa 1929), I:8; "Mémoire pour servir de réponse de la part des officiers et communautés du Canada à messieurs les fermiers généraux" (1675), AC, C11A, 4, fols. 118–20.

16 Report of the Conseil de la Marine, 12 Apr. 1717, cited by Shortt, *Documents relatifs à la monnaie*, I:376–92.

17 The bishop denounced this practice as being usurious. The merchants behave, he wrote, as if they advance the goods as a bottomry loan, whereas they do not share in the risks. Pastoral of Mgr de Saint-Vallier, 3 Mar. 1700, ASSM, copy Faillon H 645.

18 Arrêt of the Conseil d'Etat of 18 Nov. 1672, in Shortt, *Documents relatifs à la monnaie*, I:36. The measure merely attracted worthless copper coins, which colonial merchants would not take at par. Minutes of 10 Jan. 1667 and 28 Nov. 1679, JDCS, I and II.

19 Report by Jean Oudiette's guarantors and objections by M. Savary, AN (France), G7, vol. 1312, items 62 and 63.

20 Royal declaration of 5 July 1717, in Shortt, *Documents relatifs à la monnaie*, I:398.

21 Official parity only, since French coin circulated above its nominal rate, dictated by market conditions. This aspect still needs to be studied.

22 Most came in the form of merchandise sold in the colony for a profit. This suited the colonial administrators. See the report by Talon of 10

Nov. 1670, asking Colbert not to give in to the pleas of merchants who were demanding specie. Shortt, *Documents relatifs à la monnaie*, I:30. For the effect on agriculture, see below, chap. 11.

23 In 1680 the Sulpicians received about a third of their annual income of about 10,000 livres in gold pistoles and the rest in merchandise. Letter from M. Tronson, 20 Mar. 1680, ASSP, XIII:201.

24 J.-B. Migeon, *bailli* and merchant, paid a 3,000-livre dowry in silver écus. Marriage contract, Not. Rec., 20 Apr. 1692, A. Adhémar. Travel in France, or educating one's children there, demanded cash. The French heirs of the Montreal merchant François Pougnet received their share in gold and silver pieces. Ibid., 1 Oct. 1691. On the basis of a few ordinances setting the rate of piastres, A.J.E. Lunn and other historians concluded that foreign coin proliferated in New France as a result of illicit trade. But the shortage of coin was also severe in the English colonies, and contraband involved exchange of goods. What little Spanish currency entered the colony tended to come rather from France. A.J.E. Lunn, "Economic Development in New France, 1713–1760," PhD dissertation, McGill 1942.

25 The bulk of this currency was reserved for the West Indies. See E. Lacombe, *Histoire monétaire de Saint-Domingue et de la république d'Haïti jusqu'en 1874* (Paris 1958).

26 See chap. 11.

27 Prior to 1663, in 23 out of the 38 registered land sales the payments were stipulated in kind; 38 out of 57 in 1667–70; 10 out of 31 in 1680–81; 1 out of 27 in 1690, and none in 1700.

28 Letters from Frontenac, 2 Nov. 1672 and 12 Nov. 1690, AC, C11A, 3, fol. 245, and vol. 11, fol. 347. Jean Hamelin, *Economie et société en Nouvelle-France*, 37. W.J. Eccles, *France in America* (Toronto and Montreal 1972), 114, and others.

29 We hesitate to use the term "barter" since the Europeans dealt primarily with middlemen in deferred exchanges.

30 Beaver was not used as a standard either in exchanges between colonists or with France, as was the case with West Indian sugar.

31 The period prior to 1685 may be too short for any firm conclusions, but one should note that specie did not rise, that the price of goods did not drop, something that would inevitably have occurred had the colony really been short of means of payment. See Roger W. Weiss, "The Issue of Paper Money in the American Colonies, 1720–1745," *Journal of Economic History* 30 (Dec. 1970): 770–85. The author argues that the monetary situation was not significantly worse in the colonies than in England and that the issue of paper money was therefore not inevitable.

32 Paper money was also issued in the English colonies to finance mili-

tary expeditions, with disastrous results. In the central colonies, however, the Land Bank System would prove quite successful. This particular attempt was very different from the irrational procedures used in Canada. See Theodore Thayer, "The Land-Bank System in the American colonies," *Journal of Economic History* 13 (1953): 141–59.

33 Ranging from 1 to 32 livres. They continued to be referred to as "cards" although the intendant had long ceased to use playing cards, which had been a mere expedient for the first issues.

34 Arrêt of 7 Jan. 1689, JDCS, vol III; ordinance of 19 Nov. 1689, by the intendant, and of 13 Nov. 1690, by the *bailli* of Montreal, *bailliage*, 2nd ser., vol. 2; protest by N. Gervaise *v.* Isaac Nafréchoux, 6 Sept. 1690, ibid.

35 Letter from the intendant, 21 Sept. 1692, AC, C11A, 12, fol. 55v.

36 Letter by the same, concerning a 200,000-livre loan from the colonial merchants, 12 Oct. 1691, Shortt, *Documents relatifs à la monnaie*, I:96; letter from the minister to Lubert, 16 Feb. 1695, ibid., 100; other letter from 1710 in which the intendant explains the need to issue 244,092 livres' worth of cards, since the merchants refused to lend any more money, ibid., 206–7. We assume that the 33.3 per cent profit on exchange rates applied to these loans.

37 "Mémoire de l'estat présent du Canada," (1712), ibid., 224–6.

38 See Paul Harsin, "La Finance et l'État jusqu'au système de Law," in F. Braudel and E. Labrousse, eds., *Histoire économique et sociale de la France*, vol. II (Paris 1970), 270–6. "There is an outcry against the bills of exchange on the Treasurer of the Marine," wrote the intendant, "since the merchants prefer the cards to these notes, however much they may need them to fulfil their commitments in France." Letter of 12 Nov. 1712, in Shortt, *Documents relatifs à la monnaie*, I:232. In "Les Finances canadiennes," *Le XVIIIe siècle canadien. Etudes*, 310ff, Guy Frégault provides a good analysis of this crisis, but one over-burdened with detail and that relies too heavily on the intendant's point of view.

39 This applies to the Sulpicians of Montreal. Letters to the Seminary's procurator in Paris, June 1716, NA, M.G. 17, A7, 2, 1, vol. 2, 472–3, 514.

40 M. de Monseignat, 8 Nov. 1714, cited by Shortt, *Documents relatifs à la monnaie*, I:282.

41 Maurepas to Vaudreuil and Bégon, 26 June 1712, ibid., 220; proceedings of the Conseil de la Marine, 3 July 1713, ibid., 238.

42 The minister envisaged gradually reducing the value of the cards to stimulate their exchange. Letter from the Conseil de la Marine to Bégon, 22 Mar. 1714, ibid., 262.

43 Report from Ruette d'Auteuil, 9 Dec. 1715, ibid., 324–5.

44 The letter was dated 22 Mar. 1714, ibid., 266–70. Wheat prices doubled in Montreal in May. Yet the government only officially lowered the

remaining cards to 50 per cent of their face value in 1717. This decision legitimized the de facto situation of the previous three years. The intendant was careful not to publish this particular decree for fear that it would drive prices even higher. Ibid., 398, 432.

45 Petition by the treasurer Gaudion (1715), ibid., 306.

46 The intendant to the minister, 7 Nov. 1715, AC, C11A, 35, fol. 135v.

47 The conseil de la Marine to Law, 18 Dec. 1718, in Shortt, *Documents relatifs à la monnaie*, I:456.

48 Vaudreuil and Bégon to the minister, 16 Sept. 1714, ibid., 272.

49 Jean Hamelin writes that peasant creditors and hoarders were among the losers. *Economie et société en Nouvelle-France*, 43. But the existence of such a group still needs to be proved. As for those colonists who produced too little for their own subsistence, they had to work for others. Hiring was increasing, and wages doubled along with wheat prices. They were probably no poorer.

50 In these early years, "habitant" meant a free man resident in the colony. See below, chap. 13.

51 The well-to-do, the middling sort, and the common folk. There were four Montrealers in the first category: the governor and gentils-hommes who did not remain in the colony. Agreement between the Compagnie des Habitants and M. de la Dauversière, 18 Feb. 1645, NA, M.G. 17, A7, 2, 3, vol. 1, 28.

52 1645 ordinance forbidding the habitants, soldiers, servants, sailors, and others from taking part in the fur trade. Anyone wintering in the colony who needed furs for clothing could buy them for a reasonable price at the storehouse. P.-G. Roy, *Ordonnances, commissions*, I:6.

53 Prior to 1647 the export duty was apparently 25 per cent and the Compagnie des Cent Associés allowed free trade within the colony. The duty doubled in 1647 and was reduced again to 25 per cent in 1653. AC, C11A, 4, fols. 118–20, 175–8, and C11A, 1, fols. 494–5, cited by Innis, *The Fur Trade in Canada*, 40.

54 Prices quoted by Governor d'Argenson in his letter of 4 Aug. 1659 (copy Faillon, X140, fol. 70) and by La Chenaye in his summary (1670), AC, C11A, 3, fols. 150 –1. They are the same as those in two post-mortem inventories of May and July 1663, Not. Rec., Basset.

55 See the 1649 ordinance regarding contraband goods, which includes all the items commonly used in trading. P.-G. Roy, *Ordonnances, commissions*, I:10.

56 Innis, *The Fur Trade in Canada*, 40; M. Delafosse, "La Rochelle et le Canada au XVIIe siècle," RHAF 4, no. 4 (Mar. 1951): 476–84.

57 As long as the monopoly holders imported the trade goods, at least in theory, prices were fixed. See the tariff for goods sold by the Compagnie des Indes occidentales in 1665, AC, C11A, 2, fol. 170. As of the

following year, retail prices were no longer set and the freedom to import merchandise became established. The fact that the Compagnie des Indes occidentales relied exclusively on the export duty on furs, a weak import tax on goods, and revenues from the royal domain to defray colonial expenditures (about 36,000 livres in 1665, according to E. Salone, *La Colonisation de la Nouvelle-France*, 279–81) indicates that the profits from beaver sales in France, which they abandoned of their own accord to the colonists, could not have been exorbitant.

58 See Guy Frégault, "La Compagnie et la colonie," 243–4.

59 Ibid., 244ff.

60 The shares were set at 50 livres, and anyone who owned twenty could vote in the meetings. There were seven elected directors. The capital, which represented 339,000 livres on paper, was not paid up, but the claim could serve as collateral. Most Montreal merchants subscribed for only minimal amounts, which hardly reflected their previous turnover. They were not taking any risks. Sixteen out of the twenty-five held 1,000 livres worth of shares, if not less.

Arrêt of 31 May 1701, in *Edits, ordonnances royaux*, I:286. Prohibitions against detaining the Indians who brought furs to the colonies were never so rigorously applied. See the searches ordered in the spring and summer of 1701, *bailliage*, minutes of Apr. to Aug. passim. The ordinances were peremptory: "We forbid inhabitants of the colony, whatever their quality or station, and especially the merchants of Montreal to supply or outfit directly or indirectly any canoes, be they French or resident Indian ... under penalty of a 500-livre fine and seizure." De Beauharnois ordinance, 20 June 1703, registered at the Montreal *bailliage*.

61 From the merchant Alexis Monière's account books, passim. NA, M-847.

62 Except for the brief experiment in free trade, with an approximately 15 per cent duty on items entering France, in 1720–22. The duty was considered too high, and Canadians opted to return to a system of metropolitan monopoly.

63 Thus, illicit trade with the English colonies, which remained fairly sizable, did not affect government revenues from this trade. The one loser was the Compagnie des Indes. It received occasional help from the authorities to stop smuggling, but it took more than a few searches and lawsuits to balance out the merchants' expected profits.

64 Salone, *La Colonisation de la Nouvelle-France*, 411.

65 The very wide variety in categories, sizes, and quality makes it impossible to compare prices for the same commodity at various times. Hides and small furs rarely figured in merchants' inventories before 1700 – revealing how marginal this branch of business was – and this

deprives us of a solid basis of comparison with eighteenth-century prices. There is no doubt, however, that some, like moose hides, marten, fox, and raccoon furs were rising, while nominal prices of other small furs did not fall.

66 The merchant Monière received very little beaver, and this was also the case in other stocks inventoried between 1706 and 1717. See App. 3, Graph 12.

67 Hides and small furs other than beaver made up 50 to 75 per cent, if not more, of the furs sent to La Rochelle. Although those coming from Louisiana would need to be deducted, those originating from Canada still represented between a quarter and a half of the value of total exports of furs and hides. Lunn, "Economic Development in New France," 464.

68 The Basque word "orignal" was adopted in Canada at the end of the sixteenth century.

69 Caribou is the Algonkian word for a type of reindeer that, at the time, would stray down into the St Lawrence valley.

70 There is no precise information about tanning processes in the colony. Domestic animal hides destined for the local market were curried. Fur traders brought regular supplies of alum to the western outposts, indicating that the wild-animal hides that were exported received some elementary preparation. See J. Savary des Bruslons, *Dictionnaire universel de commerce*, vol. 4 (Copenhagen 1759–65), under the entry "Ellend."

71 Montreal retailers bought such items in Quebec.

72 The evaluation of the furs brought from the west took place in front of two witnesses who represented the interests of the fur traders if they could not be present.

73 When Alexis Monière began his career as merchant-outfitter, he sometimes cut prices to attract customers. But in general all the obligations specified that supplies would be repaid with furs "at the price set by the town merchants," a figure they all agreed to.

74 See App. 3, Graph 11. This only includes advances on credit, but all evidence indicates that cash sales were exceptional.

75 Contemporaries used the term "merchandise" to refer exclusively to imported goods, but in this study it refers to the entire stock of articles sold by the merchants.

76 Representing a value of 1,200 livres, or a third of his stock of cloth. Post-mortem inventory of Jacques Leber, Not. Rec., 1–30 Dec. 1706, Raimbault.

77 J. Coiteux' inventory, 7 Feb. 1715, Not. Rec., Senet. The family had four ells of drugget and six ells of linen woven by an artisan in the town. The intendant claimed that Montreal had twenty-five looms in

1714. Letter to the minister, 12 Nov. 1714, AC, C11A, 34, fols. 388–9. Madame de Repentigny believed that a cheap labour force consisting of prisoners captured in the English colonies would allow her to establish successful local manufacturing, but without the support of the merchants the venture could not be profitable. J.N. Fauteux, *Essai sur l'industrie au Canada sous le régime français* (Quebec 1927), II:465–70.

78 It would seem that southwestern France provided most of the woollens, but it would be futile, given the vague terminology, to try to draw up an exact map. As was the case with linens, our lists checked against Savary's produced no more than vague indications. The Castres region, for example, sold most of its woollens to Canada. Pierre Rascol, *Les Paysans de l'Albigeois à la fin de l'Ancien Régime* (Aurillac 1961), 63.

79 C. de Rochemonteix, *Relations par lettres de l'Amérique septentrionale, années 1705 et 1710*, 63. Blankets usually measured one and a half by one and a quarter ells.

80 Innis, *The Fur Trade in Canada*, 79ff, and 85. See also AC, C11A, 91, fols. 47–8.

81 Montreal merchants benefited from this smuggling, the intendant Bégon wrote in 1715. AC, C11A, 35, fol. 326. The profits that the Compagnie des Indes et Rochelais merchants made by re-exporting English cloth between 1717 and 1731 were obviously not sufficient, which is why they tried to arouse the interest of manufacturers. A.J.E. Lunn, "The Illegal Fur Trade of New France, 1713–1760," *CHAR* (1939): 61–76.

82 Monière's account books, NA, M-847.

83 The proportion is similar to the cargoes loaded in Nantes, Rouen, and Le Havre for the Guinea coast or other African factories in the eighteenth century. Gaston Martin, *Nantes au XVIIIe siècle: L'ère des négriers* (Paris 1931), 47; Pierre Dardel, *Navires et marchandises dans les ports de Rouen et du Havre au XVIIIe siècle* (Paris 1963), 139–41.

84 These are the names most frequently mentioned in sales and inventories, but a complete list would be much longer.

85 Such fabric is made out of plant fibres, spun in the East and West Indies. Savary, *Dictionnaire universel du commerce*, 314. The linen cloth in question was imported from France, but we do not know where it was made. There were some attempts to use nettles in this way in the colony, but this never went beyond domestic use. Letter from Madame de Repentigny, 13 Oct. 1705, AC, C11A, 22, fol. 343.

86 During the eighteenth century Canada provided the major outlet for Orléans hosiery, and the loss of the colony would spell the decline of that industry. See Georges Lefebvre, *Etudes orléannaises: Contribution à l'étude des structures sociales à la fin du XVIIIe siècle* (Paris 1962), I:103.

87 This includes ramrods, gun flints, and the like.

88 See, for example, the "Etat des marchandises distribuées aux Sauvages éloignés en 1693," AC, C11A, 12.

89 Inventories of cargoes sent to Canada in the eighteenth century show that such arms came primarily from Saint-Etienne. Dardel, *Navires et marchandises*, 154. The sale of munitions and shot only made up 0.6 per cent of Alexis Monière's turnover. See App. 3, Graph 11.

90 Letter from Frontenac to the minister, 14 Nov. 1674, AC, C11A, 4, fol. 64; governor's ordinance forcing the merchants Aubert and Leber to accept wheat at 50 sols a minot as payment for the guns, 24 Oct. 1682, E.-Z. Massicotte, *Répertoire des arrêts*; intendant's correspondence of 2 June 1683, and 12 June 1686, AC, C11A, 6, fol. 169, and vol. 8, fol. 63.

91 The natives wanted a light kettle and would not accept those made of copper and iron that the traders tried to impose. AC, C11A, 93, fol. 4.

92 In the middle of the eighteenth century Canada began to produce iron, although import of iron implements did not cease completely. Axes were still included in shipments from Le Havre to Canada in 1742. Dardel, *Navires et marchandises*, 153.

93 From 1670 on, merchants' stocks rarely included frying pans, hammers, or pick-axes, and no chains, ploughshares, and other ironwork used on the farms.

94 Tin utensils are the most important item in the category "tools and utensils" in Graph 11 (App. 3).

95 As the existence of spoon moulds and the like indicates.

96 It is assumed that this refers to the *barrique* as equivalent to one quarter of a *tonneau* or barrel, or to 210 litres. Based on Vachon de Belmont, *Histoire de l'eau-de-vie en Canada*, article 9.

97 Representing an average of 200–250 litres of brandy for a typical cargo, worth about 10,000 livres, transported in two canoes by two voyageurs and their four *engagés* for a trip lasting twelve to sixteen months.

98 Letter from Champigny of 4 Nov. 1693, AC, C11A, 12, fol. 285. A bottle of brandy, worth 4 livres in the colony, went for 50 or even 100, if the intendant can be believed.

99 Shipments of spirits to the interior would increase in the eighteenth century. Around 1800, when competition between fur traders reached an all-time high, Montreal would dispatch large amounts to the northwest, making up perhaps 10 or even 20 per cent of the value of the cargoes. P.A. Pendergast, "The XY company, 1798–1804," PhD dissertation, University of Ottawa 1957.

100 The only difference was that brandy or wine bought from a merchant's were not consumed on the spot. Ordinance of the intendant Raudot, Dec. 1705, copy Faillon GG192.

101 Arrêt of the Sovereign Council of 22 Oct. 1664 and 22 Apr. 1665, JDCS,

1:286, 333; ordinance by the *bailli* of Montreal of 5 May 1688, *bailliage*, copy Faillon HH15.

102 See Roger Dion, *Histoire de la vigne et du vin en France, des origines au XIXe siècle* (Paris 1959), 442–60, on the production of eau-de-vie in the Charentes.

103 *Rasade* was also sold on the Guinea coast and Senegal. See Dardel, *Navires et marchandises*, 128–43, and Savary, *Dictionnaire universel du commerce*.

104 Ordinance of the Intendant Hocquart, 25 Feb. 1747, *Edits, ordonnances royaux*, II:390; Fauteux, *Essai sur l'industrie au Canada*, II:401–4.

105 Letter from Frontenac and Champigny to the minister, 15 Sept. 1692, AC, C11A, 12, fol. 10v.

106 Letter from Frontenac, 19 Oct. 1697, ibid., vol. 15, fol. 50, and vol. 16, fol. 17.

107 See the decisions of the Conseil of 8 July and 27 Aug. 1664, JDCS, 1:226, 269.

108 Private homes were searched, and surpluses had to be brought to the *garde-sel* by order of the judge of Montreal, 22 Nov. 1704, *bailliage*, copy Faillon GG 235.

109 Salt in the colony was sold by the minot or the *barrique*, but we have no precise information about how much these contained and cannot therefore compare local prices with those in effect at Brouage, for example. M. Delafosse and C. Laveau, *Le Commerce du sel de Brouage aux XVIIe et XVIIIe siècles* (Paris 1960).

110 The flower of a plant known as "cotonnier" gave a sugar that some liked better than maple. De Rochemonteix, *Relations par lettres de l'Amérique septentrionale*, 16. Inventories make no mention of beehives. Cane sugar, like rum and molasses, would spread throughout the colony once trade with the West Indies became regular after 1720.

111 In the seventeenth century prices were set as follows: 50 per cent "profit" over the French purchase price, and another 33.3 on that first operation, "given the appreciation of the coinage in Canada." Even after the latter was abolished, eighteenth-century merchants still continued to charge twice the French price. This did not apply to liquids, which were billed separately. One can notice a similar 100 per cent increase in the price of dry goods between Bordeaux and the West Indies. J. Cavignac, *Jean Pellet, commerçant en gros, 1694–1772* (Paris 1967), 195.

112 Pierre Goubert, *Beauvais et le Beauvaisis*, 500ff.

113 Arrêts of the Sovereign Council of 17 Nov. 1663, 17 Jan. 1664, and 4 Feb. 1665, JDCS, I. Minutes of 1 Feb. and 26 Apr. 1683, JDCS, II:860–2, 870. On the question of mitigated competition, see below, chap. 5.

114 Nevertheless, stocks were appraised at the going price in Montreal.

See, for example, the inventories of J. Legras and J. Leber, Not. Rec., 24 Jan. 1704, A. Adhémar, and 1 Dec. 1706, Raimbault.

115 Since metropolitan prices remained high until the deflationary policy carried out in 1724–25. See F. Baudel and E. Labrousse, eds., *Histoire économique et sociale de la France*, II:297–8. To find out, it would have been necessary to examine a series of inventories later than 1726, which would take us beyond the confines of this study.

116 In order to chart this trend, I compared prices for the periods 1660 to 1685 and 1722–25 (at least twenty prices for each period) for a number of commonly used products with fairly stable quality standards. The items were wine, brandy, floor and shingle nails, trade woollens, *mélis* linen, *carisés*, a pound of copper (kettle), black tobacco, pepper, Saint-Maixent stockings, large-sized hempen shirts, and the ordinary large coat or *capot*. Every single one rose.

117 *Nouveaux voyages de M. le baron de La Hontan dans l'Amérique septentrionale* (The Hague 1704), I: 70–1.

118 See R. Grassby, "The Rate of Profit in Seventeenth-Century England," *English Historical Review* 84 (1969): 721–51; K.G. Davies, *The Royal African Company* (London 1960), 335–43; Ralph Davis, *Aleppo and Devonshire Square: English Traders in the Levant in the Eighteenth Century* (Toronto and London 1967), 226–42; Pierre Villar, *La Catalogne dans l'Espagne moderne: Recherches sur les fondements économiques des structures nationales* (Paris 1962), 2:139ff.

119 Anyone transporting the goods on his own ship would, of course, have an added advantage.

120 E.E. Rich, "Trade Habits and Economic Motivation among Indians," *CJEPS* (1960): 35ff; Abraham Rotstein, "Karl Polanyi's Concept of Non-Market Trade," *Journal of Economic History* 30, no. 1 (Mar. 1970): 117–26. This trade resembled the slave trade on the west coast of Africa, where, S. Berbain concludes, prices never changed. *Le Comptoir français de Juda au XVIII siècle*, cited by Rotstein in the above article.

121 Innis in *The Fur Trade in Canada* sees a direct link between the advance of Canadian fur traders to the Pacific and the effort to reach tribes that had not yet come into contact with European goods. The author too often assumes, however, that this trade was controlled by market mechanisms.

122 Account books detailing exchanges between the Indians and fur traders of New France have not been located. See terms of exchange quoted in A. Rotstein "Fur Trade and Empire: An Institutional Analysis," PhD dissertation, University of Toronto, 1967.

123 The fur trader Tonty reported that a pound of beaver was worth one and a half ells of woollen cloth in the Michilimakinac region in 1719. This was the very value noted in Albany and Hudson Bay (AC, C11A,

124, 265). See the equivalent prices for powder, guns, and shot quoted by Nicolas Perrot in *Mémoire sur les moeurs et coutumes des Sauvages*, 134.

124 At the end of the French regime, one observer remarked that "everything is bartered, so many blankets for so many beavers. The tariff is set and can be enforced. It represents a profit of around 100 per cent." "Premier mémoire sur les impôts que le Roy veut imposer sur le Canada" (ca. 1755), ASSP, mss, R1200.

125 A beaver skin weighs a pound and a half on average. Sixty-seven sols represents an average of the price of coat beaver (82 sols) and parchment beaver (52 sols). The export tax was automatically deducted from the voyageurs' profit margin.

126 The market value of these permits or *congés* was about 1,000 livres for the shipment of one canoe-load worth 3,000 livres. Fraud was common, however, and one permit served for several canoe-loads. See the sale of the permits in notarial records: Basset, 14 and 25 June, 21 July 1686; A. Adhémar, 9 June 1694 and 22 May 1698; other sales in 1692, 1697, 1698 in AC, C11A, 12, fols. 7, 15, and 81; Lahontan, *Nouveaux Voyages*, 85–6.

127 Agreement between the Notre-Dame Montreal vestry and three voyageurs of 22 Feb. 1682, APND, box 1, folder 17.

128 Agreement between J.-J. Patron, merchant, and two voyageurs for the use of a *congé* (Not. Rec., 14 May 1683, Maugue.

129 Voyageurs had to take their furs straight to the outfitter, who took what had been mutually agreed to in the obligation and usually bought up the remainder. Ordinance of the intendant De Meulles, 17 May 1685, in Massicotte, *Répertoire des arrêts*. See, for example, the obligation signed by P. Deniau to Alexis Monière, in Not. Rec., 5 Sept. 1714, J.-B. Adhémar.

130 "Considérations sur l'état présent du Canada," Oct. 1758, in *Collection de mémoires et relations sur l'histoire ancienne du Canada*, 13.

131 A. Monière paid his Rochelais supplier with 106 otters, which were credited to him at the rate current in the colony. Account books, 1719, NA, M-847.

132 Accounts of the widow Lemoyne and A. Pascaud, 1691, and 1695. See below, Table 21.

CHAPTER FIVE

1 Letter from Marie Pournin to M. Baston, sent from Montreal on 2 Oct. 1662, ANQ, Montreal, Documents judiciaires (piéces détachées). Quebec residents had enjoyed such simple trading arrangements earlier: "Mulier quaedam mediocris quaerentibus quanti negotiata fuerat:

'Mille et quinquentis tantum,' respondit, nummis." Letter by the Sieur Denys, Quebec, 28 Oct. 1651, presented by Lucien Campeau in "Un témoignage de 1651 sur la Nouvelle-France," RHAF 23, no. 4 (Mar. 1970): 601–12.

2 As shown by the presence of such trade goods in many post-mortem inventories.

3 "With time Montrealers will want to trade separately (as they already show signs of doing) and stop the Indians from coming to Trois-Rivières and Quebec, which would surely result in civil war." Letter from Governor Voyer d'Argenson, 4 Aug. 1659, ASSP, copy Faillon X 141.

4 Inventory of P. Pigeon's assets at the time of his marriage, 6 Nov. 1662, Not. Rec., Basset; inventory upon his widow's demise, 11 Oct. 1686, ANQ, Montreal, clôtures d'inventaires.

5 All officials of whatever rank had a hand in the trade. W.J. Eccles has clearly demonstrated the involvement of governors such as Frontenac and La Barre, and the same can be said of most governors, intendants, judicial officers, and other agents of the Crown. As J.F. Bosher aptly remarked, this is not a question of "corruption" but part and parcel of the administrative system of l'Ancien Régime, where private entreprise and the public sector overlapped. W.J. Eccles, Frontenac, the Courtier Governor; John F. Bosher, "Government and Private Interest in New France,' Canadian Public Administration 10 (1967): 244–57.

6 François Charon, Simon Mars, François Hazeur, Jean Gitton, and Charles Aubert.

7 Charles Lemoyne and Jacques Leber had excellent relations with the Jesuits and Sulpicians and two well-located posts, one at the island's west end and the other on the South Shore, near the Sault-Saint-Louis mission.

8 Pierre Picoté's held 6,500 livres' worth of claims when he died, two-thirds on Indians, listed as sound debts, while the rest, the widow declared, consisted of debts by insolvent Frenchmen. Inventory of 13 Mar. 1679, Not. Rec., Basset.

9 Merchants' post-mortem inventories in this period make no mention of large advances of trade goods to anyone.

10 E.R. Adair, "The Evolution of Montreal during the French Regime," CHAR (1942): 27–8.

11 Letter from Intendant Duchesneau, 13 Oct. 1680, AC, C11A, 5, fol. 161; report by Patoulet, ibid., fol. 320.

12 One should not, as did Salone, relate the number of coureurs de bois estimated by the intendant to the number of married men listed on the census (500/1475) and falsely conclude that a third of the settlers left the land. In fact there were no more than a hundred sons of

habitants out west at the time, and all were single. Most of the adventurers were non-residents who were never enumerated. At most they were potential settlers lost to the colony, if we assume that without the lure of quick wealth these young men would not have taken advantage of the free passage to France to which they were entitled. E. Salone, *La Colonisation de la Nouvelle-France*, 56.

13 E.E. Rich, *The Fur Trade and the Northwest to 1857* (Toronto 1967), 76.

14 At least one was hanged as a warning to others. Letter from Frontenac, 14 Nov. 1674, AC, C11A, 4, fol. 70.

15 W.J. Eccles, *Canada under Louis XIV* (Toronto 1964), 122–4; AC, C11A, 5 fol. 359; Rich, *The Fur Trade*, 52.

16 In 1681 the intendant complained that 20,000 pounds of beaver had been sold to the English, or one-fifth of what had gone to Quebec. The operation was supposedly carried out by a small company that consisted of a Montreal merchant, two coureurs de bois, and the governor general. Report by Duchesneau, 13 Nov. 1681, AC, C11A, 5, fols. 322–3.

17 JDCS, II:570–7, 299.

18 Letter from Duchesneau, 10 Nov. 1679, AC, C11A, 5, fol. 38, as well as vol. 6, fol. 112ff.

19 Letter from the same, 10 Nov. 1679, ibid., vol. 5, fol. 51v.

20 Two are missing. The yearly *congés* were supposed to be registered at the local clerk's office. The registers have apparently been lost. I found the 1682 list on a separate sheet mingled among other documents: ANQ, NF21, vol. 15. The list published in the *RAPQ* (1921–22): 189–225 is very incomplete for the seventeenth century.

21 The merchant who provided the permit and had a share in the returns was known as the "bourgeois du congé."

22 Letter from Denonville, 8 May 1686, AC, C11A, 8, fols. 21–2.

23 The proceeds from the sale of *congés* were assigned for defence purposes after 1688. In order to satisfy all the pension-holders, the intendant had to give out free *congés* beyond the twenty-five he sold for budgetary reasons. AC, C11A, 12, fols. 6–7. Letter from Denonville, 6 May 1686, ibid., vol. 8, fols. 21–3. The *congés* were abolished in 1696, re-established between 1716 and 1719, suppressed again, and finally revived in 1726.

24 Among a total of 439 urban and rural households listed in the 1697 tenant book of the Séminaire de Montréal, ASSM. Records of the obligations held by outfitters support the enumeration data.

25 A typical voyageur partnership: Paul Bouchard, Jean Coton Fleur d'Epée, and François Bigras agreed to go to the upper country with the following provisos: they would take up one canoe-load of goods under joint ownership and trade them for the best possible terms; the canoe, goods, food supplies, and wages (they hired an *engagé*) would

be paid by their company; potential losses, "the Lord forbid," would be shared equally among the three, as would whatever profits "the Lord should see fit to grant them." Not Rec., 30 May 1714, A. Adhémar.

26 The analysis of the seasonal distribution of conceptions showed that few married men took part in this far-flung trade. See chap. 3, sec. 3 above.

27 La Mothe Cadillac in Detroit, Laforest and Tonty in the territory of the Illinois.

28 For further details, see sec. 5, below.

29 Marcel Giraud, *Histoire de la Louisiane* (Paris 1953), I:45–7, 136. In 1702 there were still sixty Canadians in Mobile despite the deaths and departures. Traders wintered around the Illinois missions. Some of the young Montrealers who accompanied Juchereau down the Wabash did not return.

30 This picture is based on an analysis of all notarial deeds related to the fur trade: partnerships, obligations, hiring, and so on. The compilation covered the years up to and including 1717. The figures for 1727, 1737, and 1747, added for comparative purposes, are based on *RAPQ* (1921–22), 191–466 and ibid., (1930–31), 353–453. In 1709, for example, there were only forty-five recorded departures west, including those of five *engagés* and eighteen outfitters who financed small cargoes.

31 Innis, *The Fur Trade in Canada*, chap. 5.

32 See below, sec. 5, and App. 3, Graph 15.

33 Around 1664 the drop in beaver prices had more severe repercussions. Once merchant profits were solely based on trade goods, they were far less affected by the lower price in furs than were the voyageurs. On the whole the merchants had little reason to close ranks. As their turnover was limited by their credit in France, increases in the volume of fur exports signify increases in the number of merchants.

34 Canadians such as Charly, Soumande, Neveu, and others trailed close behind.

35 Prior to 1700 they had not been overly successful. Without any specific role they had to push their way into the network, entering into partnerships with the voyageurs and remaining dependent upon the merchants.

36 See, for example, the permits given to Louvigny, which he endorsed and then sold. Not. Rec., 12 Mar. 1717, J.-B. Adhémar.

37 See below, chap. 13, sec. 8. Cameron Nish, in *Les Bourgeois-gentils-hommes de la Nouvelle-France, 1729–1748* (Montreal 1968), looks at these associations when they were already in place and presents as a permanent social feature what was in fact the result of an economic and political process.

38 See Graph 12 in App. 3.
39 As long as the cards circulated, hard currency quite naturally remained hidden. Cash payments began only in 1719 and thus were relatively more important thereafter than shown on the graph.
40 Three shoemakers delivered shoes to Monière that were credited to the tanner who had supplied them leather. The product moved less quickly than wheat, so the merchant eventually asked to be paid another way. See the accounts of Poidevin, Sansterre and Moreau, shoemakers, and of the tanner Bélair, the smith Lavallée, etc., in NA, M-847 and M-848.
41 On this aspect, see also Maurice Dobb, *Studies in the Development of Capitalism* (London 1946).
42 Monière regularly gave out work to six women. Each could sew about 100 coats a year, for 15 sols apiece. She would have had to make 2 a day to earn as much as a labourer, an impossible feat given the coarse and heavy material. He paid out 6 sols per shirt. A large coat took 3.5 ells of serge, worth 4 livres retail, and 1 livre's worth of thread, buttons, and so on. The merchant sold the outerwear for 17 livres 10 sols, netting 11 per cent. See the accounts of Nelsont, Homénie, Payet, and others, in NA, M-847 and M-848.
43 He made a slight profit on the sale of pork and tobacco, but apparently none from flour.
44 The range of services increased as the voyageurs' position improved. In the seventeenth century they still came to Montreal, where they organized the next trip personally. By 1717 many of the voyageurs lived in Michilimakinac and relied on their outfitters to receive the furs, prepare the cargoes, and organize the transport.
45 The names most frequently mentioned were those of Guillet, Trottier-Desauniers and daughters, and Catignon, royal storekeeper.
46 Since every merchant outfitted illegally at some time or other, one could easily denounce a competitor and see him sentenced to a heavy fine.
47 Fur merchants' account books dating from the second half of the eighteenth century, NA, M-848–53, M-1005; P.A. Pendergast, *The XY Company, 1798–1804*; see also G.V. Taylor, "Some Business Partnerships at Lyon, 1785–1793," *Journal of Economic History* 23 (1963): 46–70.
48 "Au nom de Dieu et de la Très Saint Vierge soit commencé le présent Livre Journal de Vente à Credit et Argent Resus pour servir à moy Monière à Montréal Ce 15ᵉ octobre 1715," NA, M-847. Entries from the daybook were consigned to the current-account books on opposite sheets, and regularly brought up to date. The list of books in post-mortem inventories do not reveal any personal accounts. See R. De Roover, "Aux Origines d'une technique intellectuelle: la formation et

l'expansion de la comptabilité à partie double," *Annales d'histoire economique et sociale* 9 (1937): 171–93.

49 These were the same archaic methods that appalled Pierre Deyon, *Amiens, capitale provinciale* (Paris 1967), 99.

50 See, for example, the accounts of the company formed by the Widow Lemoyne with Antoine Pascaud, Not. Rec., 5 Dec. 1690, Basset.

51 This practice differs from the more rigid ones encountered in some French regions in this period. Pierre Guichard noted that in the Andance, "every written transaction corresponded to an actual transfer of funds." "Evolution socio-économique de la région d'Andance," in P. Léon, *Structures économiques ... dans la France du Sud-Est* (Paris 1966), 182.

52 The merchant who advanced supplies to a coureur de bois was liable to a heavy fine, half of which went to the informer. See, for example, the 1,500 livres to which Soumande was sentenced on 17 Oct. 1707. *JDCS*, V:690. Holders of promissory notes had to obtain a sentence against their debtors before they could make a claim on their property. Olivier Martin, *Histoire de la coutume de la prévôté et vicomté de Paris* (Paris 1922), II:580. For an example of a contested payment, see Not. Rec., 31 July 1684, Basset.

53 Adhémar and son specialized in the fur trade. See André Vachon, *Histoire du notariat canadien 1621–1960* (Quebec 1962).

54 The approximate date of return was included. A typical contract would state "next August or, at the latest, at the beginning of October." In half the cases the obligation specified the value of small furs and of beaver as well as the desired quality: coat or parchment, etc. When debts were earmarked to more than one individual, the outfitter who had advanced the goods that had returned in the shape of the contested furs had first picking if another creditor with a prior obligation had not obtained a sentence. If there was a sentence, the last supplier, who disregarded it, became responsible for the debt to the first creditor. This called for diligence. Minutes of 19 Oct. 1682 and 7 Mar. 1689, *JDCS*, II and III.

55 Either at another merchant's or at the home of one of their partners who resided within the notary's district.

56 At least in the seventeenth century.

57 See, for example, the proceedings by Jean Plattier against André Heneau for his share in a binding agreement, amounting to 2,214 livres. *Bailliage*, ser. 2, reg. 2, fol. 169v.

58 Wages, of course, took precedence. See the minutes of 9 Oct. 1681, *bailliage*, ser. 1, reg. 1.

59 These small claims matured much faster, for most *engagés* were only absent three to four months.

60 See App. 3, Graph 13. Receipts were jotted down on the merchant's copy of the obligation, but rarely on the original notary's draft, so it is impossible to assess the delays in payments on the basis of notarial records. This is why the present calculations are limited to a single merchant's returns.

61 Merchants recently arrived from France, without good information on traders, were at a disadvantage.

62 Post-mortem inventory of P. Lemoyne de Maricourt, Not. Rec., 9 Dec. 1703, A. Adhémar.

63 Charles de Couagne, a reckless lender, relied on this method to secure part of his loans to the traders. See Not. Rec., A. Adhémar, 3 Jan. and 9 July 1703, and 23 Jan. 1699; P. Raimbault, 15 July 1700, etc.

64 Agreement between de Couagne and Alexandre Turpin, ibid., 8 July 1699, A. Adhémar.

65 Between the merchant P. Perthuis and the voyageur P. Millet, ibid., 3 Sept. 1699.

66 Legal proceedings against traders accounted for fewer than 10 per cent of the three hundred cases brought before the magistrate each year between 1688 and 1698. This was not a large caseload, given the importance of the fur trade in the colony.

67 See, for example, the bill drawn by a Quebec merchant on a Montreal one, 5 Apr. 1696, bailliage, ser. 2, reg. 3, fols. 394 and 396v.

68 Sale to the royal attorney Pierre Raimbault by the Sulpicians, Feb. 1716, Not. Rec., J.-B. Adhémar.

69 The Hôtel-Dieu created bills of exchange on Paris on behalf of Montreal merchants for the merchandise it had received in the colony. See the community's account books, 1696–1726, passim.

70 J. Meuvret, "Manuels et traités à l'usage des négociants aux premières époques de l'âge moderne," Etudes d'histoire économiques (Paris 1971), 231–50.

71 See, for one, the detail of J.-B. Bauvais' succession, 17 Apr. 1705, Not. Rec., A. Adhémar, and that of Jean Legras, 24 Jan. 1704, ibid.

72 Based on Alexis Monière's account books and the debts listed among current accounts in merchants' post-mortem inventories.

73 See the quarterly movement of payments and sales in App. 3, Graph 14.

74 This applies to normal years. When there were crop failures, there would be longer delays.

75 According to 1673 royal ordinance on commerce, the liability for this kind of debt was limited to one year, but signed tallies were subject to the thirty-year statute, like any bill or obligation. Oeuvres de Pothier, annotées et mises en correlation avec le code civil et la législation actuelle, 10 vols. (Paris 1847), II, items 706 to 713.

76 The last specification was merely a turn of phrase, since the blanket mortgage included in the notarized contract achieved the same end. Olivier Martin, *Histoire de la coutume*, II:580.

77 The first case is illustrated by the deeds dated 4 Apr. and 13 Aug. 1699. Not. Rec., A. Adhémar. Charles de Couagne's post-mortem inventory offers many examples of the second type of loan. Ibid., 28 Aug. 1706.

78 A silver cup for a loan of 25 livres figures in the notary A. Adhémar's post-mortem inventory, Not. Rec., 14 May 1714, Le Pailleur; another pawned object found in Charles Lemoyne's, ibid., 27 Mar. 1685, Basset.

79 See Deyon, *Amiens, capitale provinciale*, 560–1, and below, chaps. 9 and 11.

80 Quick tallies show that the number of notarial deeds rose from about one hundred a year in 1680 to over 400 in 1700.

81 For example, a rente of 30 livres for a loan of 600 livres' worth of cards on 6 Apr. 1699 was refunded with a single card payment by Aug. 1704. Not. Rec., A. Adhémar. Yet again, a rente created for 544 livres on 3 Jan. 1703 was repaid in full with cards in Aug. 1704, ibid.

82 Contracts of 13 Aug. and 14 Sept. 1716, ibid., J.-B. Adhémar.

83 See, for example, the rentes acquired by Charles de Couagne, ibid., on 23 Jan., 20 Mar., 6 Apr. 1699, 3 Jan., 9 July 1703, etc., as well as those created on behalf of the seigneurs, usually to cover arrears in seigneurial dues or land purchases, etc.

84 Pastoral of Bishop Saint-Vallier of 3 Mar. 1700, ASSM, copy Faillon, H 645.

85 I verified this by comparing debts listed in Monière's accounts with the notarized obligations that settled them – for example, the obligation of 19 Feb. 1702, Not. Rec., J. David.

86 "I will pay the Sieur Médart Mézeret the sum of 1,500 livres in local currency at the end of October, twelve-month. For which sum the Sieur Mézeret sets the interest at 7 per cent ... done in Quebec, 18 Oct. 1695." The note is described in Mézeret's post-mortem inventory of 6 July 1696. Not. Rec., Basset. For another example of such a note at 5 per cent, see 29 Aug. 1692, *bailliage*, ser. 2, reg. 2, fols. 545 and 548v. See also the 10 per cent interest charged by the seigneurs of Montreal for a short-term loan to Charles de Couagne, listed in the latter's post-mortem inventory of 28 Aug. 1706, Not. Rec., A. Adhémar. These were not exorbitant when compared to the 24 per cent tacked on to the 3,225 livres advanced in cash by Jean Philippe, *écuyer*, to the merchant Jean Arnaud, who had to reimburse 4,000 livres' worth of beaver, interest that was justified by the standard pattern of exchange on beaver. Minutes of 28 June 1694, JDCS, III.

87 See Not. Rec., 22 May 1694, Basset.

88 Abel Poitrineau, *La Vie rurale en Basse Auvergne au XVIIIe siècle (1726–1789* (Paris 1965), 496–501. Pierre Guichard, "Evolution socio-économique de la région d'Andance," in Léon, *Structures économiques ... dans la France du Sud-Est*, 181–2.

89 See the 9,430 livres the seigneurs of Montreal loaned Charles de Couagne, for which he consigned 9,670 livres' worth of *rentes constituées*, Couagne's post-mortem inventory, 28 Aug. 1706, Not. Rec., A. Adhémar; suit between Jean Durand and Jean Arnaud, Mar. 1697, *bailliage*, ser. 2, reg. 3, fols. 549–51v.

90 Transfer to the Sieur Granmesny, 31 May 1714, Not. Rec., J.-B. Adhémar. Transfer of seventeen obligations and notes by Madame de Repentigny to Pierre Raimbault, 24 July 1714, ibid. Transfer by de Couagne to the Sieurs Peirre of Quebec, Trehet of La Rochelle, and Delisle of Tours, 1703–05. This last transaction can be followed in de Couagne's inventory and in *JDCS*, V:54ff.

91 Transfer by P. Couillard of Lachine to the merchant Etienne Véron, 31 May 1714, Not. Rec., J.-B. Adhémar.

92 Obligation signed by Jean-Baptiste Deniau, 13 Aug. 1699, ibid., A. Adhémar.

93 Pothier, *Oeuvres de Pothier*, III:205–6. See also, for example, the contracts of 26 May 1692, Not. Rec., Basset; 25 June 1690, ibid., Pottier; 14 July 1700, ibid., Raimbault; 11 Sept. 1697, ibid., Basset, and so on.

94 Deeds dated 26 Oct. 1703, ibid., A. Adhémar; and 21 Aug. 1667, ibid., Basset.

95 The claim was sold for 520 livres by the family of Toussaint Hunault to a Montreal merchant who transferred it to a metropolitan merchant. Deed of 10 Oct. 1690, ibid., Basset.

96 Not all merchants' post-mortem inventories give details on the sums invested in trade. That is why numbers here are smaller than those in Table 41 below.

97 Inventory of 1 Dec. 1706, Not. Rec., P. Raimbault, notary. Cash was just as insignificant in the fortunes left behind by Amiens merchants between 1672 and 1703. Deyon, *Amiens, capitale provinciale*, 106–8.

98 Charly's bad claims are not included in this table. See also the sidenotes on the state of the claims in the Aubuchon succession, 17 Feb. 1688, Not. Rec., Maugue.

99 Pierre Goubert observes a similar phenomenon among far better-established and wealthier merchants in *Les Danse et les Motte de Beauvais, familles marchandes sous l'Ancien Régime* (Paris 1959), 74–5.

100 Born in Pitres, in the diocese of Rouen, he had come to the colony as a merchant in 1657. Entry by Yves Zoltvany, *DCB*, vol. II.

101 That is, eighteen to twenty-four months for fur traders and less than

twelve months for others. Any extension would have entailed an obligation or note and cancelled the credit listed in the ledgers.

102 Charles Renaud *dit* de Couagne (he never used his real name in the colony) was born in Clion, in the Bourbonnais. He began as Governor Frontenac's steward, which must have facilitated his first ventures.

103 See his previously mentioned dealings with Peirre, Trahet, Delisle (n 91 above).

104 A total of 13,575 livres had been advanced to five small merchants in 1700: 11,065 livres to Tonty in 1701; 7,000 livres to Nicolas Demers, a shopkeeper who fled leaving wife and children behind as well as a string of creditors; 6,000 livres to Janvrin-Dufresne; 4,000 livres to Milot, a Lachine merchant, etc. In normal times all these small merchants received their supplies from Quebec or France and settled them ahead of time.

105 He either acted as the company's unofficial sub-contractor or else illegally tried to get around the company's monopoly by setting up a parallel distribution system. The evidence is unavailable on this point, but what is sure is that his ventures at this juncture rocked what had previously been a solid concern.

106 She married Pierre You in 1697, an adventurer who had come with La Salle and knew how to make useful connections, and who apparently continued the business quite successfully.

107 The others were Charron, Migeon, Perthuis, Charly fils, and perhaps J.-J. Patron and Jean Quenet, not to mention the Quebec merchants who did business in Montreal, such as Aubert, Hazeur, and others.

108 His day-to-day expenses were slight and incorporated into those of his business. He drew out his house payments over six years. He settled everything with merchandise, so that he increased his turnover while repaying debts.

109 The tutor of Jacques Bizard's heirs invested 2,600 livres, of an unspecified nature, with the merchant Bertrand Arnaud, 13 Aug. 1700, Not. Rec., A. Adhémar. The tutor of Mathieu Fay's heirs, resident of La Prairie, invested 600 livres' worth of beaver with the merchant Soumande, at 7 per cent interest, 6 Oct. 1693, ibid. A Sulpician gave 1,000 livres' worth of trade goods to two young Indians, which were to be invested with a merchant until they came of age, 6 July 1699, ibid., Basset.

110 A large segment of the merchants' liabilities, at least half, were family debts. See, for example, the 17,175 livres Couagne owed his father-in-law and brother-in-law out of a total debit of 32,900 livres. 7 Aug. 1686, ibid., Maugue.

111 The shares that the Lemoynes possessed in the Compagnie de la Baie d'Hudson brought them initial high dividends that far outweighed the

losses of these "shares" (which had little face value) once the English regained control of the Bay's outposts. Leber and Lemoyne had long owned ships that travelled between France, Canada, Acadia, and the West Indies. The outbreak of war as well as their advanced years made them abandon shipping. Leber also owned fishing and coasting vessels. AC, C11A, 4, fol. 56.

112 Petition addressed to Governor Frontenac, followed by an ordinance of 14 July 1674, *bailliage*, copy Faillon, QQ57.

113 On this question, see Richard Pares, "The Economic Factors in the History of the Empire," in *Economic History Review*, ser. 1, vol. 7, no. 2 (May 1937): 119–44, and *Yankees and Creoles: The Trade between North America and the West Indies before the American Revolution* (London 1956).

114 M. Delafosse, "La Rochelle et le Canada au XVIIe siècle," *RHAF* 4, no. 4 (Mar. 1951): 469–511, and "Le Trafic franco-canadien (1695–1717)."

115 The business of Leber, Lemoyne, Soumande, Hazeur, and Pacaud showed such reciprocity in commercial dealings.

116 Such was the situation up to the 1720s. Later in the eighteenth-century, major Bordelais shippers, attracted by military expenditures, would pounce on the Canada trade, pushing aside the Canadian-Rochelais merchants. See James Pritchard, "The Pattern of French Colonial Shipping to Canada before 1760," in *Revue française d'histoire d'outre-mer* 63 (1976): 189–210.

117 In 1683, Jean Gitton from La Rochelle requested the status of resident on the basis of his trading activities in Canada, and those of his father before him, "from which he had amassed over 120,000 livres' worth of debts and notes, which made him decide to settle here." *JDCS*, II:873–4.

118 Jean Grignon died in La Rochelle, leaving three children behind: two daughters married in Canada and a son with a Canadian wife who took on the business. Charles Lemoyne died in Montreal, and a large part of his inheritance was used by his sons to launch various foreign ventures elsewhere and to buy a seigneury near Rochefort for 94,000 livres. How can one assess how much of this commercial capital remained in the colony?

119 M. Delafosse, "La Rochelle et le Canada au XVIIe siècle," *RHAF* 4, no. 4 (Mar. 1951): 469–511. The list of small merchants who disappeared after a few disastrous seasons is a long one: Raymond Amyault, Dupuis, Jean Boudor, Hattanville, Guillaume Boutillers, Jacques Passard, Louis Boucher Bouval, Pierre Bailly, Jean Arnaud, and so on.

120 By marrying in the colony, merchants could shorten the probation period and avoid heavy deposits. See the regulations of 1 Apr. 1674, 14 June 1676, 13 Apr. and 11 May 1676, and 1 Feb. 1683, E.Z. Massicotte, *Repertoire des arrêts*.

121 See the petition by Simon Mars "pour obtenir les privileges accordés aux bourgeois et habitants," putting forth a property of some 2,400 livres in Montreal. *JDCS*, II, 28 June 1677; that of Jean Gitton, who had recently acquired a house in Montreal for 2,500 livres, ibid., 873–4; the lawsuit against Jacques de Faye, Mars's nephew, ibid., 874–5.

122 Montrealers were quick to include among *marchands-forains* such persons as Aubert, Hazeur, or Charron, who were in fact well established in Quebec. There is a danger in taking these petitions as proof that foreigners controlled the trade. W.J. Eccles, *The Canadian Frontier*, 124.

123 Ruling of the Council of 1 Feb. 1683, *JDCS*, II:860–2.

124 Excerpt from a petition of 1 Apr. 1718 by Canadian merchants denouncing *forains* who retailed their wares during the winter, took out money from the colony, and did not contribute to its expenditures. AC, C11A, 124, fol. 365 or fol. 140: double pagination.

125 It is interesting to see how all the Montreal merchants, including fresh arrivals (Jean Pauthier, F. Poisset, who resided in France, Du Chouquet, Pierre Biron) united against Antoine Pacaud, who had traded in Montreal for thirty years and who, thanks to an agreement with Néret and Gayot of Paris, was in a position to negotiate other merchants' bills of exchange and to monopolize imports. Letter of 5 Oct. 1716, in Adam Shortt, *Documents Relating to Canadian Currency, Exchange and Finance during the French Period*, I (Ottawa 1925), 354–6.

126 Against the government when it tried to impose French annuities in exchange for the cards, or against the lessees of the Western Domain. On several occasions, all merchants joined forces.

127 This interpretation is largely based on intendants' reports, especially those of Duchesneau, a dour and superficial observer, or those of Champigny, who exaggerated in order to parry criticisms.

128 To obtain a large and representative sample, it was necessary to choose a period when fur-trade agreements were normally recorded by notaries and to bypass the worst years of the crisis. All related deeds, such as obligations, partnerships, or hirings, instrumented by notaries in and around Montreal were used to construct a file of participants. I was able to ascertain that very few fur-trade operations were recorded by Quebec notaries, and that when the case arose there would be a complementary deed in the Montreal archives for these people. Genealogical studies, in particular C. Tanguay, *Dictionnaire généalogique*, were used to identify the participants. In the case of Montrealers, I was often able to add information on occupations. There were never more than thirty outfitters a year, but many of them including some Quebec merchants, appeared only once in that decade, and this explains the relatively large number of individuals in the category. The officers in the sample contracted obligations for trade

goods, alone or in association with voyageurs. The few who acted as outfitters were listed as such. Together, voyageurs, traders, and en-gagés total 668, but the breakdown between the two groups is not clear-cut, for a few individuals figured in both over the decade. (See Table 22.)

129 See App. 3, Graph 15.

130 See above, sec. 1, on the consolidation of 1700–25.

131 Merchants were still outfitting the occasional trader during this peri-od. Ten years later, however, credit was restricted to professional traders, and others had to accept the status of wage-labourers.

132 See App. 3, Graph 17. Whenever no mention was made of the parish of origin of the parties to the contract, it was located through C. Tan-guay, *Dictionnaire généalogique* using a demographic event close to the date of contract: place of baptism of a child in the case of married men, of siblings in the case of bachelors, or a burial. The fact that most men were first-generation native-born facilitated the linkage procedure. Thirty-five doubtful cases, five Indians and six Detroit residents were discarded, leaving 622 men with families in various parts of the colony.

133 Especially Cap-de-la-Madelaine, Champlain, and Batiscan.

134 With the highest concentration in Boucherville.

135 There were only five Indians among the *engagés*, but there may have been more among the thirty-five who could not be traced. They appear to have been slaves with French names, and in at least one case the wages were paid to the master.

136 See also the Deniaus, Hubert-Lacroix, Tessiers, Trottiers, Saint-Yves, and Vandrys from Montreal, as well as the Ménards, Réaumes, Garea-us, and so on. Three married Rivard brothers went west with their sons and nephews, totalling fourteen participants in that single kin group between 1708 and 1717.

137 Occupations are rarely stated on the contracts or in Tanguay's diction-ary. From other sources I was able to find this information for Mont-realers, but not for the rest.

138 This last group would make the rounds of the Indian settlements, where arms and utensils always needed fixing. A.J.E. Lunn, "The Illegal Fur Trade Out of New France 1713–1760," CHAR (1939): 61–76.

139 For example, Pachot, Mailhot, Robutel, Trottier, Gamelin, Lemoyne, and Perthuis all had sons who figured among the voyageurs between 1708 and 1717.

140 See App. 3, Graph 16.

141 The mean age was 29.2, though the figure is meaningless since this was not the first voyage for many of these men. Given the large proportion of new recruits, the modal age is more significant. The parents were not present when those legally under-age signed on. In

only a few instances did merchants insist that the father guarantee the loan. See the contract of 1 Oct. 1713, Not. Rec., A. Adhémar.

142 Between 1 and 1.5 per cent, according to Duvillard's tables.

143 *Relations par lettres de l'Amérique septentrionale, années 1709 et 1710*, 8.

144 There were some attempts to minimize the risks between Montreal and the outposts by sending out convoys, but isolated canoes often departed before or after the flotillas or in the off-season.

145 Taking for granted that the traders' earnings were superior to those of their *engagés*, and since an experienced canoeman earned up to 400 livres, traders should have netted at least 500 livres of profits annually.

146 Later on, in the eighteenth century, the employer paid more for those who paddled at the rear and less for the new recruits seated in the middle. Although such distinctions may already have been in effect, they were not yet spelled out in the contracts.

147 See, for example, the accounts of G. Longpré, Stébesse, and Brisebois, in Monière's account books, NA, M-847.

148 About thirty beavers. See the indentureships made by La Forest, La Tourette, and Cadillac from 1686 on. Not. Rec., Maugue and A. Adhémar.

149 Indentureship contracts by Rocbert on behalf of the Compagnie de la Colonie, 30 May 1705, ibid., A. Adhémar; and by Dumontier, 10 July 1703, ibid.

150 Based on 109 fur-trade indentureship contracts in J.-B. Adhémar's notarial records, 1714–16.

151 See chap. 13, sec. 5. In the colony a labourer employed all year round, with room and board provided, earned at most 125 livres, while a trip west would earn him 250 livres, his own little barter included.

152 See H.A. Innis, *The Cod Fisheries: The History of an International Economy* (Toronto 1954), and *The Fur Trade in Canada*; W.T. Easterbrook and H.C.J. Aitken, *Canadian Economic History* (Toronto 1956); M.H. Watkins, "A Staple Theory of Economic Growth," in W.T. Easterbrook and M.H. Watkins, *Approaches to Canadian Economic History* (Toronto 1969), 49–74; V.C. Fowke, in *Canadian Agricultural Policy: The Historical Pattern* (Toronto 1946), provides some interesting insights.

153 See Pierre Vilar's discussion of these questions in *La Catalogne dans L'Espagne moderne: Recherches sur les fondements économiques des structures nationales* (Paris 1962), III, passim but espec. 9–12.

CHAPTER SIX

1 Raoul Blanchard, *Etudes canadiennes: L'Ouest du Canada français. Montréal et sa région* (Montreal 1953); P. Lajoie and R. Baril, *Les Sols de l'île de Montréal, de l'île Jésus et de l'île Bizard* (Ottawa 1956).

2 In 1664 Pierre Boucher described Montreal's black soil and how well suited it was to growing melons and onions. *Histoire véritable et naturelle des moeurs et productions du pays de la Nouvelle-France, vulgairement dite le Canada*, Société historique de Boucherville, no. 1 (1964), 232. In the twentieth century, after centuries of neglect, this properly drained soil permitted the development of market gardening.

3 The first yields following clearing were high on the poor and sandy soils of the lower St Lawrence. Montreal's comparative advantage only became apparent over time, and after the necessary improvements.

4 The earliest descriptions confuse meadows and marshes. The terms "mouillères" and "prairies noyées" appear interchangeably in the texts. See the declarations for the 1666 *aveu et dénombrement*, NA, M.G. 17, A7, 2, 3, vol. 2, passim. For a reference to the beavers, see the deed of 29 Nov. 1701, Not. Rec., A. Adhémar.

5 They included the fort mill and that of the Côteau Saint-Louis, built before 1657, Not. Rec., Basset, 10 Jan. 1658; the Sainte-Anne mill at Pointe Saint-Charles, ibid., A. Adhémar, 12 Sept. 1703, and Raimbault, 19 July 1707; that of Lachine, built in 1670, ibid., Basset, 11 June 1670; that of Pointe-aux-Trembles, built about the same time, ibid., 5 Apr. 1677; of Rivière-des-Prairies, ibid., Raimbault, 22 Feb. 1707; and at the end of the island, ibid., Basset, 19 Aug. 1686. These were all the windmills built in the seventeenth century, and the returns, though uneven, were considered better than those of the two or three water mills.

6 Louis-Edmond Hamelin, *Le Canada*, (Paris 1969), 12ff.

7 At first, the nuns of the Hôtel-Dieu had to toast their bread to defrost it while water froze inside the jugs within fifteen minutes. Soeur Marie Morin, *Annales de l'Hôtel-Dieu de Montréal*, 122. The Sulpicians only had one heated room where their ten or so priests huddled together when they read or worked. Letter of M. de Bretonvilliers, 17 Mar. 1676, ASSP, XIII:3–36. The settlers' log cabins, which had no floors or fireplaces, only shielded them from the snow. See chap. 9, sec. 1.

8 Ordinance of Duchesneau, 27 Aug. 1680, ASSM, copy Faillon H 593–4, and another by Raudot, 22 June 1706, *Edits, ordonnances royaux*, II.

9 Things have not really changed in Quebec. Roofs need to be redone, houses shift, beams cave in, impassable streets or roads have to be repaired, involving large expenditures each spring. It is hardly surprising, therefore, that such damages could not be prevented in the seventeenth century, although people were quick to put the blame on the masons and carpenters.

10 The Montreal court went into recess from mid-April to the end of May in the sowing season.

11 There are a minimum of 160 frost-free days.

12 C. de Rochemonteix, *Relations par lettres de l'Amérique septentrionale, années 1709 et 1710,* 14.

13 Imported glass panes were limited to those better off.

14 Two ordinances by the intendant dated 2 Sept. 1670 and 17 Jan. 1671, registered at the *bailliage,* forbade the cutting of oaks before they had been inspected by the royal shipwrights, but the regulations were never enforced. Massicotte, *Répertoire des arrêts.*

15 Based on the buildings described in notarial records. See also Boucher, *Histoire véritable et naturelle des moeurs,* 34–50. Jacques Rousseau, "La forêt mixte du Québec dans la perspective historique," *Cahiers de géographie du Québec* 13 (Oct. 1962–Mar. 1963): 111–20.

16 Currants, strawberries, and raspberry bushes grew on the fringes of cleared plots, as did blueberries.

17 Soeur Marie-Morin, *Annales de l'Hôtel-Dieu de Montréal,* 121–2; as well as de Rochemonteix, *Relations par lettres de l'Amérique septentrionale,* 13–29.

18 The judge split the moose in two between the plaintiffs and the hunters. Report of 19 Mar. 1695, *bailliage,* ser. 2, reg. 3, fol. 255. Post-mortem inventories include neither salted nor smoked venison. Winter prices run as follows: 4 sols for a pound of beef or moose, 8 sols for partridge, and 6 sols for chicken.

19 H.P. Biggar, *The Works of Samuel de Champlain,* 6 vols. (Toronto 1922–36), II:176.

CHAPTER SEVEN

1 The Société de Notre-Dame held the seigneury from the Compagnie des Cent Associés, which held it from the king.

2 R.C. Harris, *The Seigneurial System in Early Canada,* 191.

3 This was the most widespread form of tenure in France and was extended to Canada in 1627. Dues known as *champarts, tasques,* and *terrages* did not exist in the colony.

4 These were private agreements, kept in the archives of the Saint-Sulpice Seminary in Montreal. An examination of all land transactions in this period shows that this was practically all that was granted at the time. Other land may have been occupied without title. E.-Z. Massicotte, "Les Premières concessions de terres à Montréal sous Maisonneuve, 1648–1665," *TCRS* (19143): 215ff; NA, M.G. 17, A7, 2, 3, vol. I, passim.

5 E.-M. Faillon, *Histoire de la colonie française au Canada,* vols. II and III.

6 These are the terms of the governor's (Maisonneuve's) ordinance of 14 Nov. 1662. Massicotte, *Répertoire des arrêts.* But a letter sent by Voyer

d'Argenson on 4 Aug. 1659 indicates that this agreement had already existed for several years. ASSP, copy Faillon x 141.

7 Two hundred arpents were being tilled in 1659, where "the produce did not go solely to the Society because they had been cleared by people who had been granted the fruit of their labour." Ibid.

8 Agreements of 11 Nov. 1657, 15 Aug., 5 Oct., 2 Dec. 1659, 1 Dec. 1662, and 25 Apr. 1663. Not. Rec., Basset.

9 On this particular question, see the minutes of the lawsuit between Jobar and Charles Lemoyne of 10 Nov. 1662, bailliage, copy Faillon KK 292. For the several transactions concerning these rights, see the deeds of 5 Nov. 1658, 18 Feb., 4 Mar., and 24 Aug. 1675,. 20 Feb. 1676, and so on. Not. Rec., Basset. For the movement in prices, see below chap. 11, sec. 2.

10 Freedom was sometimes contingent on the acceptance of such an agreement. Deed of 1 Mar. 1663, Not. Rec., Basset.

11 Decree of 18 July 1664, NA, M-1654, sec. III, no. 1.

12 People even built on each other's property: 17 June 1649, Not. Rec., Saint-Père. It was quite common for a settler to own the right to an arpent of A's land, and another on B's, and a house on C's land.

13 Lawsuit between Jean Leduc and M. Hurtubise, 1688, bailliage, ser. 2, reg. 1, appealed to the Sovereign Council, 17 Jan. 1689. JDCS, vol. III. Ordinance of 11 May 1676, in Massicotte, Répertoire des arrêts.

14 Intendant's ordinance of 1 Nov. 1666, in P.-G. Roy, Ordonnances, commissions, etc., I:47.

15 It is impossible to know the exact number of concessions between 1665 and 1680 because few of these private agreements have survived.

16 There are scattered references to these concession tickets, but the deeds have not survived and we cannot tell if they were issued systematically.

17 Register of censitaires, 1697–1708, ASSM; Aveu et dénombrement of 1731, RAPQ (1941–42): 3-176.

18 Following the publication of Marcel Trudel's Le Régime seigneurial (Ottawa 1956), textbooks have described the Canadian seigneury as a means of populating the colony, although that was not its purpose. The ordinances that forced seigneurs to grant their land or else lose their fief never went into effect. Concessions were unavoidable, since a pool of labour had to exist on the seigneury before a seigneur could find tenants for his domain.

19 Post-mortem inventory of B. Juillet, 20 June 1660, Not. Rec., Basset.

20 At the end of the seventeenth century, uncleared plots in undevelopped areas went for 2 livres an arpent, meaning the cens and rentes to which they were subject. It is interesting to note that their

value was based on an artificially set rent. Uncleared properties in well-occupied areas were worth more. See land sales in the Côte-des-Neiges, 1699–1700, Not. Rec., Raimbault and A. Adhémar, passim.

21 I will be repeating in the next few pages some of the arguments that appeared in my article "L'Evolution du régime seigneurial au Canada: le cas de Montréal aux XVIIe et XVIIIe siècles," *Recherches sociographiques* 12, no. 2 (May–Aug. 1971): 143–83.

22 The rates current at first in Montreal were almost the same as those raised by the abbey of Saint-Germain-des-Prés from the fifteenth to the early sixteenth centuries, at a time when the man-to-land ratio was as favourable as it would be in the colony. Yvonne Bézard, *La Vie rurale dans le sud de la région parisienne de 1450 à 1560* (Paris 1929), 93. See also the tenures in the forests of Orléans from the end of the sixteenth century to the beginning of the seventeenth century, which owed 8 to 12 deniers per arpent. Georges Lefebvre, *Etudes orléannaises: contribution à l'étude des structures sociales à la fin du XVIIIe siècle*, 36.

23 This is worth comparing to the examples cited by P. de Saint-Jacob in *Les Paysans de la Bourgogne du Nord au dernier siècle de l'Ancien Régime* (Paris 1960), 38–40.

24 See the contracts signed with Milot, Tailhandier, Saint-Père, Gadois, Prudhomme, and Richaume between 1648 and 1650. NA, M.G.17, A7, 2, 3, vol. 1.

25 "With the obligation to bring every year to the dwellings of the said seigneurs 6 deniers tournois of cens per arpent ... as well as three capons in rent." Concession deed of 2 Dec. 1667, ASSM, copy Faillon, DD 267. "It is essential to convert to wheat or to other grains or fowl, the cens and rentes of every concession ... because this will steadily increase the seigneurs' revenues as every seigneur in France has learned." Letter from M. Magnien, 5 Apr. 1702, ASSP, XIV:412.

26 "The said property owes 1 livre 10 sols in cash and 1.5 minots of wheat for every twenty arpents, as non-repurchasable seigneurial cens and rente." Concession of 5 Nov. 1750, Not. Rec., Danré de Blanzy.

27 Letters to Messieurs Leschassier and Magnien of 5 Apr. 1677 and 5 Apr. 1702, ASSP, XIII:74, and XIV:412.

28 The average in the Saint-Joseph *côte* ought to have been 3 and not 10 deniers. These properties received more acreage at an increased rate, and several had to sign a new deed.

29 Answer to a Canadian report, NA, M-1584, 88.

30 F.-J. Cugnet, *Traité de la loi des fiefs qui a toujours été suivie en Canada* (Quebec 1775), 44. This is a fundamental work on the question. The author, a seigneur, wrote it for the British subjects to help them make the best from the seigneuries they acquired.

31 Letter from M. Magnien of 6 June 1723, NA, M.G.17, A7, 2, 1, II:735.

32 Harris, *The Seigneurial system*, 71.

33 For more on the Communauté des Habitants, see below, chap. 12, sec. 4.

34 According to the statement of the Seminary's holdings and fees in 1701 (copy Faillon R 612), a document I cite with reservations. Most transactions involved plots that had barely been improved. They therefore brought in only minimal profit for the seigneurs, although these eventually added up. Most of the revenues came from *lods et ventes* on the sale of urban property.

35 M. Magnien, 6 June 1716 and 10 Apr. 1720, NA, M.G.17, A7, 2, 1, II:497, 614. Transfer fees were collected not only on actual sales but on redeemable ground-rent leases, annuities, gifts of payment, sales between fathers and sons prior to the division of an estate, etc. The seigneurs were as eager to levy these fees as the censitaires were to evade them. Relying on the Coutume and commentaries to support their claim, they demanded payment of the *lods* on cessions between co-heirs who contravened formalities, on donations *inter vivos*, on sales disguised as leases and so on. See the numerous arguments about these rights in ibid., I:315, and II:198–500, 690; ibid., M-1584, no. 77.

36 Louis XIV established these new fees on his domains by a series of edicts and allowed seigneurs in the rest of the kingdom to levy them on their lands as long as they paid him a certain sum, should such fees prove contrary to local custom. The Sulpicians did not have to pay for this right because they had ceded to the Crown their judicial prerogatives. *Oeuvres de Pothier*, IX:764; F. de Boutaric, *Traité des droits seigneuriaux et des matières féodales* (Nîmes 1781), 140–1; M. Marion, *Dictionnaire des institutions de la France aux XVIIe et XVIIIe siècles*, 2nd ed. (Paris 1969), 195.

37 Ordinance of 23 Aug. 1667, P.-G. Roy, *Ordonnances, commissions*, I:70. The tithe had never been levied at one-thirteenth in Montreal, but in August 1668 a communal assembly agreed to set aside the twenty-first sheaf of wheat and oats as the tithe. That decision was revoked, and the rate was fixed at 1 / 26 on wheat, oats, peas, and maize. APND, cahier A, 42. The lower rate was supposed to remain in effect only twenty years, yet despite pressure from the bishops, the Sovereign Council retained it throughout. Decree of 18 Nov. 1705, *Edits, ordonnances royaux*, II.

38 In the French countryside tithes often rose as high as 8 to 10 per cent; the tithes on new lands varied from 21/2 to 3 per cent, and during the eighteenth century new lands would be exempt for the first twenty years.

39 See below, chap. 12, sec. 3.

40 F.-J. Cugnet, *Traité de la loi des fiefs*, 42.

41 Letter from M. Magnien, 6 June 1723, NA, M.G. 17, A7, 2, 1, II:722.

42 After the Conquest, British officials would abolish seigneurial courts. The Sulpicians and other fief owners were quite distressed. NA, M-1584, sec. 3.

43 The edict ordered seigneurs to build "banal mills." Cugnet, *Traité de la loi des fiefs*, 36–7.

44 Several studies show that it varied between one-sixteenth and one twenty-fourth.

45 Grains purchased to nourish the troops were given preference, as were those of any important personage.

46 Ordinance of the *bailli* of 8 Feb. 1672, *bailliage*, ser. 1, reg. 1; letter of M. Leschassier, 18 Mar. 1705, ASSP,m XIV:344. Report of 1717, NA, M-1584, no. 86. Proceedings of 22 and 26 Mar., 14 May, 21 June 1697, and so on, *bailliage*, ser. 2, reg. 3; letters from M. Magnien, 26 Mar. 1706, NA, M.G. 17, A7, 2, 1, II:355–66, 496.

47 The privilege could not be farmed out. Otherwise, it might well have been organized as a monopoly.

48 Intendant's ordinance of 27 Sept. 1678, NA, M-1584, no. 32. See also the report on the running of the seigneury, 1712–13, ibid., no. 85; various leases, ibid., sec. IV, nos. 21–2, and lawsuits, nos. 80 and 83.

49 This was no mere convention, although the process cannot be quantified, for expropriation rarely appears in the records except in the case of renewed subinfeudation.

50 Decisions of 10 Nov. 1707 and 5 May 1717, AC, G1, fol. 462; F.-J. Cugnet, *Traité de la loi des fiefs*, 20.

51 Letter from M. Magnien, 1705, NA, M.G. 17, 2, 1, I:342. One should keep in mind that these *retraits* or expropriations were not intended as in Europe to increase the domain. See L. Verriest, *Le Régime seigneurial dans le comté de Hainaut du XIe siècle à la Révolution* (Louvain 1956), 172–3; Louis Merle, *La Métairie et l'évolution de la Gâtine poitevine de la fin du Moyen Age à la Révolution* (Paris 1958), 52–6.

52 The repossession of vacant lots, called *droit de réunion*, was legalized by a decree of 6 July 1711. *Edits, ordonnances royaux*, I:324–6. The seigneurs of Montreal had been doing it since 1675.

53 Land with a few felled trees was recovered with no further formality; more complicated cases, where the property had been worked on, belonged to under-age children, or carried mortgages, were examined by the intendant or by a judge. See the minutes of the Conseil de la marine, 31 Mar. 1716, concerning forty-eight vacant farms on seigneuries belonging to the Sulpicians, AC, G1, vol. 462. Since the intendant did not reside in Montreal, such cases dragged on. The seigneurs complained and in 1716 obtained the right to have the issue settled by a local judge. BN, mss fr., 23664, minutes des sessions du conseil de la Régence, 5 May 1716; M. Magnien, 6 June 1716, NA, M.G. 17, A7, 2, 1,

II:480–501; suits to reclaim about twenty-five abandoned properties, 1706–08, NA, M-1584m, nos. 57, 64, and 71.

54 Petition by the seigneurs to the judge to carry out appraisals, 5 Apr. 1710, NA, M-1584, no. 74.

55 See the wording of the concession deeds, notarial records, passim, as well as the letters from M. Magnien of 1 June 1715 and 6 June 1716, NA, M.G. 17, A7, 2, 1, II:455, 494.

56 This privilege was upheld by several decisions of the intendant cited by Cugnet, *Traité de la loi des fiefs*, 52. A commission of inquiry correctly reported in 1843 that the privilege appeared after 1711. *Pièces et documents relatifs à la tenure seigneuriale* (Quebec 1852), I:34.

57 Marc Bloch, *Les Caractères originaux de l'histoire rurale française*, 2 vols. (Paris 1961), I:137.

58 Adjudication of the tithes and seigneurial dues, 12 Aug. 1705, ASSP, copy Faillon, II91; contract of 12 Dec. 1684, Not. Rec., Maugue; and of 20 Jan. 1689 and 9 Sept. 1704, ibid., A. Adhémar.

59 Letter from Magnien, 18 June 1718, NA, M.G 17, A7,. 2, 1, II:560, and report on the running of the seigneury, 1716–17, NA, M-1584, no. 85.

60 Cited by M. Leschassier (1716), NA, M-1584, no. 85.

CHAPTER EIGHT

1 In the seventeenth century, the term "habitation" was also used for an entire seigneury.

2 Pierre Deffontaines, *L'Homme et l'hiver au Canada* (Paris 1957), 92; and *Le Rang: Type de peuplement rural au Canada français* (Quebec 1953).

3 L.F. Gates, *Land Policies of Upper Canada* (Toronto 1968). R.C. Harris, who carefully studied settlement patterns in Canada before the Conquest, did not notice strict parallel alignments either. *The Seigneurial System in Early Canada*, 176–88.

4 They were, from east to west, Fort Cuillerier, built around 1676; Fort Rémy, built around 1670 on the arrière-fief originally granted to Cavelier de la Salle; Fort Rolland, built around the same time, and Fort de la Présentation, which housed the old Gentilly mission, built around 1668. D. Girouard, *Lake St. Louis, Old and New* (Montreal 1893). All the forts on the island consisted of large palisade enclosures that included a few permanent buildings and a number of huts occasionally used as temporary shelters.

5 There were over one hundred farms on the southwestern side of the island in 1721, but only forty-five resident families. Ile Perrot and other small islands in Lake of Two Mountains can be included in the western part of the seigneury. These had for a long time served merely as outposts for illegal fur trading. The name of one of these

islands, "Petit Gain" (small gain), speaks clearly of the activities of its owners. Concession deed, 15 Feb. 1684, Not. Rec., Basset; "Procès-verbal sur la commodité et l'incommodité ... des paroisses," by M.-B. Collet, 19 Feb. 1721, RAPQ (1921–22): 262ff.

6 Besides the church and windmill, there were also a few houses and huts at Fort Rémy in Lachine, Pointe-Claire, and Rivière-des-Prairies. Yet, as in Pointe-aux-Trembles, it took a while for basic services to develop. Fur traders, carters, and artisans who settled on the western side of the island lived on their farms.

7 The habitant, Denonville wrote, "likes having elbow-room near his wood or his field, without anyone looking on." 27 Oct. 1687, AC, C11A, 9, fol. 127v.

8 These geographic and economic factors did not escape R.C. Harris, who nevertheless unfortunately begins with a lengthy discussion of the habitants' insubordination, which sheds no light on the question of scattered habitat. *The Seigneurial System in Early Canada*, 178–86.

9 Deffontaines, *Le Rang*, 98.

10 The power of attorney granted the supérieur général of the Montreal Seminary on 17 June 1701 stated that he should stick to 60 arpents as a general rule and never grant more than 120 arpents, whatever pressures were applied. ASSP, copy Faillon, GG 165.

11 Thus the 1:10 ratio between the width and the length of a field expressed by the English measures of furlong and rod. Gaston Roupnel, *Histoire de la campagne française* (Paris 1932), 174–9.

12 Roads were no problem in winter, for travellers could cross the fields on the hard, windswept snow. The roads were not kept up. It is therefore difficult to link the initial shape of the farms to "snow clearance," as does Deffontaines, *L'Homme et l'hiver au Canada*, 89.

13 Harris, *The Seigneurial System in Early Canada*, 119–21.

14 A household needed between 12 and 20 cords of wood, representing about 50 cubic meters. That is what landowners had their farmers deliver each winter. P. Deffontaines, *L'Homme et l'hiver au Canada*, 79. Darrett B. Rutman estimates that three-fifths of an acre were used in New England, where winters were both shorter and milder. *Husbandmen of Plymouth: Farms and Villages in the Old Colony, 1620–1692* (Boston 1967), 42.

15 A few properties were granted for that very purpose: *bail à cens* to P. Gadois, 5 Nov. 1667, Not. Rec., Basset. Religious communities made the most demands. Their requests annoyed the seigneurs, who refused to grant the most outrageous. See the letter dated 7 Mar. 1701, ASSP, XIV:417; report of 1712–13, NA, M-1584, no. 77; letters by M. Magnien, 1 June 1715 and 6 June 1716, NA, M.G. 17, A7, 2, 1, I:455, 494–5.

16 Commission registered on 20 Jan. 1682, *bailliage*, ser. 1, reg. 2.

17 See App. 3. This *côte* included three large properties granted to the Hôtel-Dieu and Hôpital général which do not appear on graph 18.

18 See App. 3, Graph 19.

19 See App. 3, Graph 20.

20 Post-mortem inventory of M. Leclerc, J. Blois' wife, of 27 Sept. 1704, Not. Rec., Raimbault; division of Blois' property, 21 Oct. 1719, ibid., Le Pailleur.

21 Raoul Blanchard, *Etudes canadiennes: La plaine de Montréal* (Montreal 1953). The author was relying on Canadian censuses and so does not go back further than the late nineteenth century. Comparisons with the present are impossible, the area having been invaded by towns and suburbs.

22 Kenneth A. Lockridge, *A New England Town: The First Hundred Years* (New York 1970), 71.

CHAPTER NINE

1 The following hypothetical example is based on the analysis of about fifty land-clearing transactions, signed between 1650 and 1720 by a variety of inhabitants. It also relies on property descriptions found in leases, estimates of movables, post-mortem inventories, and sales. The sources also provide descriptions of the buildings.

2 "Cabane" is the name assigned in the records to this type of building.

3 This involved cutting round the bark and cambium at ground level. The same methods were used by the Plymouth settlers. See D.B. Rutman, *Husbandmen of Plymouth: Farms and Villages in the Old Colony 1620–1692* (Boston 1969), 7.

4 Catalogue report on the seigneuries, 1715, AC, F3, vol. 2, fols. 386–7.

5 Contemporaries reckoned that an average of two arpents was cleared each year. Lucien Campeau, "Un témoignage de 1651 sur la Nouvelle-France," RHAF 23, no. 4 (Mar. 1970): 601–2. Martin L. Primack has calculated that in the 1860s in the United States it took thirty-three man-days to clear an acre (about one arpent). Given that there were other things to do, he assigns a maximum of five acres a year. Although methods have remained much the same, men were stronger two centuries later, and had better tools. In Montreal, once the most urgent building had been taken care of the threshhold was around three arpents at best. M.L. Primack, "Land Clearing under Nineteenth-Century Techniques: Some Preliminary Calculations," *Journal of Economic History* 22, no. 4 (1962): 484–97.

6 Talon's ordinance of 22 May 1667 required that two arpents be felled and cultivated each year. Roy, *Ordonnances, commissions*, 1:66.

7 This required capital of 200 to 250 livres for the first eighteen months

and at least as much over the next two years to buy animals, seed, hay, and so forth.

8 Around 1670 the intendant paid top price for ashes to make potash, so that a burnt arpent could bring in a 30-livre profit. This agreement, which weighed heavily on the Treasury, only lasted two or three years and only benefited colonists around Quebec. Report made by the Intendant Talon in 1673, AN, C11A, 4, fols. 32–43. Montreal had no potash works. The ash remained on the ground and enriched the soil. It was also used for the domestic manufacture of soap.

9 At best we can determine some relative costs. A land-clearer with room and board received 10 livres for every arpent he felled, another 10 to turn the same soil, and a further 25 to put it under plough. This last step was the longest and most expensive. Guardianship accounts, 25 Jan. 1677, Judicial Archives, *Tutelles et curatelles*, I: minutes of 13 Mar. 1684, *JDCS*, vol. 2, 933.

10 Or he might be remunerated for specific tasks: so many livres for felling and clearing one arpent, "déserter et nettoyer un arpent." The same wording is used in fifteenth-century contracts in the countryside south of Paris. Yvonne Bézard, *La Vie rurale dans le sud de la région parisienne de 1450 à 1560*, 145.

11 Clauses varied from one lease to the next. The tenant was sometimes compelled and at other times allowed to clear land. Under no circumstances was he to open up new land as he pleased. All leases manifest the same concern to protect wooded areas. See, for example, the leases dated 23 Sept. 1668, 17 Mar. 1676, Not. Rec., Basset; and 13 Sept. 1699, ibid., A. Adhémar; or 14 July 1720, ibid., Le Pailleur.

12 See App. 3, Graphs 21 and 22.

13 Louis Merle, *La Métairie et l'évolution de la Gâtine poitevine de la fin du Moyen Age à la Révolution*, 107.

14 It lay between 2 and 3 per cent annually between 1667 and 1739. See App. 3, Graph 24.

15 Obviously they are not proprietors in the full sense of the word since on this seigneurial land there were only hereditary landholders, or censitaires, and some ten vassals. This percentage is based on the number of owners and not on the number of lots. The distribution in terms of acreage is not provided in the 1697 roll but only in the *Aveu* of 1731, where, however, the censitaires are poorly identified. Thus this last measure cannot be used.

16 The Congregation nuns owned about 700 arpents in 1697, and the Hôtel-Dieu 500. The seigneurs used over 1,000 arpents. The relative weight of church property increased as time went on.

17 Until 1680, for example, the seigneurs managed their lands and hired labour. The system had to be properly overseen, and the supérieur

général insisted that the land be farmed out. Letter of M. Tronson, 26 May 1682, ASSP, XIII:284.

18 R.C. Harris also mentions that about one-fifth of censives were occasionally leased at Sainte-Famille on the Ile d'Orléans, but does not raise the possibility of urban ownership. The greater the distance from Montreal or Quebec, the less likely was this type of arrangement.

19 *RAPQ* (1921–22): 262ff.

20 The former include Jean Fournier, Milot's farmer, Molinier and Jacques Morin, who farmed the seigneurs' property, Thomas Monnier, Saint-Yves, and so on.

21 See the case of Paul Dazé, the seigneurs' tenant farmer who signed contracts to have his land cleared, 7 Aug. and 6 Nov. 1672, Not. Rec., Basset.

22 See the deeds of 29 Dec. 1681 and 1 Nov. 1682, ibid., Maugue; land sale to Renouart, the Hôtel-Dieu farmer, 26 May 1684, ibid., Basset.

23 Short-term leases would not always be consigned in notarized contracts. They cannot therefore be quantified. We often see the following sentence in leases – "Ladite terre que led. preneur a dit connaistre pour estre en sa possession depuis longtemps" (the property that the taker says he knows he has occupied for a long time) – without being able to locate the earlier agreement. All we can say is that is was extremely rare for leases to be renewed beyond a second term. See the lease of 20 July 1719, ibid., Le Pailleur.

24 This local custom spread gradually and was definitely adopted by the middle of the eighteenth century. See below, chap. 13, sec. 8.

25 I took a sample of some one hundred leases, meaning all those signed between 1660 and 1680, in 1690, and between 1716 and 1720, from the records of the following notaries: Basset, Maugue, A. Adhémar, Raimbault, Tailhandier, Le Pailleur, and David.

26 There were only four in the sample, including that of the fermier général of the seigneurie de Lachenaye. Ibid., Adhémar, 19 July 1689; Basset, 13 Nov. 1675. Meadows were usually leased for cash. See below, chap. 10, sec. 2.

27 Pierre de Saint-Jacob observed the same thing, *Les Paysans de la Bourgogne du Nord*, 42.

28 The word "métairie" was used by religious communities to refer to the lands they managed themselves or farmed out for a fixed sum. They sometimes used the term "grange." See, for example, the lease of 5 June 1672, Not. Rec., Basset.

29 Pierre Goubert, "Les Campagnes françaises," in Braudel and Labrousse, *Histoire économique et sociale de la France*, II:142, and Merle, *La Métairie*, passim.

30 The bishop railed against this practice. See the pastoral against usury, 3 Mar. 1700, ASSM, copy Faillon H 645.

31 Lawsuits for unpaid rent shot up in 1692–93. Some rents were reduced. Suits at the *bailliage* court, 1692, ser. 2, reg. 2, fols. 607v, 613v, 109, 429, 649v, 412v, etc.

32 Abel Poitrineau, *La Vie rurale en Basse Auvergne au XVIIIe siècle (1726–1789)* (Paris 1965), 171–4.

33 The owner also received half the wool if there were any sheep, but there were no more than three or four herds on the island in the seventeenth century. All these extra burdens resemble the *suffrages* in Poitou, described by Merle, *La Métairie*, 169–75.

34 Owners hired labourers to prepare the firewood. The tenant was only responsible for the cartage.

35 Hogs on the feast of St Michael or All-Saints Day; capons on St Martin's Day; eggs in springtime, summer, and fall; wood in winter; grain between Christmas and Candlemas or Easter, in several deliveries, first to the mill and then from the mill to the owner's residence.

36 Lease of Saint-Gabriel, 6 Dec. 1704, renewed 6 Dec. 1708, Not. Rec., Raimbault.

37 There is, however, a very liberal lease granted by the Jesuits allowing the taker to have the two horses haul for his own profit. Ibid., Le Pailleur, 14 Apr. 1720.

38 I did not account for fertility and geographic location. In the seventeenth century the latter certainly benefited landowners who owned properties close to the town. But fertility was high enough everywhere on the island, and few areas could be considered marginal.

39 In terms of cultivated land, religious communities increased their holdings, but most remained uncultivated. The Hôtel-Dieu is a good example of such negligence.

40 Tenant book, ASSM. Some had farms outside the seigneury, but at least 40 per cent of the people in these social categories had no rural property, and whenever a merchant seized some land, he quickly resold it.

41 Urban properties also conferred the status of habitant, but they had to be bought, whereas rural holdings were free.

42 This is where geographic location came into play. A farm located in an inhabited *côte* was worth more than a recently granted censive in some far-off place.

43 For example, the land of the baker Etienne Forestier at Rivière-des-Prairies. Inventory of 6 Mar. 1700, Not. Rec., A. Adhémar.

44 Seigneurs' ordinances of 20 May 1673 and 12 Jan. 1675, with a supplementary intendant's ordinance of 30 Oct. 1676. NA, M-1584; intendant's ordinance, 24 Aug. 1682, Roy, *Ordonnances, commissions*, 1:308–10.

45 Declaration of 25 June 1694, Not. Rec., A. Adhémar.

46 For example, Etienne Pothier, who spent five years with his family on a Lachine farm, went into debt, and left. Seigneurs repossessed the

land and his heirs protested. Petition of 21 Aug. 1697, NA, M.G. 17, A7, 2, 3, vol. 5, 34–5.

47 Since land prices dropped throughout the whole period, this was rarely worthwhile, and there were few settlers in this category. The case of Jean Hardouin, an unmarried ex-*engagé* who concluded five real-estate transactions within nine months that left him with a 200-livre debt, whereupon he disappeared, illustrates the dangers of this sort of speculation. Deeds of Oct. 1668, 18 Jan., 1 Feb., 28 Feb., and 23 June 1669, Not. Rec., Basset.

48 One censitaire "begged the Seigneurs to allow him to abandon a certain habitation he had acquired in *côte* Saint-Sulpice ... since he was unable and unwilling to cultivate it." Ibid., Raimbault, 13 Mar. 1710.

49 Exchanges formed another relatively important category of transactions (as high as one-quarter of sales) and are more difficult to interpret. In general, properties that were exchanged had less value than those that were sold.

50 For a long time other seigneuries had no notaries and the residents used those of Montreal.

51 The sellers disobeyed the ordinances forbidding the sale of uncultivated land, which were never applied. There were no sanctions, and according to customary law the habitants were within their rights.

52 In such cases the merchant who employed them often bought the land on their behalf through an advance on their wages. Sales to Jacques Henry and Pierre Lelat financed by Couagne, 17 Jan. and 20 Aug. 1700, Not. Rec., A. Adhémar; sale to Michel Baribeau, Monière's *engagé*, in his account books, May 1720, NA, M-847.

53 For example, the voyageurs Jacques Cardinal, Joseph Leduc, Antoine Trudel, Louis Hubert-Lacroix, and Nicolas Duclos, who bought land worth between 1,200 and 10,000 livres, 29 Dec. 1675, Not. Rec., Basset; 24 Apr. 1687 and 24 Dec. 1703, ibid., A. Adhémar; 27 Jan. 1691, ibid., Pottier.

54 R.C. Harris did the same for seventy-one censives at Sainte-Famille d'Orléans. One-third of these properties were sold within ten years. Harris, *The Seigneurial System in Early Canada*, 141–4. In the Seigneury of Notre-Dame-des-Anges, half the land changed owners in the first years. Ibid.

55 It is easy to trace property from father to son, less so when a son-in-law took over. I may have made a few errors of identification but not enough to skew the overall picture.

56 R.C. Harris observed a four-phase cycle in the movement of acreage near Quebec: original size, extension, subdivision, and final equilibrium of a holding somewhat larger than the original. *The Seigneurial*

System in Early Canada, 138. In Montreal the equilibrium followed the second phase and lasted at least a century.

57 This assumption has been shared by a number of anglophone writers and is illustrated by the following: "Subdivision of frontage generation after generation at last meant farms of infinite length and no breadth. There is a tradition that, at one point on the St. Lawrence, one great elm tree used to shade the frontage of three farms." A.R.M. Lower, *From Colony to Nation* (Toronto 1946), 43.

58 Ordinance of 28 Apr. 1745, *Edits, ordonnances royaux*, I:585–6. Besides being based on false premises, this decree was in direct contradiction to seventeenth-century legislation that sought to bring the farms closer together.

59 Harris, *The Seigneurial System in Early Canada*, 131–6.

60 Fernand Ouellet has studied this question. See, for example, "Répartition de la propriété foncière et types d'exploitation agricole dans la seigneurie de Laprairie durant les années 1830," in *Eléments d'histoire sociale du Bas-Canada* (Montreal 1972), 114–49.

61 *Recensement du Canada de 1851.* Jean Hamelin and Yves Roby, *Histoire économique du Québec 1851–1896* (Montreal 1972), 6. Yet at this juncture forestry, which proletarianized the habitants for seven months of the year, did much to dull the old hopes of creating an ideal farm property. See Gérard Fortin, *La Fin d'un règne* (Montreal 1971), passim.

62 In France as well property proved resilient. See René Baehrel, *Une croissance: la Basse-Provence rurale (fin du XVIe siècle–1789)* (Paris 1961), 439–40.

63 For example, the successions of M. Lorion, 24 June 1680, Not. Rec., Maugue; 1 Mar. 1694, ibid., A. Adhémar; that of P. Goguet, 2 Nov. 1703, ibid.; of André Dumers, 24 July 1699, ibid.; and description of the property of the Dumers' inheritance in 1731, *RAPQ* (1942–42).

64 Division of the inheritance of F. Brunet, 16 and 17 Oct. 1703, Not. Rec., Le Pailleur.

65 This was an expensive procedure. At the end of the seventeenth century four to ten properties were auctioned a year, mainly in town. See the adjudication of P. Pigeon, L. Guertin, and J. Beauchamps' possessions, 9 Mar. 1688, 6 Mar. 1692, and Apr. 1694, *bailliage*, ser. 2, reg. 1, fol. 331, reg. 2, fol. 427, and reg. 3, fol. 92.

66 Cuillerier's will, deposited with the notary Adhémar on 28 Apr. 1716.

67 Deeds touching the Baudry inheritance, 29 Aug. 1695, 16–17 Sept., 12–17 Nov. 1698, Not. Rec., A. Adhémar; description of these properties in 1731 in *RAPQ* (1941–42).

68 Philippe Leduc bought back from his brothers and sisters land in the *côte* Saint-Joseph that his father had amassed. His debt rose to 6,000 livres. The merchant de Couagne paid the other heirs right away and

Leduc's debt towards him took the form of a *rente constituée* and an *obligation* on request. Contracts of 14 and 25 May 1702, Not. Rec., Raimbault.

CHAPTER TEN

1 Pierre Goubert, *Beauvais et la Beauvaisis de 1600 à 1730*, 115.
2 Isaac Weld, *Travel through the States of North America and the Provinces of Upper and Lower Canada during the Years 1795, 1796, 1797*, 4th ed., 2 vols. (London 1807); John Lambert, *Travels through Canada and the United States of North America in the Years 1806, 1807 and 1808*, 2 vols. (London 1811); and others.
3 See Lord Ernle, *Histoire rurale de l'Angleterre* (Paris 1952), chap. 6: "Les derniers Stuarts et la Révolution"; W.G. Hoskins, "English Agriculture in the 17th and 18th Centuries," Xe *Congrès international des sciences historiques* (Rome 1955), vol. 4, 203ff.
4 As shown in chap. 9, members of all social groups, including peasants, were likely to lease out their land when the head of household died or retired. The 125 leases used in this section are sufficiently diverse to express general tendencies, and exceptional practices are noted as such. The agriculture of New France still awaits its historian. Robert-Lionel Séguin's work merely inventories the habitant's implements from the early days of the colony to the nineteenth century. *L'Equipement de la ferme canadienne aux XVIIe et XVIIIe siècles* (Montreal 1959); *La Civilisation traditionnelle de l'habitant aux XVIIe et XVIIIe siècles: Fonds matériel* (Montreal 1967); and numerous articles.
5 Sieur Liber, *La Nouvelle Maison rustique ou économie générale de tous les biens de campagne: la manière de les entretenir et de les multiplier*, 2 vols. (Paris 1792), I:463.
6 For about twenty years the settlers grew corn Indian-fashion, after which European cereals took over. Darrett B. Rutman, *Husbandmen of Plymouth: Farms and Villages in the Old Colony, 1620–1692* (Boston 1967), 7.
7 Concerning the corn and oats ground at the mills, minutes of 30 Dec. 1692 and 21 June 1697, *bailliage*, ser. 2, reg. 2, fol. 610v.–11 and reg. 3, fol. 583v.
8 Report of 2 Nov. 1671, AC, C11A, 3, fol. 166. Historians always refer to the years 1665–72 as a golden age. They argue that under the leadership of a dynamic intendant, agriculture and industry suddenly took off. Then, once Talon left, the habitants reverted to their natural lethargy. All this is based on the reports that the intendant sent to the French minister, where one is hard put to separate ambitious projects from actual achievements. By dipping into the colonial treasury, Talon

set up a number of premature undertakings that disappeared as soon as the government stopped its subsidies. This intendant had no more impact on the internal economy than did his successors. Official policy could neither create needs nor ensure the viability of what were in fact non-viable activities.

9 Report by Catalogne (1715), AC, F3, vol. 3, fol. 387.

10 See Paul-Emile Renaud, *Les Origines Economiques du Canada: l'oeuvre de la France* (Paris 1928), 352–3, based on Pehr Kalm, *Voyage de Pehr Kalm en Amérique* (Montreal 1880), I:50–1.

11 According to the census figures. Fernand Ouellet and Jean Hamelin, "La Crise agricole dans le Bas-Canada, 1802–1837," *Etudes Rurales* (1962–63): 36–57.

12 See the farm leases in A. Adhémar's notarial records, 9 July 1689 and Apr. 7 1693; in Le Pailleur's of 7 Apr. 1721 and Basset's of 23 Oct. 1658; the lawsuit by Fezeret against his tenant-farmer who did not divide his land in three sections: minutes of 9 Mar. 1700, *bailliage*, ser. 2, reg. 4, fols. 275 and 283:

13 According to land leases the proportion of wheat was greater, but is it not conceivable that the owners left the legumes and poorer cereals to the tenant, partly for feed, and took a larger share of the wheat? Another example of triennel rotation can be found on the Malbaie farm, which belonged to the Domaine d'Occident. Report from Hocquart, 1 Sept. 1733, AC, C11A, 59, fol. 366.

14 Even the most accommodating of owners demanded that the tenant leave the same amount of worked-over fallow as he had found when he came. Not. Rec., Adhémar, 14 Oct. 1688, 15 Oct. 1693; Le Pailleur, 22 Oct. 1720; minutes of 30 Sept., 11 Oct. 1695, and 11 Apr. 1698, *bailliage*, ser. 2, reg. 3, fols. 345, 351, and 759.

15 I presume that there were also more complex forms of rotation where wheat alternated with hay in a looser and much longer cycle.

16 These exceptions confirm the rule of rotation over two or three years. One owner declared that since his land had become exhausted and only produced bad wheat, he had had to let it rest for three years. Lawsuit by the Widow Dudevoir of 12 Nov. 1697, *bailliage*, ser. 2, reg. 3, fol. 694v.

17 Lease of Jean Leduc, habitant, to his son, 28 June 1700, Not. Rec., Raimbault; and Basset, 9 May 1669, 25 Aug. 1672; Le Pailleur, 19 Jan. 1716; Basset, 10 Aug. 1667; Le Pailleur, 22 Oct. 1720; David, 19 June 1721, and so on.

18 See, for example, the entry for June 1717 in their account books: receipts for 134 cartloads at 2 livres each.

19 Minutes of 19 Oct. 1696 and 2 Nov. 1697, *bailliage*, ser. 2, reg. 3, fols. 483v., 701, and 781v.

20 Slicher Van Bath, *The Agrarian History of Western Europe, 1500–1800 A.D.* (London 1963), chap. 1, passim.

21 See leases of meadows and the clauses detailing their care in farm leases, as well as the testimony of Peter Bréhaut, from Guernesey, to an inquiry into the state of agriculture in 1816. He claimed that there was not enough fertilizer because the farmers used everything they had for their vegetables and meadows. *Journal de l'Assemblée législative du Bas-Canada,* 1816, app. E. Nothing had changed.

22 Letter from Intendant De Meulles to the Court, 28 Sept. 1685, AC, C11A, 7, fol. 144.

23 Transaction of 10 Feb. 1670, Not. Rec., Basset.

24 Transactions of 15 Apr. 1665 and 5 June 1667: closure of interventories; intendant's ordinance of 3 July 1680, NA, M-1584, no. 34; petition by the residents of the *côte* Saint-Joseph, 21 June 1706, ibid., no. 56; proceedings by J. Blois against a neighbour who did not take care of his ditches, 28 Oct. 1694, *bailliage,* ser. 2, reg. 3, fol. 168v.

25 According to Jacques Rousseau and Marius Barbeau, cited by A.G. Haudricourt, *L'Homme et la charrue à travers le monde* (Paris 1955), 411. "The plough used in this region is rather adequate," the English expert noted in 1816. See n 21.

26 Isaac Weld, *Travels,* 250; John Lambert, *Travels,* I:131.

27 In the eighteenth century, horses were sometimes hitched up to a team of oxen. One commonly attached the yoke to the horns in most parts of France, especially on Poitou farms, where this was done until very recently. Louis Merle, *La métairie poitevine,* 111. It provided as much traction as harnessing with shafts and collar harnesses, and there is no need to consider this form of yoke a sign of backwardness. Marcel Trudel, *Initiation à la Nouvelle-France: Histoire et institutions* (Montreal 1968), 221; Denis Delage, "Les Structures économiques de la Nouvelle-France et de la Nouvelle-York," *L'Actualité économique* 46, no. 1 (Apr.-June 1970), 104–5.

28 Worth about one-third the one described above. One cannot tell whether the implement in question is different or merely the same one, but in a worse state.

29 A Sulpician reported that wheat had been sown on 5, 6, and 7, Apr. "although it had been very cold and there had been a strong frost." ASSP, sec. Canada, doss. 20, item 4.

30 A French agronomy manual of the period mentioned that in Canada grains and vegetables were sown with their husks, "which protected them on these new plots." This seems rather surprising, for the crops were threshed, whatever they were meant for. Sieur Liger, *La Nouvelle Maison rustique,* I:472.

31 Catalogne's report on the seigneuries (1715), AC, F3, vol. 2, fol. 387.

32 Baudry succession, 12–14 Nov. 1698, Not. Rec., A. Adhémar.

33 Report by De Meulles on Canada, AC, F3, vol. 2, fol. 202v.

34 They were paid 1 livre 10 sols for a day's harvesting, or 4 livres to cut down one arpent of wheat or oats. Accounts in the Gasteau succession, Apr. 1692, Not. Rec., A. Adhémar.

35 This was when sharecroppers had to make their first wheat delivery, and the rest followed at Candlemas or Easter.

36 P. Kalm, *Voyage de Kalm en Amérique*, 51, 118–19. Walking around Quebec, Kalm identified a mixture of *poa angusti folia* and white clover, which earned his admiration, and in Montreal, the *poa capillaris*, less dense than the above. On the origin of these plants see Marie-Victorin, *Flore laurentienne* (Montreal 1947), 360, 769–71. There was a market in Montreal for grass seed.

37 Not. Rec., David, 9 June 1721; Bourgine, 22 May 1685; Moreau, 20 May 1690; A. Adhémar, 11 June 1693; etc.

38 Lawsuit between several habitants of Lachine, when some denied others access to the communal ground, 3 June 1698, *bailliage*, ser. 2, reg. 3, fol. 779v. In Lachine, for example, only fourteen habitants had access to the 270 arpents of commons granted as meadows and reserve of wood. Contract of 21 Aug. 1697, NA, M.G. 17, A7, 2, 3, vol. 5, 34–45.

39 The residents of the Côte Saint-Joseph complained to the intendant that the seigneurs had taken away one of the communal pastures that had been theirs for the past forty-nine years: 22 June 1699, NA, M.G. 17, A7, 2, 1, vol. 1, 231–2. The same complaint was made in Lachine: July 1705, ibid., 352–4.

40 Ordinance by Raudot, 2 July 1706 and 1 July 1707, concerning Montreal's commons. *Edits, ordonnances royaux*, II:262, III:135.

41 Raudot ordinance of 8 May 1708, after the seigneury of Varennes complained that the Pointe-aux-Trembles residents were using his islets, ibid., III; minutes of 10 Nov. 1676, *bailliage*, ser. 1, reg. 1. The widow Giart declared that she owned two calves "who are on the islands but they might well be lost, for no one has seen them for a long time," post-mortem inventory, 17 July 1710, Not. Rec., A. Adhémar.

42 In 1714 the intendant observed that there were very few fences on the island of Montreal and that even the seigneurs' domain lay open. 19 June 1714, *Edits, ordonnances royaux*, II:441.

43 See the ordinances dated 25 May 1670; 14 May 1672; 28 Apr. 1674; 13 May 1679; 10 May 1686; 19 May 1687; 21 May 1690; 24 Apr. 1693; 4 May 1697; 8 May 1699; 8 May 1709; and so on. *Bailliage*, passim.

44 *Bailli*'s ordinance of 5 Oct. 1686, *bailliage*, ser. 1, reg. 2.

45 Proceedings by P. Gadois *v* Tessier concerning four oxen and two

horses that had wandered into his meadow while the cowherd was asleep. Ibid., 1 June 1686.

46 The first ordinance that allowed habitants to kill roaming pigs, probably dated from about 1663, was not located.

47 E.-Z. Massicotte, *Répertoire des arrêts*, ordinance of 19 May 1687. It was the turn of the owners of the slaughtered animals to sue. Petition by Pierre Chauvin *v* J. Blois, "who maliciously killed three of his pigs that he claimed to have found on his fields" (1690), *bailliage*, vol. 545; ibid., 23 Aug. 1695, fol. 311; 10 Nov. 1680, for a sow "killed in a stack of peas," with witnesses who swore that it had not gone there; etc.

48 Ordinance of Intendant Dupuis of 31 Oct. 1727, in *Edits, ordonnances royaux*, III:452.

49 Ordinances of the intendants, 19 June 1714 and 10 June 1724, endlessly reiterated. Ibid., II:441, 305.

50 See the regulation by the Sovereign Council, 13 Apr. 1725, the ordinances by the Montreal judge of 14 May 1741 and 11 May 1744 (copy Faillon, II 16 and SS 86); and the by-law of 1790 cited by V.C. Fowke, *Canadian Agricultural Policy: The Historical Pattern* (Toronto 1946), 101. Animals were let loose in other parts of the colony, but it seems that nowhere outside Montreal did the custom meet with official approval and last so long.

51 Paul-Emile Renaud, *Les Origines économiques du Canada: l'oeuvre de la France* (Paris 1928), 365.

52 Sixty-five inventories. Bourgeois and religious properties were not included in this table.

53 It is interesting to compare the number of cattle per capita in Montreal and in Acadia as calculated by Andrew H. Clarke, using the same method: the units varied between 0.9 and 1.4 in Montreal, whereas they were above 2.0 on most Acadian farms. Both New England and Ile Royale provided a market stimulus that did not exist for Montreal. *Acadia: The Geography of Early Nova Scotia to 1760* (Madison, Wisc. 1968), 166–75.

54 For the ration of an ox, see the contract of 8 Oct. 1673, Not. Rec., Basset.

55 R.-L. Séguin and other writers have advanced several hypotheses. The agronomic literature of the early nineteenth century should contain useful information on this question.

56 Since the new breed was shared equally, the seigneurs made about 5 to 6 per cent interest annually on their initial cattle investment, once costs had been deducted.

57 That is, 10 livres a year for animals valued at 30 livres, or a 33 per cent interest. The owner would then share the risks.

58 The declaration of 1667 forbade the seizure of plough animals. But the

habitants owned little else but their oxen. See BN, Cinq cent Colbert, 251, fols. 661–4. JDSC, vol. 1, 2 Oct. 1663, 5 Apr. 1664. The royal decree of 6 Nov. 1683, registered by the council on 12 Nov. 1686 and by the *bailliage* on 5 Mar. 1687, Massicotte, *Répertoire des arrêts*.

59 See Not. Rec., Maugue, 23 May 1691, and A. Adhémar, 4 Jan. 1700.

60 Instead of one cow and three lambs or goats, as stipulated in the kingdom. Article 14, item 32, of the ordinance of 1667, and decree of 24 Jan. 1707, *Edits, ordonnances royaux*, I, II.

61 These were partly descended from the animals imported thirty years earlier and partly from the horses that the voyageurs and militiamen brought back from Illinois (Spanish stock) or from New England. Not. Rec., Maugue, 14 May 1690; letter from the intendant, 26 May 1699, AC, C11A, 17, 87.

62 To be used for carting, harrowing, for getting about the countryside, and less often for ploughing (where horses would be coupled to a team of oxen).

63 Letter from the intendant to the Court, 1710, AC, C11A, 31, fols. 15 and 67. Ordinance of 13 June 1709. *Edits et ordonnances royaux*, II:273. In 1731, alarmed by such reports, the minister suggested that horses be taxed to keep their numbers down. Administrators then had to backtrack and declare that horses were indispensable. AC, B55, 538, and C11A, 57, 40v.

64 In Acadia the cabbages that had been pulled up were kept outside all winter long, face down. In Canada they may have been kept in cellars. Sieur de Diéreville, *Relation of the Voyage to Port-Royal in Acadia or New France* (Toronto 1933), v:241.

65 Charlevoix, *Histoire et description générale de la Nouvelle France* (Paris 1744), v:241.

66 Biography of Michel Sarrazin by Jacques Rousseau in *DCB*, vol. 2. Before his death the geographer had begun to put together some of the manuscripts for publication. A. Vallée's book, *Un Biologiste canadien, Michel Sarrazin 1659–1735* (Québec 1927), does not cover these aspects.

67 Based on Charlevoix's list, *Histoire et description générale de la Nouvelle France*, IV:299ff. His description of plants owed much to Sarrazin. See also Pierre Boucher, *Histoire véritable et naturelle des moeurs et productions du pays de la Nouvelle-France, vulgairement dite le Canada* (Paris 1664; Boucherville 1964), passim. Cattail or bullrushes: any of the genus of *Typha*.

68 Account book of the nuns of the Congrégation de Notre-Dame, 1742–45.

69 Orchard leases of 9 Feb. and 15 July 1719, Le Pailleur; letter by M. Forget, PSS, concerning the seminary's apple produce. NA, M.G. 17, A7, 2, 1, vol. 2, 367–8.

70 For a brief description of interiors and habitants' standard of living, see below, chap. 13, sec. 6.

71 Contracts for the haulage of houses and small barns, Not. Rec., Maugue, 11 Mar. 1681; Adhémar, 6 Mar. 1702; inventory of Jean Leduc, ibid., Raimbault, 26 Apr. 1702.

72 *RAPQ* (1941–42): 3–176.

73 To illustrate his thesis of an arcadian New France, W.J. Eccles claims that the habitants enjoyed iced drinks and desserts all summer. *The Canadian Frontier*, 95. Only merchants or innkeepers could stock meat in the hot season in these cedar buildings, which were insulated with straw and maintained by an outer wall of stakes, with a grid to drain the ice water. Transaction of 11 Oct. 1704, copy Faillon, DD 302; reference to the innkeeper Nafréchoux's ice house, 13 Oct. 1687, JDCS, vol. 3.

74 Louis Merle, *La Métairie poitevine*; Pierre Goubert in Braudel and Labrousse, *Histoire économique et sociale de la France*, II:108–11; Gabriel Debien, *En Haut-Poitou. Défricheurs au travail, XVe–XVIIIe siècles* (Paris 1952); Paul Bois, *Paysans de l'Ouest* (Paris 1971).

CHAPTER ELEVEN

1 These settlers did run into pockets of good land, here and there – in the Saguenay region, for example – but this was exceptional. On the whole, the marginal land that was cleared in the late nineteenth and early twentieth centuries had to be abandoned, after more than half a century of useless toil and poverty. See Raoul Blanchard's *Etudes canadiennes*.

2 Fernand Ouellet and Jean Hamelin, "Les Crises agricoles dans le Bas-Canada, 1802–1837," *Etudes rurales* (1962–63), 36–57. Several articles by Fernand Ouellet in collaboration with Jean Hamelin in Claude Galarneau and E. Lavoie, *France et Canada français du XVIe au XXe siècle* (Quebec 1966). Fernand Ouellet, *Histoire économique et sociale du Quiébec 1760–1850* (Montreal 1966). Elizabeth J. Lunn, "Agriculture and War in Canada 1740–1760," CHR 16, 123–36.

3 Reported by M. de Tronson, who warned the priests to avoid such generalizations. 13 Mar. 1683, ASSP, XIII:320.

4 *Annales de l'Hôtel-Dieu de Montréal rédigées par la soeur Morin*, 114.

5 Between 1655 and 1665, plots of one to three arpents were leased fairly frequently and the rent was set according to the area sown. Later on, rented properties grew larger, land use more diversified, and the clauses in contracts more complex, so it therefore becomes impossible to perceive this relation.

6 M. de Belmont noted a yield of between 10 and 12 to 1, 13 Mar. 1683, ASSP, XIII:320. Pehr Kalm reported a ratio of 15 to 20 minots to 1 in

1750 after his visit to Sault-au-Récollet. *Voyage de Pehr Kalm*, 221. The results of the 1793 surveys are cited by Fernand Ouellet, *Histoire économique et sociale du Québec*, 154–5.

7 Using the 1739 census, R.C. Harris calculated a seed-to-yield ratio of 1 to 4.4 on the Island of Montreal and of 1 to 9.2 in the seigneury of Notre-Dame-des-Anges, which was settled in the same period. One is equally hard put to explain why ratios were respectively 1 to 9.4 and 1 to 3.6 in the neighbouring seigneuries of Varennes and Contrecoeur, with similar soils and types of settlement. R.C. Harris, *The Seigneurial System in Early Canada: A Geographical Study* (Quebec and Madison, Wisc. 1967), 153. F. Ouellet and J. Hamelin, in "Les Crises agricoles dans le Bas-Canada, 1802–1837," assume that three-quarters of the arable land was sown over with wheat every year and do not account for the fallow. They therefore obtain lower yields than does Harris, who supposes a general biennial rotation.

8 For example, the Saint-Gabriel estate, and the farms owned by Leber, d'Ailleboust, J.-B. Migeon, Jean Milot, Nicolas Jetté, J. Messier, Richard, etc.

9 One does not have to go back to the Middle Ages to find yields as low as 4 to 1. Cole Harris, *The Seigneurial System in Early Canada*, 154.

10 The arable land in 1715 can be roughly categorized as follows: 33 per cent newly cleared plots; 16 per cent older plots with excellent yields; and 50 per cent with mediocre yields. For comparisons see Michel Morineau, *Les Faux-semblants d'un démarrage économique: agriculture et démographie en France au XVIIIe siècle* (Paris 1970), 24–31.

11 See, for example, the yields on Charles Juillet's farm during the 1691–93 crisis, trusteeship accounts, 24 Mar. 1696, Not. Rec., A. Adhémar.

12 This is the explanation offered by Fernand Ouellet and Cole Harris. But one might bring up the Acadians, who arrived in the middle of the seventeenth century from the west of France, as did the Montrealers, and were not selected any more carefully. Yet by a mixture of hard work and savvy they managed to create a thriving agriculture by diking the fertile lowlands. In the eighteenth century Acadians were prosperous farmers who exported cereals and meat as far as Boston. Andrew H. Clarke, *Acadia: The Geography of Early Nova Scotia to 1760*, passim.

13 Testimonies of Meiklijohn and Anderson to the Assembly (1793), mentioned by Fernand Ouellet in *Histoire économique et sociale du Québec*, 154–5.

14 See App. 2, Table D listing the values and App. 3, Graph 23. Prices quoted in notarized contracts were used only when it was explicitly stated that a price was the current one. The assessments of grain and cattle in post-mortem inventories were based on the market value, as I

was able to ascertain. The prices collected from such disparate sources coincided with those listed in the Hôtel-Dieu's account books between 1698 and 1723. The seasonal pattern obtained from this last source provided a base on which to establish the annual average in those years with two few monthly quotations.

15 Quebec prices were calculated according to the calendar year. J. Hamelin, *Economie et société en Nouvelle-France*, 61.

16 The habitants' grain supplies, which were normally quite sufficient at the end of the harvest, confirm this.

17 In 1666 the grains were harvested before they had ripened. Soldiers wanting bread pillaged the fields. Talon ordinance of 22 May 1667; Massicotte, *Répertoire des arrêts*.

18 The regulation has not survived and we only know of its existence from the decree of 19 May 1665, which repealed it upon the request of the merchants, who refused to accept wheat at that rate. *JDCS*, vol. 1. In 1651 it was worth only 50 sols in Quebec. Lucien Campeau, "Un Témoignage de 1651 sur la Nouvelle-France," *RHAF* 23, no. 4 (Mar. 1970): 601–12. After 1665 wheat prices were no longer regulated. We should nevertheless mention two official interventions on behalf of the peasants: on 19 November 1669 the Council ordered the merchants to accept wheat at 60 sols for three months to repay old debts; and on 24 October 1682 to accept it at 50 sols in payment of the guns that every inhabitant had to buy for the safety of the colony. Both measures were temporary.

19 The deflation represented a reduction of 3/8 (1/2 x 3/4), which is what the merchant calculated when accounts were settled in cash. See A. Monière's account books, NA, M-847, passim.

20 There were some grain exports in 1710, 1712,m and 1713. Report by M. Magnien (1713), ibid., M-1584, no. 77.

21 After 1670 Montreal prices were generally lower than those in Quebec. The land was more productive and the region was further removed from the markets. The price of Montreal grains would bear the cost of transport once they were exported through Quebec.

22 Ernest Labrousse, "D'une Economie contrôlée à une économie en expansion," in Braudel and Labrousse, *Histoire économique et sociale de la France*, II:333.

23 I based myself on Pierre Goubert's averages: 14.32 and 21.9 livres tournois for the two periods in question. *Beauvais et le Beauvaisis de 1600 à 1730*, 424.

24 This phenomenon might be contrasted to the coincidence observed by Fernand Ouellet between Canadian and English price fluctuations in the last quarter of the eighteenth century. *Histoire économique et sociale du Québec 1760–1850*, passim.

25 It was not possible to define the capacity of a minot of oats, pulses, or corn.

26 There were very few quotations for hay, and these did not specify the quality.

27 Division of the estate of J. Blois, 28 Sept. 1704, Not. Rec., Raimbault.

28 As might be expected, these products were more expensive in winter than in summer. It is interesting to see that the Hôtel-Dieu consumed milk even in winter, which indicates that cows did not completely dry up. The butter was salted to preserve it.

29 Goubert, *Beauvais et le Beauvaisis*, graph 105, 104–5. Beef and veal prices were regulated, and the prices cited above are those charged by butchers and not the price received by the habitant when he brought the animal to town. The habitants kept no salted beef.

30 For example, a farm that had cost 3,262 Canadian livres in 1687 went for 2,100 livres in 1709, despite all the labour expended on it. Contract of 12 Sept. 1709, Not. Rec., A. Adhémar.

31 For examples of rentes or peasant savings, see the property of J. Averty, sale of 25 Aug. 1669, ibid., Basset; the Beaudry inheritance, 15 Nov. 1698; the Milot inheritance, 8 Feb. 1702.

32 Letter from M. de Tronson 20 Apr. 1684, ASSP, XIII:392.

33 Letter by the same, 4 May 1686, ibid., 476. The seigneurs finally managed to negotiate an exchange for la Présentation with a habitant and his sons, long-time farmers of their Sainte-Marie domain.

34 Report from La Barre to the king, 13 Nov. 1684, AC, C11A, 6, fols. 351–2.

35 Letter from M. Leschassier, 18 Mar. 1706, ASSP, XIV:358.

36 François Quesnay, *Oeuvres économiques et philosophiques*, quoted by Slicher Van Bath in *The Agrarian History of Western Europe*, 246.

37 J. Hamelin in *Economie et société en Nouvelle-France*, 38–71, places all the emphasis on the crises, as does Fernand Ouellet for a later period. Without denying the scarcities, we must recognize that good harvests were much more common and the bad ones were rarely catastrophic.

38 "There is too much wheat in the colony," Patoulet wrote the Court. AC, C11A, 3, fol. 65v.

39 This problem is clearly discussed in Duchesneau's letters to the minister in 1680 and 1681. AC, C11A, 5, fols. 173, 100–1. Charles Lemoyne exported some wheat to France: post-mortem inventory of 30 Jan. 1685, Not. Rec., Basset. The official correspondence sometimes includes partial information about such exports: AC, C11A, 6, fol. 402 (1684); C11A, 7, fol. 140ff (1685); C11A, 8, fols. 143v., and 44 (1686–87).

40 The habitants were supposed to sell the livestock to the butchers and were forbidden to sell meat. They disobeyed these regulations. There was no grain market, which explains why we find no official price lists. See the various market regulations in *bailliage* registers.

41 Instead of twice a week. Report of the lieutenant général, 20–21 Nov. 1721, *bailliage*, copy Faillon HH 116. See P. Kalm, *Voyage de Kalm en Amérique*, 57.

42 The minister wrote to the intendant in 1671 that it was important "to go on sending supplies and to keep money within the kingdom," AC, B3, fol. 30v.

43 Letter from De Meulles of 12 Nov. 1684 stressing that the king had paid 9 livres 14 sols in France for a quintal, which went for 7 livres in Quebec. AC, C11A, 6, fol. 402; similar report by the governor, ibid., fol. 346. Letter from Frontenac, 21 Nov. 1672, ibid., vol. 3, vols. 238–9. Report by Talon (1670), ibid., fol. 105.

44 Ibid. This occurred in 1684–88. Letters from De Meulles of 12 Nov. 1684, 24 Sept. 1685, ibid., vol. 6, fol. 402, vol. 7, fols. 140, 152; "Mémoire des choses nécessaires à l'entreprise de guerre à faire en 1687," ibid., vol. 9, fols. 168–73; "Etat des dépenses de 1688," ibid., vol. 10, fols. 130–9.

45 Letter from M. Tronson, 25 Mar. 1686, ASSP, XIII:443.

46 Letter from Duchesneau, 13 Nov. 1680, AC, C11A, 5, fols. 177–8.

47 Letter from Frontenac, 2 Nov. 1672, ibid., vol. 3, fols. 238–9.

48 Letter from De Meulles, 12 Nov. 1682, ibid., vol. 6, fol. 81.

49 Letter from Champigny, 10 Mar. 1691, ibid., vol. 11, fol. 262.

50 The assize of bread was interrupted because none was sold. Letter by the same of 12 Oct. 1691, ibid., fol. 292v.

51 Declaration of the curé Rémy, May 1693, *bailliage*, ser. 2, reg. 2.

52 A report from Saint-Sulpice to the Court, around 1697, recalled "the wheat that the Seminary had always made available at a very moderate price to feed the troops in times of urgent necessity." "They always opened their granaries to the intendant without trying to take any advantage." NA, M.G. 17, A7, 2, 1, vol. 1, 221–6.

53 In 1694–95 the situation righted itself. "To avoid price rises" the intendant continued to order flour for the troops. AC, C11A, 13, fol. 309, and vol. 5, fol. 45. Henceforth, if the colonial budget was sent in kind, this was due to necessity rather than to a fixed policy. These shipments usually arrived in the spring. The intendant requisitioned wheat from the population in the fall to feed the troops over the winter and gave it back in the spring. The producers made no profit from this troublesome transaction, which slowed down trading and payments and made them grumble. See, for example, the testimonies of 22 Feb. and 12 Mar. 1697, *bailliage*, ser. 2, reg. 3, rols. 533, 543–4.

54 The problem of overproduction was not confined to the seventeenth century. Livestock prices remained low, and the habitants were not encouraged to raise animals. Letter from Beauharnois and Hocquart of 4 Oct. 1731, AC, C11A, 54, fols. 54–7.

55 The adult settler's ration was at least as high as that of the soldier and more varied. It was widely believed that puny recruits who spent some time on the *côtes* got stronger. One intendant claimed in 1706 that the habitant ate two pounds of bread and six ounces of lard a day, which represents 1,338 + 2,352 = 3,690 calories – plentiful rations that cannot be presumed to apply to the entire population. AC, C11A, 24, fol. 226. C. Clark and M.R. Hoswell, *The Economics of Subsistence Agriculture* (New York 1967), 53–4.

56 A fifth was set aside for seeds. This calculation includes all the island's rural parishes, and is based on the census data for production and population.

57 Report on the state of the parishes, 1721, RAPQ (1921–22): 262ff. Thirty-two habitants thus declared that their tithes in wheat and peas amounted to an average of 300 minots a year, meaning that they harvested 7,800 minots, 5,200 of them in wheat. At Pointe-aux-Trembles, eighteenth-century censuses convey similar averages.

58 "If the Canadians had been willing to work hard they could all have been very prosperous" wrote W.J. Eccles, *The Canadian Frontier, 1534–1760* (New York 1969), 96.

59 See my discussion of the population movement in times of crisis, chap. 3, sec. 5, and App. 3, Graphs 9 and 10.

60 Slicher Van Bath, *The Agrarian History of Western Europe*, 120–1.

61 This was how an anonymous observer saw the problem in Canadian food supplies in 1739. AC, C11A, 57, fols. 182–3.

62 By adding a few foodstuffs to the soldier's basic ration, we easily reach the 4,000 calories needed by a hard-working adult.

63 Hogs about to be or already fatted, depending on the time of the year, figured in every post-mortem inventory.

64 The Canadian farmer, who had never been able to afford coffee, took up tea after the Conquest to accompany his meals.

65 The peasant diet only has been considered. The upper classes could count on more varied and better-balanced menus, supplemented with imported foodstuffs, beef, etc. The meals that were provided for the sick of the Hôtel-Dieu, with their regular diet of veal, eggs, chicken, geese, and milk as well as wine, fit what we know of other hospital diets. Robert Mandrou, "Le Ravitaillement d'une ville dans la ville. La ration alimentaire de restauration à l'assistance publique à Paris (1820–1870)," in *Jahrbucher fur Nationaloekonomie und Statistik* 3 (1966) (Paris 1967), 189–99.

66 The daily wage of the soldiers "loaned" by their captains varied between 9 and 15 sols. They could be found throughout the countryside at harvest time.

67 L.R. MacDonald, "France and New France: The Internal Contradic-

tions," CHR (June 1971): 121–43. The author recasts an old theory in a Marxist framework.

1 See the descriptions of pillage in the first half of the century in Gaston Roupnel, *La Ville et la campagne au XVIIe siècle. Etudes sur les populations dijonnaises* (Paris 1955), 18–24. W.J. Eccles holds that the military and civil populations lived in perfect harmony: "The Social, Economic and Political Significance of the Military Establishment in New France," CHR 52, no. 1 (Mar. 1971): 5–6.

2 Duelling appeared the way to settle disputes in the Free Companies of the Marine. Unless one of them died, the duellists were usually absolved. The *bailli* did not prosecute such cases, and those we know about were recorded in the registers of the Sovereign council. St-Paul, a soldier, meeting one of his comrades in the street drew his sword to force him to stand him a drink. The other tried to disarm him and was killed by a thrust in the stomach. Report of 27 Feb. 1688, Not. Rec., Basset. Such incidents were not infrequent. See also the murder of T. Hunault, habitant, by lieutenant Dumont, on 10 Oct. 1690, ibid., Basset; that of Lachaume by a soldier planning to flee to France with his victim's wife, 4 July 1702, *bailliage*, ser. 2, reg. 4; the assaults on the apothecary St-Olive and the butcher Henri Catin, 25 Feb. 1709 and 20 Apr. 1707, ibid., reg. 5, and JDCS, V:584.

3 Brief against Governor Pérot, presented to M. de Seignelay by the Sulpicians (ASSP, vol. XIII, separate item); inquiry against Captain la Freydière, Sept. 1667, *bailliage*, ser. 1, reg. 1; threats by Captain Vergnon against a sergeant of the *bailliage*, 16 Jan. 1688, ibid., ser. 2, reg. 1; etc.

4 Only the briefest references in official correspondence.

5 There was a high rate of desertion; officers gave their soldiers leave to go trading with the Indians and employed them as servants, despite the regulations. "Règlement pour la conduite, marche, police et discipline des compagnies que Sa Majesté entretient dans le Canada," 30 Mar. 1695, AN (France), F3, AD, VII, art. 2b.

6 Letter from M. Magnien, 1719, NA, M.G.17, A7, 2, 1, vol. 2, 584–5.

7 See the 1673 tax assessment in BRH (1926): 265–79.

8 Ordinance of De Meulles, 15 May 1685, E.-A. Massicotte, *Répertoire des arrêts*.

9 Regarding soldiers' work, see above, chap. 2, sec. 6; André Corvisier, *L'Armée française de la fin du XVIIe siècle au ministère de Choiseul. Le Soldat*, 95–7.

10 Statement by Pierre Paris, habitant of St Sulpice, 12 July 1722, *bailliage*, copy Faillon HH 128.

11 Minutes of 16 Nov. 1672, *bailliage*, ser. 1, reg. 1; regulation concerning the guardhouse of 3 Dec. 1673, followed by the tax assessment, BRH (1926): 265–79. Barracks were never built, and the above arrangement did not survive the arrival of the Free Companies of the Marine ten years later.

12 Rental lease, 21 Oct. 1669, Not. Rec., Basset.

13 This is suggested in a letter from Frontenac and de Champigny: "In Montreal, the garrison is billeted and the officers are provided with a private heated room by their host whenever this can be arranged. Some prefer to choose their own lodgings, in which case the accommodations are paid for by those who were supposed to take them in." 10 Nov. 1695, AC, C11A, 13, fol. 103.

14 Letter from the commissaire de la Marine in Montreal, 15 Oct. 1697, ibid., vol. 15, fol. 162.

15 E.-M. Faillon, *Histoire de la colonie française au Canada*, II:15–18; RAPQ (1949–51): 429–34.

16 In 1688 the intendant made those who stayed behind, namely the merchants, pay for the militiamen's board. AC, C11A, 10, fol. 121.

17 Intendant's report, 16 July 1687, ibid., vol. 9, fols. 32s., and 69s.

18 6 and 24 July 1684, Not. Rec., Maugue.

19 Letter from Champigny, 6 Nov. 1687, AC, C11A, 9, fol. 13; letter from Callières, ibid., vol. 10, fols. 148–9.

20 Letter from De Meulles, 24 Sept. 1685, ibid., vol. 7, fol. 140.

21 Before 1690 Charles Lemoyne, a merchant ennobled by Louis XIV, his eldest son, and the nephews of a previous governor, d'Ailleboust, served as captains with the urban militias.

22 In 1714 four of the six captains were merchants who had never done any fighting, and neither had J.-B. Charly, major in 1729, etc. See the provisional list in RAPQ (1949–51): 423–527; Cameron Nish, *Les Bourgeois-gentilshommes de la Nouvelle-France, 1729–1748*, 155–6.

23 Like providing certificates of non-residency, which allowed the seigneurs to repossess unoccupied parcels of land, the least pleasant of their tasks.

24 What historians have described as a novel institution, a quasi-democratic body, was but a bastardized version of French communal structures. The habitant who had been "named" performed the same duties as the elected syndics. See Benjamin Sulte, "The Captains of the Militia," CHR 1, no. 2 (1920): 241; C. de Bonnault, "Le Canada militaire," RAPQ (1949–51): 264.

25 Raudot ordinance of 25 June 1710, in *Edits, ordonnances royaux*, II:275.

26 W.J. Eccles believes that commoners rose to military command positions and therefore scaled the social hierarchy via the militia. The examples he mentions, Lemoyne, Boucher, Charly, and so on, had

been propelled by commercial success, and it was only once they had been promoted, and ennobled in the first two cases, that they served as officers. W.J. Eccles, *Frontenac, the Courtier Governor*, 214, and "The Social, Economic and Political Significance of the Military Establishment in New France."

27 See the accounts of these campaigns in AC, C11A, 4, fols. 12–18, vol. 6, fols. 297–8, vol. 9, fols. 32ff, 69ff.

28 List of vacant posts of 1691, ibid., vol. 11, fols. 221–4.

29 Besides d'Iberville's well-known prizes we might cite the example of Testard de Montigny, who obtained 260 pounds sterling as his share of the ransom for Bonavista, a Newfoundland fishing village. Arbitration verdict of 13 Sept. 1715, Not. Rec., J.-B. Adhémar.

30 Report from 1673, AC, C11A, 4, fol. 6.

31 Letters from the governors and intendants, 14 Nov. 1684, 12 Nov. 1691, ibid., vol. 6, fols. 382–5, and vol. 11, fol. 291.

32 J.-B. Dumers, who had three children, Louis Ducharme and his brother Pierre, both married men, "were ordered to go to war" and were killed. Jean Lelat, a married man recruited for convoy duty, was reported missing, etc. So declared the widows during post-mortem inventories.

33 AC, C11A, 4, fol. 13.

34 Letter from de Callières, 15 Oct. 1698, ibid., vol. 16, fols. 164–70. Etat du Canada (1699), ibid., vol. 3, fols. 37–8.

35 They were assessed for so many stakes, which they had to prepare and cart over. Those who failed to do so were prosecuted by the *bailliage* authorities. Further references can be found in the inventories of J. Beauvais, 6 Apr. 1691, Not. Rec., Maugue, and J. Millet, 9 July 1714, ibid., Senet.

36 See the decree of the Conseil d'Etat of 1 May 1743, *Edits, ordonnances royaux*; P.-G. Roy, *Inventaire des papiers de Léry*, I, passim.

37 Robert Rumilly, *Histoire de Montréal* (Montreal 1970), I:321–3.

38 This description is based on the *aveu et dénombrement* of 1731, the search for illegal goods carried out by the India Company in 1741, and earlier census material. We must work backwards to get an idea of what the town looked like at the beginning of the century. See Louise Dechêne, "La Croissance de Montréal au XVIIIe siècle," RHAF 27, no. 2 (Sept. 1973): 163–79.

39 *Bailli*'s ordinance of 24 Sept. 1676, establishing market days on Tuesdays and Fridays: *bailliage*, copy Faillon GG 7.

40 General regulations of 11 May 1676. Every item had to be reiterated nearly annually by the *baillis* and intendants. E.-Z. Massicotte, *Répertoire des arrêts*. Ordinance of June 1689, *bailliage*, copy Faillon KK 233. Raudot ordinance of 27 June 1707, *Edits, ordonnances royaux*, III:418.

41 Vaudreuil ordinance of 25 June 1721, copy Faillon H 638; other ordinance of 21 Aug. of the same year regarding Notre-Dame street, ibid., FF 153.

42 Petition by the sisters of the Congrégation, 27 Aug. 1680, followed by an ordinance by Duchesneau, ibid., H 593–4.

43 Aveu et dénombrement, 1731, RAPQ (1941–42).

44 In 1741 70 per cent of the residents were householders: minutes of the search carried out by the India Company, published by E.-Z. Massicotte in MSRC 3, no. 15 (1921).

45 There were 900 toises in an arpent.

46 Contract of 2 Oct. 1651, which included a return clause, NA, M.G. 17, A7, 2, 3, vol. 1.

47 Petition by the residents of Montreal, June 1706, NA, M-1584, 59.

48 Letter from M. Magnien, 6 June 1716, NA, M.G. 17, A7,. 2, 1, vol. 1, 488.

49 Brief concerning the running of the seigneury (1716–17), NA, M-1584, 86.

50 Boutaric cites it among a number of curious, archaic dues. F. de Boutaric, Traité des droits seigneuriaux et des matières féodales (Nîmes 1781), 656.

51 The Sulpicians readily admitted among themselves that their staff was mediocre and that its exactions raised protests. Letters from M. Tronson from 1677, 1679, 1681, and 1685, ASSP, XIII:74–7, 233–5, 422, etc.

52 See the minutes of the bailliage and those of the Sovereign Council, especially between 1690 and 1693.

53 They retained the right of basse justice and property rights on the clerk's office. Edict of Mar. 1693, Edits et ordonnances royaux, I.

54 NA, M-1584, 28; letter from M. Tronson, 22 June 1689, ASSP, XIII:564.

55 Cost evaluations of 28 June 1706 and 11 Feb. 1707, bailliage, APQ, NF 21, vol. 13.

56 Deed of 6 Mar. 1676, Not. Rec., Basset.

57 Jacques Mathieu reached the same conclusion in "Les Causes devant la prévôté de Québec en 1667," Histoire Sociale 3 Apr. 1969): 101–13.

58 For instance, de Couagne's seizure, from a habitant, of 35 minots of wheat, met immediately by the seigneurs' claim for 18 livres, 8 minots of wheat, and 24 capons, which represented four years' arrears of dues. Bailliage, ser. 2, reg. 3, fols. 719v., 722, 724.

59 Report of 1716–17, NA, M-1584, 86.

60 According to Faillon, town meetings started as early as 1644, but the surviving minutes only begin in 1656. E.-M. Faillon, Histoire de la colonie française au Canada, II:199, and bailliage, pièces détachées passim.

61 Inventory of the communauté's papers, 5 June 1667, bailliage, closing of inventories. The communauté owned a "shed" where it held its

meetings and which it sold to the seigneurs on 23 June 1672: Not. Rec., Basset.

62 See the list in Massicotte, *Répertoire des arrêts*.

63 Contract of 9 Dec. 1657, Not. Rec., Basset.

64 Ordinance of 23 Mar. 1677, registered at the *bailliage* on 3 Apr., Massicotte, *Répertoire des arrêts*.

65 Election of a syndic, 15 May 1672, *bailliage*, ser. 1, reg. 1, copy Faillon GG 273.

66 At least up to 1675, the communauté continued to fight for what it believed was its property against the usurpers: see the lawsuit by the syndic, 5 Nov. 1675, ibid., GG 295. On the communautés in France, see Pierre de Saint-Jacob, *Les Paysans de la Bourgogne du Nord au dernier siècle de l'Ancien régime*, 75–93; Pierre Goubert, "L'Assemblée des habitants," in F. Braudel and E. Labrousse, eds., *Histoire économique et sociale de la France*, II:575–8.

67 Ordinances of 3 Apr. 1687, 30 Mar. 1688, 22 June 1703, 23 June 1711, etc., contained in the registers of the *bailliage*, passim.

68 Assembly concerning the building of the wall, NA, M.G. 17, A7, 2, 1, vol. 2, 487ff; lawsuits, 15 Apr. 1667, 7 Sept. 1679, and 5 Nov. 1722, *bailliage*, dossier series.

69 The merchants grouped together and held meetings long before the ruling of 11 May 1717 that authorized them to do so. *Edits et ordonnances royaux*, I.

70 Report concerning the fortifications, Mar. 1729, NA, M.G. 17, A7, 2, 3, vol. 6, 742–6.

71 On this aspect, see Guy Frégault, "Politique et politiciens," in *Le XVIIIe Siècle canadien. Etudes*, 159–241.

72 "There is nothing fairer nor better conceived than the rulings that govern this country, but I assure you that none are so poorly observed." Letter from the colonial governor, 13 Nov. 1685, AC, C11A, 7, fol. 91.

73 John F. Bosher, "Government and Private Interest in New France," *Canadian Public Administration* 10 (1967): 244–57.

74 Thus Juchereau succeeded his father-in-law Migeon, and Adhémar's son took over as notary.

75 A few Montrealers made it to the Sovereign Council, whose membership grew from seven to twelve members.

CHAPTER THIRTEEN

1 No single source provides a good picture of the occupational structure after 1681. The following approximation combines census quantitative data with partial information found in a 1715 tax roll and in the 1731

seigneurial survey, supplemented with genealogical sources and my own index of Montreal families from Notarial Records.

2 NA, M.G. 17, A7, 2, 1, vol. 2, 487ff.

3 See App. 3, Graph 25. The two highest assessments, of 400 and 200 livres for the Sulpicians and Jesuits respectively, were not included.

4 J. Dupâquier, "Problème de mesure et de représentation graphique en histoire sociale," *Actes du 89ᵉ congrès des sociétés savantes* (1964), vol. 3; Régine Robin, *La Société française en 1789: Semur-en-Auxois* (Paris 1970), 157ff.

5 René Baehrel, *Une Croissance: la Basse-Provence rurale (fin du XVIᵉ siècle– 1789)*, 441–2.

6 This represents the totality of those extant prior to 1700, and seventy-five others dating from 1700 to 1730, related to the families observed in the earlier period.

7 See the debts owed to notaries listed in the inventories, e.g. that of Brunet *dit* Bourbonnais, 16 Oct. 1709, Not. Rec., Le Pailleur.

8 Pierre Gadois' inventory, 3–4 Nov. 1667, ibid., Basset.

9 The *cru* actually only applied to non-productive items that would wear out in time.

10 According to the method used by A. Hansen-Jones, based on the classification of the American Bureau of Statistics: "La Fortune privée en Pennsylvanie, New Jersey, Delaware: 1774," *Annales ESC* (Mar.–Apr. 1969): 235–49.

11 Despite the evidence, historians such as Emile Salone, W.B. Munro, F. Parkman, B. Sulte, Rameau de Saint-Père, and others, have described the whole social structure in terms of the seigneury.

12 The vassals were the two female convents and the gentlemen-soldiers who had to protect the island against invasion in return for their strategically located fiefs. The arrival of the troops rendered such arrangements unnecessary.

13 As opposed to the distribution of seigneurial revenues in France, where *fermages* held first place. G. Le Marchand, "Le Féodalisme dans la France rurale des temps modernes: essai de caractérisation," *Annales historiques de la Révolution française*, no. 190 (1969): 77–108.

14 Letter from M. Leschassier, 5 Apr. 1702, ASSP, vol. 14, 411.

15 So Pehr Kalm reported, *Voyage de Kalm en Amérique*, 111.

16 See below, chap. 15, sec. 1.

17 P.-G. Roy, *Lettres de noblesse, généalogies, érections de comté et baronies instituées par le Conseil souverain de la Nouvelle-France*, 2 vols. (Beauceville 1920), passim.

18 Letter of 13 Nov. 1685, AC, C11A, 7, fol. 93v.

19 Letters from the intendants between 1679 and 1690, passim, and especially ibid., vol. 5, fols. 49–50, and vol. 8, fol. 145v.

20 Commissions in the Compagnies Franches de la Marine were not venal.

21 The expression is Robert Mandrou's: "oisiveté en armes," in *Classes et luttes de classes en France au début du XVIIe siècle* (Florence 1965), 31.

22 Testimony of 23 Oct. 1683, *bailliage*, ser. 1, reg. 2; another of 17 Apr. 1684 before the Conseil, *JDCS*, vol. 2, 947–8. The names of the culprits do not figure in the records of the Conseil.

23 Letter from the governor, 8 May 1686, C11A, 8, fol. 12v.

24 Ibid., vol. 7, 147. See Gaston Zeller, "Une Notion de caractère historico-social: la dérogeance," in *Aspects de la politique française sous l'Ancien Régime* (Paris 1964), 336–74.

25 Letter from the governor, 20 Nov. 1686, AC, C11A, 8, fols. 144–144v. The father threatened to take his ten children back to France, "where they might earn their bread and go into service here or there." Official correspondence is full of such wails and blackmail.

26 See Cameron Nish, *Les Bourgeois-gentilshommes de la Nouvelle-France, 1729–1748*, 113–15.

27 AC, C11A, 7, fols. 97v.–98, and vol. 8, fols. 12–123v.

28 They left behind between 20,000 and 40,000 livres. Not. Rec., Maugue, 13 Mar. 1679, 21 Dec. 1683; Basset, 5 Dec. 1684.

29 Those of Captains Dugué, Pécaudy, Daneau, Blaise, d'Ailleboust, Duplessis, Gresolon, Marganne, Dufresnel, of Lieutenants de Ganne, de Gauthier, Bizard, and Piot, staff officers, and Lamothe, Picoté, Carion, and La Fresnaye, militia officers. All were called "écuyer."

30 Inventory of René Gauthier of Varennes, an officer retired from the Carignan regiment, governor of Trois-Rivières: Not. Rec., A. Adhémar, 1 July 1693.

31 See, for example, the inventory of the lieutenant de roi Piot de Langloiserie, 5 Dec. 1722, ibid., Senet.

32 About 2,000 livres. Inventory of Antoine Pécaudy de Contrecoeur, 10 Apr. 1792, ibid., Basset.

33 Six of the seventeen were tenants.

34 He corresponded with Vauban. See L. Dechêne, ed., *La Correspondence de Vauban relative au Canada*, 15–22.

35 The Sulpician Rémy wrote that d'Ailleboust was entirely relying on his advice: ASSM, copy Faillon H 339–46. Appointment of Migeon, 6 Aug. 1677, *bailliage*, copy Faillon H 213.

36 Charles Juchereau de Saint-Denis, lieutenant-général until he died in 1704.

37 Letter from M. Tronson, 20 Apr. 1677, ASSP, vol. XIII, 422; minutes of *bailliage*, Feb.–Mar. 1678, ser. 1, reg. 1; E.-Z. Massicotte, "L'Hôtel-Dieu et la famille Basset," *Le Journal de l'Hôtel-Dieu* (Nov. 1942): 431ff.

38 André Vachon, *Histoire du notariat canadien, 1621–1960*.

39 Inventory of 14 May 1714, Not. Rec., Le Pailleur.
40 Inventory of 25 Mar. 1693, ibid., A. Adhémar.
41 Hilaire Bourgine, son of a La Rochelle merchant and F. Pougnet's clerk.
42 See the examples of the seventeenth-century Montreal notaries Pierre Cabazié, Claude Maugue, Nicolas Senet, and J.-B. Pottier.
43 Inventory of 29 Oct. 1700, Not. Rec., Raimbault.
44 E.-Z. Massicotte, biography of Raimbault, in BRH, vol. 21, 78, and vol. 27, 182; entry in the DCB, vol. II.
45 Post-mortem inventory of his first wife, 10 Dec. 1706, Not. Rec., A. Adhémar.
46 Soumande and Lestage. See AC, C11A, 124, fol. 393, and ASSP, doss. 20, item 4.
47 Inventory of 18 Apr. 1708, Not. Rec., A. Adhémar; and of 14 Apr. 1712, ibid., Le Pailleur.
48 According to the description of the two inventories of 1 Dec. 1693 and 1 Dec. 1706, ibid., Basset and Raimbault.
49 Yves Zoltvany noticed a similar sobriety in Aubert de La Chenaye, a major Quebec merchant. DCB, II:27–36.
50 Couagne's inventory of 7 Aug. 1686, ibid., Maugue; and 26 Aug. 1706, ibid., A. Adhémar.
51 Inventories of Jean Magnan, René Malet, Jacques Hubert-Lacroix, ibid., 14 Mar. 1694, 23 Mar. 1698, Adhémar; 20 Mar. 1720, Le Pailleur.
52 Inventories of 10 Oct. 1687, ibid., Cabazié; and 28 Jan. 1704, ibid., A. Adhémar.
53 Ten livres and confiscation for public disturbance on a Sunday to Vincent Dugast, for whom this was the umpteenth condemnation. Jan. 1689, bailliage, ser. 2, reg. 1.
54 See, for example, the list of licenses granted by the court, 10 Dec. 1694, ibid., reg. 3.
55 Inventory of 30 Dec. 1698, Not. Rec., A. Adhémar.
56 Petition of the armourer Fezeret to obtain a certificate, and that of the cartwright Brazeau for the establishment of a craft guild. AC, C11A, 12, fols. 333v. and 310v.
57 Contract of 16 Dec. 1675, Not. Rec., Basset.
58 See the regulations contained in the bailliage registers, passim.
59 Petition by the butchers, 4 June 1709, bailliage, ANQ, NF 21, vol. 13.
60 Brunet, Bouchard, and Lecour were sentenced to a 35-livre fine each, 4 June 1709, bailliage, ser. 2, reg. 5.
61 Inventories of 3 Nov. 1689, 11 Apr. 1699, and 6 Mar. 1700, ibid., A. Adhémar.
62 Dated 20 July 1706, Raudot, Edits, ordonnances royaux, II:265.
63 De Launay, Barsalou, Bélair, Noir.

64 Including what he advanced to his children prior to his death. Inventories of 6 July 1663, Not. Rec., Basset, and 21 Aug. 1700, ibid., A. Adhémar.
65 Ibid., Maugue, 28 Apr. 1684; David, 4 Nov. 1720.
66 Inventory of Tessier, 2 Aug. 1689, and of Dumets, 9 Feb. 1691, ibid., A. Adhémar.
67 Elizabeth J. Lunn, *Economic Development in New France 1713–1760*, 185.
68 Leber hired a blacksmith. See the seigneurs' leases, 16 Dec. 1669 and 17 June 1677, Not. Rec., Basset.
69 In 1691, for instance, there were some fifty such lawsuits, one-sixth of all civil litigations.
70 René Allary, Moise Hilleret, Janson *dit* Lapalme, Jourdain, etc.
71 Inventory of 5 Oct. 1699, Not. Rec., A. Adhémar.
72 See the case of Martinet *dit* Fontblanche and that of Antoine Forestier.
73 According to Peter N. Moogk, who made a systematic study of these contracts: "Apprenticeship Indentures: A Key to Life in New France," CHAR (1971): 68.
74 Laurent Tessier's apprenticeship indenture to Gilles Lauson, 1 Nov. 1673, Not. Rec., Basset. Butchers and millers also took over from generation to generation.
75 Letter from Frontenac and Champigny, 4 Nov. 1693, AC, C11A, 12, fol. 209v.
76 A man employed all year round earned between 100 and 120 livres, which was therefore a better deal.
77 The Hôpital général, founded in 1694 and supported by grants and charitable donations, was poorly administered until 1747 and did very little to help the residents. Only seven people (mentally ill, aged, or paupers) were admitted during the twenty years following its creation, another fifty or thereabouts between 1714 and 1747, but these mainly consisted of disabled soldiers. "Mouvement annuel des pauvres reçus à l'Hôpital général, 1694–1747," archives of the Montreal Hôpital général.
78 Inventory of 25 Oct. 1695, Not. Rec., Pottier.
79 He had come to Canada as an indentured servant in 1659 and had lived on the same property for twenty-five years. He is a good example of the reasonable though modest achievement of most immigrants.
80 This view, based on one or two superficial accounts of colonial mores, received wide acdeptance. See W.J. Eccles, *The Canadian Frontier*, 94; F. Ouellet, "La Mentalité et l'outillage économique de l'habitant canadien 1760," in BRH 63, no. 3 (1956).
81 Clothes were not always inventoried. Only forty decent descriptions were found.

82 Jean Leduc was among them. He died when he was eighty-one, leaving behind six enterprising sons and net assets of 18,000 livres.

83 Marcel Trudel, "Sur les mutations sociales d'avant 1663: la recherche d'une explication," paper presented to the Colonial History Conference, Ottawa, Mar. 1970, and "Les Débuts d'une société: Montréal 1642–1663," *RHAF* 23, no. 2 (Sept. 1969): 185–208.

84 The term was also used in its broad sense, meaning someone who has elected residence somewhere. The second meaning appears in Trévoux's dictionary (1752): "Habitant ou colon en parlant des colonies se dit d'un particulier auquel le souverain a accordé des terres pour les défricher et les cultiver à son profit."

85 Fiefs were also known as "habitations," but noble seigneurs were not called "habitants." See Conrad Filion, "Essai sur l'évolution du mot habitant, XVIIe–XVIIIe siècles," *RHAF* 24, no. 3 (Dec. 1970): 375–401. This discussion follows that author's argument but relies on different sources, closer to common usage and shift of meaning over time.

86 Post-mortem inventory, 14 June 1693, Not. Rec., A. Adhémar.

87 Abel Poitrineau, *La Vie rurale en Basse-Auvergne au XVIIIe siècle (1726–1789)*, 76.

88 Statement of 3 Apr. 1675, Not. Rec., Basset. The term *manant*, unlike that of *paysan*, survived in the colony. "He lived off lard and peas like an artisan or *manant*," wrote the merchant La Chesnaye. BN mss r., N.A., 9273.

89 *Histoire de l'Amérique septentrionale* (1722), quoted by Filion, "Essai sur l'évolution du mot habitant,"

90 André Corvisier, *L'Armée française de la fin du XVIIe siècle au ministère de Choiseul. Le Soldat*, II:851–61. The author's lists reveal a sizeable sample of present-day Canadian last names, from Belhumeur to Vadeboncoeur by way of Dechêne and Sanfaçon.

91 Alexis Lemoine, for example, never put down more than his surname, "Monière," on whatever he signed.

92 Inventory of Jacques Leber, 1 Dec. 1706, Not. Rec., Raimbault. The family had just acquired a title, which explains the heir's sensitivity to the issue.

93 Lawrence Stone, "Social Mobility in England, 1500–1700," *Past and Present* 33 (Apr. 1966): 16–55.

94 See S. Thernstrom, "Notes on the Historical Study of Social Mobility," *Comparative Studies in History and Society* 10 no. 2 (Jan. 1968): 171.

95 This includes very ordinary cases of social ascension, such as soldiers or indentured servants who became notaries or small merchants. Only eight families can be said to have really broken with their roots: the Lemoyne, Dupuis, Closse, Robutel, Charly, Culerié, Godé, and for a while, the Milot families.

96 Accounts of the year 1707–08 by J.-J. Lebé, then warden, archives of the Notre-Dame parish, A-14.

97 The bridegroom was Gabriel De Thiersant de Genlis. See the entry by Jules Bazin in the DCB, II:229.

98 He was related to Louis Rouer de Villeray, a merchant and controller of the ferme du Canada and a conseiller du roi. DCB, I:593–6. Two other Perthuis, Nicolas and Charles, hailing from the same parts, no doubt his cousins, arrived in Canada in 1690. Charles left a greater mark on the society.

99 "He is an old propertied merchant," the intendant wrote about him. AC, C11A, 125, fol. 365ff; inventory of 18 Apr. 1708, Not. Rec., A. Adhémar; and other deeds concerning the inheritance, from the same notary.

100 One son was killed in New England in 1709; another, a voyageur, settled at Détroit; one of his sons-in-law, Pierre Maguet, lost the little he had brought with him to Canada through trading and lived on his farm; another son-in-law, Louis Lefebvre-Duchouquet, spent his life as a voyageur. Desroche, Gervaise, and Caron were habitants. P.-G. Roy, "La Famille Perthuis," BRH 41: 449–77.

101 P.-G. Roy, Lettres de noblesse, généaologies, etc., passim.

102 AN (Paris), ser. P, item 6119; the biography by Yves Zoltvany in the DCB, II: 389–90.

103 Pierre Goubert, L'Ancien Régime (Paris 1969), I:172.

104 Letter from the governor and the intendant, 15 Oct. 1736, cited by R.C. Harris, The Seigneurial System in Early Canada, 44–5. Harris clearly recognizes that the ownership of a seigneury was not the key to social prestige.

105 Census of La Guillaudière, 31 Aug. 1677, Not. Rec., Basset.

106 Aveu et dénombrement of the fief of Bellevue, 24 Aug. 1683, ibid., Basset. His widow refused the estate but the sons managed to buy back the fief from the main creditor.

107 List of creditors in the Gervaise inventory, 14 Sept. 1700, ibid., A. Adhémar; verdict of the intendant of 11 May 1685, ibid., Basset.

108 See, for example, the fiefs purchased by Louis Lecomte-Dupré, René Fezeret, J.-B. Neveu, and Jacques Charbonnier.

109 Contracts of 2 Mar. 1684, Not. Rec., Basset, and 27 Apr. 1703, ibid., A. Adhémar. Bouat did much better by buying Terrebonne for 5,268 livres and selling it for 10,000 livres two years later: Cameron Nish, Les Bourgeois-gentilshommes de la Nouvelle-France, 1729–1748 (Ottawa 1968), 118. But such speculation usually brought only moderate returns.

110 Contract drawn up in Quebec on 6 Oct. 1699, ANQ, Chamballon; tenancy lease of 30 Oct. 1699, Not. Rec., A. Adhémar; Couagne's inventory of 26 Aug. 1706, ibid.

111 As Habbakuk has noted for England, we cannot always approch land purchases in terms of social prestige. They were often good investments that, in the long term, compared favourably with the returns from trade. But since this was not the case in Montreal, merchants bought little land, and the question of prestige was not usually a consideration. H.J. Habbakuk, ''The English Land Market in Eighteenth-Century Britain and the Netherlands,'' in J.S. Bromley and Kossmann, eds., *Britain and the Netherlands* (Oxford 1960), 154–73. See also Robert Mandrou, *Les Fugger, propriétaires fonciers en Souabe, 1560–1618* (Paris 1969), 235ff.

112 Testart was already forty-three and had fought many a glorious campaign as leader of the militia when he received his first commission in the Troupes de la Marine. Some of the men with Cavelier de La Salle, such as La Forest and You, also rose in this way. *DCB*, II:176, 653, 702.

113 On military careers in France, see Elinor G. Barber, *The Bourgeoisie in 18th Century France* (Princeton 1967), 117–25.

114 Letter from Frontenac, 20 Oct. 1691, AC, C11A, 11, fol. 242.

115 Letter from Talon, 10 Nov. 1670, concerning the marriage of Morel de la Durantaye with the widow of Jean Madry, in Quebec, ibid., vol. 3, fol. 82.

116 Letter from Vaudreuil, 8 Nov. 1718, ibid., vol. 124, fol. 393. See also Frontenac's attempts to arrange a marriage for the major of Montreal, ibid., vol. 12, fols. 236v–237.

117 This includes officers residing in Montreal and others found in Tanguay's dictionary under the letters ''d'' and ''l'' in order to broaden the sample. René Jetté's article, ''La Stratification sociale: une direction de recherche,'' *RHAF* 26, no. 1 (June 1972): 48–52, is interesting, but his rates could not be used since he incorporated too many of the lower categories into his upper class.

118 There were only two such cases in our sample: the marriages of Jean Tessier and Jean-Baptiste Charly.

119 Cameron Nish, *Les Bourgeois-gentilshommes de la Nouvelle-France*. The author attempts to show that officers and merchants formed an homogeneous group, a single ''class.'' Yet one needs only to look at the emergence and eruption of conflicts after 1760 to realize how fragile this alliance had been. The Conquest loosened the economic ties, leaving two fundamentally and consciously opposed groups. See also Guy Frégault, *La Société canadienne sous le régime français* (Ottawa 1954), 14.

CHAPTER FOURTEEN

1 Criminality is no doubt an interesting field of study, but dangerous when normal behaviour remains largely unknown. See, for example, Robert-Lionel Séguin, *Le Vie libertine en Nouvelle-France au XVIIᵉ siècle* (Montreal 1972).

2 Léon Gérin's work appeared in *La Science sociale suivant la méthode d'observation*, published between 1891 and 1894. See also "L'Habitant de Saint-Justin. contribution à la géographie sociale du Canada," MRCS, ser. 2, IV (May 1898): 139–216; Jean-Charles Falardeau and Philippe Garigue, *Léon Gérin et l'habitant de Saint-Justin* (Montreal 1968), reprint of the latter article, with excellent comments and a very useful bibliography.

3 For a summary of these debates, see Marcel Rioux, Yves Martin, et al., *La Société canadienne-française* (Montreal 1971).

4 I am using the terminology suggested by Peter Laslett in *Household and Family in Past Time* (Cambridge University Press 1972).

5 The co-residence of Perroy and Rouiller lasted, while other similar legal and residential arrangements were temporary, awaiting marriage, when each would recover his personal property and half the censive.

6 Inventory of 7 May 1661, Not. Rec., Basset. Register of the Notre-Dame parish, May 1661.

7 John Demos, *A Little Commonwealth Family in Plymouth Colony* (Oxford 1970), 77–8.

8 The aggregate census provide the number of families, that of children aged 0–14 and of children aged 15 and over. I estimated that 20 per cent of the latter lived with their parents. This estimation is based on the 1681 nominal census, where the proportion was 17 per cent, at a time when girls were still marrying very early. The results are 3.9 in 1707, the high point and 3.4 in 1716, 3.0 between 1720 and 1730, and 2.7 in 1736 and 1739.

9 It seemed reasonable to presume that at the time they married, these people could expect to reach the age of sixty.

10 The custom of Paris was imposed in 1664 with the creation of the Compagnie des Indes occidentales.

11 Yves J. Tremblay, "La Société montréalaise au début du régime anglais," MA thesis, University of Ottawa 1970. The author located 2,773 marriage contracts and 2,875 marriages. The ratio is far higher than the 70 per cent found by A. Daumard and F. Furet, "Méthodes de l'histoire sociale. Les achives notariales et la mécanographie," *Annales ESC* (1959): 676–93.

12 *Oeuvres de Pothier*, VI, "Traité du contrat de mariage et du douaire"; Olivier Martin, *Histoire de la coutume de Paris et vicomté de Paris*, IV.
13 *Oeuvres de Pothier*, VIII, "Traité des propres." At first, land was sometimes granted to the marriage community.
14 Marriage contract of Jean Simon, 3 Nov. 1708, Not. Rec., A. Adhémar; other examples: 16 Oct. 1711, ibid., Raimbault; 24, 31 Jan. 1717, ibid., J.-B. Adhémar. Since all the examples cited in this chapter come from notarial records, only the name of the notary will be indicated.
15 "... which property will be incorporated into the marriage community," 21 Nov. 1683. See also 25 Sept. 1713, Raimbault, as well as others.
16 Fully 98 per cent of contracts between 1750 and 1770 included a *douaire préfix*. See Tremblay, *La Société montréalaise*.
17 Marriage contracts of the officers La Fresnaye, Bizard, Le Gardeur, Juchereau, des Bergères, La Corne, Céloron, 26 Nov. 1685, Basset, as well as those of 11 Aug. 1678 (Maugue), 20 Apr. 1692, 8 Nov. 1694, 9 June 1695 (A. Adhémar), and 28 Oct. 1724 (Le Pailleur).
18 For the lower classes the amount ranged between 100 and 200 livres.
19 The royal bounties that were granted in this period were included in the marriage community.
20 The Hurtebises, Juillets, Prud'hommes, Courtemances, Dumets, Celles, Desroches, and Brunets may have been better-off habitants, but they did not endow their children.
21 Girls rarely worked outside the home and married young, which explains why they brought no personal savings. Men included theirs within the marriage community without mentioning them.
22 "Livestock worth 300 livres, according to the valuation of experts," 20 Aug. 1679, Maugue. "A four-year-old cow, a one-year-old pig, a dozen fowl, a suit of clothes worth about fifty livres," 25 July, ibid. "Ploughing with four oxen for five days in the proper season during three years," 22 Oct. 1679, ibid.
23 "Description of what I, Jean Leduc, have given Paul Desroches in fulfilment of what I promised in his marriage contract." A long list is appended, covering furniture, tools, grain, animals and various services provided in the two years following the marriage of his daughter. 8 Jan. 1691, Maugue.
24 The marriage contracts of the children Beauvais contained an advance on the inheritance, but their mother stated in her will that none had received it. 11 Oct. 1692, A. Adhémar.
25 Such was the case with the merchants, Lemoyne, Leber, and Charly.
26 For example, Elisabeth Charly did not receive a dowry but interited about 15,000 livres when her parents died. 26 Sept. 1677, Basset. In this social stratum the range of possibilities in the nature and the

value of endowments was far broader, and our sample is too small to permit generalizations.

27 Marriage contract of Migeon-Juchereau, 20 Apr. 1692, A. Adhémar. The bride brought 4,000 livres in silver écus, half of which was legally her personal property, "for her and those of her stock." These were officer families.

28 Marriage contracts of 21 Nov. 1683, Cabazié, and of 11 Jan. and 16 Oct. 1701, Raimbault.

29 Olivier Martin, *Histoire de la coutume de la Prévôté et vicomté de Paris*, II:292–5; C. De Ferrière, *Dictionnaire de droit et de pratique* (Toulouse 1779), I, "Sur les libéralites entre époux"; *Oeuvres de Pothier*, VII:494ff.

30 The marriage contract could also be used to establish that there would be no community of goods between spouses. I met only one such case; Yves Tremblay found only 4 out of 1,032 contracts for the mid-eighteenth century. According to Olivier Martin, the practice was widespread among the Parisian upper classes at the end of the eighteenth century: *Histoire de la coutume*, II:226.

31 See Jean Yver, *Egalité entre héritiers et exclusion des enfants dotés. Essai de géographie coutumière* (Paris 1966), and the comments by Emmanuel Le Roy Ladurie, "Système de la coutume. Structures familiales et coutumes d'héritage en France au XVIe siècle," *Annales ESC* 27, nos. 4–5 (July–Oct. 1972): 833.

32 Jean Yver, "Les Caractères originaux du groupe de coutumes de l'Ouest de la France," *Revue d'histoire du droit français et étranger* (1951): 51ff.

33 "L'Apparition de la succession testamentaire," *Revue du Barreau* 26 (1966): 499ff. "There is nothing easier in the *coutume de Paris* than to undermine this prohibition against favouring one more than the other." Text by Basnage (1778), cited by Jean Yver, *Egalité entre héritiers*, 301.

34 The *légitime* represented half of what each would have received if the inheritance had been divided equally.

35 The *réserve*, or obligation of the father to leave four-fifths of his personal property (*propres*) to his heirs did not apply either, since personal property was rare and fathers were not inclined to deprive their children.

36 One dowry in some one hundred and fifty contracts: a daughter received land from her parents "in recognition of the important labour and services she had performed for them, [they] desiring her to have it above and beyond her share in their inheritance." 25 Sept. 1713, Raimbault.

37 *Oeuvres de Pothier*, VIII:13.

38 Pierre Chauvin's will, 28 July 1699, A. Adhémar.

39 Will of 25 June 1701, ibid.
40 The daughter, injured in her rights, fought the will, "full of injustices and nullities." The suit dragged on, and she agreed before she died to end her opposition, leaving her personal wealth to her prodigal brother. Will of Jeanne Leber, 18 Sept. 1713, Raimbault.
41 See another instance of entailed succession in the will of René Fezeret, 18 Feb. 1720, David.
42 26 Aug. 1686, Basset; 14 July 1695, A. Adhémar; 10 Sept. 1779, Faucher.
43 Wills of R. Cuillerier, P. Perthuis, Jacques Lebé, C. de Couagne, and the widow Lemoyne, 22 Mar. 1712 and 10 July 1708, Le Pailleur; 22 Aug. 1706 and 8 Apr. 1708, A. Adhémar; 18 Mar. 1690, Basset.
44 24 June 1680, Maugue, and 1 Mar. 1694, A. Adhémar.
45 The seigneurs wondered about the real nature of such sales. Should they be subject to the *lods et ventes*? They were advised against it because the sales were fictitious and the parents were only looking for a way of ensuring their subsistence. "Besides, children who acquire such land are usually the losers, because their parents consume more than the property produces." NA, M.G. 17, A7, 2, 2, vol. 1, 315.
46 For other donations, see 10 Oct. 1684 and 26 May 1692, Basset; 7 July 1690 and 30 Dec. 1698, A. Adhémar; 19 May 1690, Maugue, etc.
47 For example, the succession of the widow Le Roy, wife of P. Pigeon, 6 and 17 Mar. 1662, 6 Dec. 1676, 25 Jan. and 22 Apr. 1677, Basset; and that of the widow Gasteau, 3 Jan. 1704, Le Pailleur.
48 Marriage contract between A. Turpin, aged sixty, and Marie Gauthier, aged eighteen, 10 Feb. 1701, Raimbault; that of P. Perthuis, 13 Apr. 1707, A. Adhémar; and that of the widow Couagne, 11 Nov. 1712, ibid.
49 Marriage contract, 12 June 1679, Maugue.
50 Ibid., 16 Nov. 1679. See also 3 Nov. 1677, Basset; 3 Nov. 1680, Maugue; 25 Mar. 1693, A. Adhémar. Maisonneuve, the first governor, who thought he had rights over people's private lives, would take back the deceased's land and grant it anew to the new husband and have him promise to hand a sizeable stipend to the orphans when they came of age. These few contracts created many problems and were quite unlike subsequent adoptions, which were spontaneous and reasonable.
51 5 Apr. 1685, Bourgine. Lamouroux' first wife was an Indian. Apparently, no guardian had been appointed to protect her children's interests. See also the Tabaut-Barban marriage, 19 Jan. 1688, Pottier.
52 Examples of this can be found in the settlement of the inheritance of François Brunet, 16 Oct. 1703, Le Pailleur; and of Jean Leduc, 9 Sewpt. and 2 Nov. 1701, 26 Apr. 14 and 25 May, 1702, Raimbault.
53 Above, chap. 9, sec. 4. In order to facilitate matters, especially where minors were involved, movable effects were auctioned off. The heirs,

the guardian, or else the widow's future husband would then buy up
most of them.

54 Le Roy Ladurie, "Système de la coutume. Structures familiales et
coutumes d'héritage en France au XVIe siècle," 842.

55 Transactions over inheritance shares usually took place after the
inventory. As all these procedures are notarized, one can easily follow
the whole process.

56 See the renunciations with an option on the mother's *douaire*: Gabriel
Noir and J.-B. Dugast, 3 Apr. 1713, 4 July 1714, Le Pailleur. The lifestyle and inflated *douaires* common in officer families led frequently to
conditional acceptance of the estate, followed by renunciation when
the inventory revealed the extent of indebtedness. Lawsuits for the
dissolution of the marriage community were not rare either in this
group. See the cases of Daneau de Muy, Bissot de Vincennes, Juchereau, Gauthier de Varennes, d'Ailleboust, and others.

57 I was unable to compare Canadian practices with those of peasant
communities in the northern parts of France. Pierre Guichard and G.
Sabatier's work, which focuses on the same issues, concerns areas with
primogeniture. P. Léon, *Structures économiques ... dans la France du Sud-
Est*.

58 For the economic consequences of partible inheritance, see above,
chap. 9, sec. 4.

59 Historians have tended to overemphasize the legal constraints and to
bypass the socio-cultural factors. Yves Zoltvany, "Esquisse de la
Coutume de Paris," RHAF 25, no. 3 (Dec. 1971): 383–4. For a discussion
of the spontaneous evolution of inheritance ties towards greater equality in the English colonies, see Alexis de Tocqueville, *La Démocratie en
Amérique* (Paris 1951), chap. 3, 74–85.

60 André Morel, *Les Limites de la liberté testamentaire dans le droit civil de
Québec* (Paris 1960), 30ff.

61 H.J. Habakkuk, "Family Structure and Economic Change in Nineteenth-Century Europe," *Journal of Economic History* 15 (1955): 1–2.

62 Philippe Ariès, *L'Enfant et la vie familiale sous L'Ancien Régime* (Paris
1960), 421–2.

63 Ibid., 441ff.

64 The evolution of the colonial family reinforces, if necessary, Ariès'
argument. My conclusions are similar to those of J. Rothman, "A Note
on the Study of the Colonial Family," *William and Mary Quarterly* (Oct.
1966): 627–34.

65 Letter from Intendant Raudot, June 1706, cited by Robert Rumilly,
Histoire de Montréal, I (Montreal 1970), 294.

66 This is the interpretation advanced by Eccles in *The Canadian Frontier*,
88ff; and in "Opulence et biculturalisme," in *La Société canadienne sous
le régime français* (Montreal 1968).

67 H. Tête and C.-O. Gagnon, *Mandements, lettres pastorales et circulaires des évêques de Québec*, I:376. Developments were similar in France. A. Burguière, "De Malthus à Max Weber: le mariage tardif et l'esprit d'entreprise," *Annales ESC* 27, nos. 4–5 (July–Oct. 1972): 1136.

68 Saint-Vallier, *Rituel du diocèse de Québec* (Paris 1703), 359.

69 As Jacques Henripin seems to imply in *La Population canadienne*, 101. For further information on this custom, see Olivier Martin, *Histoire de la coutume de la Prévôté et vicomté de Paris*, II:226.

70 ASSP, copies Faillon HH89 and FF132. See the description of such a marriage *à la gaulmine* in Alain Lottin, *Vie et mentalité d'un Lillois sous Louis XIV* (Lille 1968), 272. The circumstances were identical to those in Canada.

71 Last will and testament of 13 Dec. 1683, Not. Rec., Maugue. The marriage took place the following year.

72 Such as the widow Couagne's opposition to her son's marriage, 10 Oct. 1716, ibid., J.-B. Adhémar.

73 Will of the widow Forestier, who asked that her children take care of their sister Angélique, aged thirty-six. 25 Jan. 1719, ibid., Le Pailleur.

74 "Statement of what Ignace Hubert contributed towards the subsistence of his father's household, to which he is entitled above and beyond his share.' 14 Feb. 1682, ibid., Maugue. Other specific instances: 26 Sept. 1723, David; 14 Dec. 1691, A. Adhémar.

75 *La Population canadienne*, 55, and by the same author, *Tendances et facteurs*, 8. This-was higher than in Beauvaisis (1 per cent), Quercy (5 per cent), Crulai (3 per cent), or Melun (8 per cent), but lower than in three Ile-de-France villages (14 per cent).

76 Namely, the wife of the surgeon Bouchard, and female tavern-keepers such as Folleville, André, Fournier, Cardinal. Robert-Lionel Séguin, *La Vie libertine en Nouvelle-France au XVIIe siècle*, passim.

77 24 Oct. 1672, Basset.

78 See the annulment of the Gadois-Pontonnier union, which involved a bizarre story of evil spells, in the registers of the Notre-Dame parish, 30 Aug. 1660. See also R. Boyer, *Les Crimes et les châtiments au Canada français du XVIIe au XXe siècles* (Montreal 1966), 293–5.

79 John Demos also observed that in Plymouth married men were not prosecuted for adultery but merely appeared as correspondents when married women were involved. John Demos, *A Little Commonwealth Family Life in Plymouth Colony* (Oxford 1970), 97.

80 Inquiry against La Freynière, Sept. 1667, *bailliage*, ser. 1, reg. 1.

81 Inquiry of 17 June 1660, ibid.; statement made to Basset, a notary, 10 July 1676.

82 Minutes of 23 Aug. 1689 and May 1695, ibid., regs. 1, 2.

83 Sentenced to death by the *bailli*, he appealed to the Quebec Council,

which granted him temporary release from prison. The sentence seems to have been commuted in the end. 5 Dec. 1684, *JDCS*, II:969.

84 I. Foulche-Delbosc, "Women of New France," *CHR* 21, no. 2 (June 1940): 132–49; P. Garigue, *La Vie familiale des Canadiens français* (Montreal 1962), 16.

85 This was the term used by the local commander, who urged husbands to exercise this power over their wives to stop their verbal and physical abuse. Ordinance of 20 Sept. 1662, E.-Z. Massicotte, *Répertoire des arrêts*.

86 Last will and testament of René Cuillerier, 22 Mar. 1712, Le Pailleur.

87 Monière's account books, NA, M-847.

88 Henripin, *La Population canadienne*, 99.

89 Their clothing was rarely inventoried, and there was no mention of toys or special furniture. Children would long continue to wear clogs, unlike their parents, who quickly adopted shoes suited to the climate.

90 For more on schools, see below, chap. 15, sec. 2.

91 Peter Moogk, "Apprenticeship Indentures: A Key to Artisan Life in New France," *CHAR* (1971): 75–83, 70.

92 According to the 1784 census, children under fifteen represented only one-ninth of the 1,184 domestic servants. See W. Kinsford, *The History of Canada* (Toronto 1887), VII:204.

93 This proportion only applies to the Island of Montreal and a few surrounding seigneuries. See above, chap. 5, sec. 5.

94 Letters from La Barre and Denonville, 4 Nov. 1683, 13 Nov. 1685, AC, C11A, 6, fol. 153, and vol. 7, fols. 89v–90.

95 Petition of the widow Biron, 14 July 1723, *bailliage*, copy Faillon HH 125.

96 This story was traced through notarial records: 9 Oct. and 11 Nov. 1684, 30 May 1692, 24 Nov. 1693, Basset; 23 and 24 Apr. 1706, A. Adhémar.

97 23 Dec., 1677, ibid., Basset.

98 The three cases of multiple family households that figure in the 1681 census represent the same proportion of recent unions. If there were no such clauses in the first decades, it is more than likely that such agreements were reached informally.

99 Sales of 28 July 1680 and 9 Dec. 1681, ibid., Maugue; of 23 July 1713, ibid., Raimbault; etc.

100 31 Mar. 1700, ibid., A. Adhémar.

101 P.J. Greven observed the opposite in a Massachusetts village. The fathers held on to their properties until they died. The sons who ran them merely had the usufruct. "Family Structure in Seventeenth-Century Andover," *William and Mary Quarterly* (Apr. 1966): 234–56.

102 Agreement reached between the children of J. Archambault to give

their father 100 livres a year, "meaning that each would contribute 25 towards his room and board, and that he would be free to live where he liked, and either to rent a house or to live with the above." 25 June 1678, Not. Rec., Basset.

103 Agreement between the Godé heirs concerning their mother's pension, 29 June 1676, ibid., Basset.

104 Laurent Archambault offered to share his property among his children so that each would provide him and his wife with a reasonable allowance. Upon "mature reflection they decided they would rather turn over the usufruct to a single one." 26 Sept. 1706, ibid., Senet.

105 25 June 1678, ibid., Basset.

106 These observations are based on ninety-three guardianship deeds (tutelles et curatelles) involving families who left an inventory. This question should be more thoroughly examined for the eighteenth century, where the records are more complete.

107 See the cases of the families of J. Beauchamp, A. Dumers, J. Descaris, J. Gervaise, P. Pigeon, A. Forestier, P. Lorain, and so on. M. Baulant notes that brothers played a similar role in the Meaux region: "La Famille en miettes: sur un aspect de la démographie du XVIIe siècle," *Annales ESC* 27, nos. 4–5 (July–Oct. 1972): 967.

108 Inventory, guardianship accounts, division of succession, and sales of the inheritance claims, 29 Aug. 1695, 12–14 Nov. 1698, A. Adhémar.

109 Thus we find the brothers Cardinal, coureurs de bois and a bad lot, taking care of their blind brother and then their mother, who lived on to be ninety. 6 July 1689, *bailliage*, ser. 2, reg. 1; 9 Feb. 1720, Not. Rec., Raimbault. When Madeleine Leblanc, who worked as a maid in one of the inns, was accused of theft, her brother took the innkeeper to court to force him to retract the accusation. 19–22 Feb. 1689, *bailliage*, Boudor case.

110 24 June 1691, Not. Rec., Maugue; 18 June 1694, 5 July 1695, 22 July 1698, ibid., A. Adhémar, etc.

111 7 Oct. 1719, ibid., David.

112 Will of René Cuillerier, 22 Mar. 1712, ibid., Le Pailleur.

113 "Should it prove impossible to reach an amicable and charitable arrangement, they should have their dispute arbitrated without any legal proceedings or other formalities of that nature." Will of 25 Jan. 1719, ibid.

114 See, for example, the relations between Trottiers and Cuilleriers; the de Couagnes and the Godés; the Leducs and the Desroches; the Perthuis and the Carons; the Bazinet-Beauchamps; the Lauson-Quesnevilles, and so on.

CHAPTER FIFTEEN

1 Dollier de Casson, *Histoire du Montréal*; E.-M. Faillon, *Histoire de la colonie française du Canada*; Léon Gérin, *Aux Sources de notre histoire*, 162–91.

2 *Annales de l'Hôtel-Dieu de Montréal rédigées par la soeur Morin*, 114–15. The nun wrote this around 1695.

3 Saint-Sulpice had obtained this arrangement, which went counter to royal policy, by explaining its expenditures and the need for priests to feel they could withdraw into its seminaries, without which they would refuse to serve. The Crown relied on this community to counterbalance the Jesuits, and so gave in. The bishop gave his permission because he hoped to obtain the same privilege for the rest of the diocese and needed the support of the Sulpicians. Arrêt of the Conseil d'Etat, 15 May 1702, *Edits, ordonnances royaux*, Vol. I; correspondence of the Sulpicians, ASSP, vols. XIII and XIV, passim.

4 Letter of 4 Nov. 1683, AC, C11A, 6, fol. 185.

5 "Don't be sorry to have given up China," M. de Tronson wrote the curé, Rémy, on 5 Apr. 1677, ASSP, XIII:66–78; see also XIV:14.

6 Letters of the supérieur général to MM. Pérot, Roche, Vachon, Geoffroy, Priat, Rémy, and Bouffandeau, 8 May 1677, ibid., XIII:82–4; 3, 5, 8 June, 18 Mar. 1706, Apr. 1707, 6 June 1708, ibid., XIV:355–6, 364–5, 366, 378, 285, 406.

7 Letter from M. de Tronson, Apr. 1685, ibid., XIII:410.

8 See the strict regulation that finally prevailed, 21 May 1694, ASSM copy Faillon H534.

9 Paris responded to Belmont's question whether priests could refuse to appear in civil courts by advising him to give in, for that was the general tendency. 26 Mar. 1706, NA, M.G. 17, A7, 2, 1, vol. 2, 355–66.

10 Colbert wrote: "Concerning your concerns about the authority wielded by the bishop de Pétrée and the Jesuits, or rather, the latter under guise of the first, I should tell you that you must act with great circumspection and tact, since there is little doubt that once the land is populated, royal authority will surpass that of the church and regain its normal parameters." AC, B1, fol. 141. That is exactly what happened. See Guy Frégault, "L'Eglise et la société canadienne," *Le XVIII*ᵉ *siècle canadien*, 114–22.

11 L. Cognet, *Le Jansénisme* (Paris 1961), 124.

12 Letters of the curé to M. Arnaud, the churchwarden, 10 Feb. 1695, NA, M.G. 17, A7, 2, 1, vol. 1; from M. de Tronson, 28 Feb. 1692, ASSP, XIV:7.

13 Fénélon was the writer's older brother. Oliver Marault, DCB, vol. I. The governor would accuse the Sulpicians by association of quietist tendencies. Letter of M. de Tronson, 12 May 1695, ASSP, XIV:125.

14 Letter from the same, 1692, ibid., 30. Report from a Sulpician (1684), referring to Kateri Tekakouitha and the people of the nearby parish of Lachine, ibid., 109, doc. 1, item 10.

15 Letter from M. de Tronson, 1 Mar. 1680, ibid., xiii:165; register of the meetings of Saint-Sulpice, minutes of 27 Jan. 1680.

16 Letter of M. de Tronson, 2 Mar. 1691, ASSP, xiii:589–602.

17 Pierre Goubert, *Beauvais et le Beauvaisis*, 204.

18 "Marguilliers de la paroisse de Notre-Dame de Ville-Marie de 1657 à 1813," *BRH* 19 (1913): 276–84.

19 Minutes of the assembly of 29 June 1654, *bailliage*; E. Faillon, *Histoire de la colonie française au Canada*, i:200.

20 Accounts of the first churchwardens, A-13; stock inventories, 19 Sept. 1660 and 9 Dec. 1661, Not. Rec., Basset.

21 3 June 1705, ibid., A. Adhémar; 28 Nov. 1710, ibid., Raimbault; report dated Mar. 1729, NA, M.G.17, A7, 2, 3, vol. 6.

22 For example, 5,000 livres from the curé Pérot to purchase a box of ornaments (in 1670). Archives of the Notre-Dame parish, box 1; minutes, 1672 (copy Faillon H 622); 1,500 livres from the king, ordinance of 3 May 1682, ASSP, xiii, separate item.

23 "Etat des Journées, dons et bienfaits qu'ont permis les habitans soubscrits pour ayder à construire et élever l'Eglise," 20 Jan. 1676, archives of the Notre-Dame parish, box 1, folder, 15.

24 In 1681 Pierre de Vanchy was sentenced to pay 32 livres and four working days for the court costs. 11 Oct. 1681, *bailliage*. Reading through these registers, I came across a number of other such cases.

25 In livres tournois. These rates were slightly higher than those in France. See Thérèse-Jean Schmitt, *L'Organisation ecclésiastique dans l'Archidiaconé d'Autun de 1650 à 1750* (Autun 1957), 146–7.

26 Accounts presented by Charly, the churchwarden from May 1706 to May 1707, archives of the Notre-Dame parish, A-14.

27 We know that dispensations from banns were frequent and quite costly: 9 livres for one bann, up to 22 livres to two and 75 for all three. The bishop made curés contribute half of that income to the Hôtel-Dieu. Letter of 10 June 1716, ASSM, copy Faillon H 533; report of 16 Aug. 1672, *bailliage*, ser. 1, reg. 1.

28 Bid of 12 Aug. 1705, ASSM (copy Faillon II 91); leases of 20 Aug. 1715 and 26 Oct. 1716, Not. Rec., J.-B. Adhémar.

29 "Procès-verbal sur la commodité ... des paroisses," *RAPQ* (1921–22): 264ff.

30 Register of the parish of l'Enfant-Jésus, minutes of the meetings (copy Faillon QQ 77–81).

31 Letter from M. de Tronson, 6 June 1708, ASSP, xiv:406.

32 See the minutes of the assemblies of all rural parishes, the intendants'

ordinances, and the bishops' pastoral letters. The same scenario would be repeated time and again throughout the colony.

33 See, for example, the proceedings of 22 July 1681, *bailliage*, ser. 1, reg. 1.

34 Ordinance of Dupuis, 21 Apr. 1727, *Edits, ordonnances royaux*, III:232.

35 Last will and testament of M. Rémy, 20 Oct. 1705 (copy Faillon LL50); petition of the curé of Lachine to Raudot, 7 Oct. 1707, ibid., DD319; petition of Bouffandeau, curé of Rivière-des-Prairies to Beauharnois, 27 Aug. 1704, Not. Rec., Raimbault. A similar declaration was made by Mgr Plessis in 1809, cited by Jean-Pierre Wallot in "Religion and French Canadian Mores," CHR 52, no. 1 (Mar. 1971): 79.

36 See, for example, the circumstances surrounding the creation of the parish of Saint-Laurent, ASSP, dossier 33, item 2.

37 22 Dec. 1688, *bailliage*, ser. 2, reg. 1. Churchwarden would wait and take a number to court at once. Ordinance by Migeon, 19 Dec. 1678, ibid., ser. 1.

38 See above, chap. 7, sec. 2; letter from Magnien, 18 Mar. 1717, NA, M.G.17, A7, 2, 1, vol. 2, 530–1.

39 Letter from M. Leschassier, 17 Mar. 1702, ASSP, XIV:249.

40 See A. Lecomte, who was prosecuted for 48 minots of grain and 27 livres, 4 July 1690, *bailliage*, ser. 2, reg. 1; and proceedings instituted by Hattanville, the collector in 1693, ibid., fols. 622–3), and by the collectors Dugast and Pottier in 1689–92, ibid., etc.

41 Letter from M. de Tronson, June 1681, ASSP, XIII:261.

42 The bishop divided them up. The total amount varied. AC, D2D, 1, and BN, mss fr., N.A., 9273, fol. 166.

43 Letters of 8 May 1677, 1 June 1681, 18 Mar. 1705, ASSP, XIII:82–4, 261, and XIV:343.

44 When a property was sold after the assessment had been drawn up, the buyer became responsible for the tax. Minutes of the assembly of the Pointe-aux-Trembles vestry, 3 July 1710 (copy Faillon HH64).

45 Lawsuit between the churchwardens and the curé of Notre-Dame concerning the sale of church property, 16 Aug. 1672, *bailliage*, ser. 1, reg. 1.

46 The Pointe-aux-Trembles parishioners asked the bishop not to make their curé serve in the Boucherville mission. Letter from M. de Tronson, 29 June 1689, ASSP, XIII:563. For the transfer of the curé Guyotte see the letters of 1694, ibid., 66 and 87.

47 Report of 12 Oct. 1715, *bailliage*, ser. 2, reg. 5 (copy Faillon HH101).

48 For example, in the missions in the western part of the island, which caused the most problems but which had no church for more than thirty years. Letter from M. Leschassier, Apr. 1704, ASSSP, XIV:317.

49 Until 1694. But funding for the school was insufficient; the curés

contributed personally towards its upkeep, and finally the vestry let the Seminary take over its direction. Contract of 13 May 1694, Not. Rec., A. Adhémar.

50 Letter from M. de Tronson, 20 Mar. 1680, ASSP, XIII:200.

51 A community of teaching brothers served the school between 1686 and 1694. Y. Poutet, "La Compagnie de Saint-Sulpice et les petites écoles au XVIIe siècle," *Bulletin du Comité des études de la Compagnie de Saint-Sulpice* 33 (Apr.–June 1961): 164–83. See also RAPQ (1923–24): 635.

52 Letter from M. de Tronson, 2 Mar. 1684, ASSP, XIII:354.

53 Letters from M. Leschassier, 24 Mar. 1702 and May 1703, ibid., XIV:260, 291.

54 Letter from the same, 1719, copy Faillon H433.

55 Mgr de Saint-Vallier, *Estat présent de l'Eglise et de la colonie française dans la Nouvelle-France* (Paris 1688), 24.

56 Deed of gift of 13,300 livres from Jeanne Leber to the Congrégation de Notre-Dame, 9 Sept. 1714, ibid., Le Pailleur.

57 For first marriages only. I had to leave out the periods 1642–57, October 1659–August 1660, and 1682–92 because the curés were not consistent in asking for signatures. The percentages are therefore based on a small number of cases: 195 men and 283 women. Drawn signatures were not included, but all the others, however crude, were kept.

58 See above, chap. 2, sec. 8.

59 The literacy level resembles that of northeastern France. It compares well with that of Bayeux (43 per cent). See M. Fleury and P. Valmary, "Les Progrès de l'instruction élémentaire de Louis XIV à Napoléon III," *Population* 1 (1957): 71–92; M. El Kordi, *Bayeux aux XVIIe et XVIIIe siècles* (Paris 1970), 85; and Louis-Philippe Audet, "La Nouvelle-France et ses dix mille colons," *Cahier des Dix* 36 (1971): 9–53.

60 See the vestry assemblies of the rural parishes. In Lachine the cantor and schoolteacher, J.-B. Pottier, received 150 livres a year (will of M. Rémy, copy Faillon LL50). The curés also had recourse to the *frères hospitaliers*, about whom they complained abundantly.

61 Report of 7 Mar. 1685, *bailliage*, ser. 2, reg. 1; letters from Vaudreuil and Bégon, 29 Nov. 1718, AC, C11A, 124, fol. 248.

62 They mostly taught children how to write. Letter from M. Leschassier, 1 May 1700, ASSP, XIV:220; reports of 22 Mar. 1689 and 20 May 1717, *bailliage*, ser. 2, reg. 1 and 6. A few bourgeois engaged them as private tutors.

63 Nearly every merchant had a stock of alphabet books.

64 A study of marriage contracts for 1750–60 yielded a literacy rate of 50 per cent for the whole of the island pointing to improvement in the countryside. Yves J. Tremblay, "La Société montréalaise au début du régime anglais," MA, University of Ottawa 1970, 73. The same study

shows that the war and the Conquest put a sudden end to this trend, and that conditions deteriorated thereafter.

65 Around 1690 there was some pressure on the Sulpicians to teach Latin, which would allow the children to further their schooling. But the Sulpicians refused to take it on. The Seminary sometimes educated two or three boys in return for their services. They took in the sons of Governor Vaudreuil, but this was obviously a special case. Letters of 24 May 1690, 3 Mar. 1704, ASSP, XIII:565, and XIV:240 and 306.

66 A. Gosselin, *L'Instruction au Canada sous le Régime français* (Quebec 1911); Louis-Philippe Audet, *Le Système scolaire dans la province de Québec de 1635 à 1800* (Quebec 1915), I, and "Programmes et professeurs du Collège de Québec, 1635–1763," *Cahier des Dix* 34 (1969): 13–18; N. Baillargeon, *Le Séminaire de Québec sous l'épiscopat de Mgr de Laval* (Quebec 1972).

67 AC, C11A, 48, 76ff.

68 The sons of Governor Vaudreuil, of Migeon, of the *bailli*, and of procureur Raimbault, etc. Letters of 9 June 1690, 19 June 1706, ASSP, XIII:583, and XIV:372; minutes of the assemblies of Saint-Sulpice, 11 Apr. 1723, I, 840.

69 Feast days brought in money for the collection plate. The churchwardens jotted down these revenues with the date, and it is thus possible to identify the festivities, which are not always named. From one year to the next it becomes possible to gauge the concordance among the records kept by various individuals. The bishops' pastorals and clerical correspondence provide supplementary information.

70 Pastoral of Mgr de Laval, 3 Dec. 1667, of Pontbriand, 24 Nov. 1744. At that point the bishop abolished nineteen of these feast days. H. Têtu and C.-O. Gagnon, eds., *Mandements, lettres pastorales et circulaire des évêques de Québec* (Quebec 1887), I.

71 At La Montagne, the missionaries heard children's confessions about four times a year. Letter from M. de Tronson, 1692, ASSP, XIV:30. A pastoral of 1751 reproached the people's "so-called respect, which excludes them from the altar." Claudette Lacelle, "Monseigneur Henry-Marie Dubreuil de Pontbriand, ses mandements et ses circulaires," MA, University of Ottawa 1971, 49.

72 Often required in the lease, as in those of 31 May 1676, 16 Apr. 1676, Not. Rec., Basset. In 1721 an arquebusier, who was thus celebrating the passage of the Blessed Sacrament, set the town on fire. Maria Mondoux, *L'Hôtel-Dieu, premier hôpital de Montréal*, 270.

73 In 1667 the bishop added two mandatory feast days, those of Ste Anne and St Francis Xavier. Neither appears to have been observed in Montreal. The first unfortunately fell during the harvest, and Saint-Sulpice must have found a good excuse not to celebrate the founder of the Jesuits, on 3 December.

74 The request was addressed to the governor around 1678. See Robert
   Rumilly, *Histoire de Montréal*, I (Montreal 1970), 205; letters from M. de
   Tronson, 24 Apr. 1680 and 8 Apr. 1684, ASSP, XIII:204 and 362. The
   residents even offered a plot of land, which they would pay for if
   Saint-Sulpice decided not to be generous.
75 Letter from M. de Tronson, 1695, ASSP, XIV:112.
76 Will of the widow Truteau, who asks to be buried in her *Tiers Ordre*
   gown, 10 May 1721, Not. Rec., Le Pailleur. Transaction by the Con-
   gregationists to build an extension to the Jesuits' house, 23 Nov. 1692,
   ibid., A. Adhémar. C. de Couagne bequeathed 200 livres to the poor,
   300 to the parish, the same to the Récollets, and 100 to the Congrégation "of which I have the honour to be a member," will of 22
   Aug. 1706, ibid.
77 Such as Masses to Sts Cosmas and Damien in September, St Eloi on 1
   December, and Crispin and Crispinian in October. The armorers' meal
   ended in noisy libations and quarrels that ended up before the court,
   and the Crown attorney called on them to give up their banquet and
   use their alms to contribute to the building of the parish church. They
   must have continued these celebrations, but more discreetly. See E.-Z.
   Massicotte, BRH 4 (1898): 376; vol. 23 (1917): 343–6; vol. 24 (1918):
   126–7; and the accounts of the churchwardens in the archives of
   Notre-Dame parish.
78 Minutes of the assembly of the churchwardens, 16 Oct. 1690, archives
   of the Notre-Dame parish, vol. A, fols. 111–12. The confraternity's
   other rules, 2 July 1691, ASSM (copy Faillon DD216). The members were
   entitled to be buried in the church.
79 For further details on this cult and on religious practices, see Alain
   Lottin, *Vie et mentalité d'un Lillois sous Louis XIV*, 207–303.
80 *Annales de l'Hôtel-Dieu de Montréal rédigées par la soeur Morin*, 85. Letter
   from the governor dated 13 Nov. 1685, AC, C11A, 7, 87v.
81 Declaration during the inventory of the belongings of Mathieu Lafaye,
   3 Oct. 1693, Not. Rec., A. Adhémar.
82 28 Nov. 1679, *bailliage*, ser. 1, reg. 1 (copy Faillon GG322).
83 Regulations of the conseil of 11 May 1676, JDCS, II; letter of 20 Nov.
   1686, AC, C11A, 8, fol. 132.
84 When these foreigners were baptized, parish registers usually mentioned their origins and the reason they had come to Canada. In the
   seventeenth century the bulk were prisoners, among them many
   children; in the following century they would be adults, merchants,
   and settlers who crossed the border of their own free will. See the
   partial list in C. Tanguay, *Dictionnaire généalogique des familles canadiennes-françaises*, I:8–10. Gabriel Chalifour, a Huguenot from La Rochelle,
   came to Montreal after spending a number of years in New England,
   and was baptized on 26 December 1699. Ibid., 111.

85 See the baptisms on 24 Aug. and 12 Sept. 1700 in the register of Notre-Dame parish.
86 The parishes kept lists of recantations. We cannot tell how complete they are and what proportion of Protestant residents they may represent.
87 This becomes clear after 1760. Canadian women showed no reluctance to marry Protestants. On 12 March 1763 the Sorbonne, concerned by these developments, rendered a decision concerning such unions. NA, M.G17, A7, 2, 1, vol. 3, 989–1026.
88 A number of pictures of the Virgin, and others of St John the Baptist, St Peter, St Anthony, Lazarus come to life, the voyage of Tobit, etc.
89 Lives of the saints, Bibles, books of meditations, etc. Notaries often left out the titles.
90 Letter from M. de Leschassier, 20 Feb. 1701, ASSP, XIV:222.
91 L.-E. Hamelin, "Evolution numérique séculaire du clergé catholique dans le Québec," Recherches sociographiques 2 (1961): 189–242.
92 Letter from Maurepas to Mgr de Pontbriand, 21 May 1743, NA, M.G.17, A7, 2, 3, vol. 3.
93 Contract of 3 Apr. 1713, Not. Rec., Le Pailleur.
94 Micheline d'Allaire, "Conditions matérielles requises pour devenir religieuse au XVIIIe siècle," in L'Hôtel-Dieu de Montréal 1642–1973 (Montreal 1973), 185–208.
95 Arrêts of the Conseil d'Etat, 31 May 1722, setting dowries at 5,000 livres. Another arrêt of 15 March brought them down to 3,000 livres. Edits, ordonnances royaux, I:464ff, 259ff.
96 Tanguay, Dictionnaire généalogiques des familles canadiennes–françaises, I, 152.
97 Micheline d'Allaire, "Conditions matérielles requises pour devenir religieuse au XVIIIe siècle," 186–7. Agreements between the family and the convent in notarial records, 14 June 1675 and 20 Dec. 1684, Basset; 11 Aug. 1679, Maugue; 12 Nov. 1699, A. Adhémar.
98 The two Leduc girls entered the convent against their parents' wishes, one in the dead of night. Adrienne Barbier was taken out by her mother, who married her off soon after. Soeur Marie Morin, Annales de l'Hôtel-Dieu de Montréal, 13, 144.
99 Letter from M. Leschassier, Apr. 1704, ASSP, XIV:317.
100 See, for example, H. Platelle, Journal d'un curé de campagne au XVIIe siècle (Paris 1965), and on similar questions, Robert Mandrou, Des Humanistes aux hommes de science, XVIe et XVIIe siècles (Paris 1973), 192–7.

CHAPTER SIXTEEN

1 For a general discussion of these issues, see, for example, K. Levitt, *Silent Surrender, The Multinational Corporation in Canada* (Toronto 1970); C. Furtado, *The Economic Growth of Brazil* (Berkeley 1963); A. Gunder Frank, *Capitalisme et sous-développement en Amérique latine* (Paris 1968).
2 See chap. 4, sec. 5, and chap. 2, passim.
3 M.H. Watkins, "The Staple Theory of Economic Growth," in W.T. Easterbrook and M.H. Watkins, *Approaches to Canadian Economic History* (Toronto 1969), 49–74; K. Levitt, *Silent Surrender*; T. Naylor, "The Rise and Fall of the Third Commercial Empire of the Saint Lawrence," in G. Teeple, *Capitalism and the National Question in Canada* (Toronto 1972).
4 Many historians view the whole of New France as a fur-trade frontier that bred a type of adventurer who was divorced from tradition. The farming frontier, despite its greater numerical importance, is not discussed: A.L. Burt, "The Frontier in the History of New France," CHAR (1940): 93–9; W.J. Eccles, *The Canadian Frontier*, 2–3; Jean Blain, "La Frontière en Nouvelle-France: Perspectives historiques nouvelles à partir d'un thème ancien," RHAF 25, no. 3 (Dec. 1971): 397–407; and also the conclusion in Andrew H. Clark, *Acadia: The Geography of Early Nova Scotia to 1760* (Wisconsin University Press 1968).
5 Which explains the large-scale departures for the United States, which we can estimate at roughly 1.5 million between 1840 and 1910, or 75 per cent of the French Canadian population at the end of this period. See Y. Lavoie, *L'Emigration des Canadiens aux Etats-Unis avant 1930, mesuré du phénomène* (Montreal 1972); Gilles Paquet, "L'Emigration des Canadiens français vers la Nouvelle-Angleterre, 1870–1910: prises de vue quantitatives," *Recherches sociographiques* (Sept.–Dec. 1964): 319ff.
6 A dispute centring on poorly defined concepts. See Robert Comeau and Paul-André Linteau's summary of this debate in "Une Question historiographique: une bourgeoisie en Nouvelle-France?" in R. Comeau, *Economie québécoise* (Montreal 1969), 311–24.
7 See, for example, the merchants' reaction to the vagaries in public finance, chap. 4, sec. 2.
8 It obtained the "trading permits" and, later, leases of the posts. See chap. 5, sec. 1; chap. 13, secs. 2, 3, and 8.
9 This emerges from the analysis of the credit system in chap. 5, sec. 2, and from the demographic changes in the town.
10 I am referring to the royal shipyards in Quebec, the Saint-Maurice ironworks, which were owned or heavily subsidized by the Crown, and to two or three other smaller premature ventures.

Note on Manuscript Sources

The documentary sources used for this study fall into two categories: local and colonial.

The notarial records of early Montreal, which were systematically searched to construct series of deeds related to trade, agriculture, or family affairs, provide the bulk of the documentation. They include all notaries who practised on the island before 1725: Jean de Saint-Père (1648–57), Lambert Closse (1651–56), Bénigne Basset (1657–99), Nicolas de Monchy (1664–67), Pierre Cabazié (1673–93), Claude Maugue (1677–96), Hilaire Bourgine (1685–90), Jean-Baptiste Pottier (1686–97), Antoine Adhémar (1688–1714), Pierre Raimbault (1697–1727), Michel Lepailleur (1703–32), Nicolas Senet (1704–31), Jean-Baptiste Adhémar (1714–54), Jacques David (1719–26).

The judicial records, which include the minutes of the Montreal Bailliage court and a number of separate but related records (such as records of criminal hearings, wills, guardianships, closures of inventories, and local ordinances) were also extensively used. Both the notarial and judicial records are located in the Archives nationales du Québec in Montreal, as are copies of the baptismal, burial, and marriage registers of the following parishes established on the island: Notre-Dame-de-Montréal (1643–), Enfant-Jésus-de-la-Pointe-aux-Trembles (1674–), Saints-Anges-de-Lachine (1676–), Saint-Joseph-de-la-Rivière-des-Prairies (1687–), Sainte-Anne-du-Bout-de-l'Ile (1703–), Saint-Joachim-de-la-Pointe-Claire (1713–). Parishes created after 1715 were not included.

Extant seigneurial records are located in the Sulpician Archives in Paris and Montreal, with copies and microfilms available at the National Archives of Canada (NA). These include the drafts of the letters written by the superior of the Compagnie de Saint-Sulpice in Paris to Sulpician priests in Montreal; the notebooks of Étienne-Michel Faillon, the nineteenth-century historian of early Montreal, which contain copies of various official and judicial documents; and tenancy books, maps, title deeds, leases, correspondance, and reports on the management of the seigneurie. The documents are listed in NA, MG 17. The account books of the Montreal seigneurie for the period under study are no longer extant.

Other local sources include the account books of the Hôtel-Dieu (1696–1726), those of the Hôpital Général (1692–99, 1705–16, 1718–46), and other documents located in the archives of these two institutions. Last, the account books of Alexis Lemoine Monière, from the archives of the Château Ramezay, were consulted on microfilm (NA, M-847 and M-848).

All the documents relating to Canada in the seventeenth and early eighteenth centuries in various archives in France were examined. Copies and microfilms can be found in the National Archives of Canada. These include the following series: Archives nationales (Paris) section outre-mer, G1 460 and 461 for census material; Archives nationales (Paris) archives des colonies, B, C11A, C11E, D2C, D2D, E, F1A and F3 for correspondance and other official records; Archives nationales (Paris), G7 or Contrôle général des finances; Bibliothèque nationale (Paris) manuscript section, Mss. Fr., NA, 9272, 9280, 9391, and Mss Fr. 20973 and 23663; Service historique de l'Armée (Paris) series A1, vol. 190–200 concerning the recruitment of the Carignan-Salières regiment.